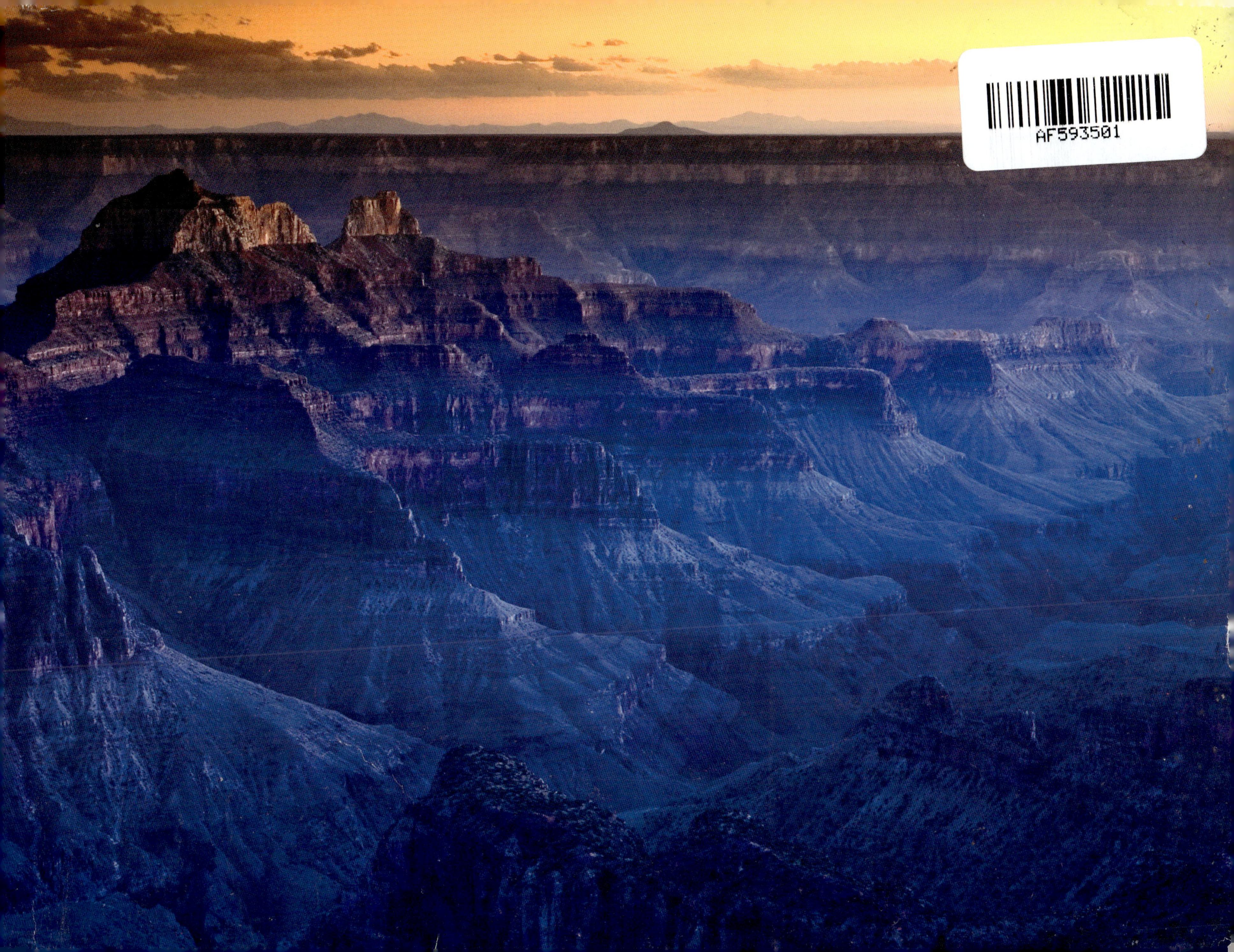
AF593501

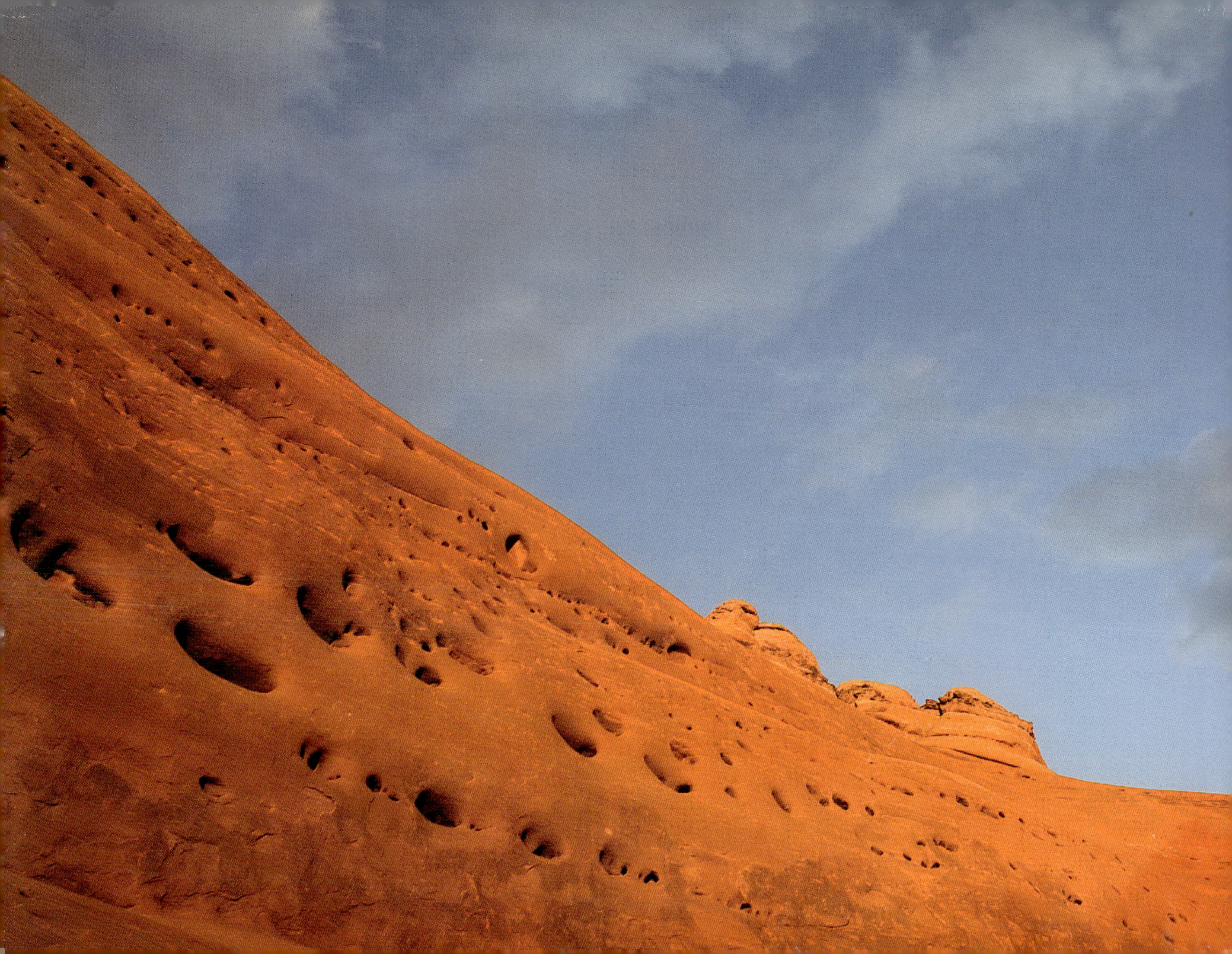

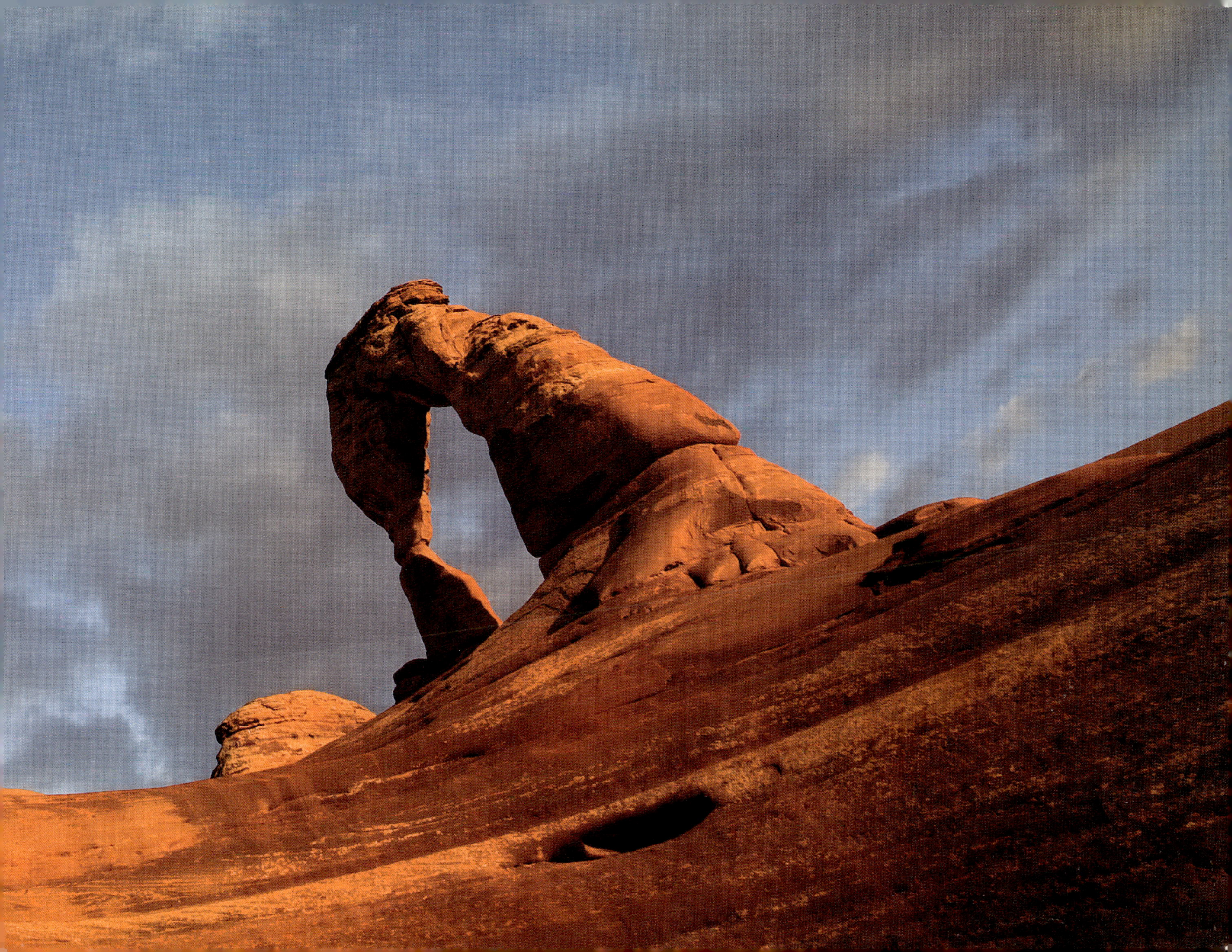

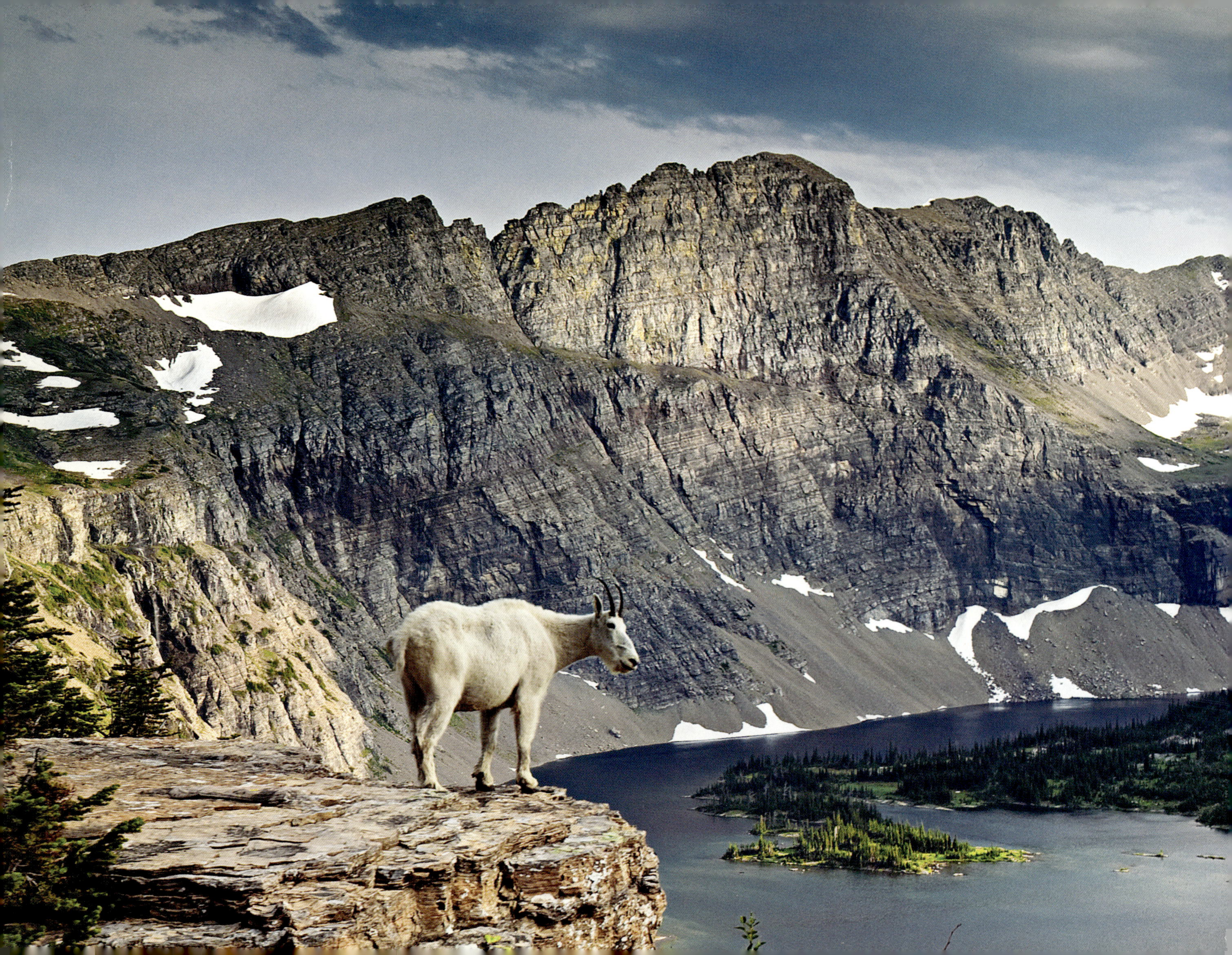

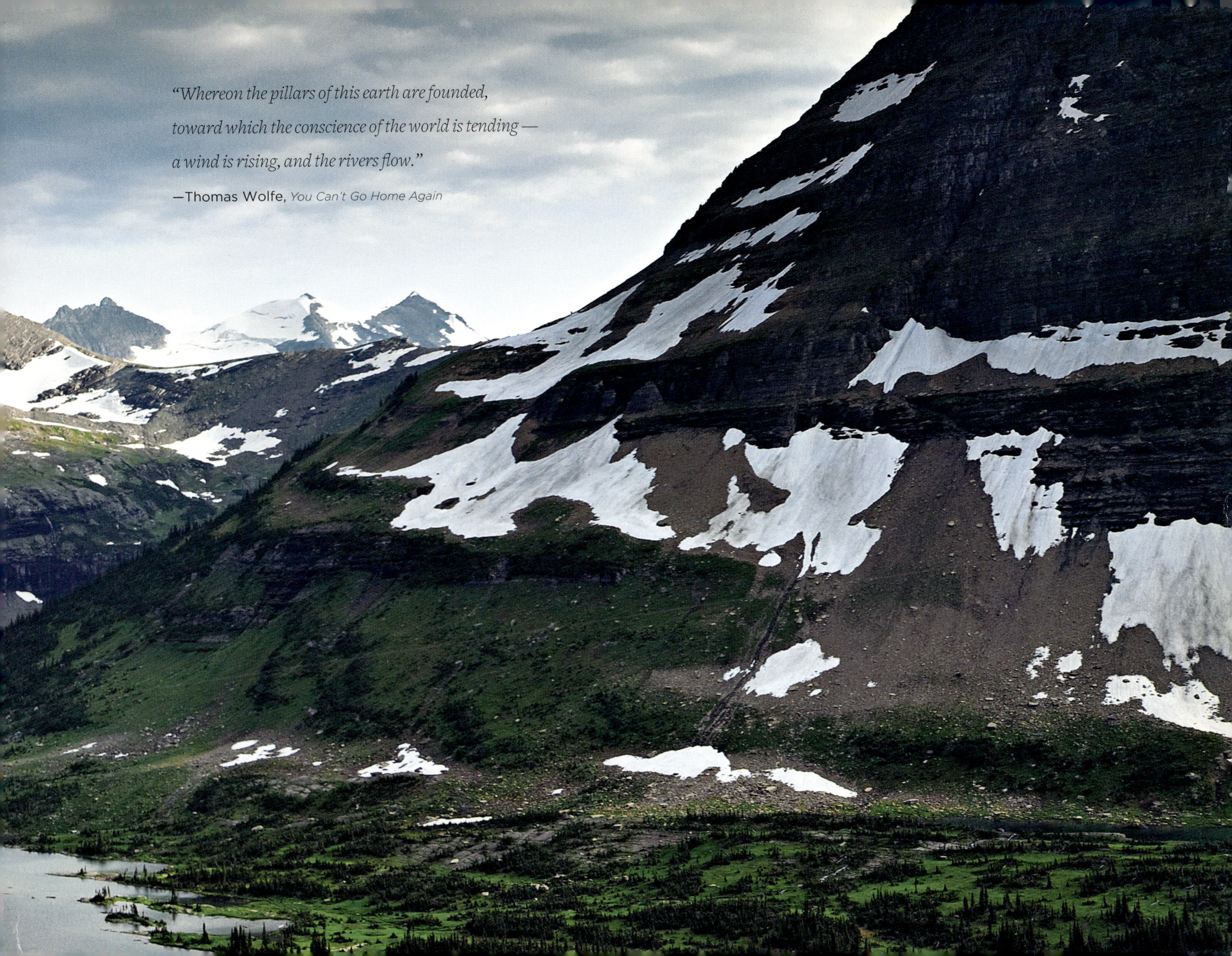

"Whereon the pillars of this earth are founded,
toward which the conscience of the world is tending—
a wind is rising, and the rivers flow."

—Thomas Wolfe, *You Can't Go Home Again*

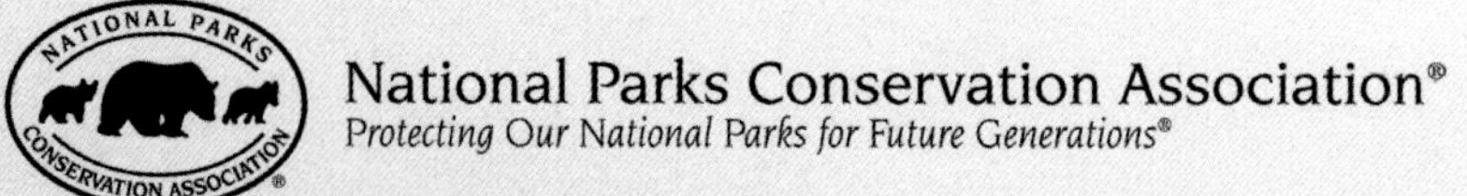

PAGE 1: **Grand Canyon National Park, Arizona**
The sun descends over the north rim of the Grand Canyon.

PAGES 2/3: **Arches National Park, Utah**
Delicate Arch.

PAGES 4/5: **Glacier National Park, Montana**
Mountain view and Hidden Lake along Hidden Lake Trail.

THIS SPREAD: **White Sands National Monument, New Mexico**
Dunes after a storm.

THE NATIONAL PARKS

OUR AMERICAN LANDSCAPE

Photography by **IAN SHIVE**

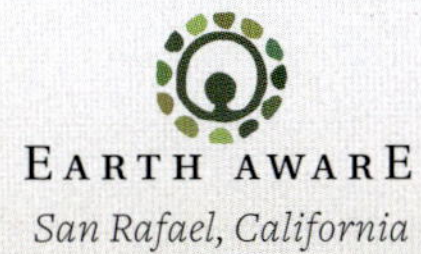

EARTH AWARE
San Rafael, California

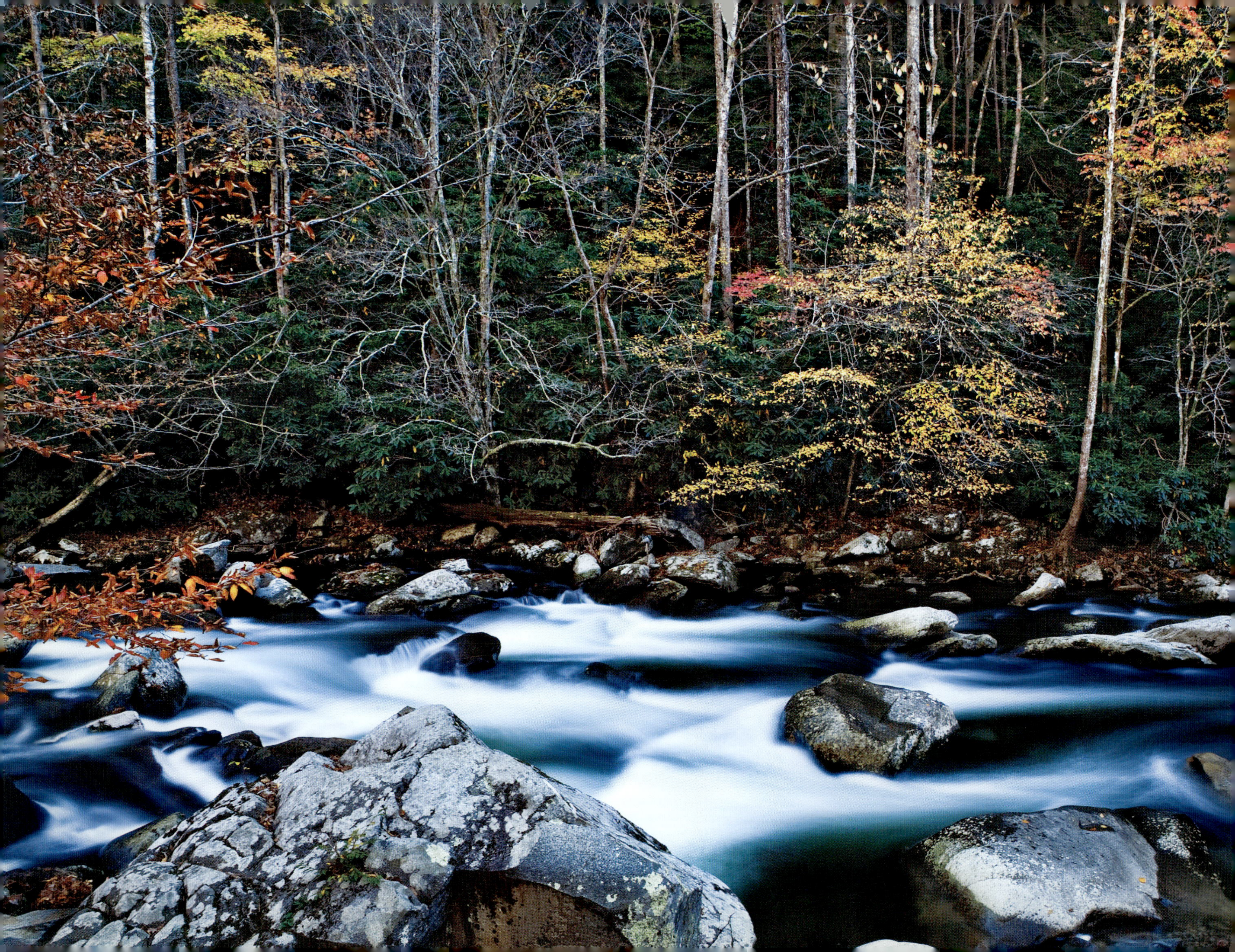

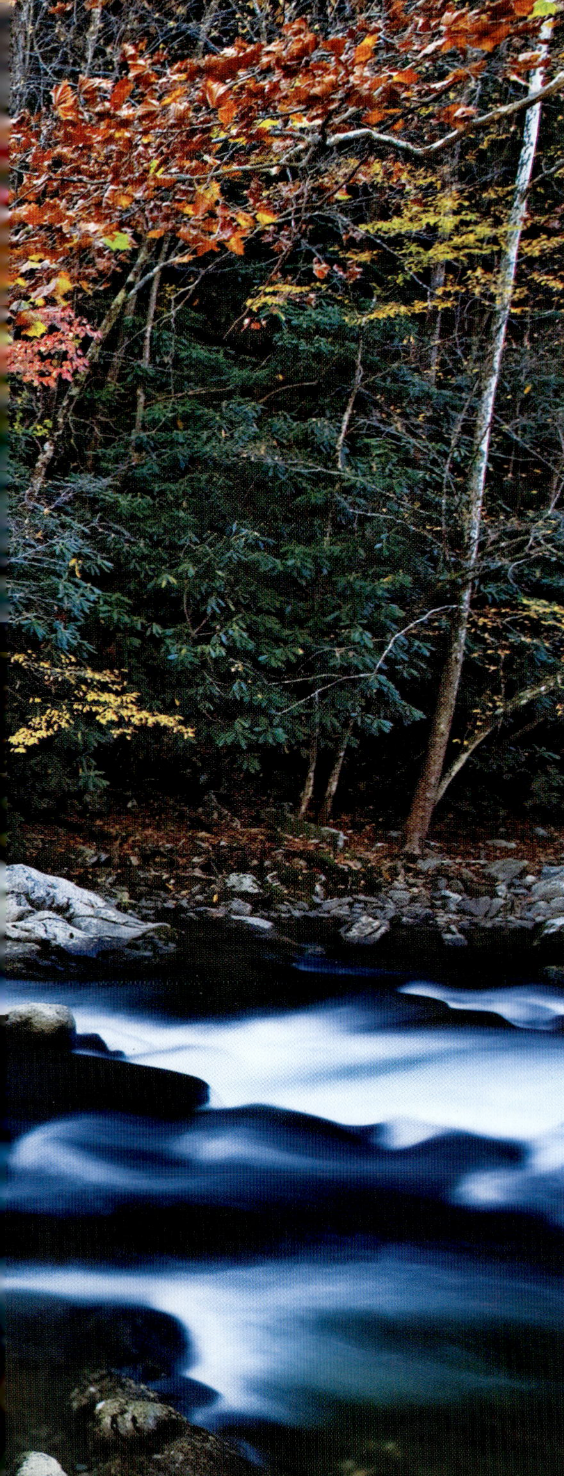

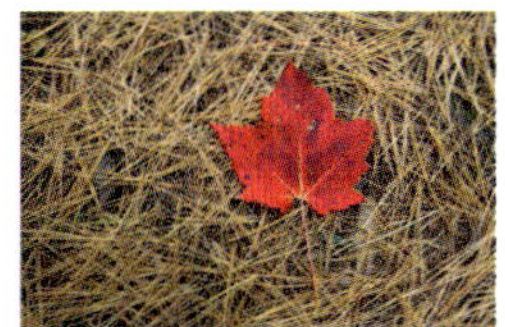

CONTENTS

LEFT: **Great Smoky Mountains National Park; Tennessee, North Carolina**
Making the most of the last days of autumn, some colors still cling to trees while the Little River below rushes over rocks, smoothing their surfaces.

RIGHT: **Acadia National Park, Maine**
A maple leaf rests on a bed of pine needles.

FOREWORD *Thomas C. Kiernan*

On May 10, 1869, the Union Pacific and Central Pacific railroads finally joined when a ceremonial golden spike was set into the earth only a few miles away from Utah's Great Salt Lake. Suddenly, east was linked to west, Atlantic to Pacific. But for years to come, most Americans knew as much about the landscapes of their own country as they knew about the landscapes of Jupiter or Mars. Photography was still in its infancy, and the most popular means of locomotion relied on steam power or horsepower—in the literal sense of the word. Artists and writers would soon set out for the West and return with fabulous images and stories of its unimaginable scenery, but there was scant evidence to persuade those who refused to believe the tales of its beauty—and the doubters were legion.

William Henry Jackson changed all of that. He changed it with a 5x8 camera and a portable darkroom. And a few simple photographs launched a nation's conservation movement.

It all began when the U. S. Geological Survey asked Ferdinand Hayden to explore the climate, geology, and natural resources of Colorado, Wyoming, and Utah in 1871. Hayden asked Jackson to leave his small photo studio in Omaha, Nebraska, and accompany him on the journey. They were joined by the respected painter and illustrator Thomas Moran. The two men recorded the scenery of the West using the methods they had mastered for years—Jackson with glass plates and chemicals that produced black-and-white images, Moran with a brush and pigments that captured the colors that escaped the camera's lens. And seven months after they returned to Washington, D.C., their handiwork played a crucial role in persuading Congress to establish our country's first national park: Yellowstone.

An intimate relationship between conservation and nature photography had begun. The work of Jackson's contemporary, Carleton Watkins, had already focused attention on Yosemite, beginning its path toward national park designation in 1890. George Masa wandered the Great Smokies, and his images helped that park become a reality in 1926. And of course, Ansel Adams captured images of California's iconic landscapes for decades, changing our understanding of photography and our understanding of nature at the same time.

Since its creation in 1916, our National Park System has grown to encompass 391 units, from the natural parks, preserves, seashores, and trails to Native American cultural sites, battlefields, and historic homes that tell our nation's stories. But make no mistake—a splotch of green ink in a road atlas doesn't make our most treasured places immune to dozens of threats. As our concept of national parks has evolved to preserve wildlife and natural habitats, tell our history, and reveal our nation's flaws, the threats to these places have evolved, too. Global warming knows no boundaries, and neither do wild animals whose habitats are shifting as our climate changes. Meanwhile, as Americans build more and more homes adjacent to these amazing natural areas, development threatens to ruin the very thing we love about these places. Wildlife like cougars, grizzlies, and pronghorn may soon find themselves marooned on

RIGHT: **Yosemite National Park, California**
Merced River beneath El Capitan.

PAGES 12/13: **Hawaii Volcanoes National Park, Hawaii**
A fern stands in stark contrast to the hardened pa'hoehoe lava.

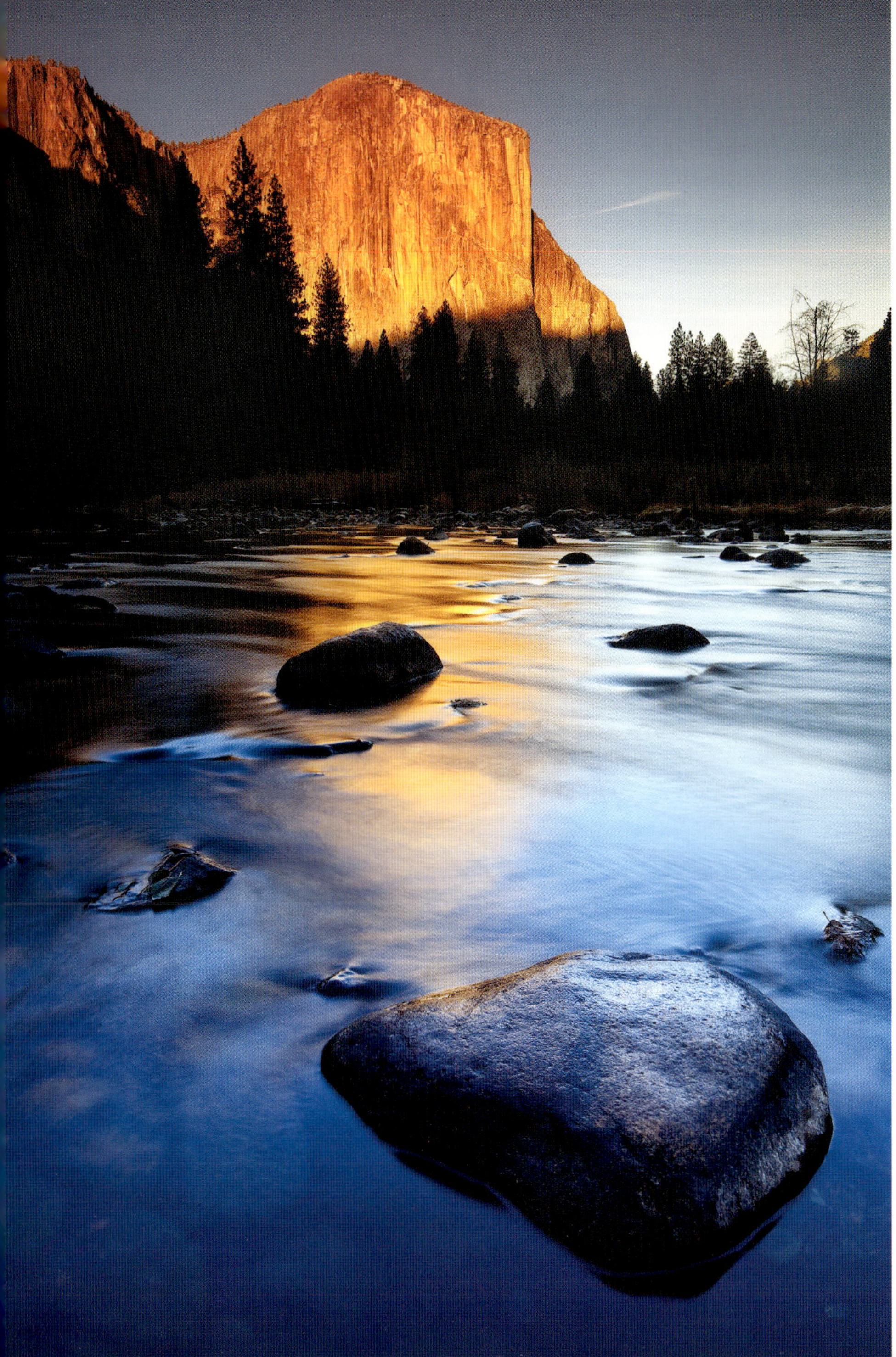

these ecological "islands," cut off from long-standing migration routes. As our nation's growing energy needs increase, we've begun to recognize the cruel irony of our continent's geology—pairing oil and gas deposits with some of our most fragile and beautiful mountains and waterways. And as coal-plant emissions cloud our landscapes, slow but irreversible damage is done to cultural sites that tell of the ancient civilizations that inhabited Mesa Verde, Canyon de Chelly, and other treasures in the Four Corners region of the southwestern desert.

But there is no need to be disheartened. These battles are not the first battles we have overcome. In 1916, when Woodrow Wilson signed legislation creating the National Park Service, Congress allocated only $4,500 for the agency—just enough to pay the director's salary. In the fall of 1939, interior secretary Harold Ickes successfully fended off government proposals to harvest Sitka spruce trees in Olympic National Park for the construction of airplanes when the timber industry insisted there were no other alternatives. And in 1955, after twenty years of controversy, park advocates successfully persuaded the Bureau of Reclamation to abandon plans to erect a dam at the confluence of Colorado's Yampa and Green rivers, sparing the paleontological treasures found at Dinosaur National Monument, whose canyons would have been flooded for hydropower, irrigation, and drinking water.

And so we continue to fight. We continue to fight because we cherish the photographs we have taken, the postcards we've gathered, the memories we have made, and the memories we have yet to make. And though we fight these battles armed with congressional testimony, with letters to the editor, with arguments and statistics and lawsuits, none of these can compare to the power of a single image. An image cannot be subject to debate, cannot be erased with statistics, cannot be swept aside with misguided appeals for progress.

Nearly 150 years after the transcontinental railroad was completed, our country has grown smaller. We can type a few characters on a keyboard and choose from dozens of flights to hundreds of destinations. We can watch news unfold on other continents before our very eyes. We can use a cell phone to capture a photograph with the push of a button and send it across the globe with the push of yet another button. But there are photographs, and then there are photographs. Few of us can capture the tension of a coyote tracking its prey and the intricacy of a dew-laden spider web, the character of a rusting locomotive and the beauty of a dry lake bed, the sweeping landscapes of Yosemite and the fragile veins of a decaying leaf. We may have the technology, but lack the artistic vision. We may have the skill, but lack the will to rise at dawn. We may have the constitution, but lack the resolve to climb a mountain. Thankfully, Ian Shive has all of these. And our national parks have an advocate whose message is plain to see, by simply turning a page.

THOMAS C. KIERNAN
President, National Parks Conservation Association

THOMAS C. KIERNAN *has been the president of the National Parks Conservation Association since January 1998, after leading the Audubon Society of New Hampshire and serving as a senior-level official in the Environmental Protection Agency. Kiernan grew up in Virginia, kayaking in the Chesapeake and Ohio Canal National Historical Park, and has paddled through Canyonlands and Grand Canyon national parks and Dinosaur National Monument. He cofounded the Rocky Mountain Outdoor Center in Colorado and achieved top-ten status in the United States in slalom kayaking in 1980. Kiernan holds an MBA from Stanford and a BA from Dartmouth College. He lives in Arlington, Virginia.*

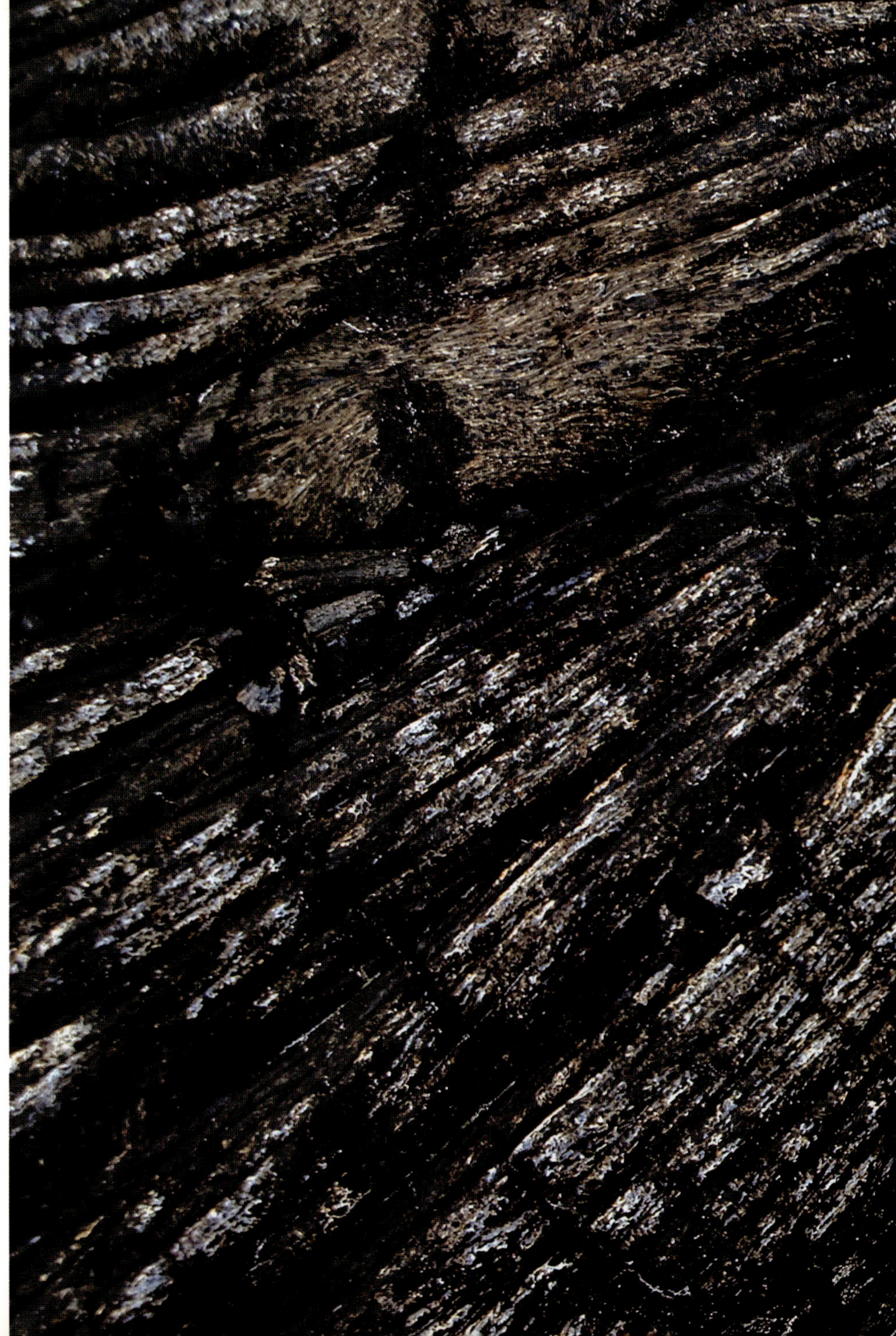

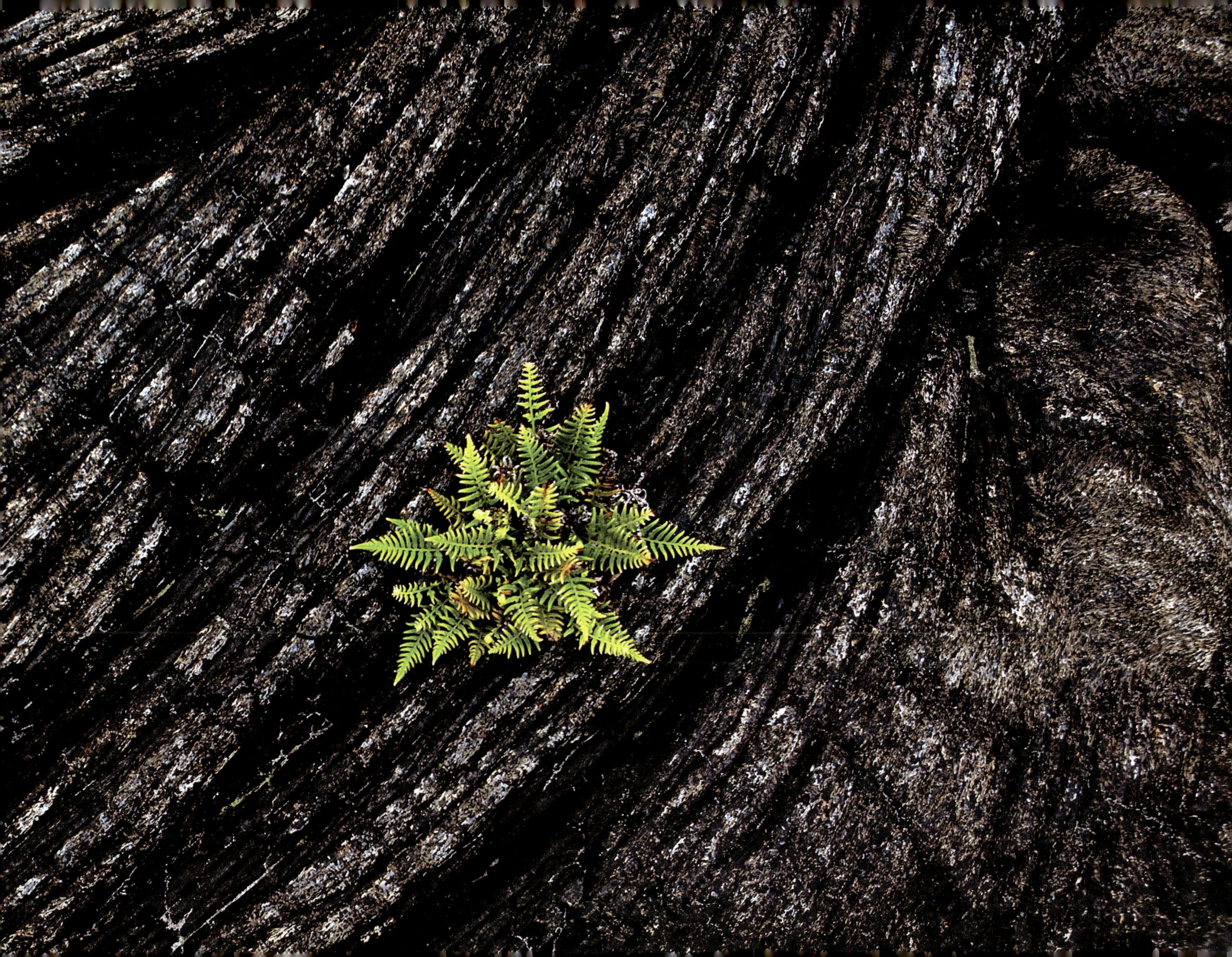

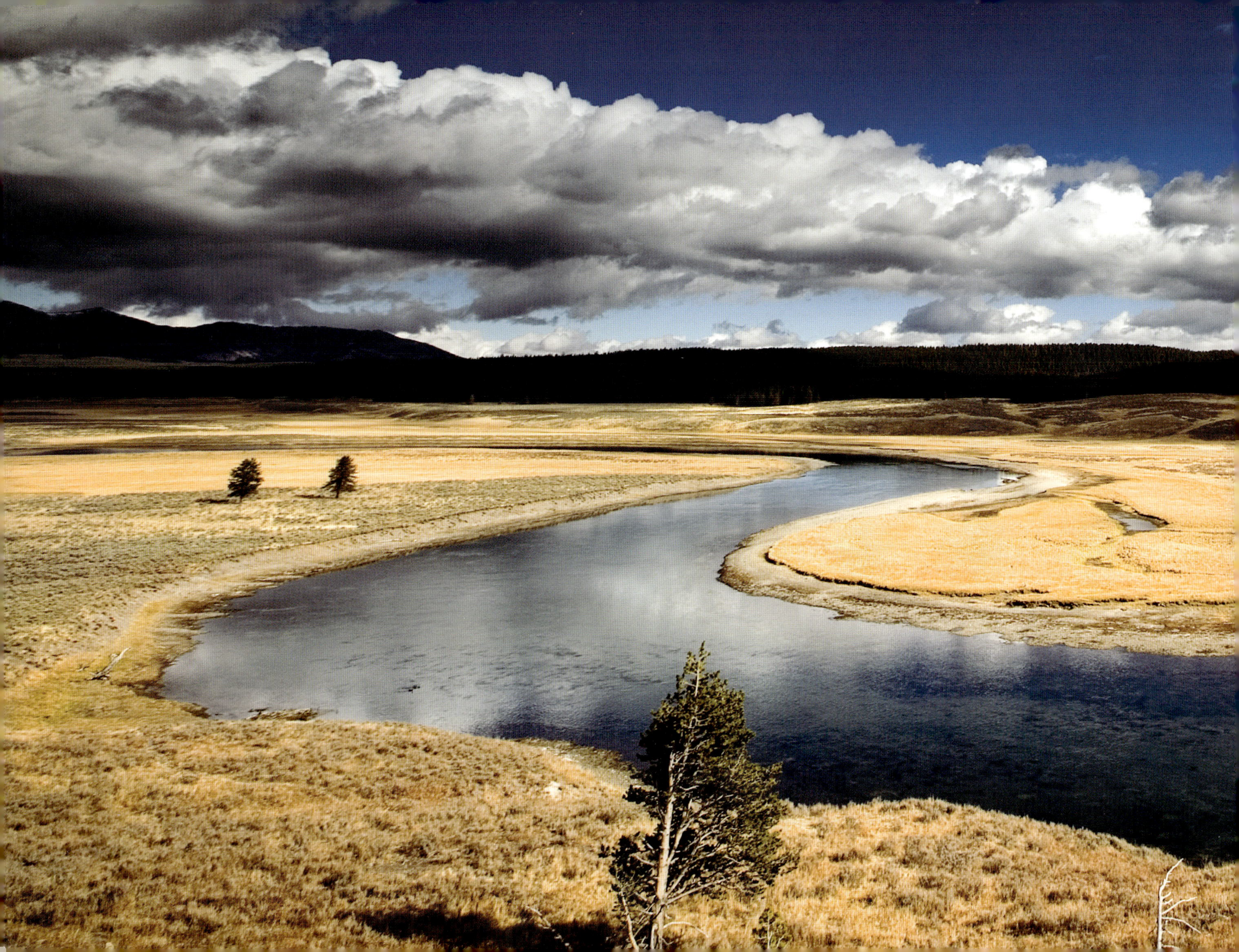

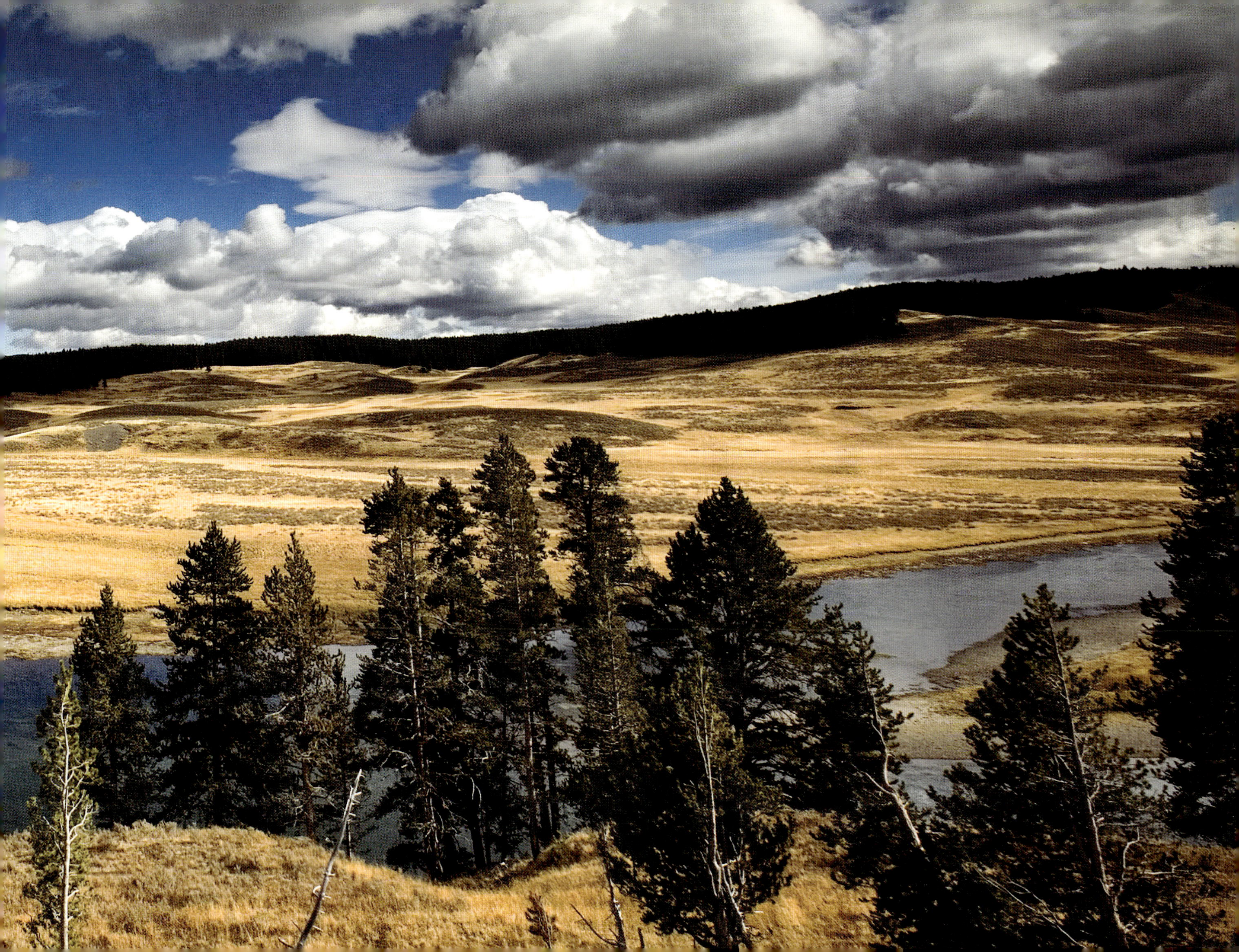

ESSAY *Scott Kirkwood*

When you're the editor of a magazine called *National Parks*, you sometimes feel a little guilty about getting a paycheck every week. Consider a few nuggets from my job description: interview park rangers, wildlife biologists, and historians as they discuss some of their favorite subjects; work with writers, photographers, and graphic designers to translate those stories onto the printed page; and, once or twice a year, visit a national park without chalking up a single vacation day. Oh, and while you're doing all that, help save an American institution that, in spite of its significance, is often overlooked in Washington, D.C.

That's not to say that it's an easy job. Trying to produce a world-class magazine on a nonprofit budget puts you at a distinct disadvantage. You're competing for the attention of eyeballs that could be surfing the Web, watching television, or reading any other publication out there. Luckily, the subject matter and the photographs in every issue of *National Parks* provide a few advantages.

But you'd be surprised how hard it is to find good photography. I see literally thousands of images of national parks every year—it's hard to imagine that anyone sees more photos of these iconic American landscapes. As much as I enjoy spending my time reviewing images of Acadia's cliffs, Zion's peaks, and everything in between, there's a point where I start to think, *seen it*. When a photographer is on assignment to Glacier National Park, he's got to execute a shot that not only screams "Glacier!" before the reader even sees a caption, but also whispers something new to those who have visited the park dozens of times. Like painting a still life that reveals something more than just a

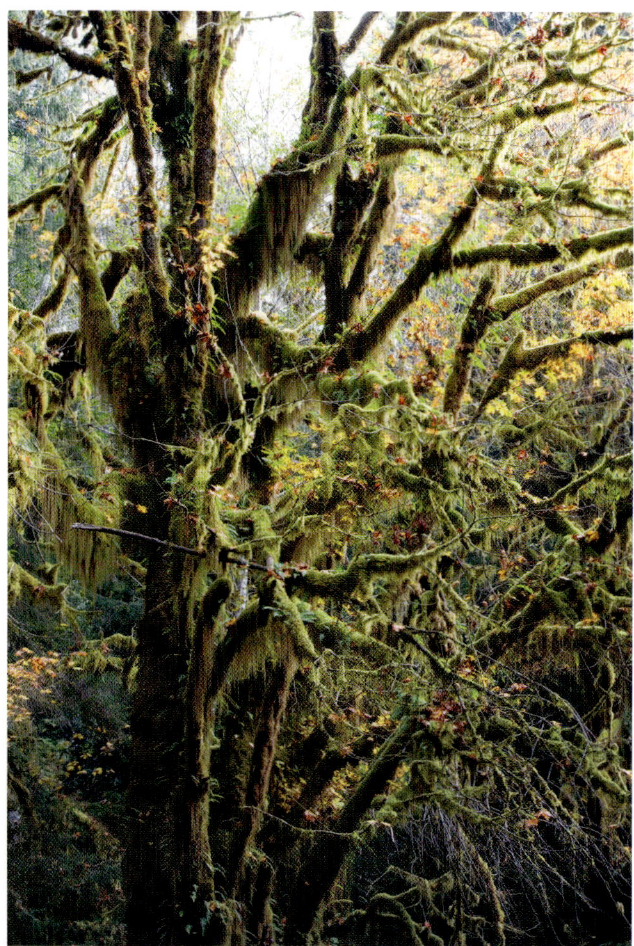

PAGES 14/15: **Yellowstone National Park; Wyoming, Montana, Idaho**
The Yellowstone River quietly flows under partly cloudy skies near Canyon Junction.

LEFT: **Olympic National Park, Washington**
Detail of a tree in the Hoh Rain Forest, one of the oldest intact old-growth rain forests in the country.

RIGHT: **Zion National Park, Utah**
A scenic view of a long exposure of river water running through the park.

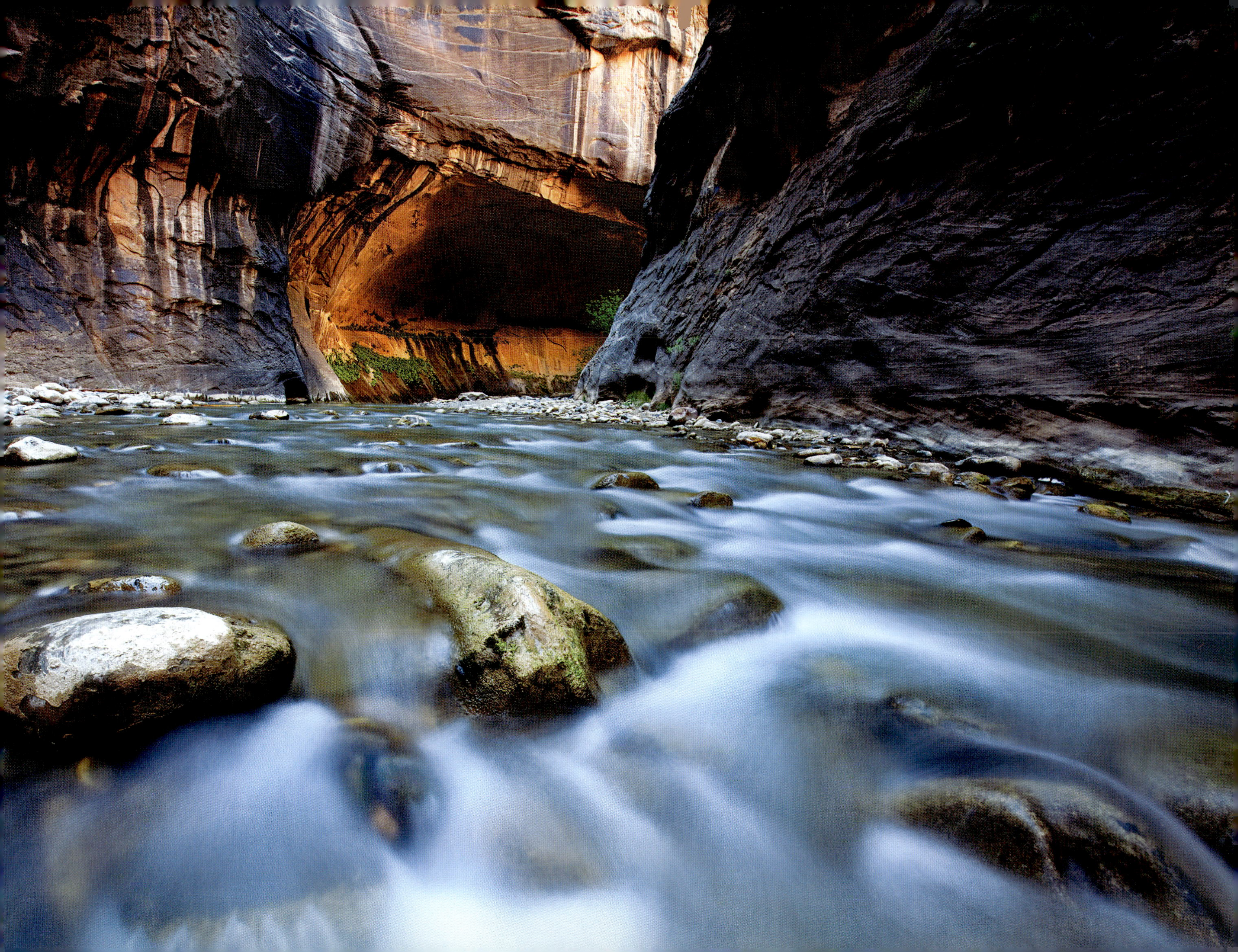

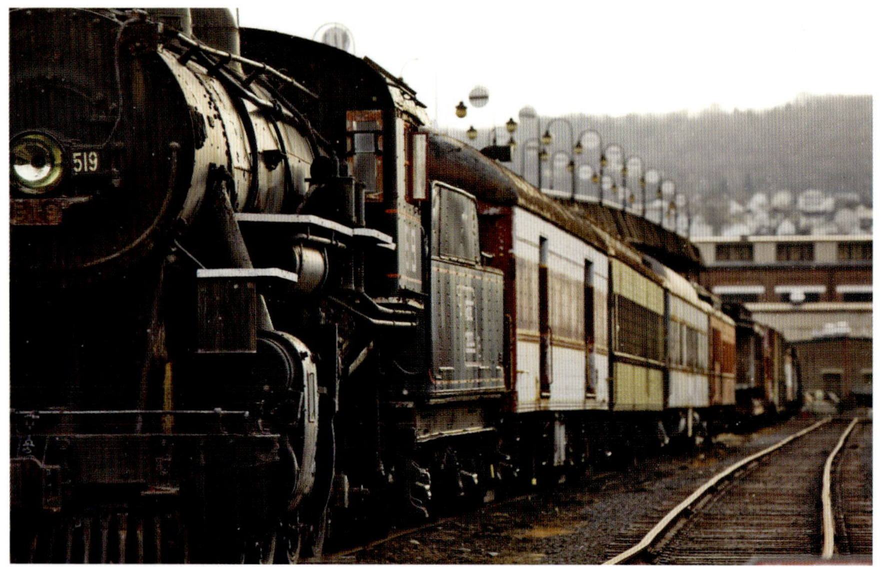

bowl of fruit, it's not easy to do. But Ian Shive does it. I'm still trying to figure out how.

In 2007 one of our editors returned from a photo conference after meeting Ian for the first time. Ian had recently visited a little-known site called Steamtown, a short drive from his grandparents' home in Browndale, Pennsylvania. Most photographers who approach us have a portfolio of the classic parks like Yellowstone and Yosemite, with the typical shots of sunsets, winding roads, and the occasional rainbow thrown in for good measure. Ian, on the other hand, had spent a cloudy afternoon in Scranton, Pennsylvania, at a national historic site that few people have ever heard of. He came back with photos of rusting steam engines and aging boxcars with torn upholstery, broken windows, and peeling paint. And they were beautiful. Our staff loved the photos' ethereal quality, and we immediately knew they belonged in our pages. But we needed some words to tell the rest of the story, so Ian wrote about his time spent wandering the vacant rail yard, listening for stories of the passengers who boarded those trains decades ago. It was simple. It spoke of our country's history. And it made clear the simple challenge facing so many Park Service sites: preserving treasures that reveal our nation's history while allowing time to have its way with those very treasures. We paired the photos with some historic black-and-white images from the romantic era of train travel, and "The Ghosts of Steamtown" won a prestigious award about a year later. But we didn't need to wait that long to know that this was the beginning of a fruitful partnership.

When faced with the grandeur of the national parks, too many photographers are tempted to treat them like museum pieces—to be put on a wall or placed under glass—to be seen but not touched. Because park landscapes change so imperceptibly year after year, paging through these photos can feel like spinning a postcard carousel in the back of a musty old gift shop—you can almost hear the squeaking metal and see the dust on the glossy images as they come around again and again. Ian's images have just a little more color, just a little more sharpness, and just a little more energy—even the clouds seem choreographed. And as you look through them, you realize these are not foreign places to be kept at a distance, somewhere "out there," something untouchable. This is your very own

THIS PAGE: **Steamtown National Historic Site, Pennsylvania**
The rusty ruins of old railroad tracks and train cars sit quietly idle, waiting for another chance at the next stop. As one walks through this rail yard, an eerie feeling settles in, like billows of steam from a forgotten era. The exterior paint whispers of a more elegant and patriotic age. It is not a far stretch to imagine passengers from a century earlier excitedly searching for their seats and stuffing luggage into overhead racks. Suddenly, I want to know their names, their stories, where they are from, and where they are headed. I do not want them to be forgotten. The Steamtown National Historic Site became part of the National Park Service on October 30, 1986, to preserve American steam locomotive history.

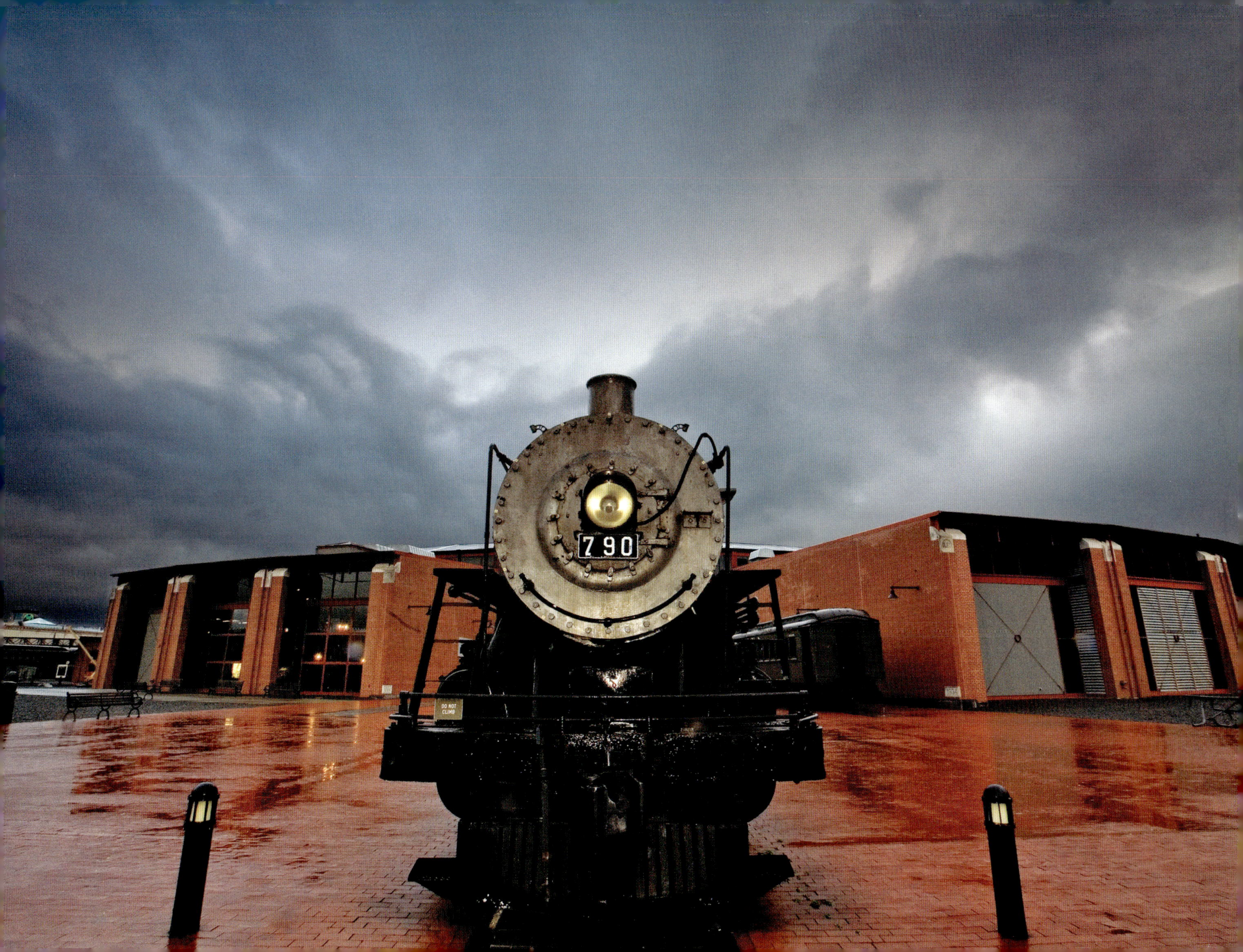
790

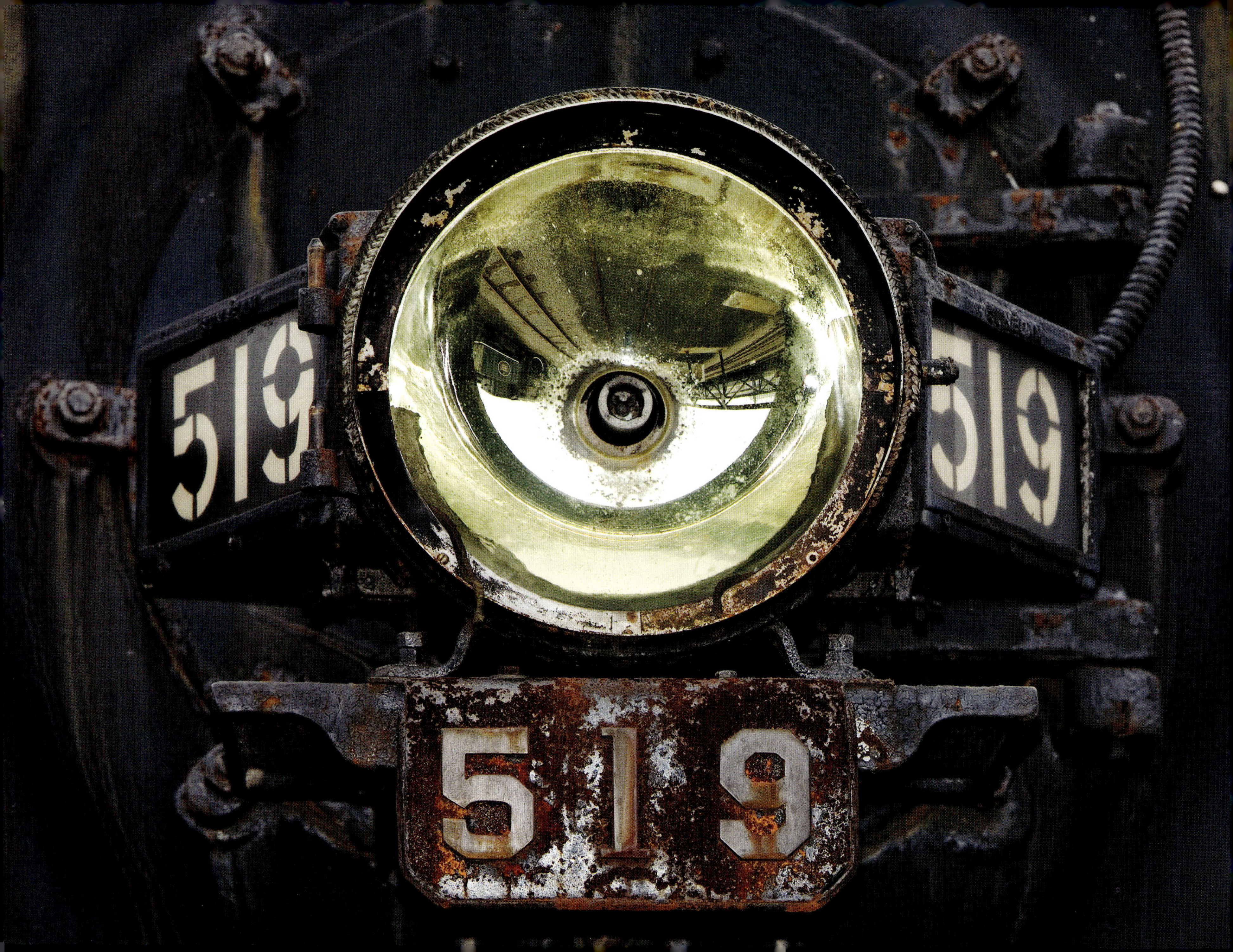
519
519
519

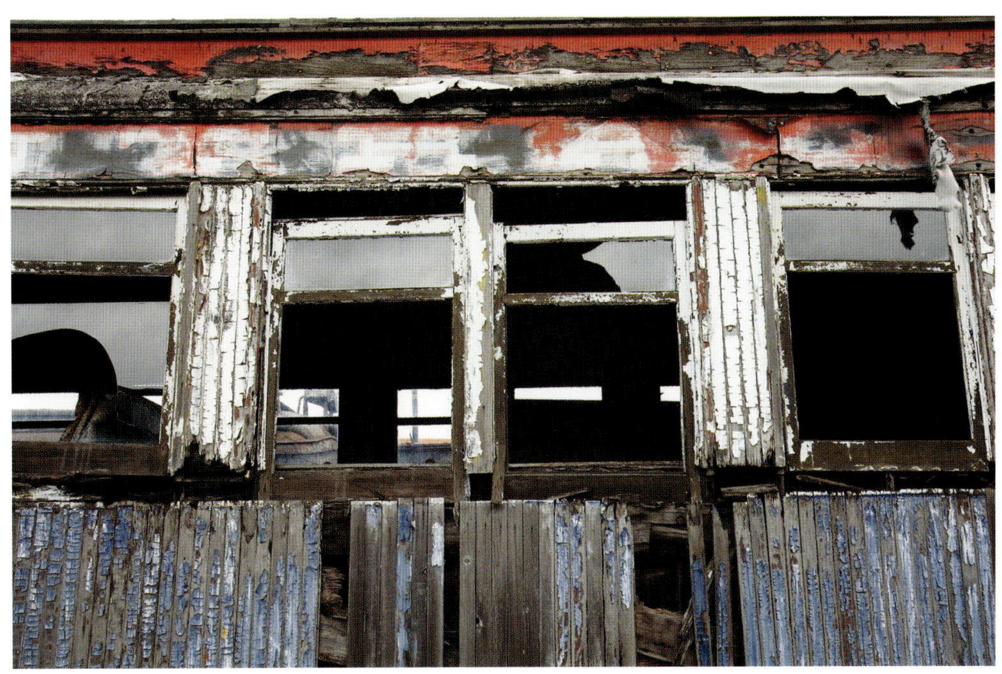

LEFT & ABOVE: **Steamtown National Historic Site, Pennsylvania**

PAGES 22/23: **Yellowstone National Park, Wyoming; Montana, Idaho**
Lights from the classic Old Faithful Snow Lodge shine behind a boardwalk, which winds through geysers and thermal features.

backyard. You are the one swimming in the waters of the Channel Islands, gasping for breath as you climb Mount McKinley, paddling the Rio Grande in Big Bend, or walking along the bustling city streets of Bar Harbor, Maine.

Hundreds of photographers are capable of showing you where they have been, and leave you a little envious in the process, but these images transport the viewer as well. Through Ian's lens, you notice a single red leaf underfoot, one that you might have otherwise overlooked. You watch the pure white gypsum of White Sands National Monument turn into an abstract painting. You find a footprint in the dried mud of Death Valley. You appreciate the detail in a fern, raindrops on a blade of grass, and mushrooms sprouting from a log. You start to understand that even scorpions and tarantulas have a beauty that you never would have expected. These are the things that children discover as they crawl on their hands and knees—while their parents are distracted by a map or a guidebook or the next scheduled showing of a film in the visitor center.

And these are the reasons that we give Ian a call whenever we need to pair images with words. Although our rates pale in comparison to many newsstand magazines or commercial shoots, he says yes every time. He drove to Lake Mead, Nevada, to dive below the water's surface with the Park Service's Submerged Resources team. He flew to Alaska to climb with Denali's search-and-rescue team. He visited Glacier National Park and shot images that scream and whisper at the same time. And when he comes back, he gives us far too many photos to run in the six or seven pages we set aside, forcing us to make painful decisions about which ones to include and which ones to leave out. Thankfully, he found a book publisher with the wisdom to print hundreds of these incredible images at once. And lucky for us, he's already out there creating even more.

SCOTT KIRKWOOD
Editor, *National Parks* magazine

SCOTT KIRKWOOD *has been writing and editing for advocacy groups in Washington, D.C., for nearly fifteen years, from the Humane Society of the United States to the Child Welfare League of America and now the National Parks Conservation Association. In his current role as editor of* National Parks *magazine, he's hiked the sand dunes of Kobuk Valley, photographed the sunrise at Dry Tortugas, and splished and splashed his way through the Narrows of Zion. When he's not collecting frequent-flier miles, he can often be found riding his bike through Rock Creek Park or playing soccer on the National Mall.*

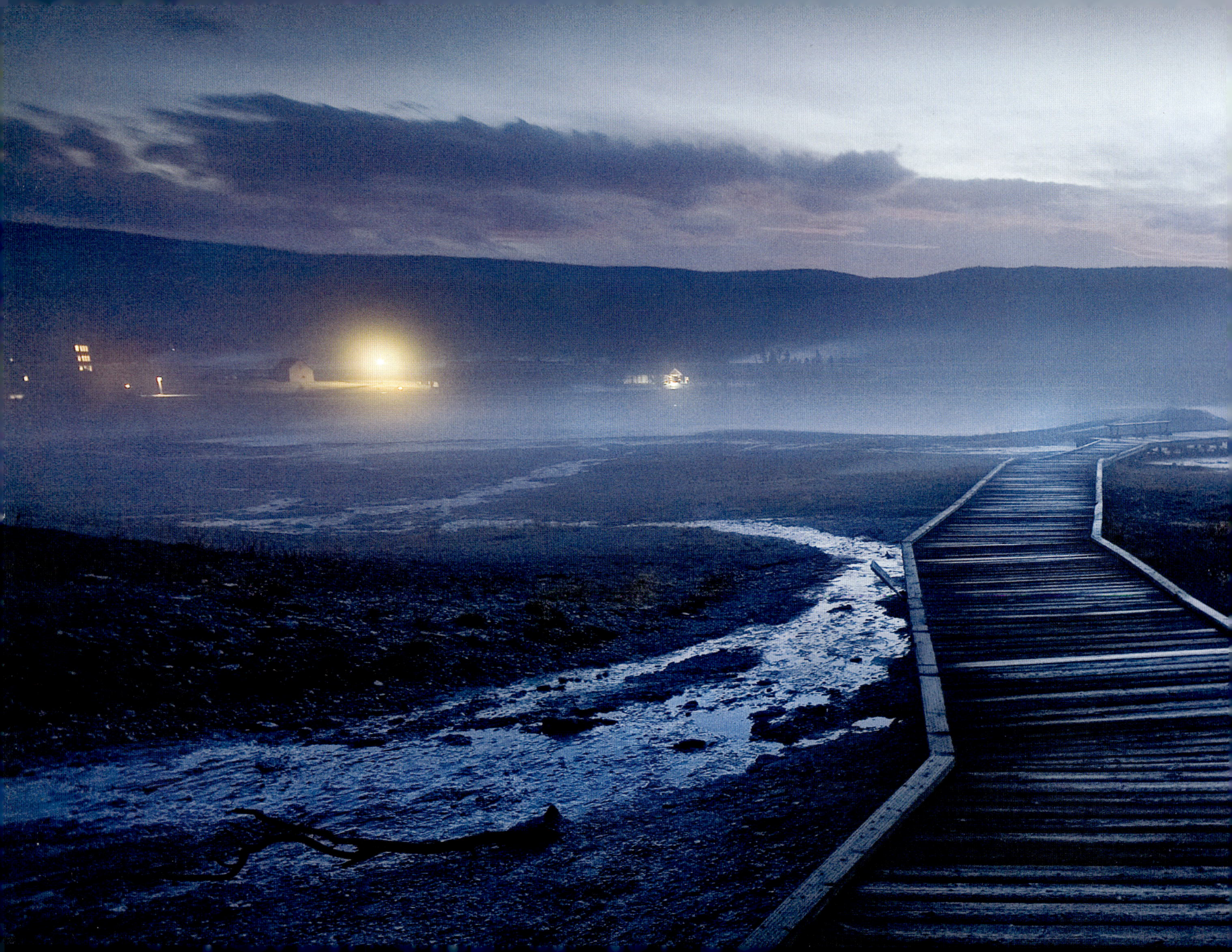

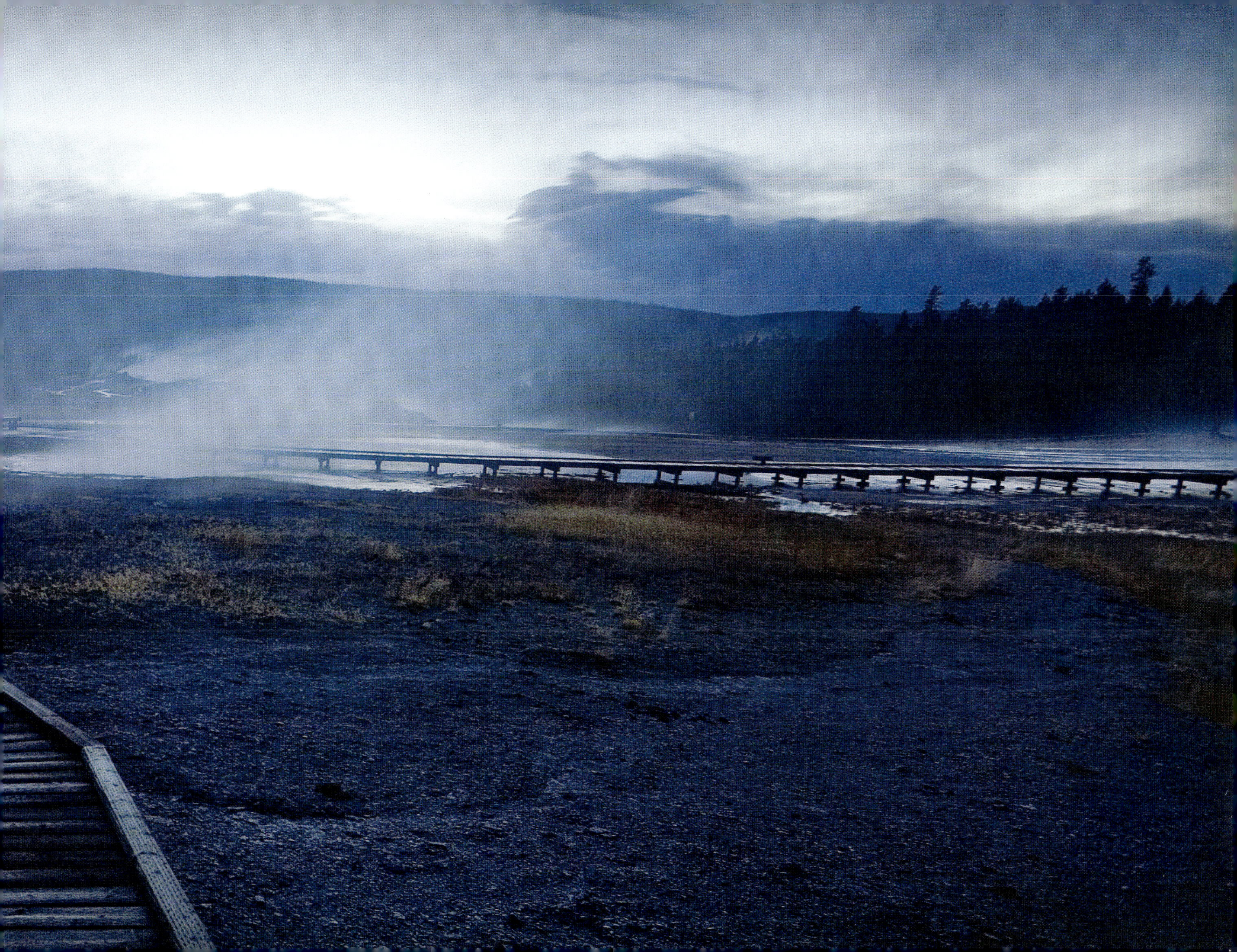

RIGHT: **Big Bend National Park, Texas**
Amy Leinbach Marquis at Big Bend.

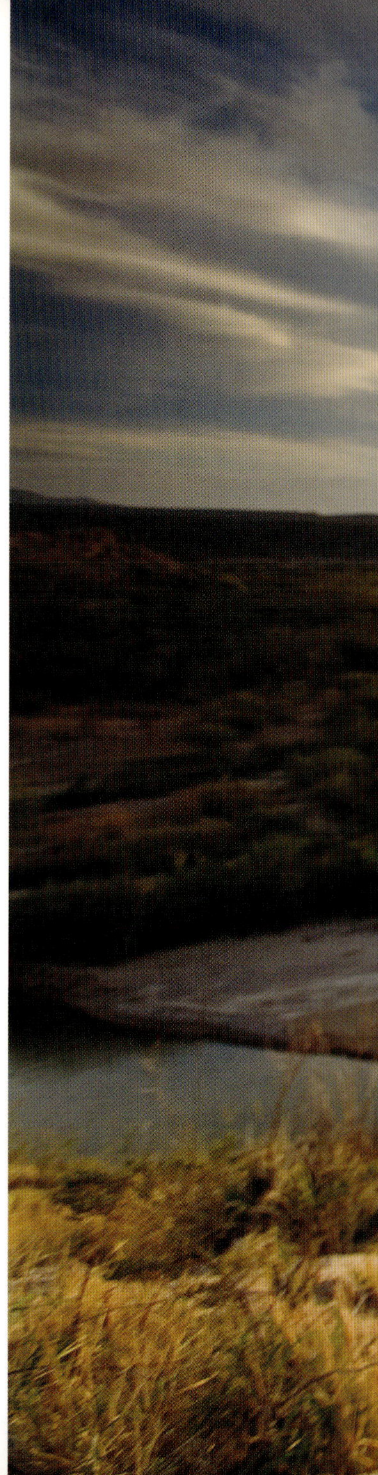

ESSAY *Amy Leinbach Marquis*

It was well after midnight and near freezing when our car broke down in the middle of the Texas desert. Ian and I were on our way back from watching a meteor shower at the river's edge in Big Bend National Park—the perfect end to a productive week on assignment for *National Parks* magazine—when our sedan bottomed out on a small boulder in the middle of a dirt road. A quick inspection confirmed a hole in the radiator, and the more coolant leaked out, the worse our situation became. We were both scheduled to fly out of Marathon—a small town about three hours north of the park—the next day.

So we began the long, methodical push to Panther Junction nearly forty miles away, where we hoped we could get a cell phone signal to call for help. As the car overheated, we fell into a measured pattern of stop and go: Gun it for one minute, cool down for four; repeat. We inched along an endless road, passing a mule deer, a coyote, and at least a dozen tarantulas, whose eyes glared back in the headlights; but we weren't interested in wildlife. With no heat, no rations, and no way to communicate with the outside world, we'd kicked into survival mode. At one point I was ready to ditch the car and continue on by foot, but the cold convinced me otherwise.

Hours later, we arrived at the ranger station and called for help. Thankfully, an employee at the park lodge works a night shift for precisely these occasions—and sometime around 3:00 a.m. his headlights came beaming down the road toward us. "What do you know," he said, "I just passed a mountain lion." Did I mention we almost walked?

Now back up for a minute and consider my typical workday as an editor of *National Parks* magazine: Wake up. Commute to work. Turn computer on. Check email. Read, write, edit. Break for a meeting. Break for lunch. Review photos. Call a park, interview a ranger. Check email again. Shut down computer. Commute home. Four times a year that routine swells into an intense phase of impromptu meetings and deadlines—stressful, but predictable. In my world, the insanity is cyclical and generally well planned, and with just two editors on staff, we generally try to avoid upsetting that flow.

But then I heard about this unique conservation partnership between an unlikely mix of people—Park Service staff, Mexican ranchers, an international cement company, and grassroots advocacy groups. Despite a recent border closing and controversial immigration debates, they had found ways to work together to protect the land and wildlife they loved. I *had* to pursue this story. After six years of photo editing, I'd just transitioned to writing, and this was the perfect chance to get a taste of life in the field. Thankfully, my boss understands the value of experiencing the parks firsthand—and of giving a young writer the space and opportunity to find her voice.

Still, I knew the work wouldn't come easy. Conservation efforts in a border park are complex, to say the least. And the story had already been broadcast from the newsstands in varying degrees. What could I say that hadn't been said already?

Thankfully, Ian turned out to be as interested in telling the story as he was in photographing it. As I conducted interviews, he hovered on the fringe—listening, observing, and occasionally stepping in to snap a portrait or guide us to a place where the composition and light worked better.

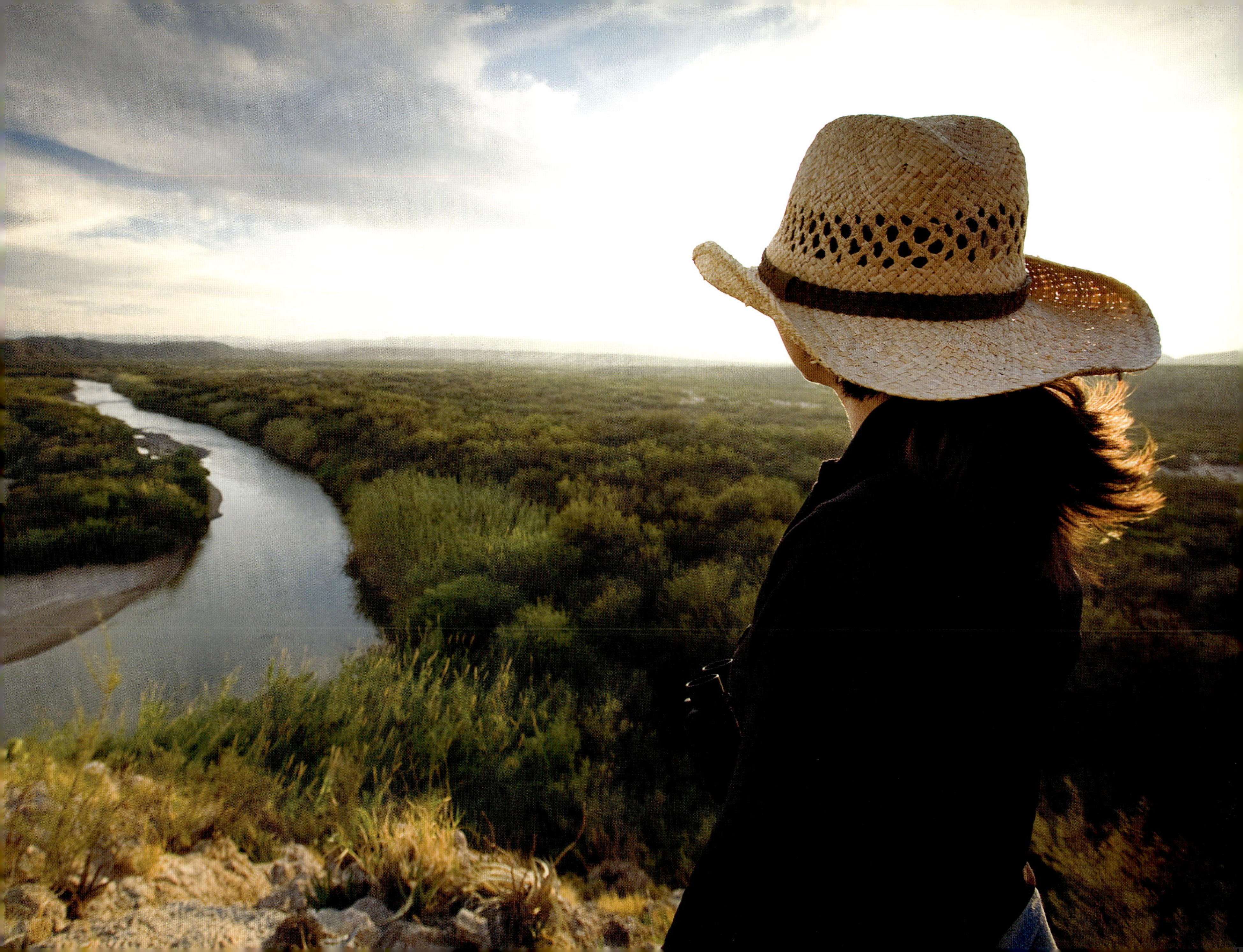

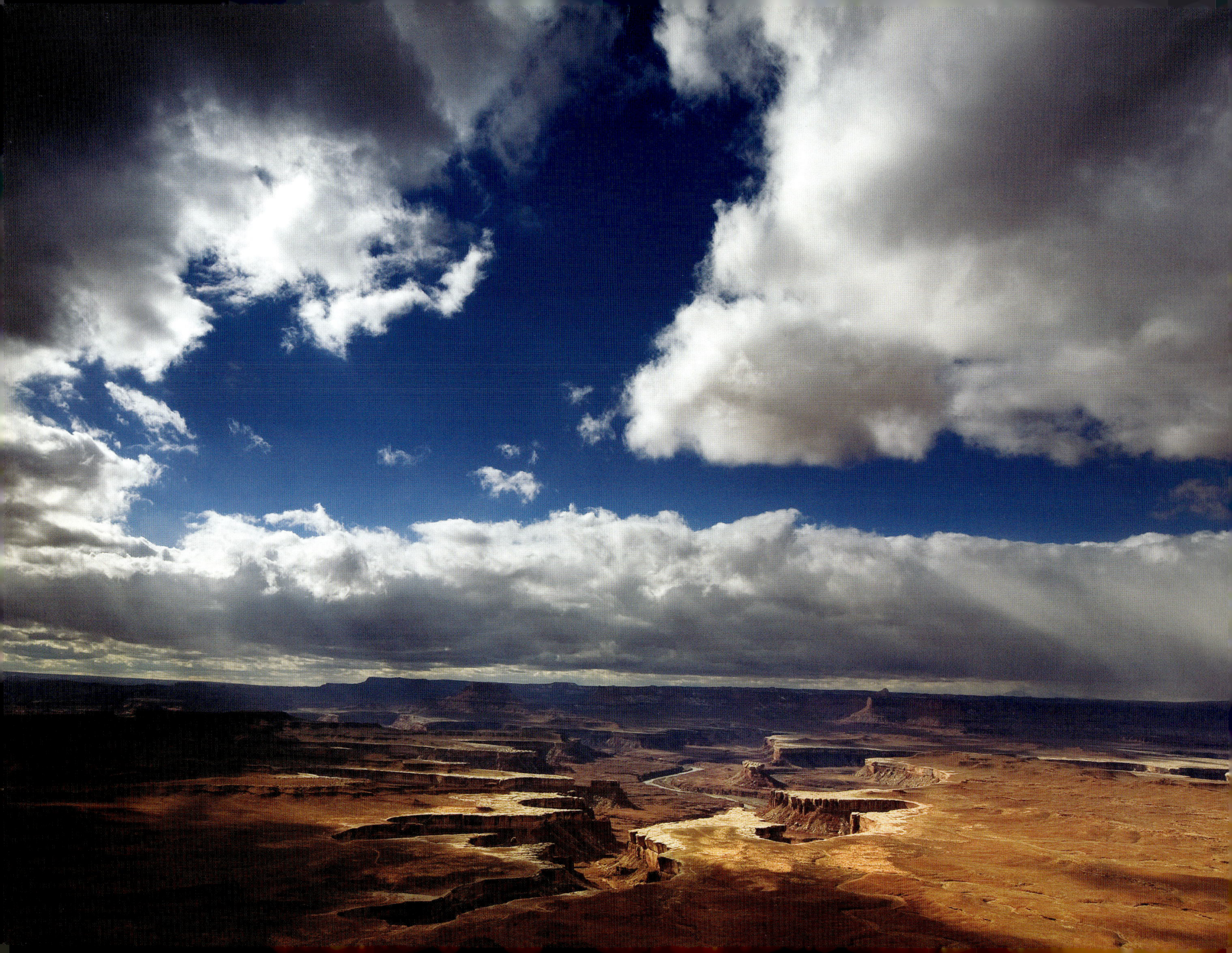

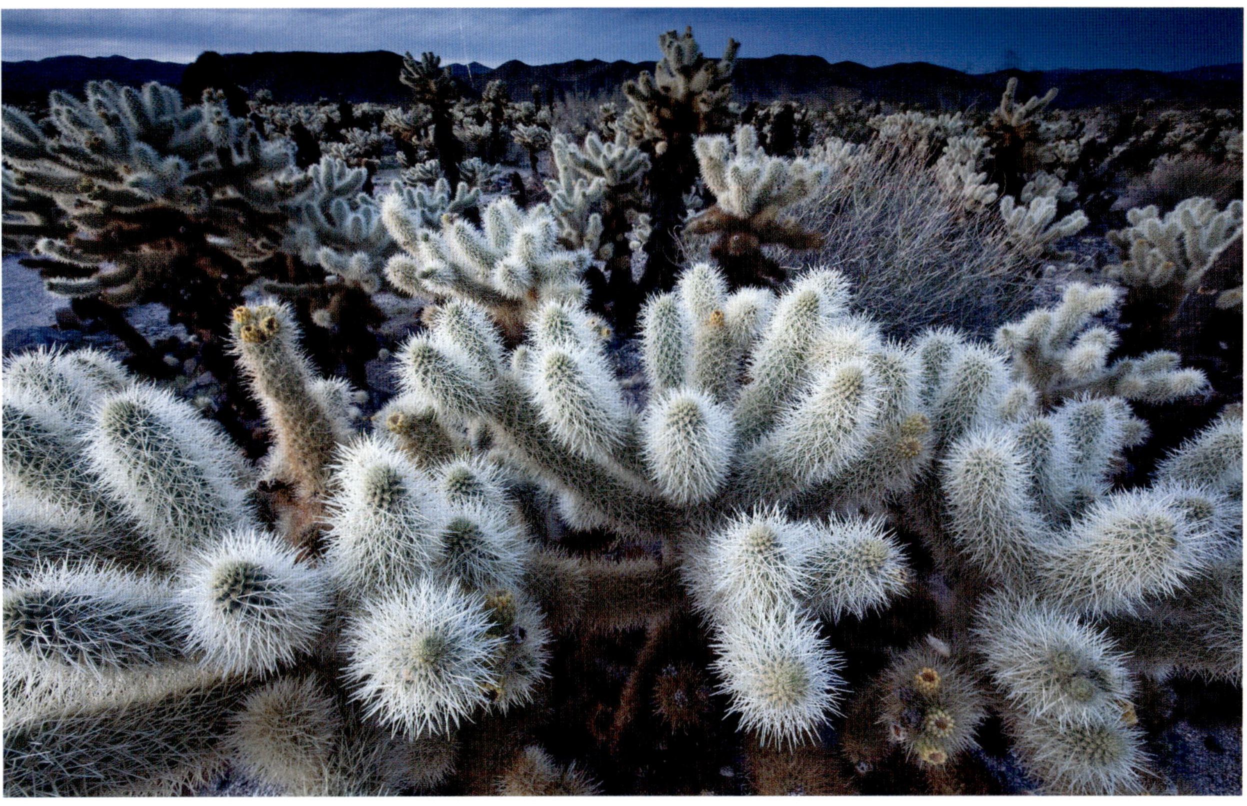

LEFT: **Canyonlands National Park, Utah**
The Green River winds below the canyon walls.

RIGHT: **Joshua Tree National Park, California**
Teddy bear cactus or jumping cholla in Joshua Tree National Park, California

After each meeting I'd turn to him and ask, "So what is this story *really* about?" We'd toss around opinions, brainstorm angles, even try crafting paragraphs out loud—all the usual tasks of my office job, but with the backdrop of a stunning desert landscape to fuel our ideas.

Sometimes, though, we'd give the words a break. We'd drive to a photogenic spot, and while I soaked in the scenery, Ian would bound swift and light footed through fields of sharp, spiky agaves and dagger-tipped cacti to capture the best light. The plants would cut right through his jeans and into his legs, and he'd return to the car shredded and bleeding and plucking out thorns. But he always exceeded his goal of capturing one good photograph a day. And by the end of the week, he had several dozen—including a magazine cover.

Other times, we'd leave the camera and journal behind and simply explore. It might have meant photos missed: the young mountain lion that leapt in front of our car, the meteors that streaked the sky during our last night in the park. But at some point you have to stop worrying about cover photos and opening spreads and just *be*.

Still, Ian had a business to run. So wherever there was a connection, he was on his phone emailing editors and responding to photo requests that didn't let up just because he was in the field. And as he built up his own portfolio with stunning images of Big Bend, he was constantly browsing other photography and multimedia Web sites, always focusing his eye on the next big project.

Honestly, it was hard to keep up sometimes. But at the end of a long day, no matter how much I wanted to retire to my room, I would stick around. Evenings were when Ian edited the day's shoot on his laptop—and I loved watching people react to his work. Waitresses and park staff would linger around our dinner table, peering wide eyed over Ian's shoulder as if seeing Big Bend for the very first time. His images weren't just illustrations of the place; they were a gift to the people who called it home.

When I returned to my desk in Washington, D.C., a week later, I kept circling back to an idea Ian had planted in my mind: Photographs are the fabric of a story, and words are the thread that stitches it all together. Whenever I couldn't find the right words, I would call up Ian's images and focus on the ones that most moved me, conjuring the park's sounds and smells all over again. And because I had something real to look at—a desert landscape saturated in late-afternoon light, the expression on a biologist's face as she gazed across the Mexican border—the story remained tangible. It was something I could grasp and shape. Through that process, I always found my voice—and by the time the article ran in the summer 2008 issue, I knew we had succeeded in telling a story that was both familiar and refreshingly new.

Our assignment in Big Bend taught me that there is always, *always*, a story behind the image. And considering the desk-bound editor's tendency to look at a photograph in its final, perfectly polished state and think, "Wow, that's pretty," I am thankful to have finally witnessed the hard work and grit that leads to the moment when the shutter clicks. I understand the challenge of chasing fickle light, of battling extreme temperatures, of racing through prickly pears bent on drawing blood.

I've had the pleasure of working with Ian on many more projects since then, and we continue to dream about our next big assignment in the field—but we never forget where we started, or the night we were stranded in Big Bend.

AMY LEINBACH MARQUIS
Editor, *National Parks* magazine

AMY LEINBACH MARQUIS *spent a summer in Malaysia eleven years ago to research and write about endangered sea turtles—an experience that sparked her career in environmental journalism. When she returned to the United States, she moved to the Washington, D.C., area and spent the next four years editing photos for* National Wildlife *magazine. In 2004, she became an editor at the National Parks Conservation Association and has covered a wide range of park issues, from global warming in Yellowstone to threats posed by the solar industry near California's desert parks. Her favorite assignments include trips to Big Bend and Great Falls, where she teamed up with talented photographers to tell park stories. In the fall of 2009, she and her husband embarked on a cross-country trip in their Airstream and settled out West, where Marquis continues to write about the parks she loves.*

RIGHT: **Big Bend National Park, Texas**
A waning crescent moon sets over the Chisos Mountains.

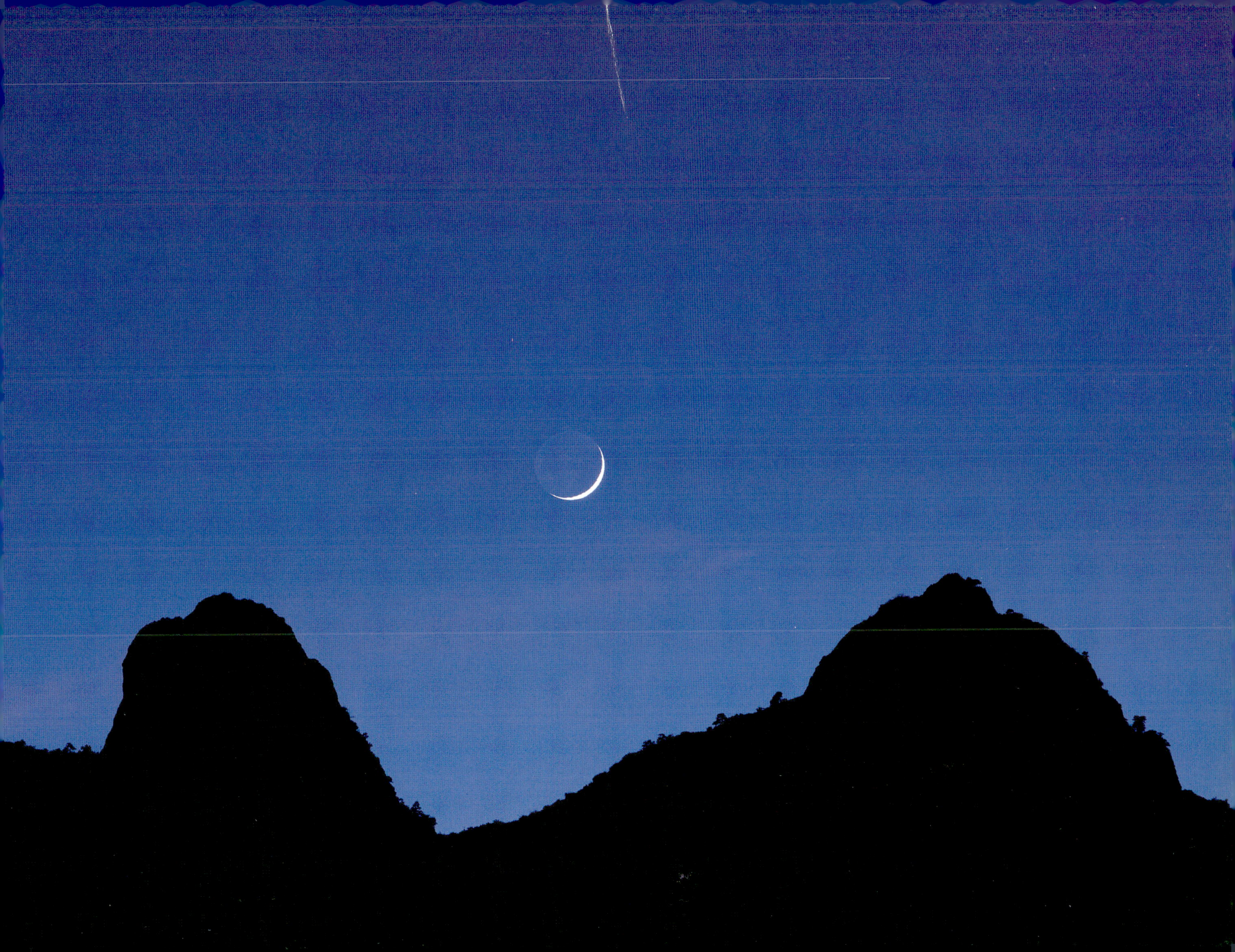

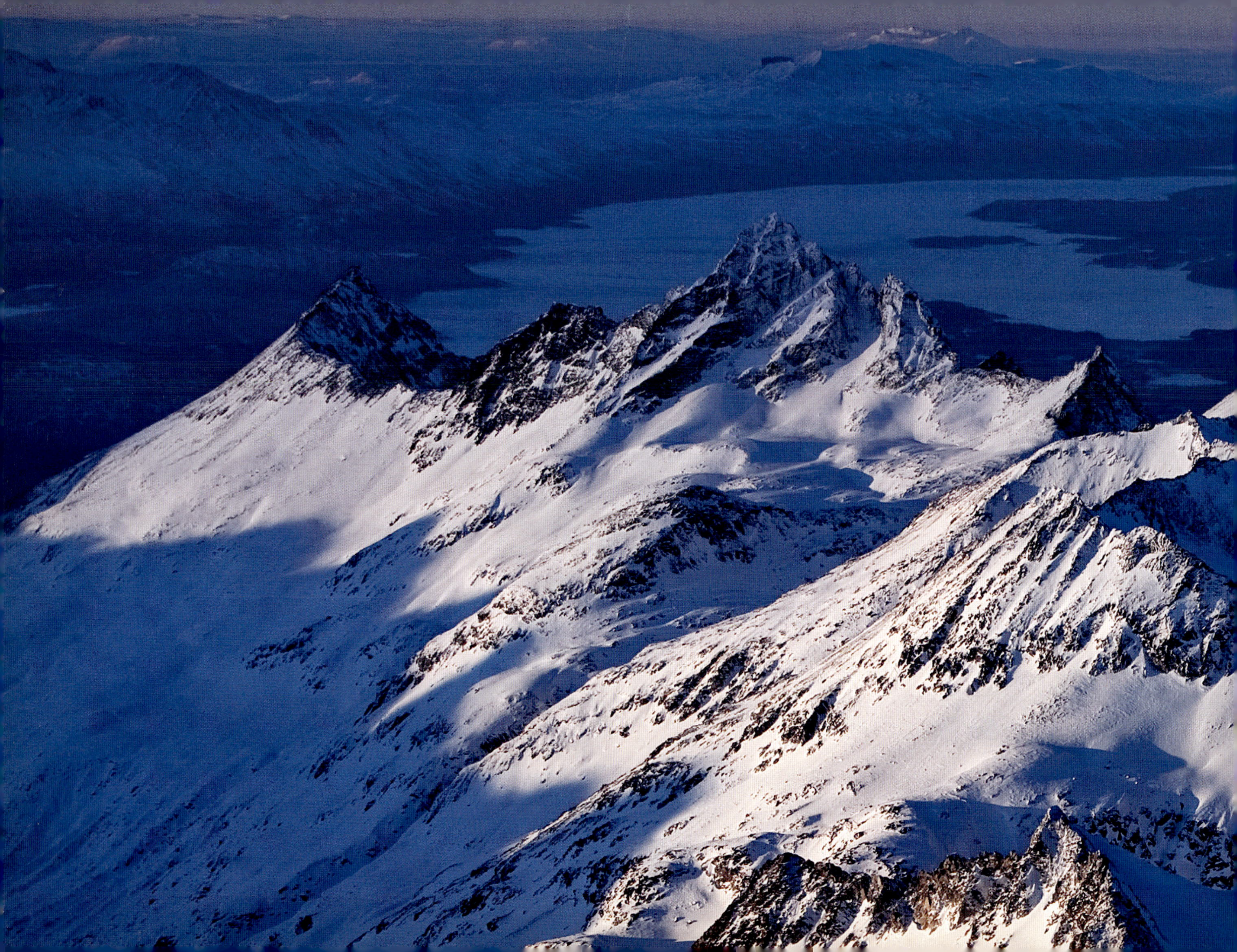

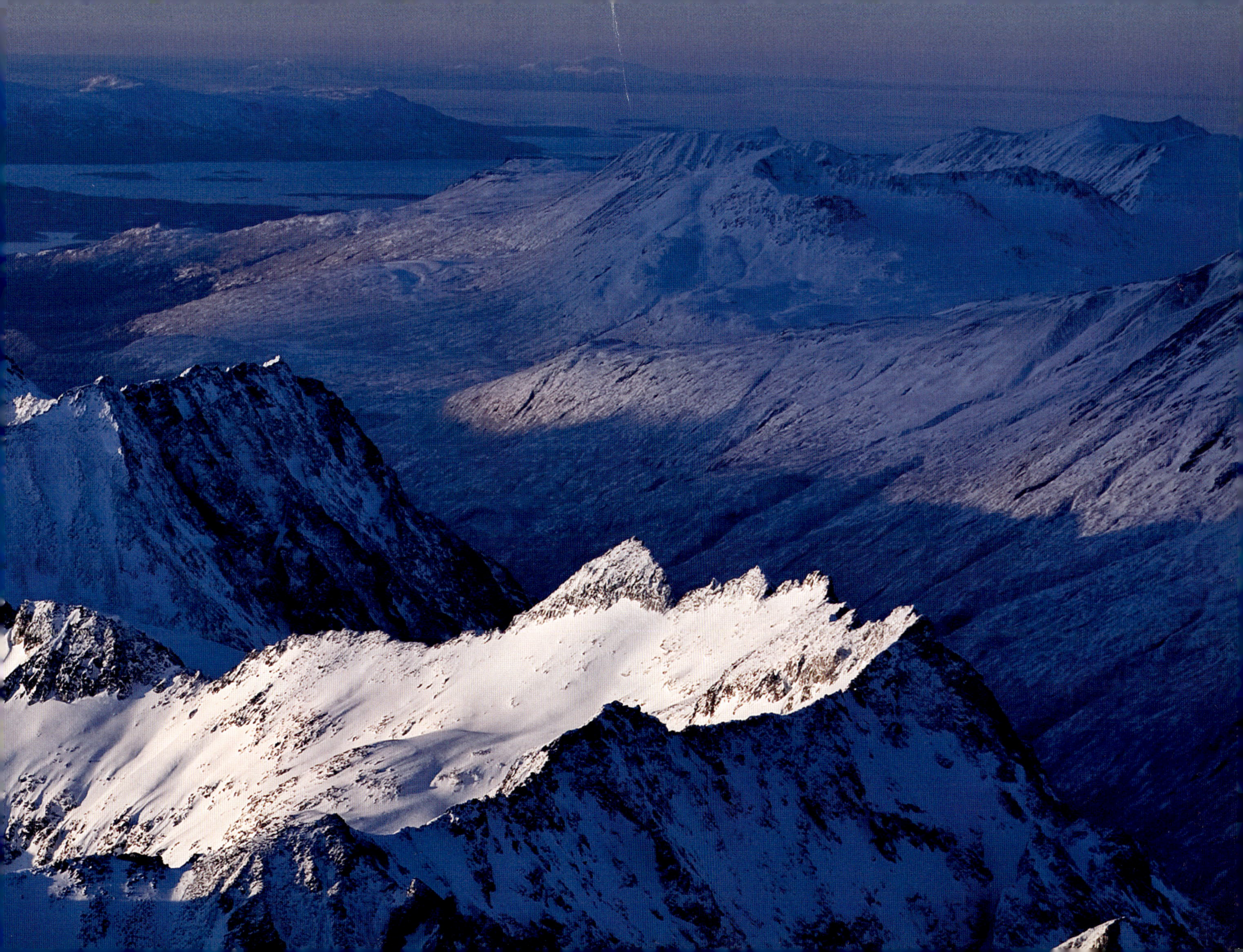

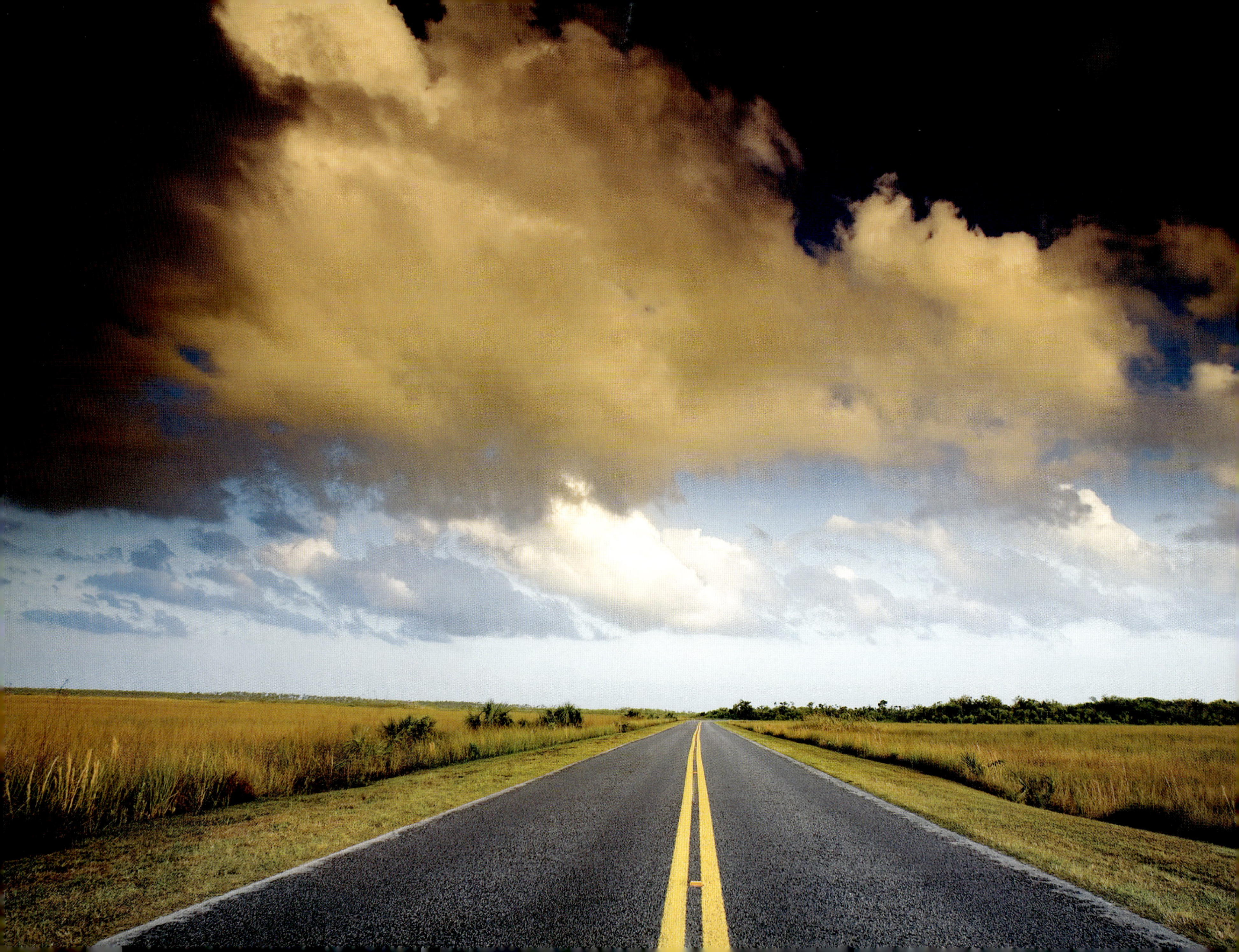

INTRODUCTION *Ian Shive*

It has often been stated that our country's national parks—Glacier, the Grand Canyon, Yosemite, Yellowstone, the Grand Tetons, Acadia, and the other 385 park units of national park status—represent that which is best in America. Oases among our fifty United States, the parks are essentially masses of land, separated and protected by invisible boundaries. Within each boundary, however, is a jewel box laden with its own unique splendor and heritage, waiting to be discovered and rediscovered.

In a 1787 letter from one American forefather to another, Thomas Jefferson wrote to James Madison, "I think our government will remain virtuous for many centuries . . . as long as there shall be vacant lands in any part of America." Nearly seventeen years later, in 1804, Meriwether Lewis and William Clark set forth west (at the urging of Jefferson) on an epic journey that would uncover both the beauty and diversity of America's landscape—a landscape of astonishing physical magnitude and aesthetic depth, which runs the gamut from austere and unforgiving to soft and verdant—as it stood ready to reveal its secrets.

Though Lewis and Clark's expedition was a milestone, it was not until 1872 that America's eighteenth president, Ulysses S. Grant, signed the Yellowstone National Park Act—effectively preserving, for perpetuity, approximately 3,300 square miles of American soil and all that sprung from it. A radical concept for the times, it was the first action that, fundamentally, established the earliest concepts of conservation—concepts that I hope readers of this book will come to understand as crucial, for if we want our great-great-grandchildren to derive the same pleasures from these parks that we have enjoyed, they are.

Since my youth, I've seen the national parks as the last authentic vestiges of America's wildest places—symbols of its one-of-a-kind spirit. Where else but in our great country can anyone stake claim to a national ancestry so vividly filled with explorers and adventurers, cowboys, pioneers, settlers and immigrants, inventors and discoverers, daredevils and dreamers? I truly believe that these vast swaths of lands represent not only my past, but also all of our collective pasts—places where, as we step beyond their gated entrances, we step back into time. For a

PAGES 30/31: **Lake Clark National Park & Preserve, Alaska**
Morning light on the Chigmit Mountains, a subrange of the Aleutians.

LEFT: **Everglades National Park, Florida**
A road through tallgrass prairie.

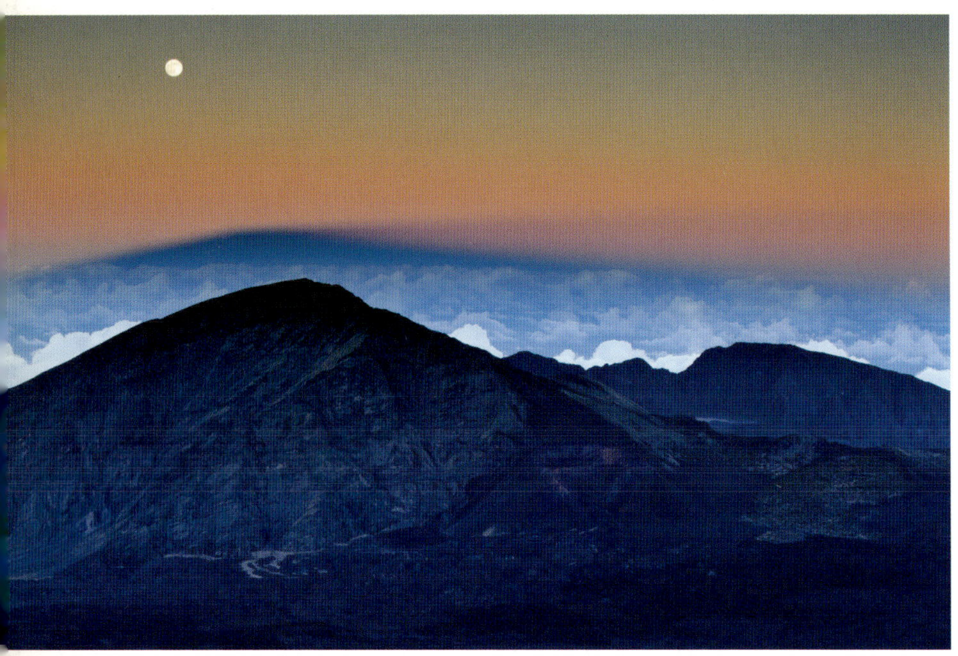

moment, we can open our eyes and see what Lewis and Clark saw in 1805 as they crossed the Continental Divide. We can imagine silhouettes on horseback galloping silently across a western horizon rough with sagebrush, covered wagons rumbling gracelessly over rutted plains, lighthouses offering beacons of hope to sailors, and locomotive steam trains hissing through the night. We can reflect back on a time when buffalo were plentiful, when there was still wild terrain to explore and dreamers who dared to explore it. Who would we be, as a nation, if we did not preserve and conserve these sites of living history and safe havens of solace? If we did not defend and care for these tracts of land, which are so inextricably tied to who we are as a people?

Throughout my life, I have been mesmerized by the natural gifts of nature and wildlife that have been bestowed upon us. Even today, from the moment I reach the entrance gate of any national park, my mind's eye leaps forward in total abandon as it conjures what lies beyond. I am instantly four and a half feet tall again and envisioning red-tailed foxes; sapphire waterfalls; emerald-green, fairy tale–sized trees; or perhaps an entire forest turned to stone. These parks are our birthright, yet it never ceases to amaze me how many visitors from other countries around the world flock in droves to these destinations. The fact that they do makes me proud. I am especially proud to be able to communicate to you, with this book and these images, a glimpse into my very special world and into two great passions of mine—photography and our American national parks.

LEFT: **Haleakala National Park, Hawaii**
With the sun setting behind me and the moon rising in front of me across the namesake Haleakala Crater, I was awestruck as the shadowy pyramid shape of the mountain I was standing on cast a long shadow into the distance and toward the moonrise.

RIGHT: **Big Bend National Park, Texas**
A woman enjoys the sunset from desert hot springs along the Rio Grande River. The natural springs are in the United States, but Mexico can be seen across the river in the distance.

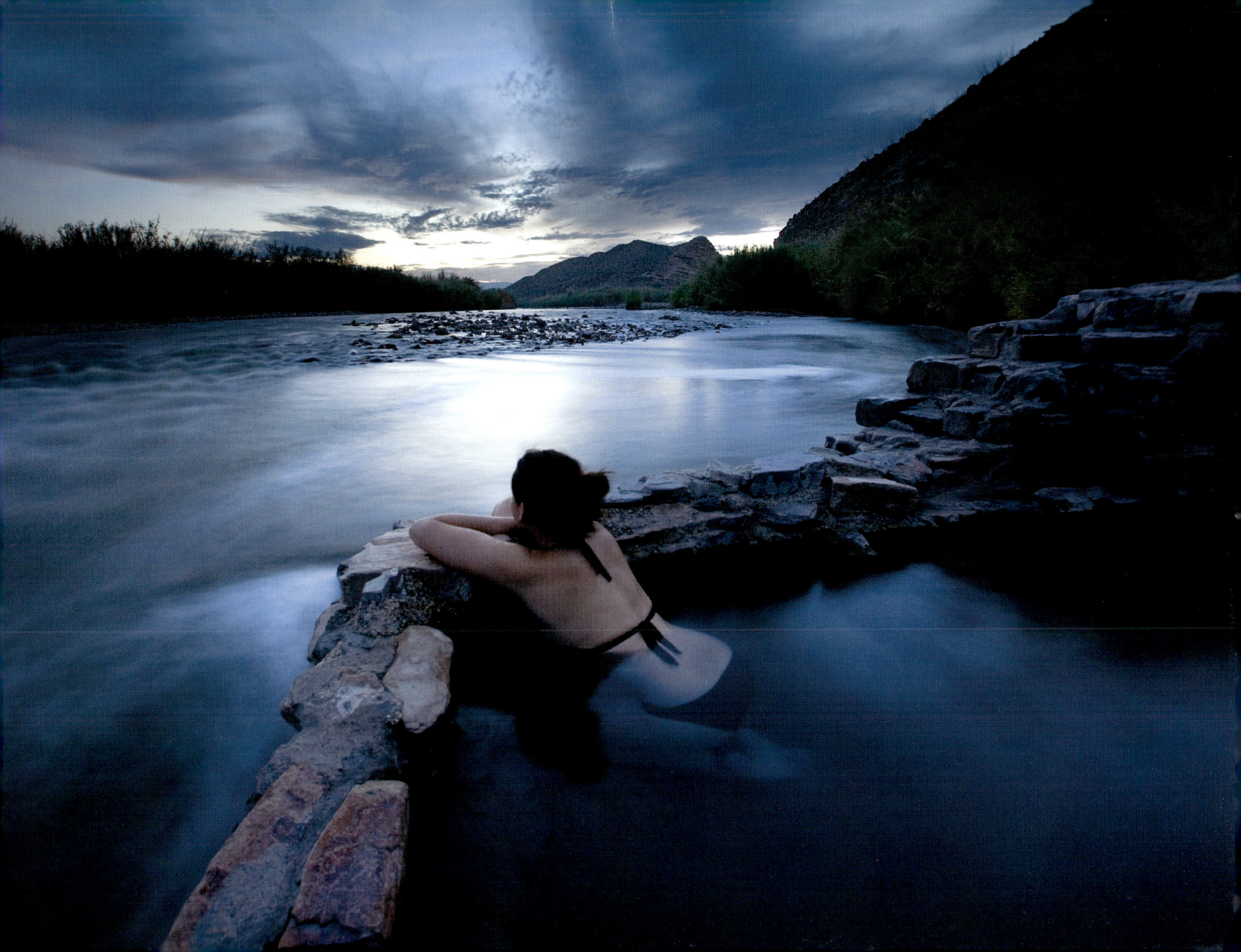

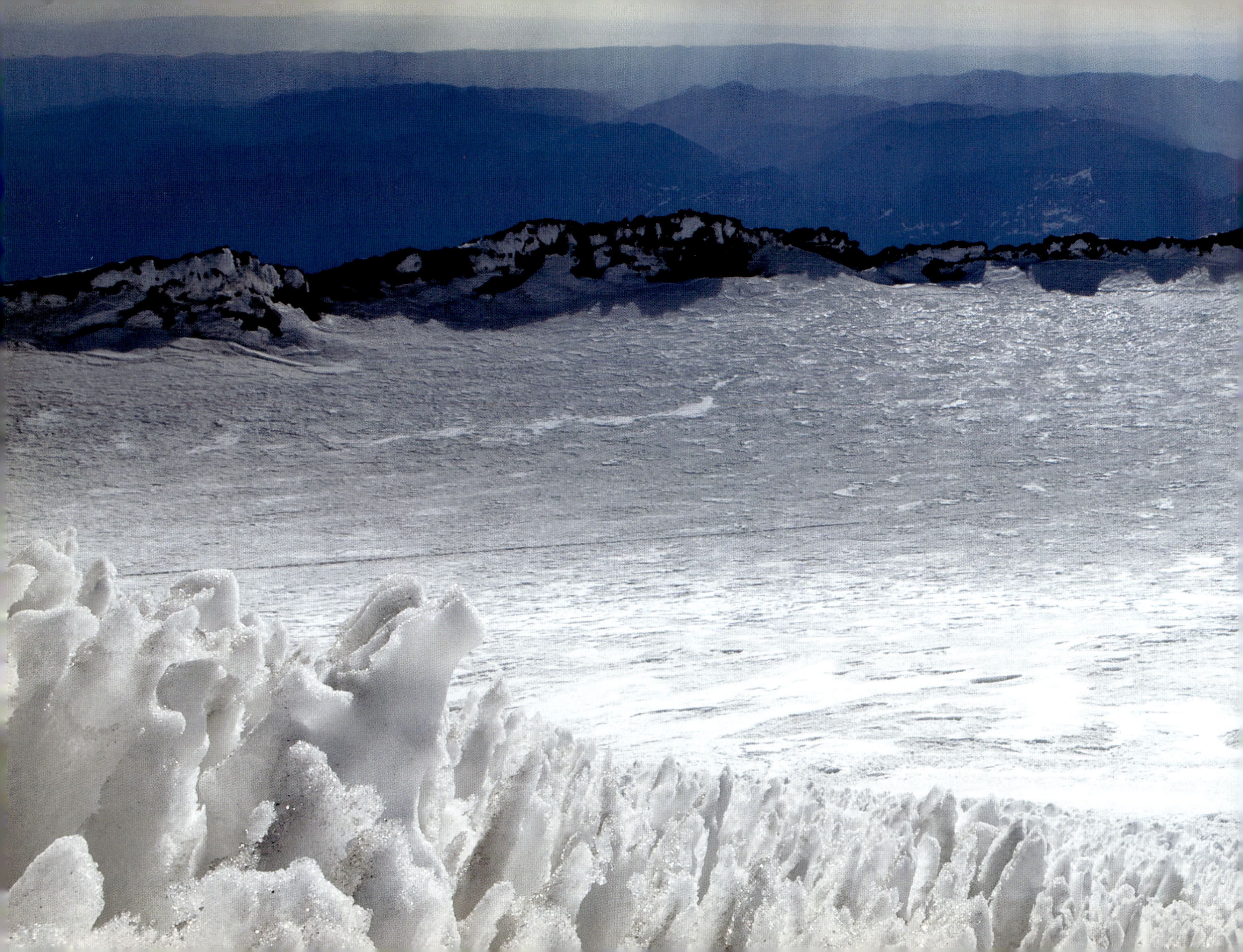

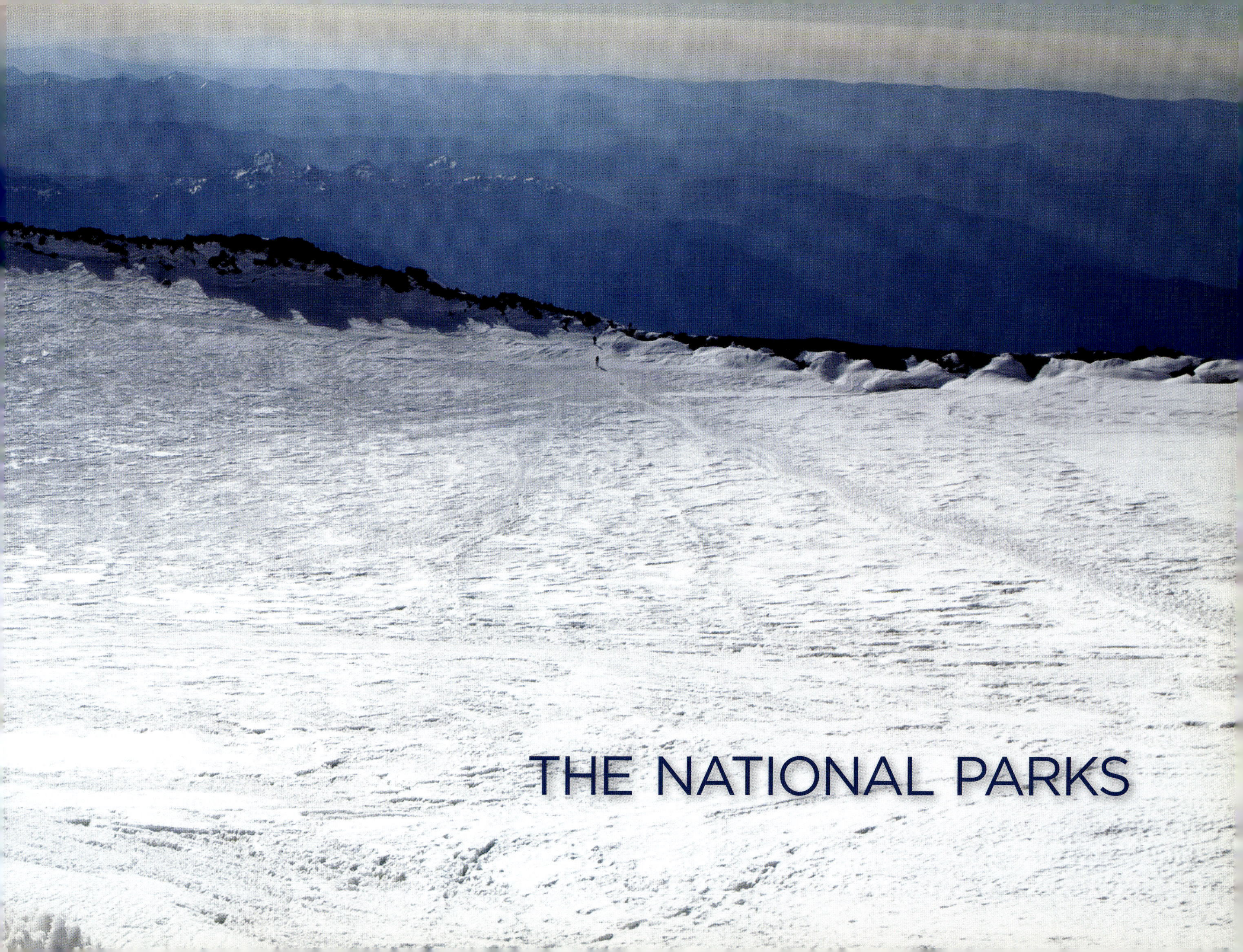

THE NATIONAL PARKS

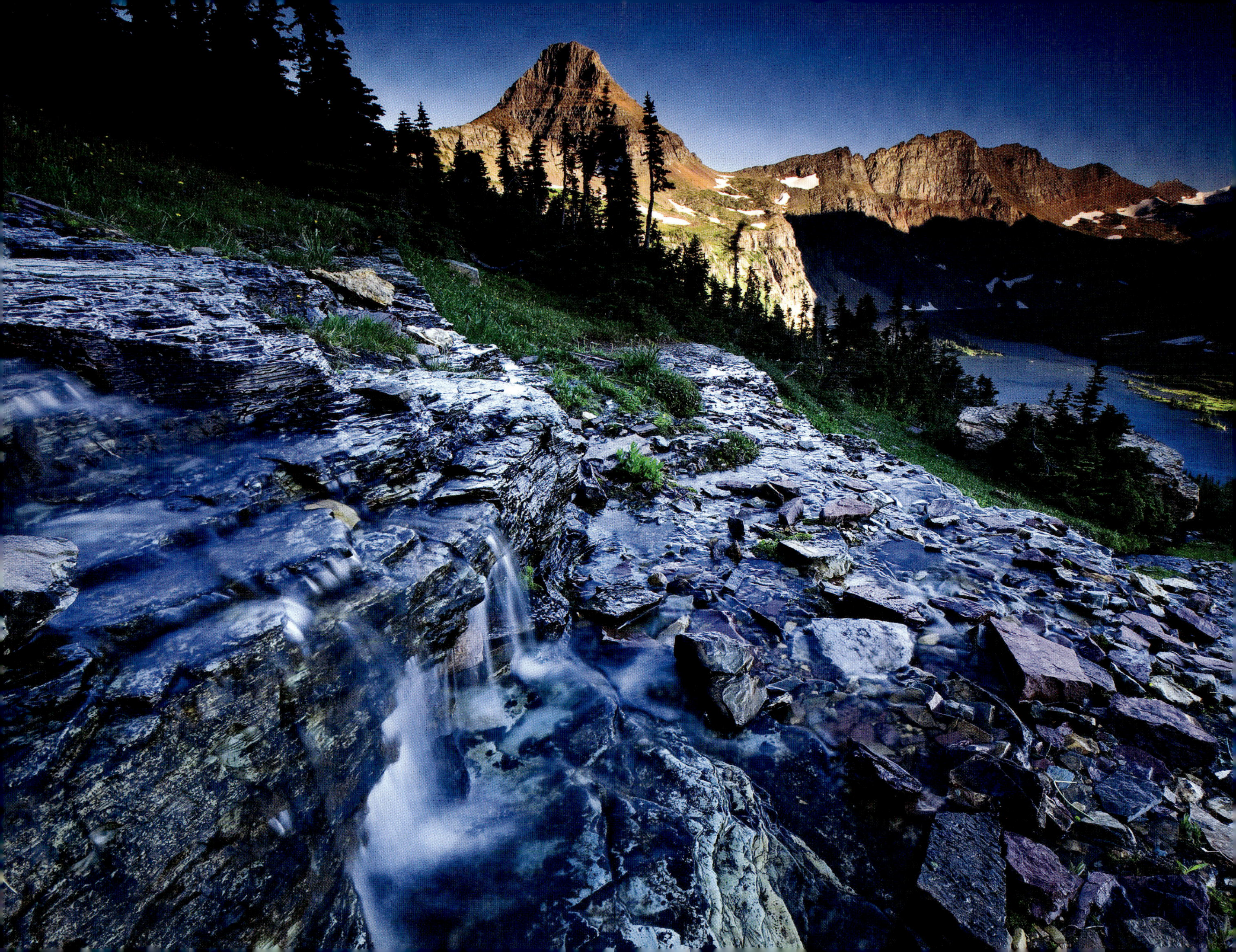

PAGES 36/37: **Mount Rainier National Park, Washington**
Detail of the summit crater as seen from the highest point on Mount Rainier.

LEFT: **Glacier National Park, Montana**
A hidden lake and waterfall along the Hidden Lake Trail out of Logan Pass.

RIGHT: **Yellowstone National Park; Wyoming, Montana, Idaho**
Soda Butte Creek. The iridescent colors are caused by the various algae that grow on this warm-water thermal feature.

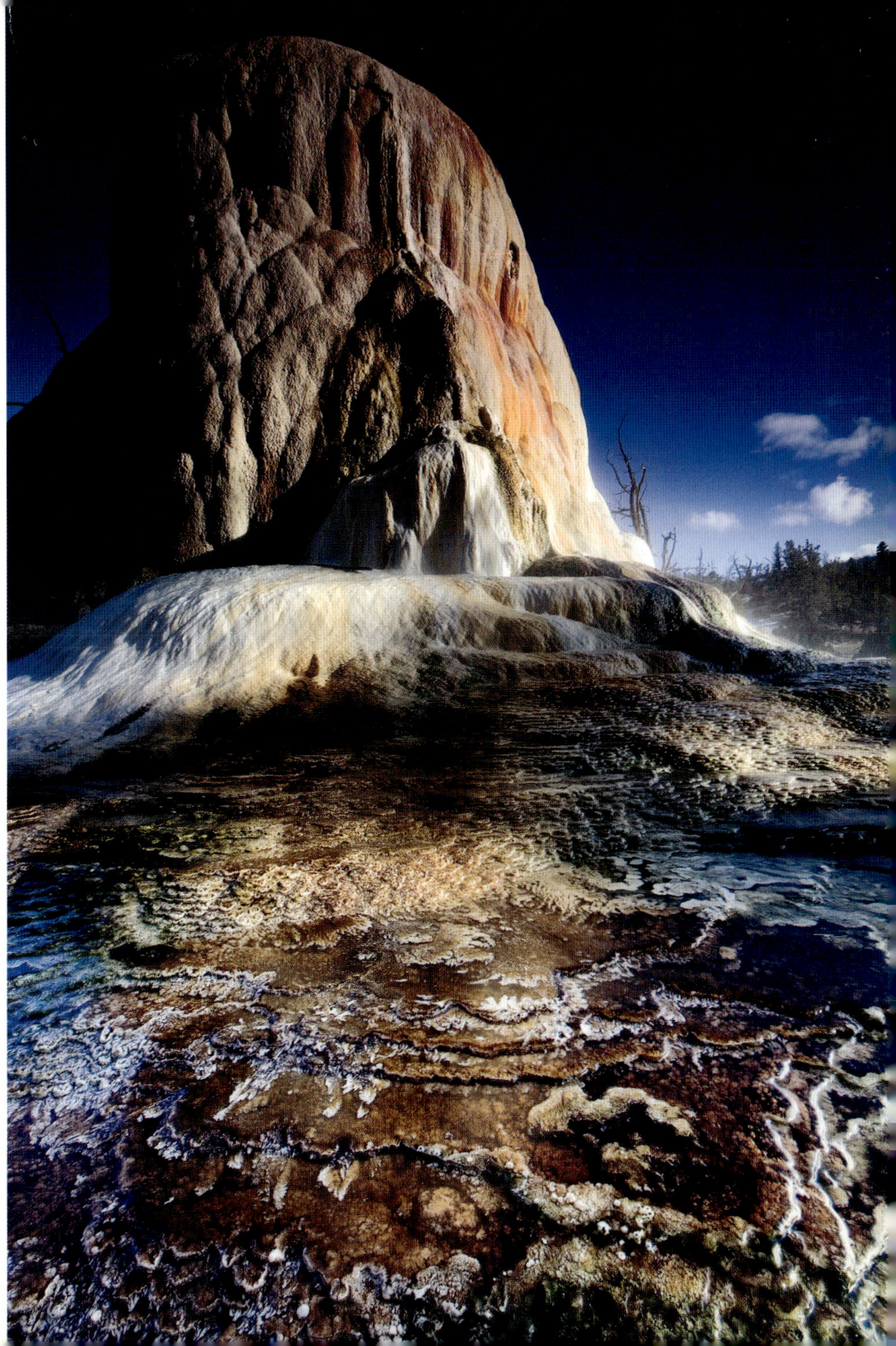

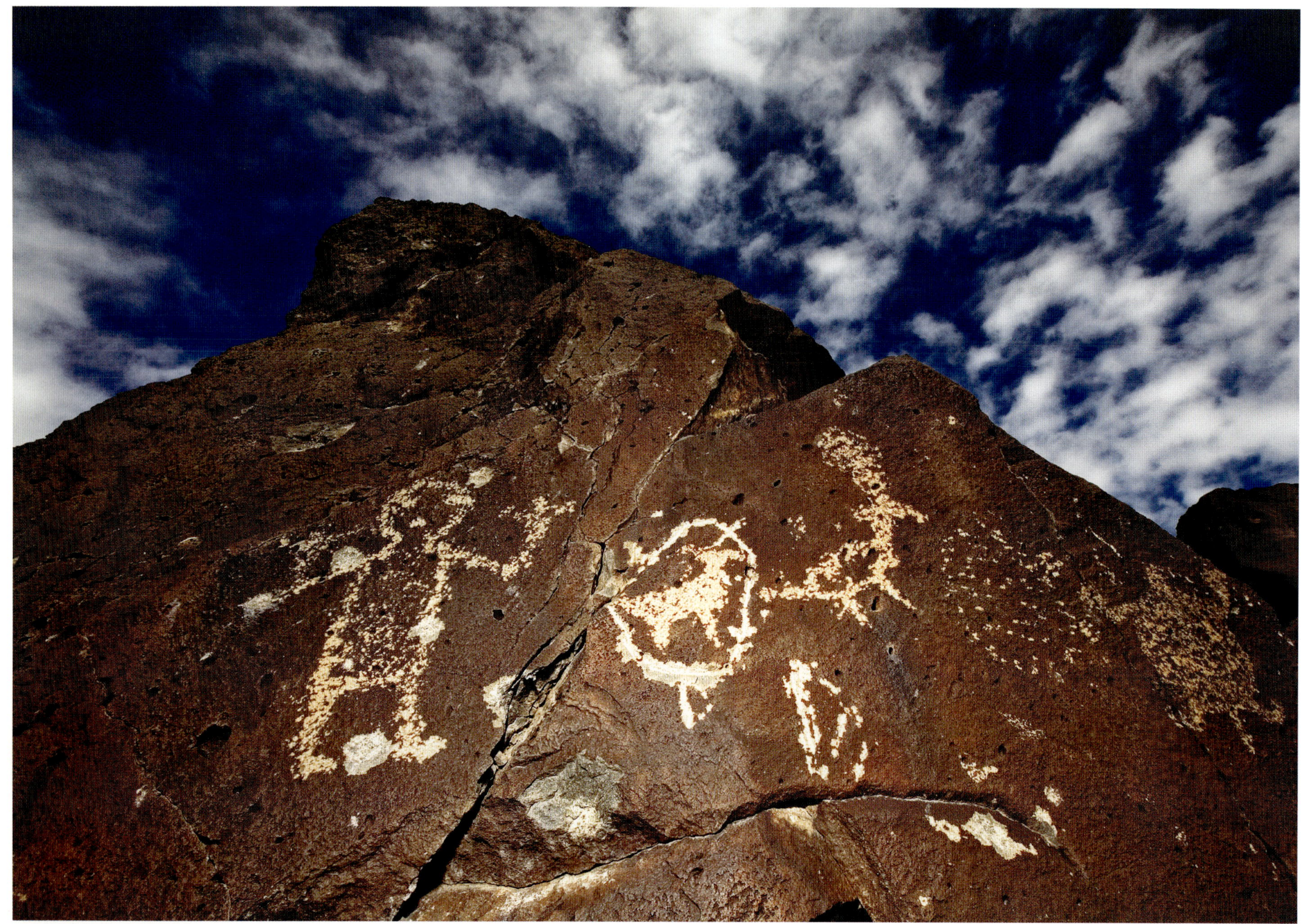

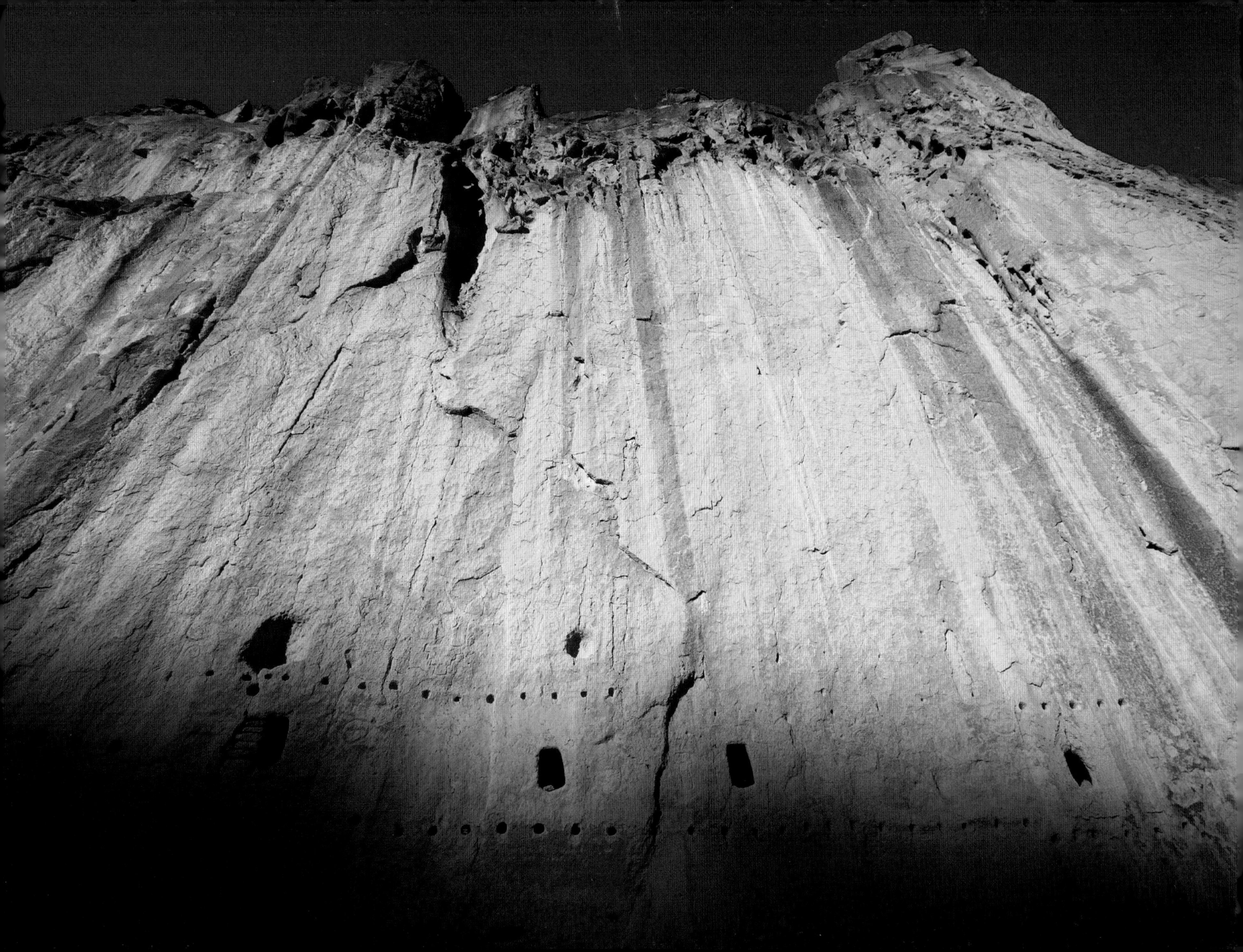

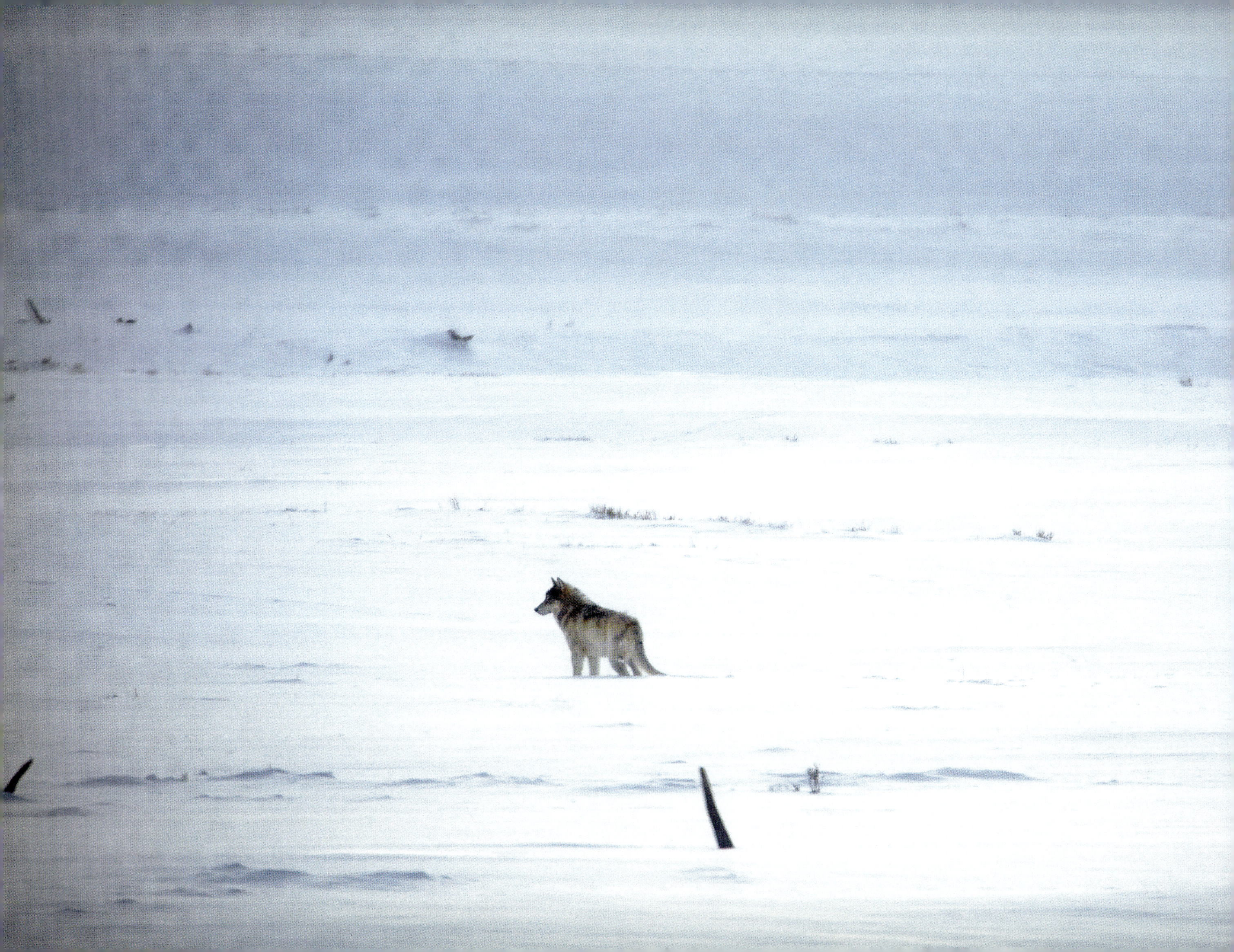

PAGE 40: **Petroglyph National Monument, New Mexico**
Ancient petroglyphs, or hand-pecked drawings on rock, are the work of ancient Native Americans, dated seven to eight hundred years old.

PAGE 41: **Bandelier National Monument, New Mexico**
The rock outcroppings in Bandelier are a reminder that this landscape was inhabited long before us. The human history here dates back more than ten thousand years—a history that can be felt in the howling wind that blows through this canyon. These small holes in the rock—known as viga holes—are indicators of a large house that was once two or three stories high.

LEFT: **Yellowstone National Park; Wyoming, Montana, Idaho**
A gray wolf walks through the snow in Lamar Valley. At first glance, the scene is simple, uncluttered. The history of the wolf in the Yellowstone ecosystem is anything but simple, however. Wolves were completely extirpated from the park, with the last wolf killed in 1926. Forty years later, changes in the ecosystem started to become obviously unbalanced: Elk populations were booming from the lack of predation, and the large herds of elk took their toll on riparian-area cottonwoods and aspen, which began to show signs of severe overgrazing. Without the keystone wolf species, coyotes began to thrive in large numbers—which, in turn, took a toll on the red fox. It took another twenty-nine years of political compromises and negotiations with the local ranching community, but finally, in 1995, the wolf was reintroduced to Yellowstone. Today it is considered by many to be a conservation success story, though it continues to stir vigorous debate in the communities surrounding Yellowstone. In 2005 it was estimated that more than 325 wolves were a part of the Yellowstone ecosystem, and in 2008 this iconic animal was removed from the "threatened" list maintained under the U.S. Fish and Wildlife Service's Endangered Species Program.

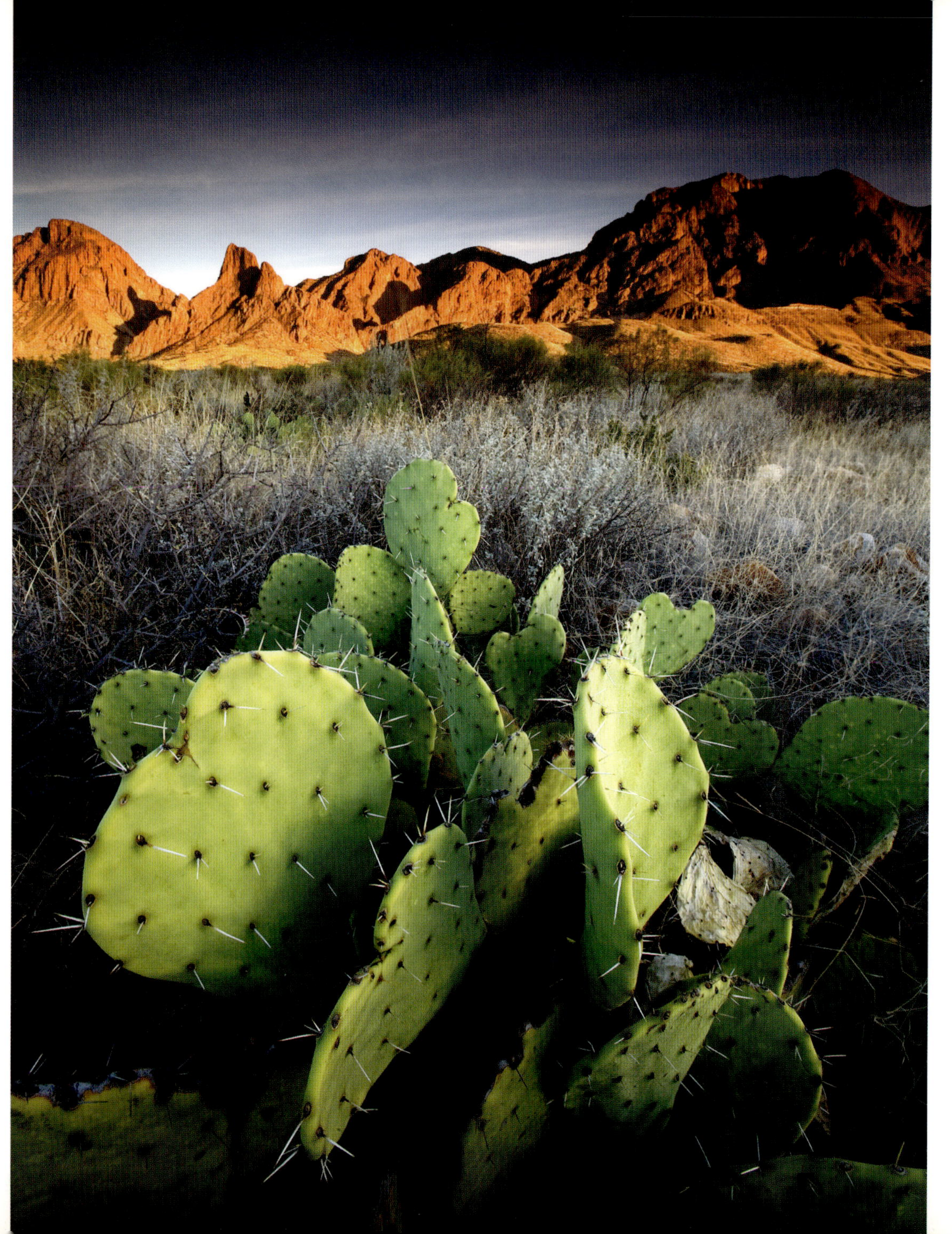

LEFT: **Big Bend National Park, Texas**
A prickly-pear cactus fills the foreground as the sunrise illuminates the Chisos Mountains.

RIGHT: **Redwood National and State Parks, California**
Detail of a fern.

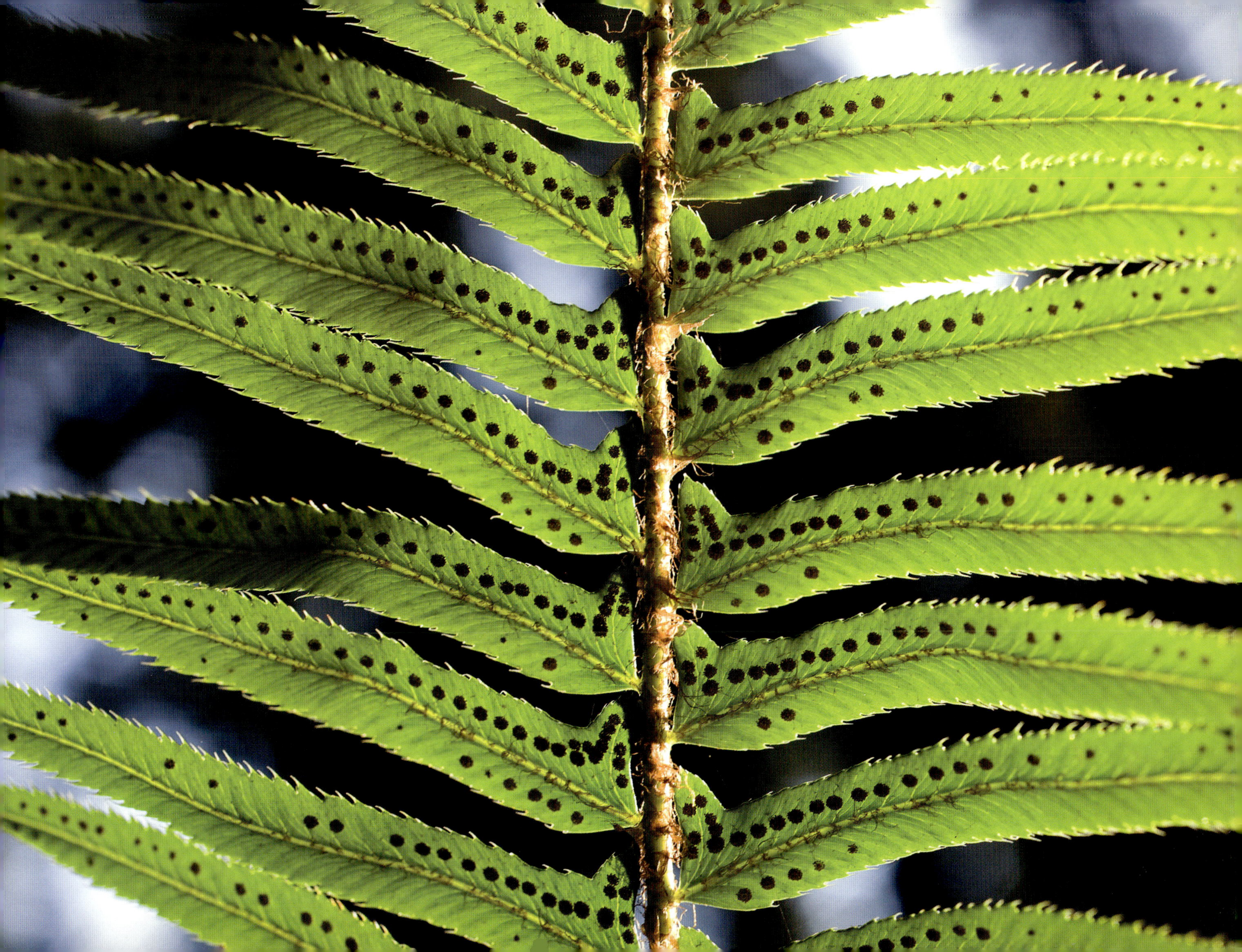

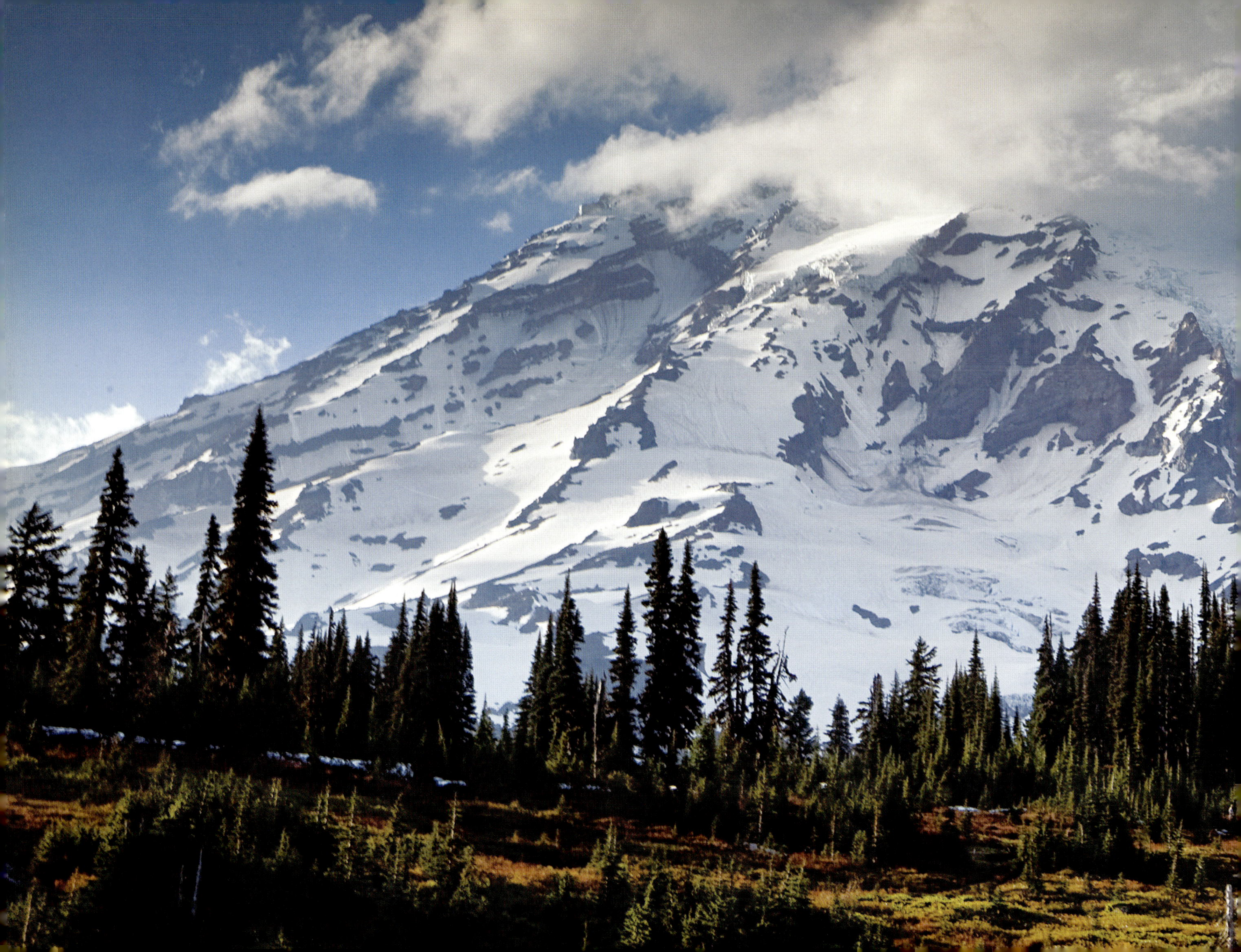

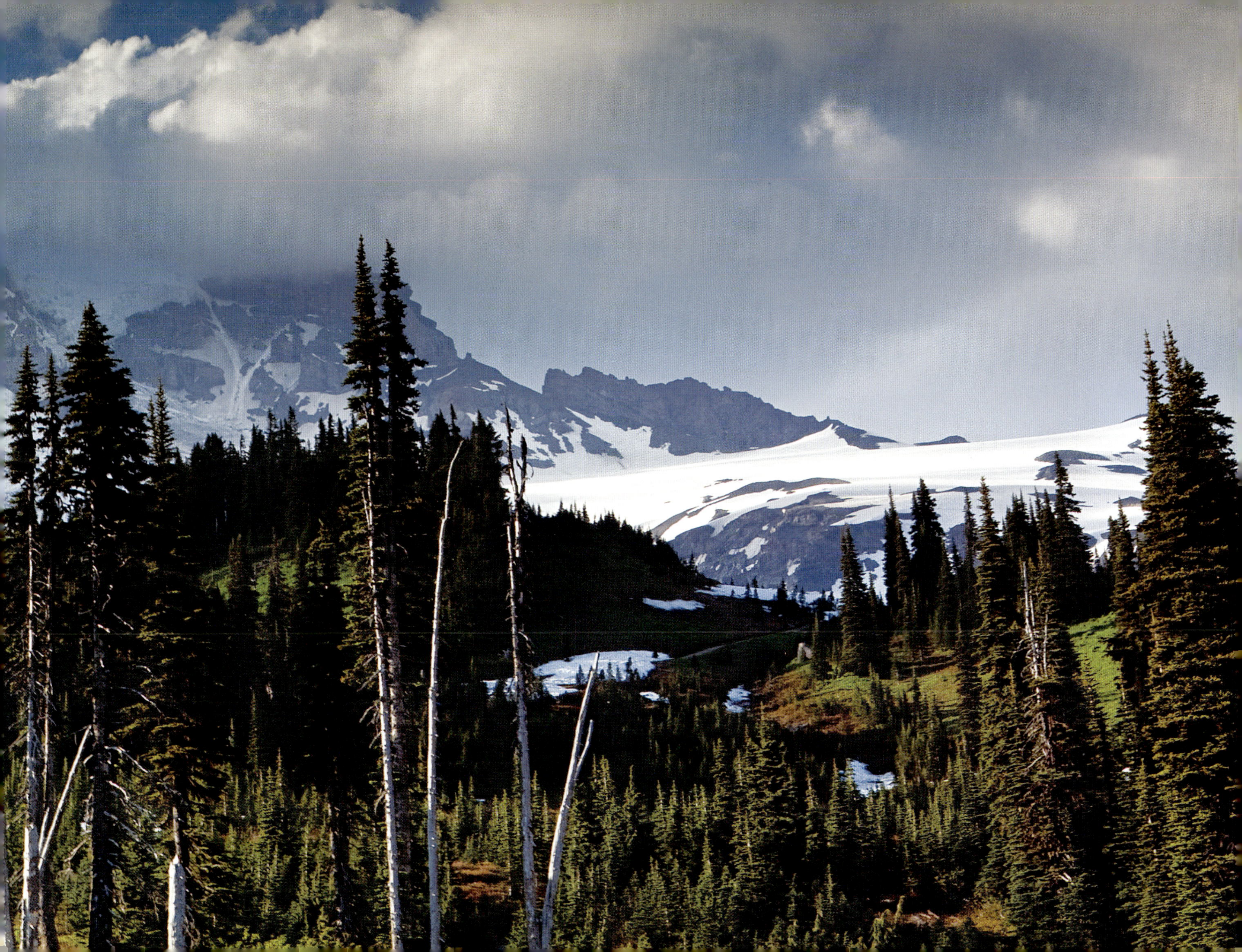

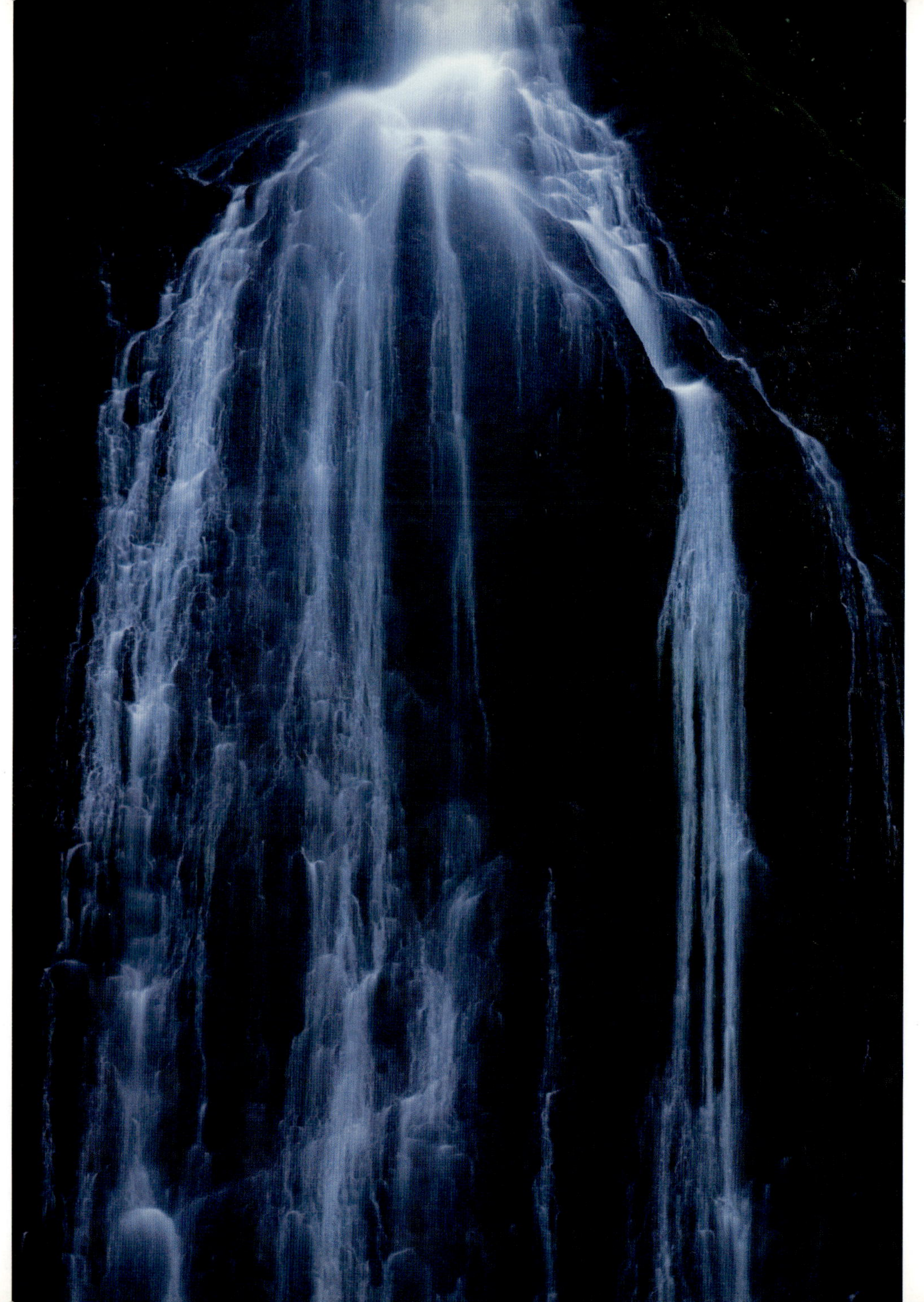

PAGES 46/47: **Mount Rainier National Park, Washington**
There is irony in this photo, though it is not immediately evident. This image was photographed from the parking lot at the base of Mount Rainier near the visitor center. However, I had just spent the last three days climbing this behemoth, summiting at 8:30am of the day I took this photo. With blue toenails and sore legs from an exhausting mountaineering exhibition, I basically crawled to my camera gear, setting up this simple shot of a beautiful mountain in the last light of the day.

LEFT: **Olympic National Park, Washington**
The blue evening light that trickles in through the tree canopy of Olympic National Park is magical, taking on a life of its own in the trickling waters of Marymere Falls.

RIGHT: **Death Valley National Park, California**
Moonrise over Badwater Basin.

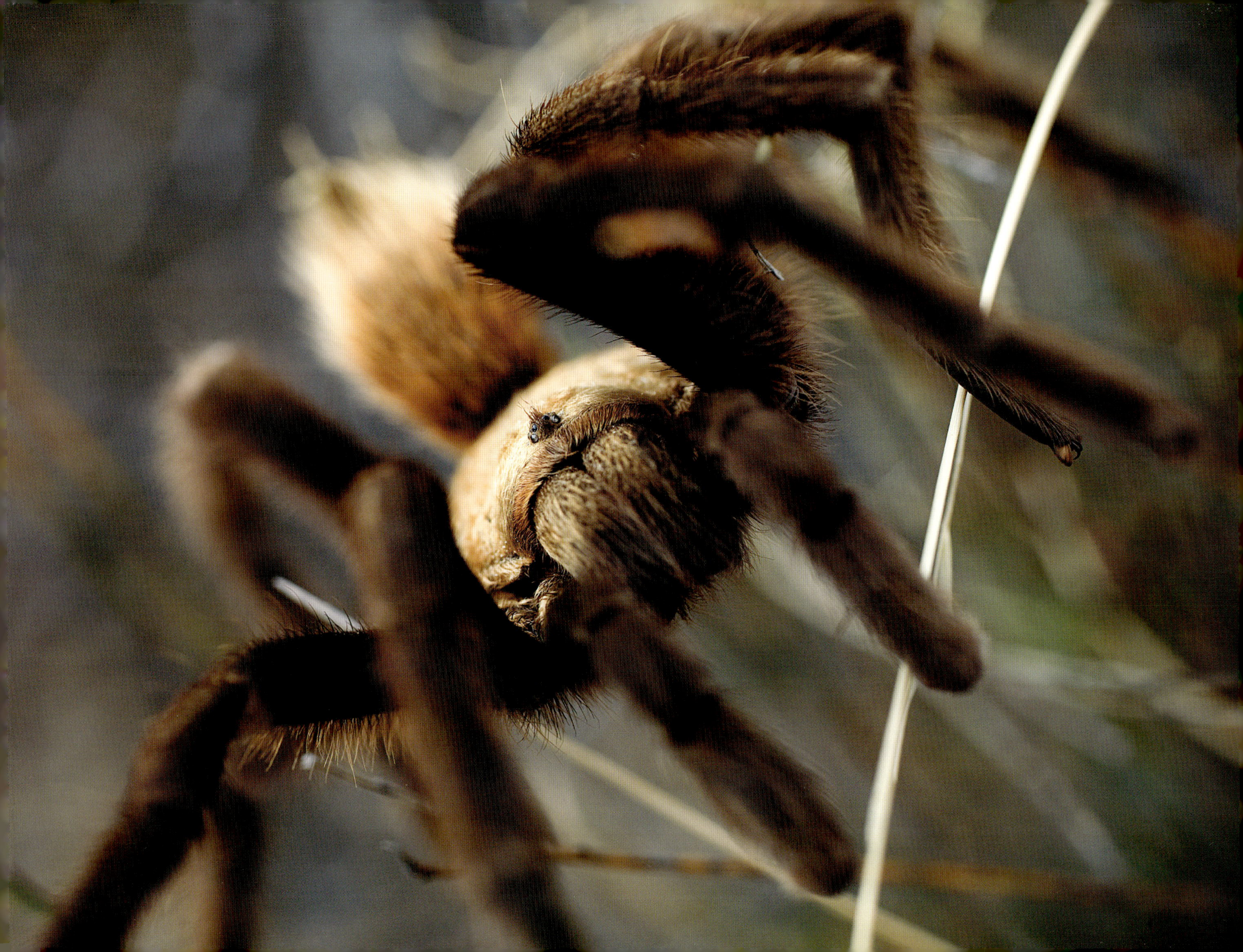

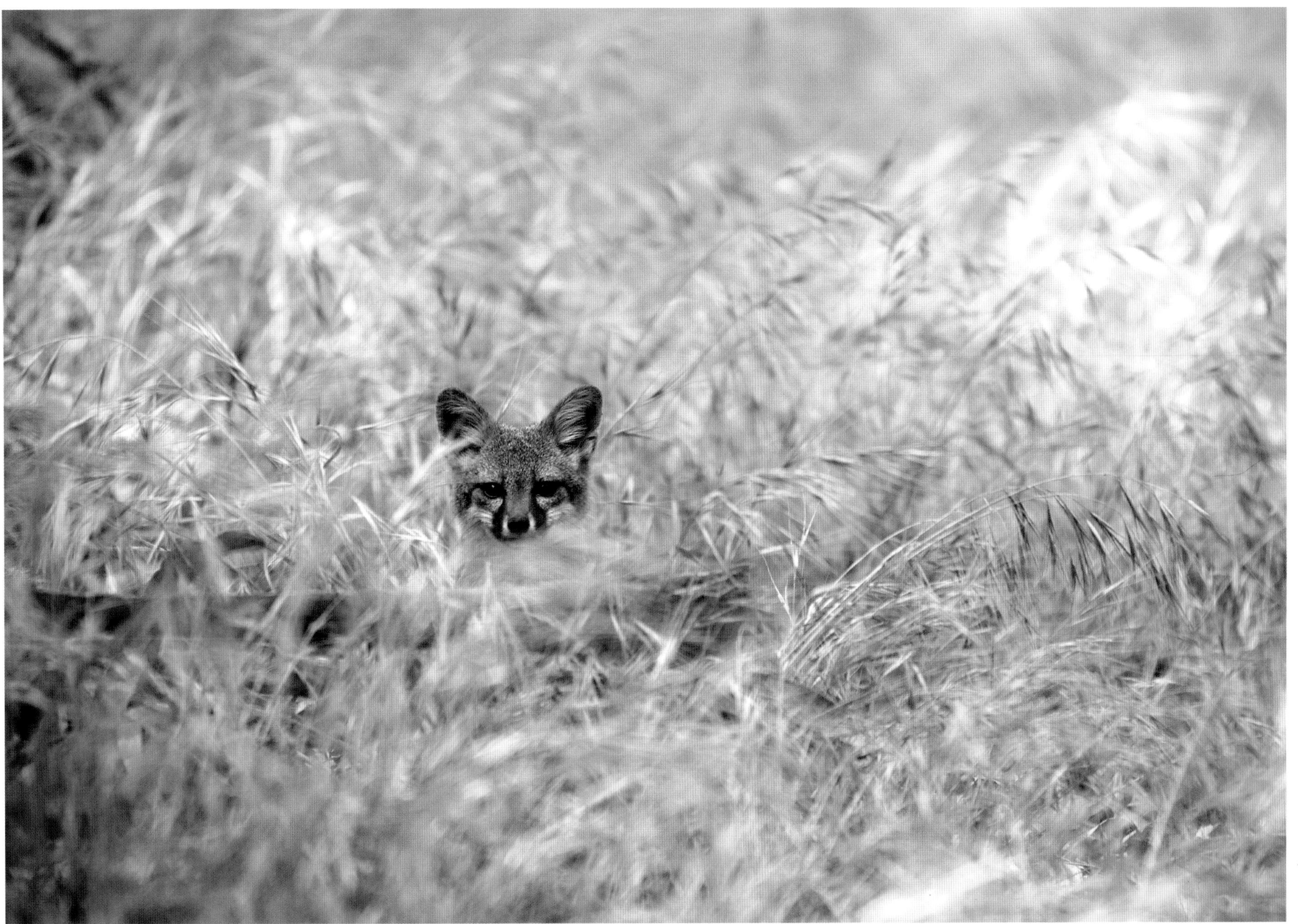

PAGE 50: **Big Bend National Park, Texas**
A wild tarantula in the Chihuahuan Desert.

PAGE 51: **Channel Islands National Park, California**
Portrait of a youthful Santa Cruz Island fox. The species has been federally listed as endangered since 2004 and is considered critically endangered by the International Union for the Conservation of Nature (IUCN) Red List. As it currently stands, this fox faces an extremely high risk of extinction in the wild, though its chances of survival are getting better with each passing day. The fox is native to six of the eight Channel Islands, and each subspecies of the fox is unique to the island it inhabits, making them unique evolutionary masterpieces. Their battle is a relatively new one, though. It was only in the 1990s that steep population declines were identified.

On Santa Cruz Island, where this fox was photographed, the number of foxes dropped from 2,000 adults in 1994 to less than 135 in 2000. On other islands, the number of foxes dropped to just fifteen adults. The primary cause was attributed to golden eagle predation. Like many environmental issues, the problems were a series of circumstances that played out over time. In this case, DDT poisoning reduced the numbers of bald eagles (which typically subsist on fish), which left room for the golden eagles to come in. Feral pigs were also common on the islands and further attracted the golden eagles, helping increase their numbers rapidly. The fox, which was the apex predator and was previously unaccustomed to being prey, was unable to adapt quickly enough, and its population plummeted. Even worse, the fox has been so isolated that it has no immunity to diseases or parasites from the mainland such as canine distemper, which wiped out 90 percent of Santa Catalina Island's population in 1998. Despite these recent challenges, quick work by conservation groups has helped eradicate the feral pigs and reduce the number of golden eagles, restoring balance. Already, the foxes have begun to recover and are often visible running through the tall, golden grass or lounging around like common house pets.

RIGHT: **Glacier National Park, Montana**
Smoke from nearby forest fires drifts into Glacier National Park, creating a blue haze on Lake McDonald. Photographed after sunset, the smoke enhanced the scene, creating an ethereal, dreamlike landscape.

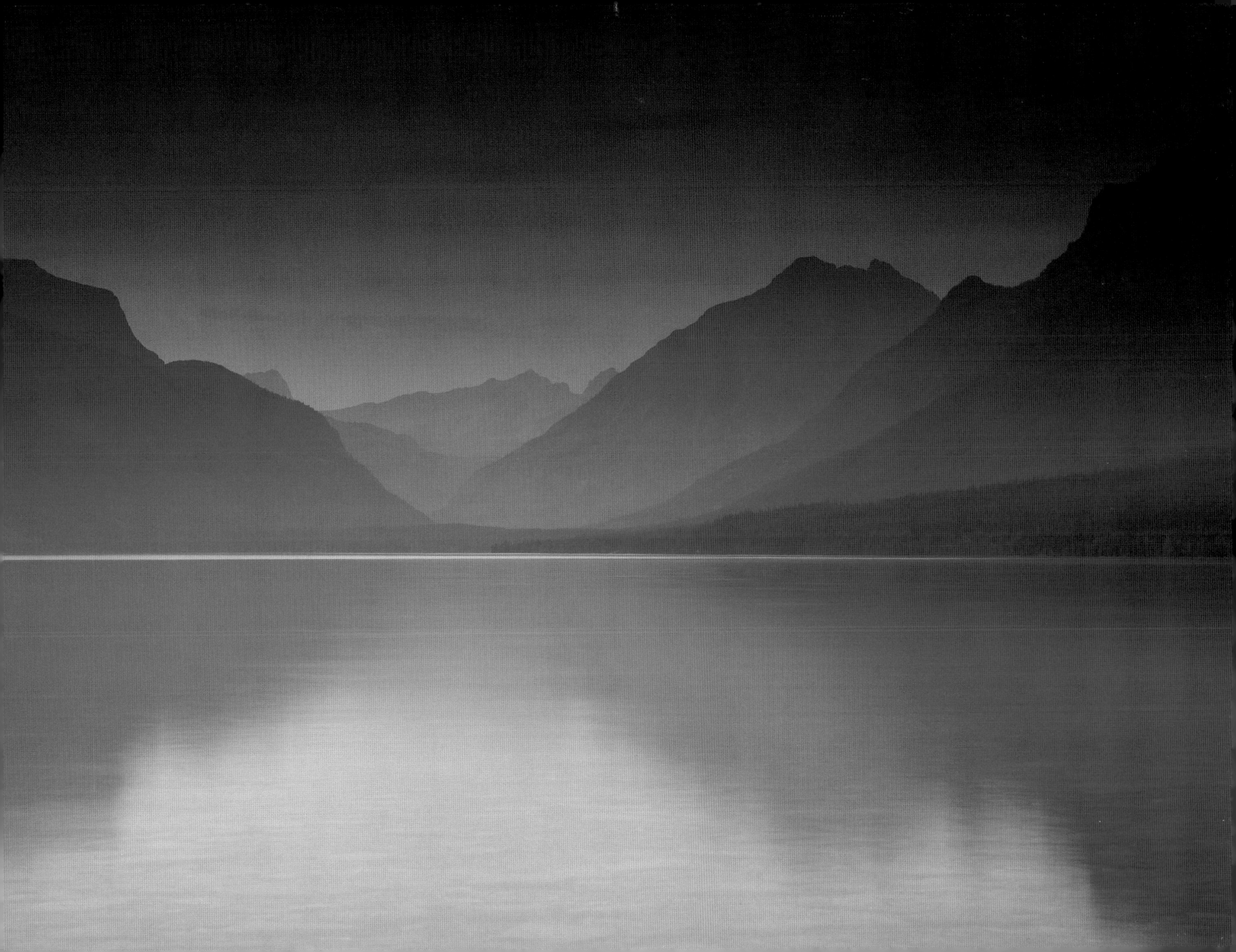

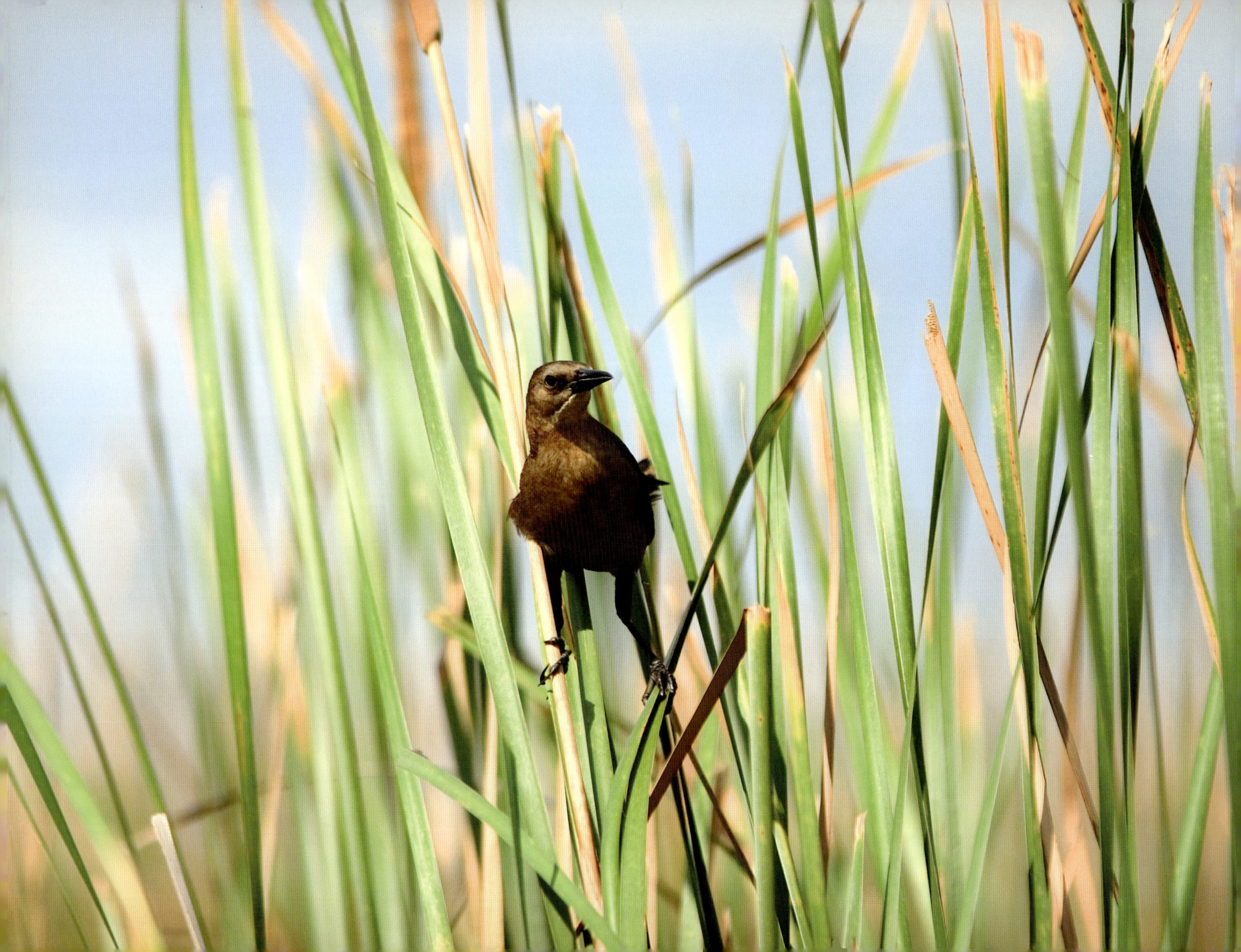

LEFT: **Everglades National Park, Florida**
A boat-tailed grackle.

RIGHT: **Lake Mead National Recreation Area, Nevada**
Sediment mixes with river water.

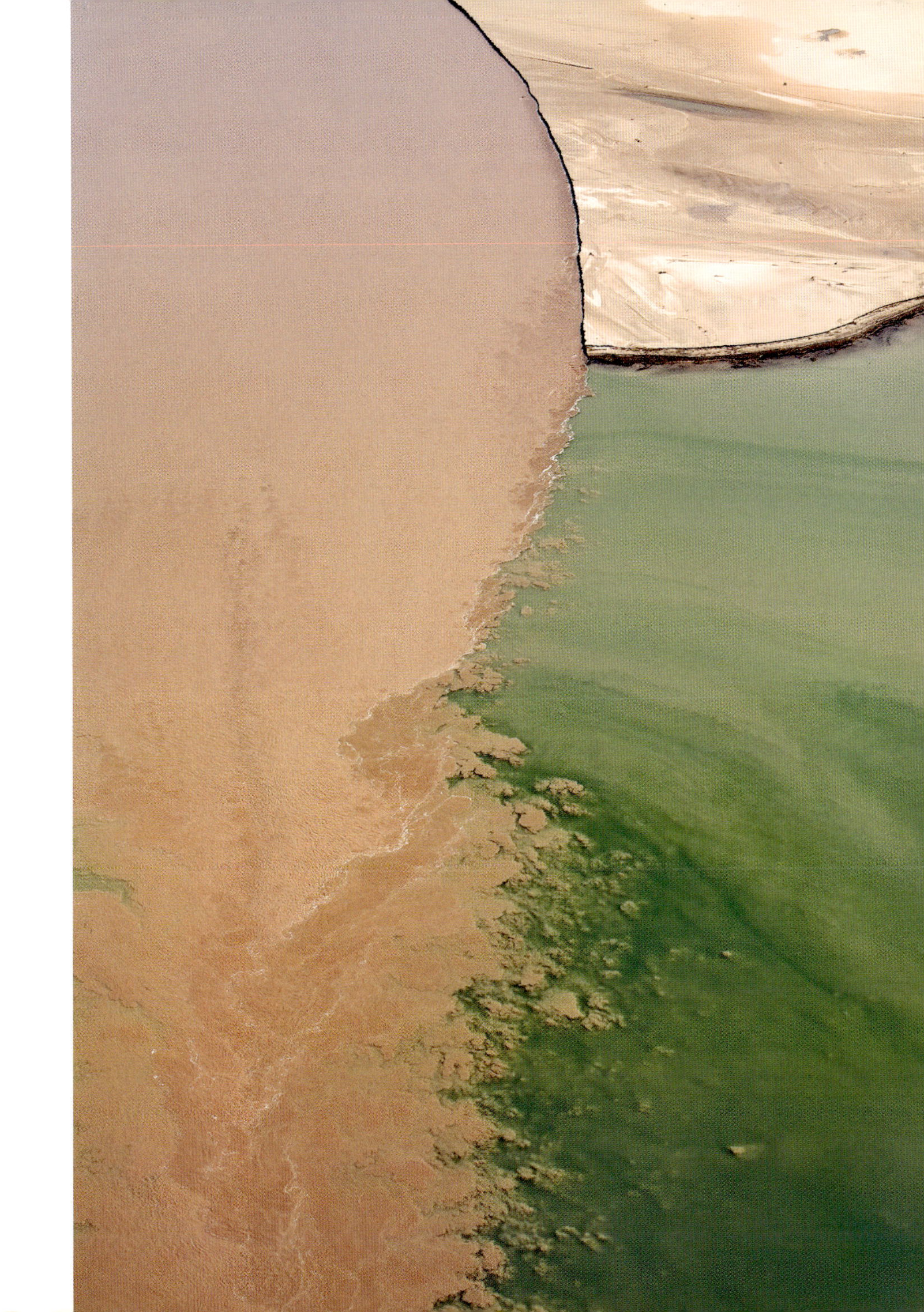

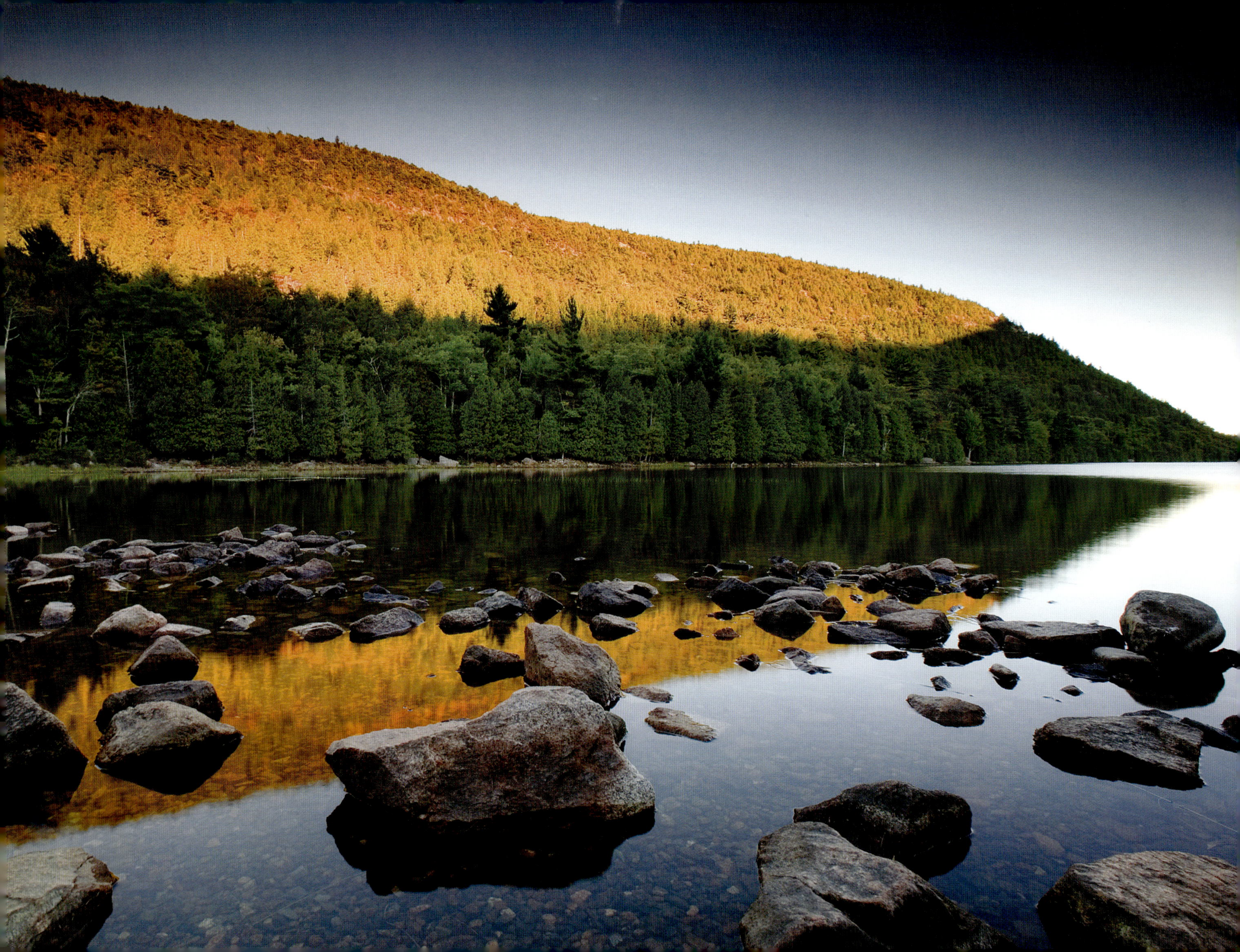

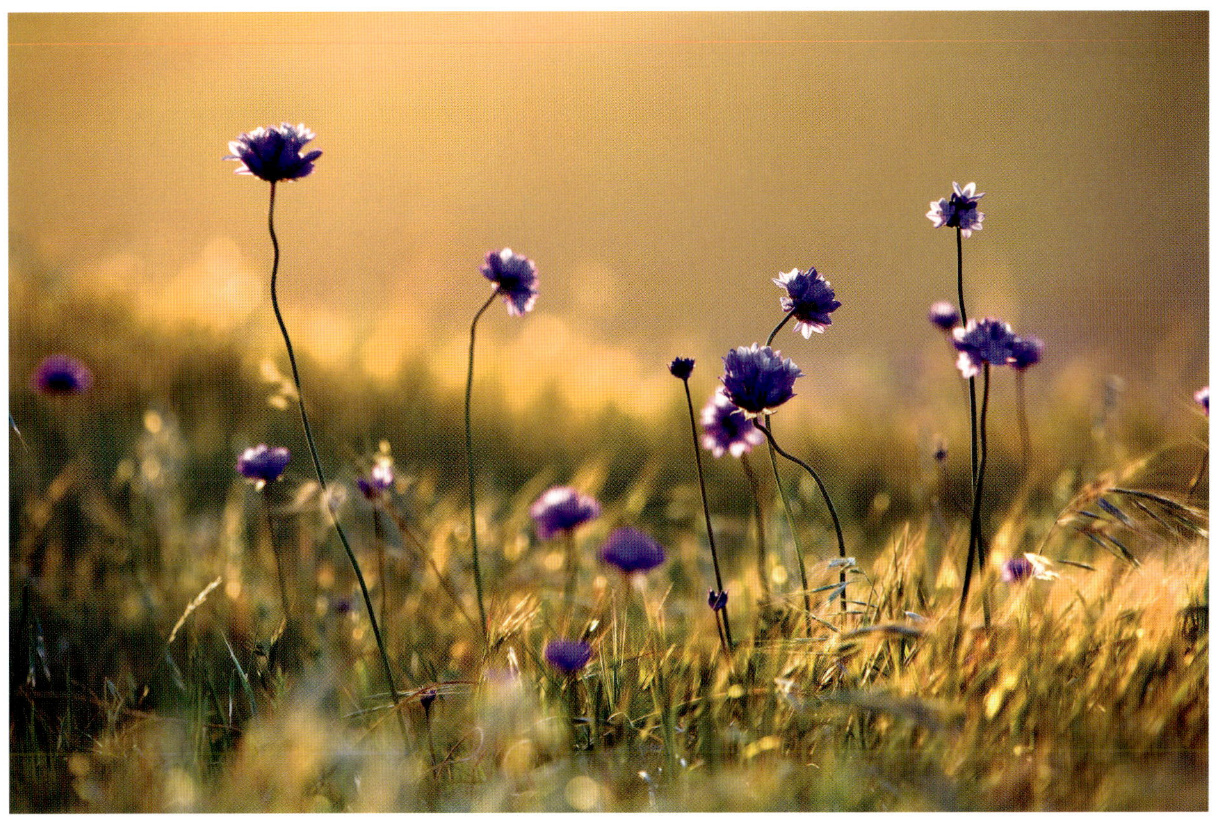

ABOVE: **Channel Islands National Park, California**
Flowers in Santa Cruz—one of the five islands that make up Channel Islands National Park.

LEFT: **Acadia National Park, Maine**
The last reflections of a setting sun along the shores of Bubble Pond. Nestled between the rolling hills of Acadia, this idyllic lake's crystal-clear waters hold no secrets, as fish are easily spotted from the shore.

RIGHT: **Point Reyes National Seashore, California**
A snowy egret waits like a patient fisherman in the shallows. The scene is immediately reminiscent of a Japanese painting, devoid of any bright colors. The fog that had begun to roll in only that evening further diffused the light, softening the edges of the grasses and helping draw the eye in toward the alcove. Only in nature could such a perfectly understated palette of colors occur.

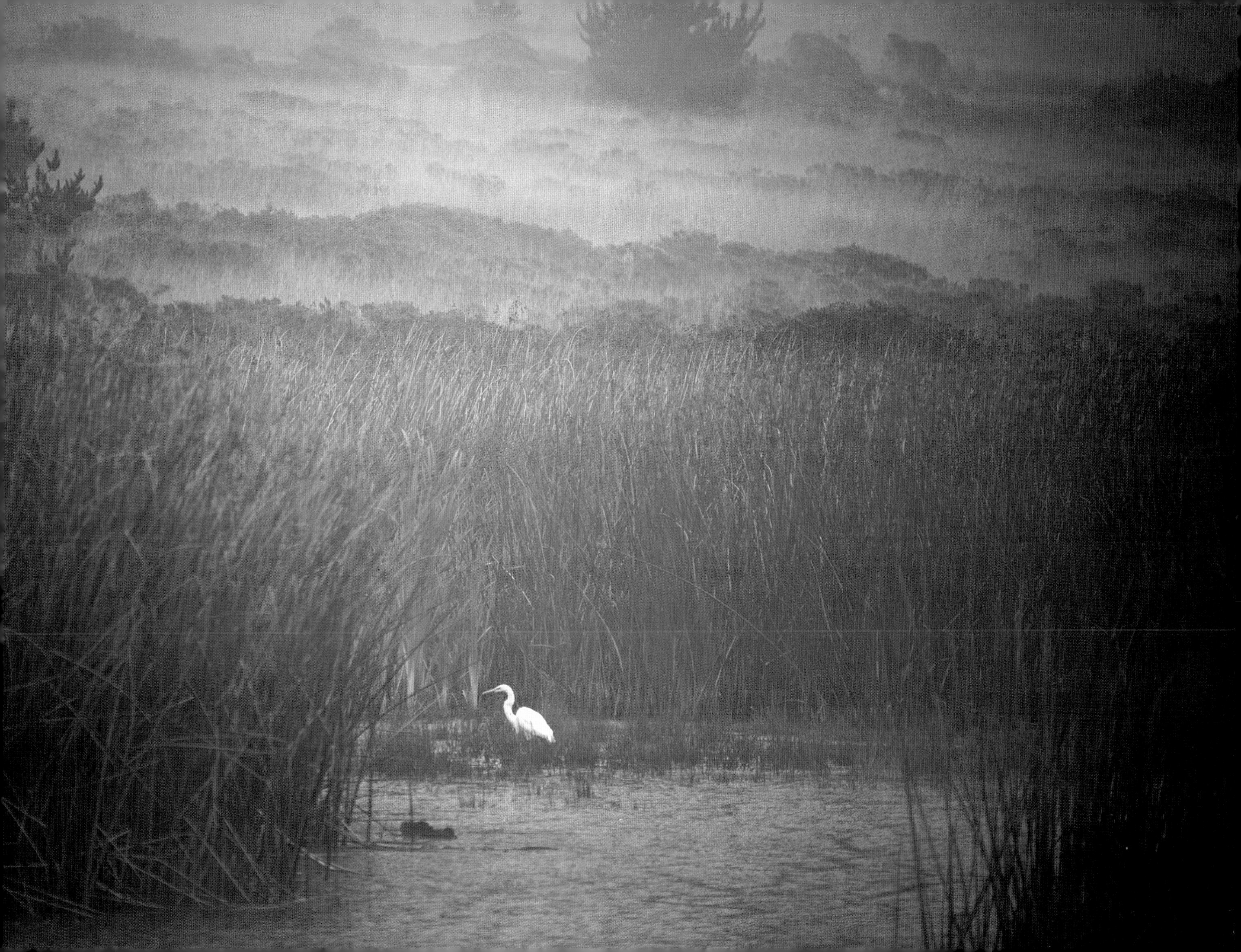

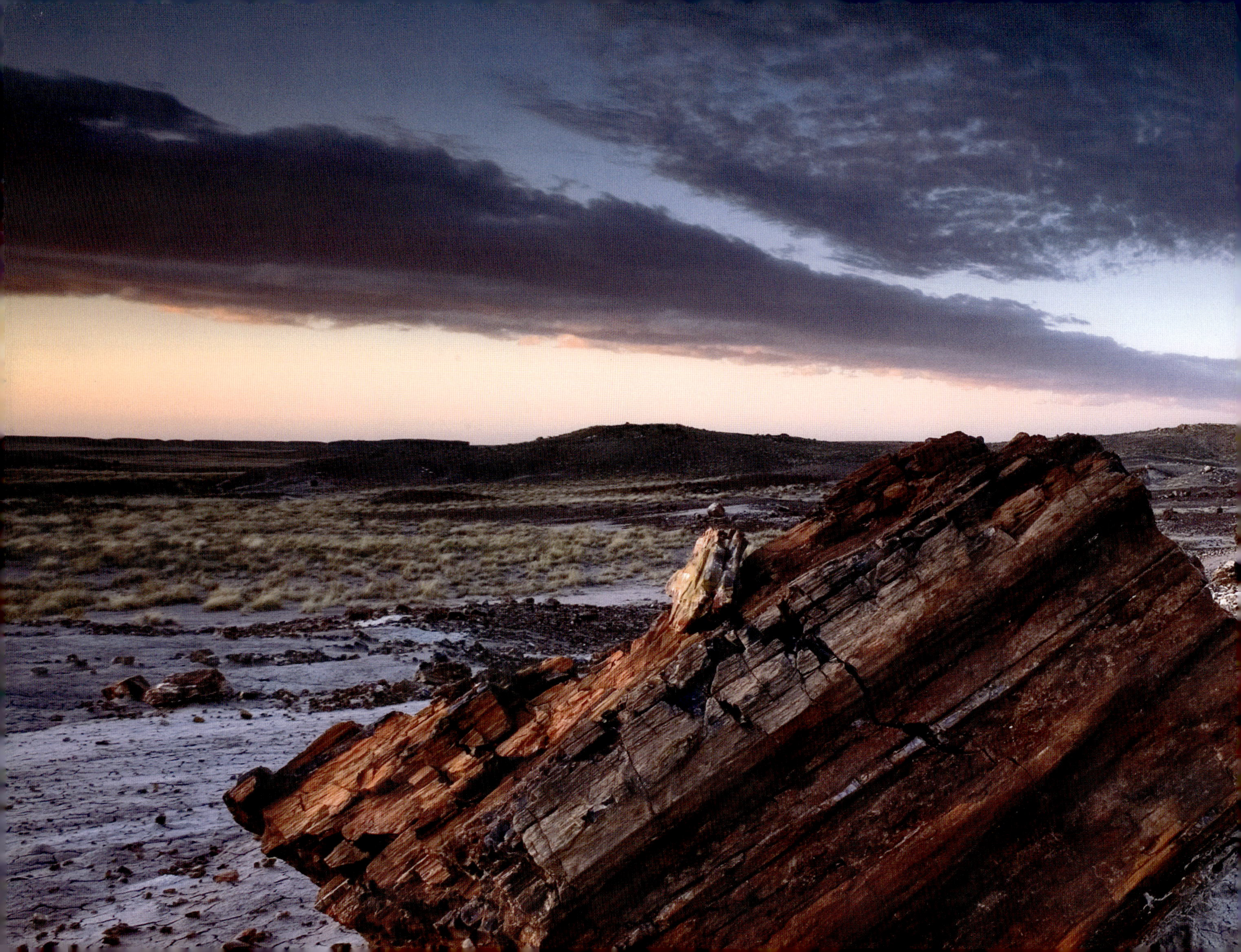

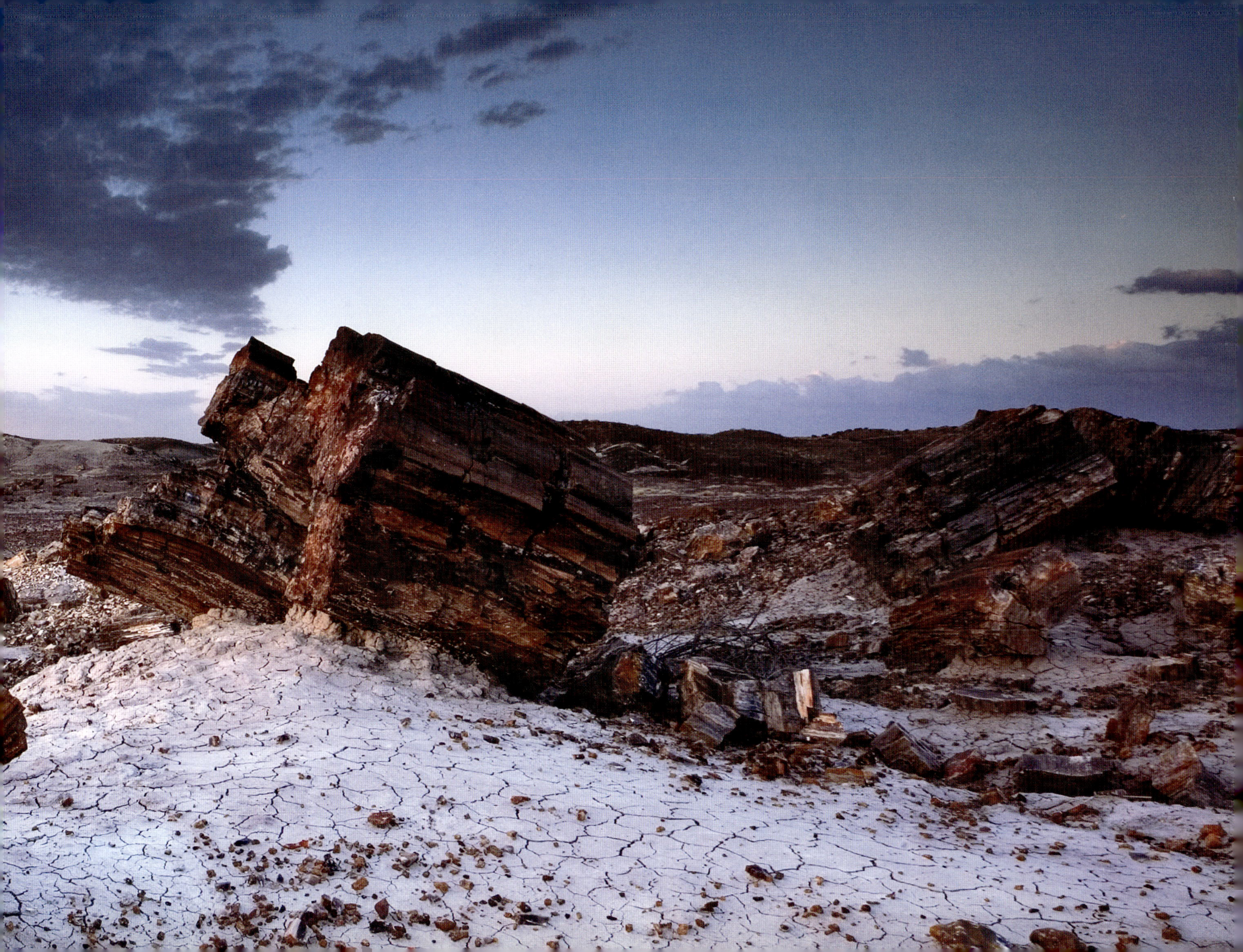

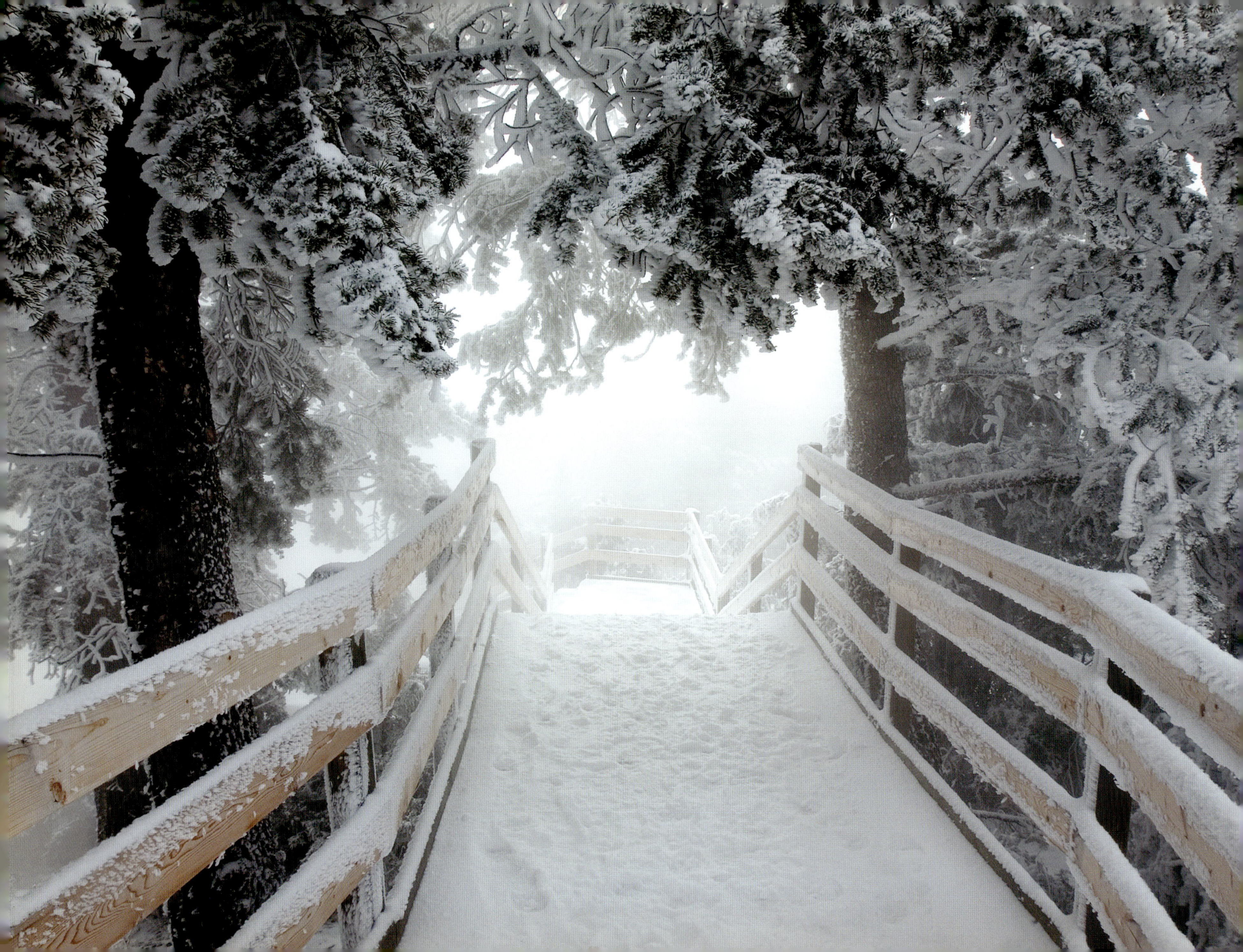

PAGES 60/61: **Petrified Forest National Park, Arizona**
The remains of a 225-million-year-old tree from the late Triassic period looks as if it were a broken log from just yesterday.

LEFT: **Yellowstone National Park; Wyoming, Montana, Idaho**
A snowy trail through Mammoth Hot Springs.

RIGHT: **Glacier National Park, Montana**
Clouds lift off the mountains at Logan Pass.

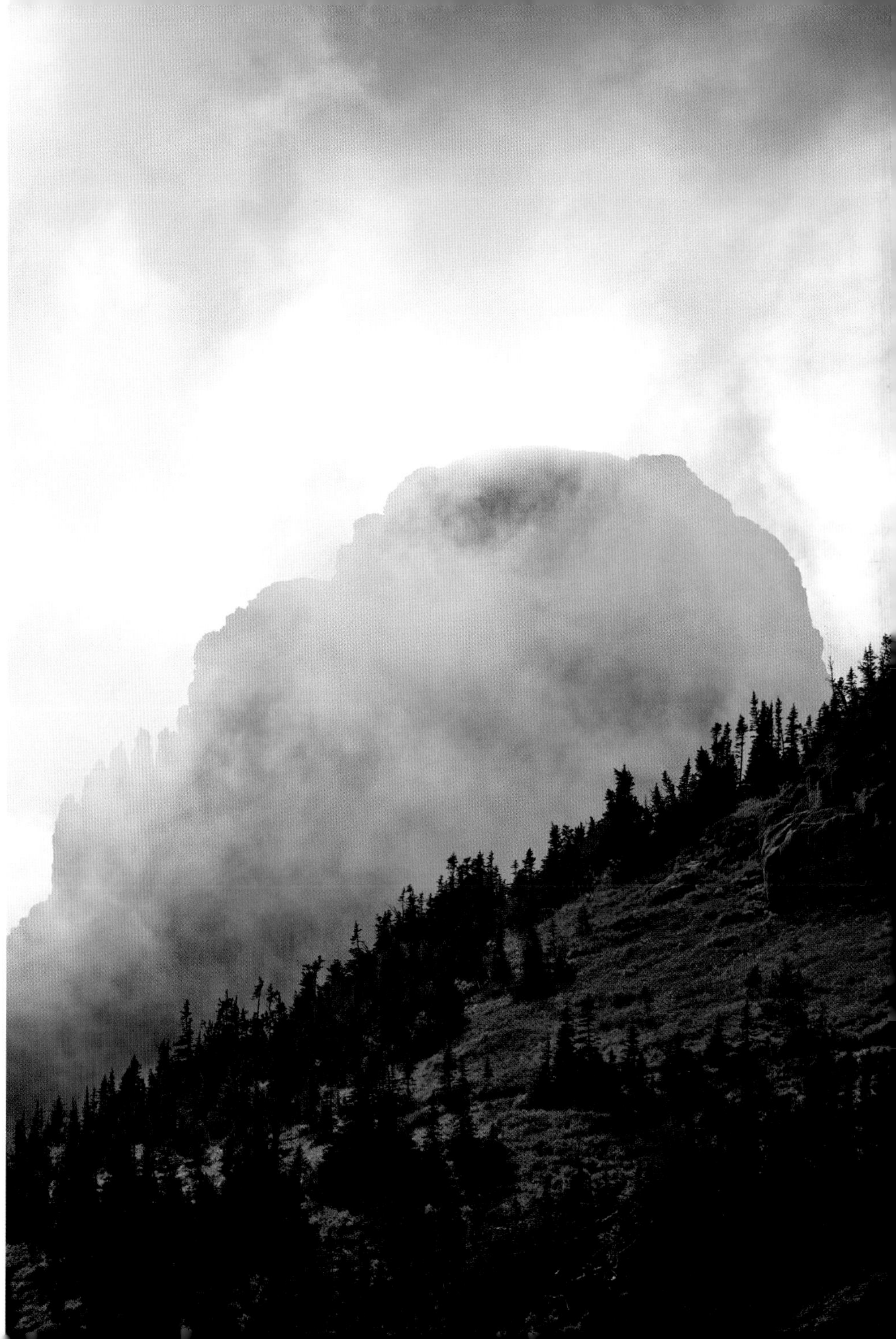

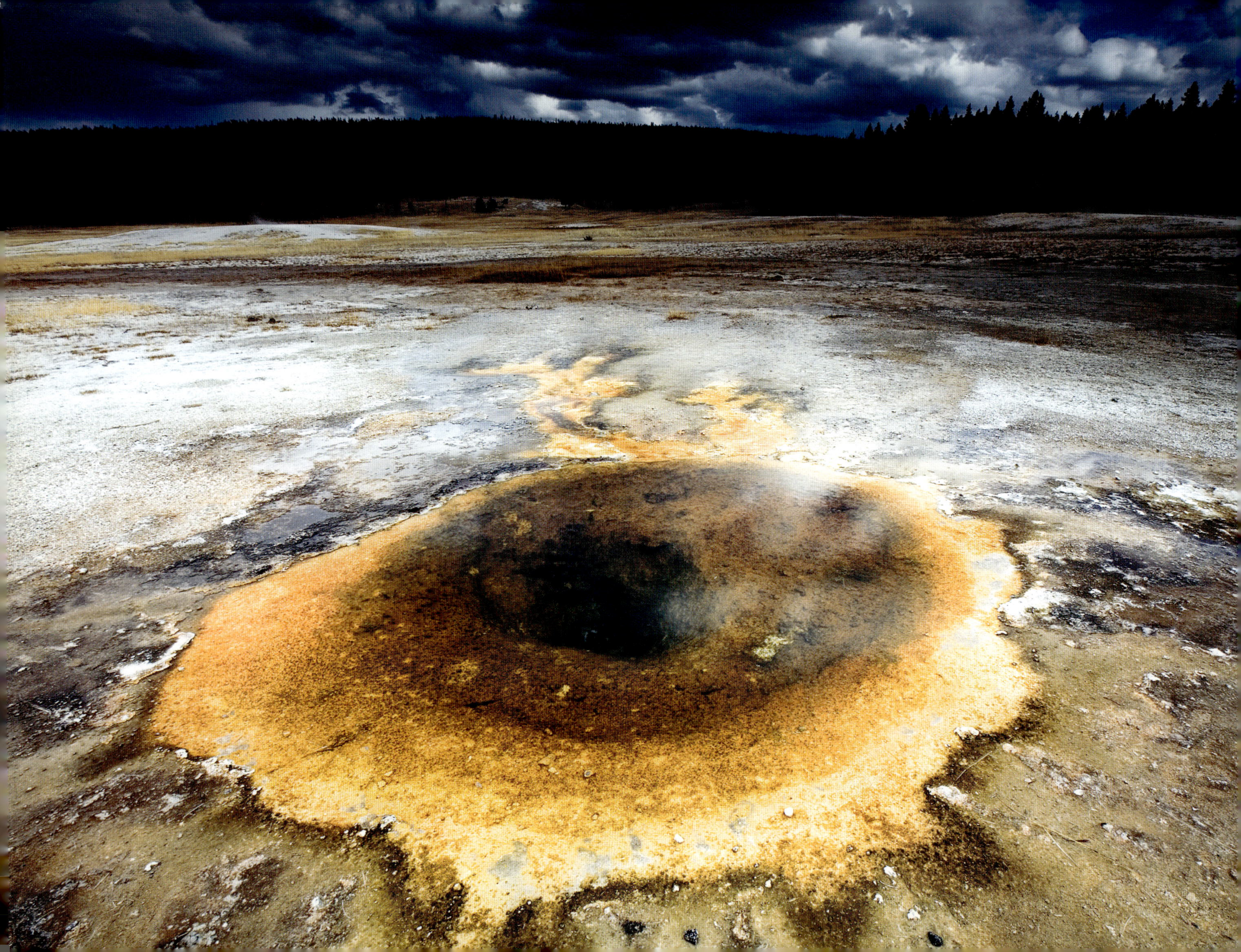

LEFT: **Yellowstone National Park; Wyoming, Montana, Idaho**
A thermal feature near Geyser Basin.

RIGHT: **Yellowstone National Park; Wyoming, Montana, Idaho**
Detail of an American bison's eye.

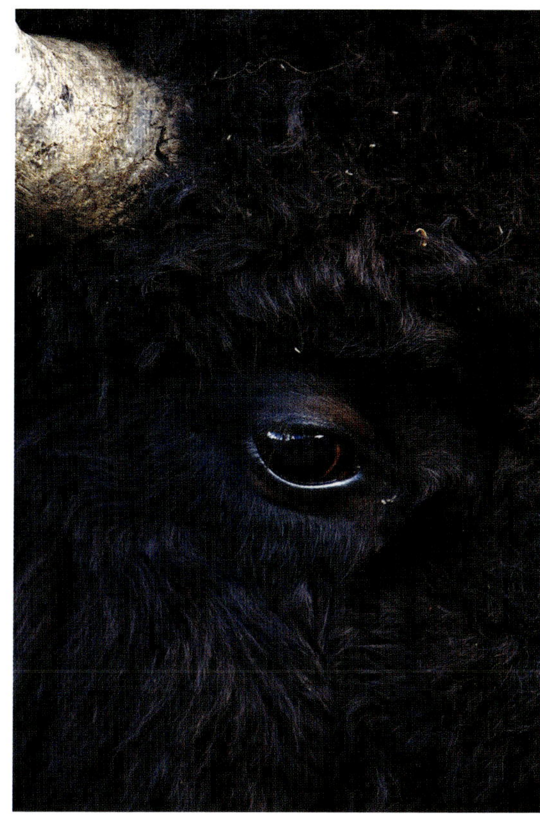

RIGHT: **Channel Islands National Park, California**
Smuggler's Cove Trail.

PAGE 68 (LEFT TO RIGHT): **Zion National Park, Utah**
It wasn't even sunrise yet, but I found myself up to my knees in silty mud and cold, rushing water. Sentinel Peak was already beginning to glow in the predawn light, and there wasn't much time to set up before the entire canyon would be flooded with light and the magic moment would be gone. Working quickly, with my toes squishing ever deeper into the river bottom and my pant legs rolled up as high on my thigh as they could go, I set up my tripod and composed the scene. Soon, the sun peeked out over the opposing canyon wall and the moment and colors were lost, but thankfully not before this frame was exposed.

Yosemite National Park, California
Merced River and El Capitan at last light.

PAGE 69 (LEFT TO RIGHT): **Glacier National Park, Montana**
A snowfield melts under the heat at Logan Pass at the Continental Divide.

Acadia National Park, Maine
The tide comes in beneath the Otter Cliffs.

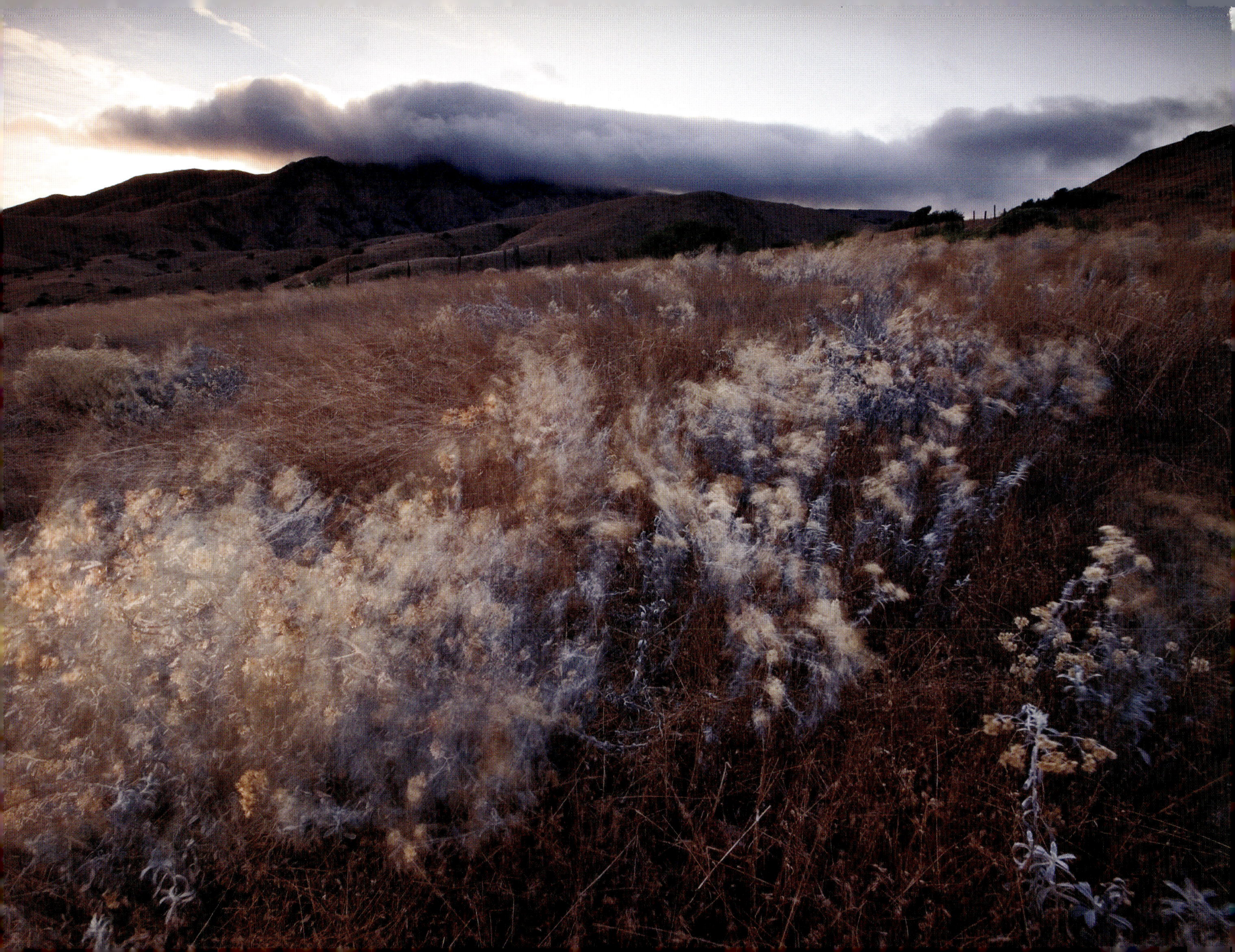

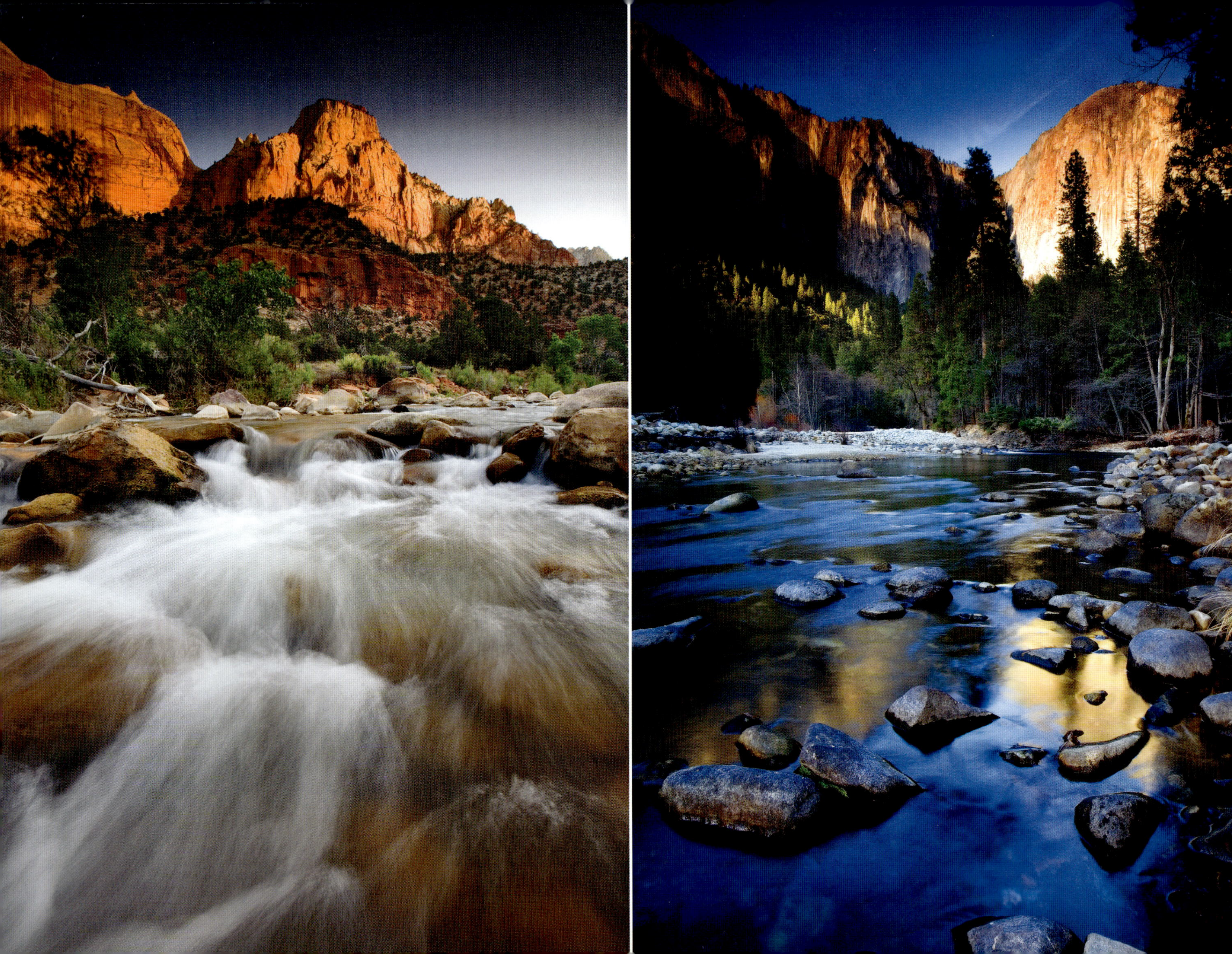

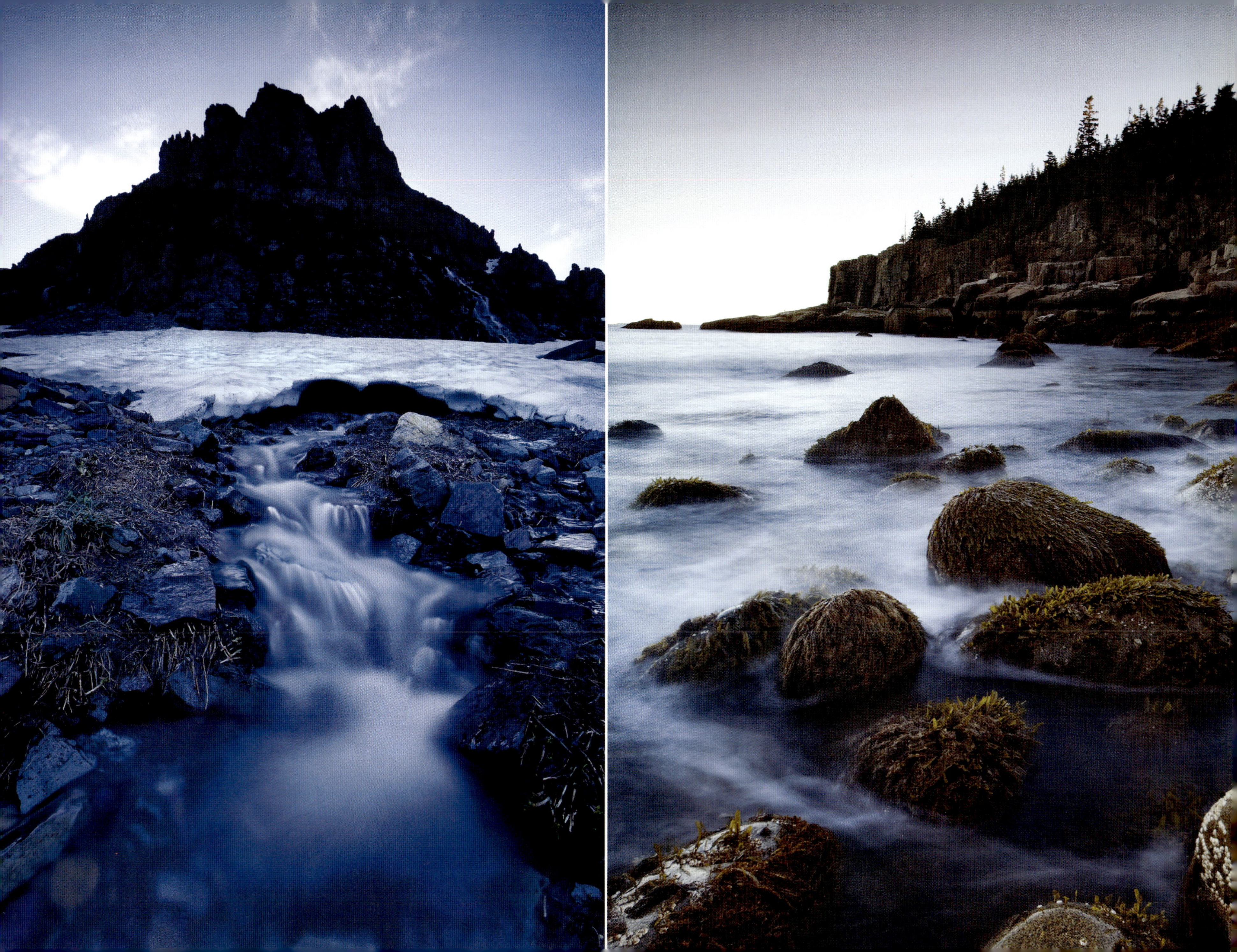

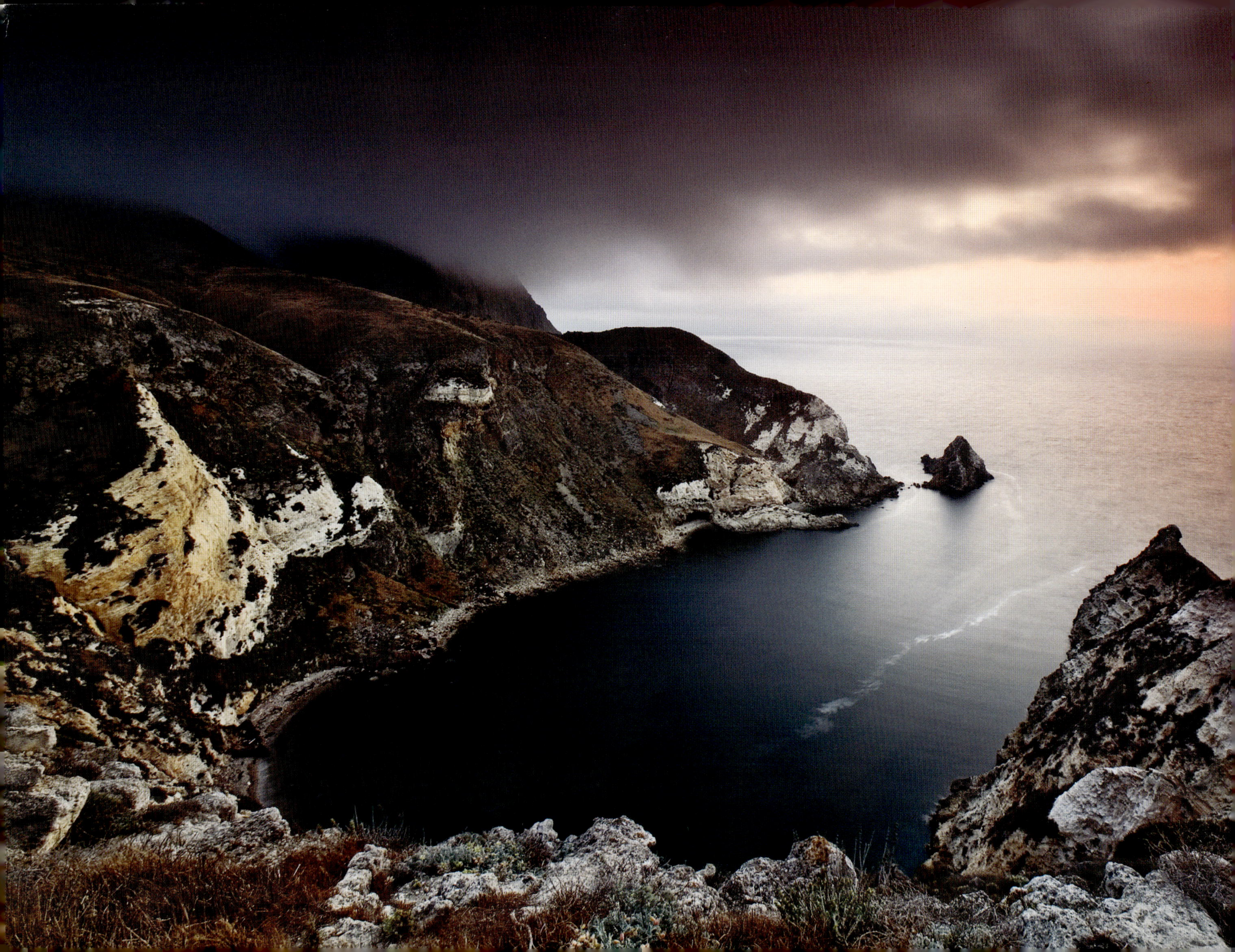

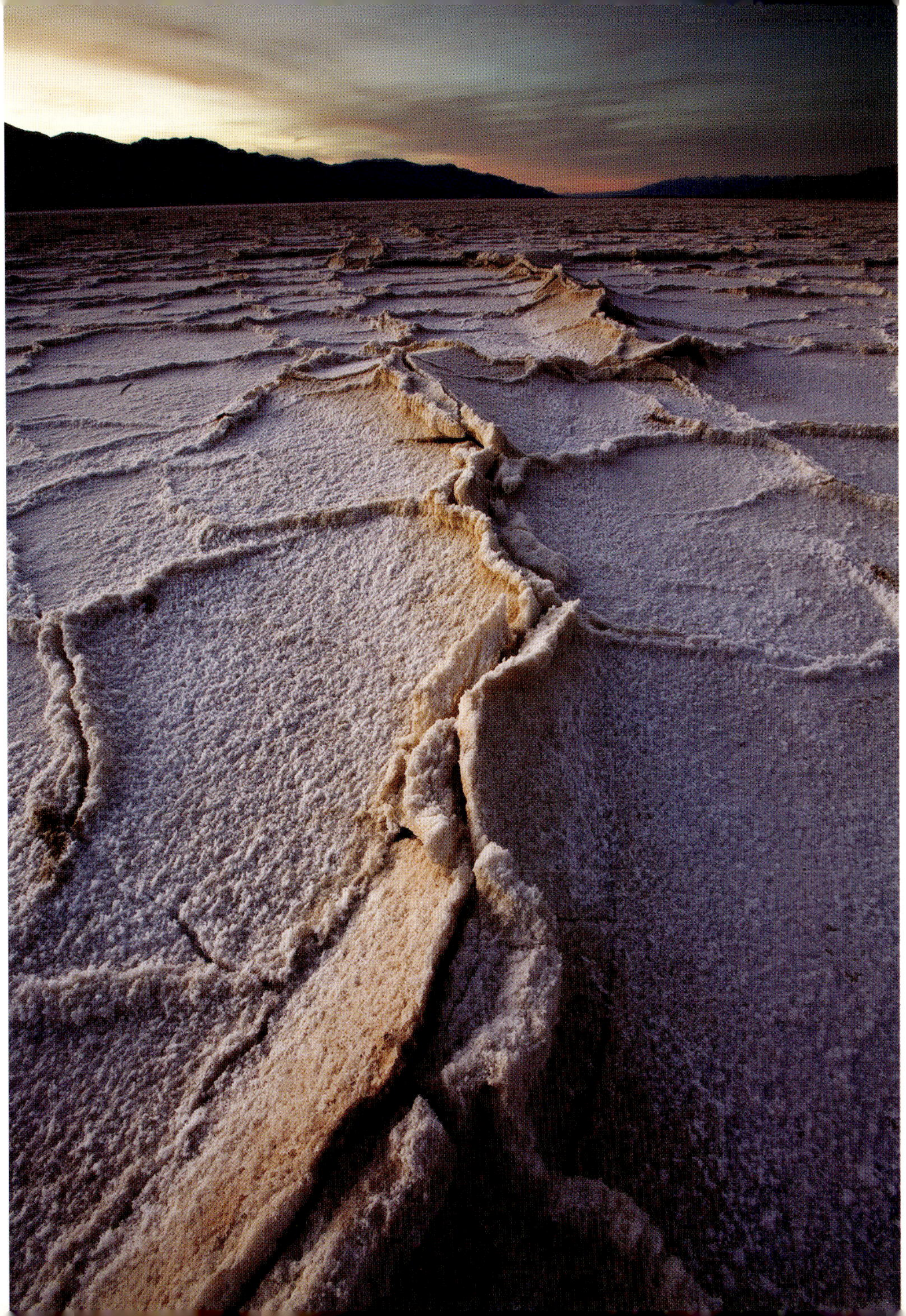

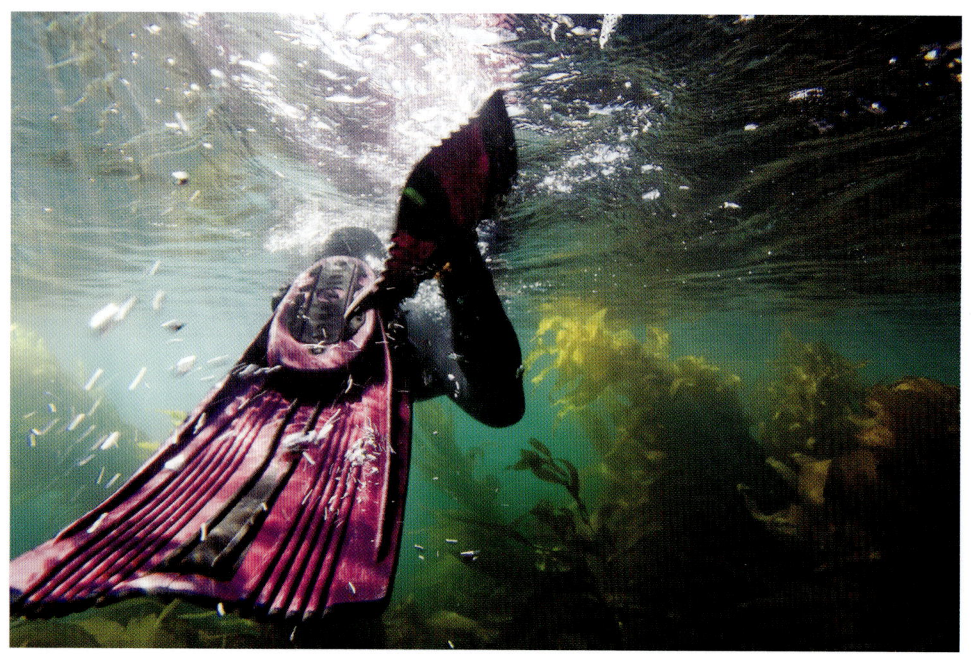

PAGE 70/71: **Channel Islands National Park, California**
A late-spring sunset over Potato Harbor on Santa Cruz Island.

PAGE 71: **Death Valley National Park, California**
Salt rises to the surface of Badwater Basin, creating interesting patterns and formations.

LEFT: **Channel Islands National Park, California**
Snorkeling in the clear waters of the marine sanctuary. A kelp forest is visible in the background.

RIGHT: **Sequoia & Kings Canyon National Parks, California**
Wildflowers caught up in morning dew and a spider web.

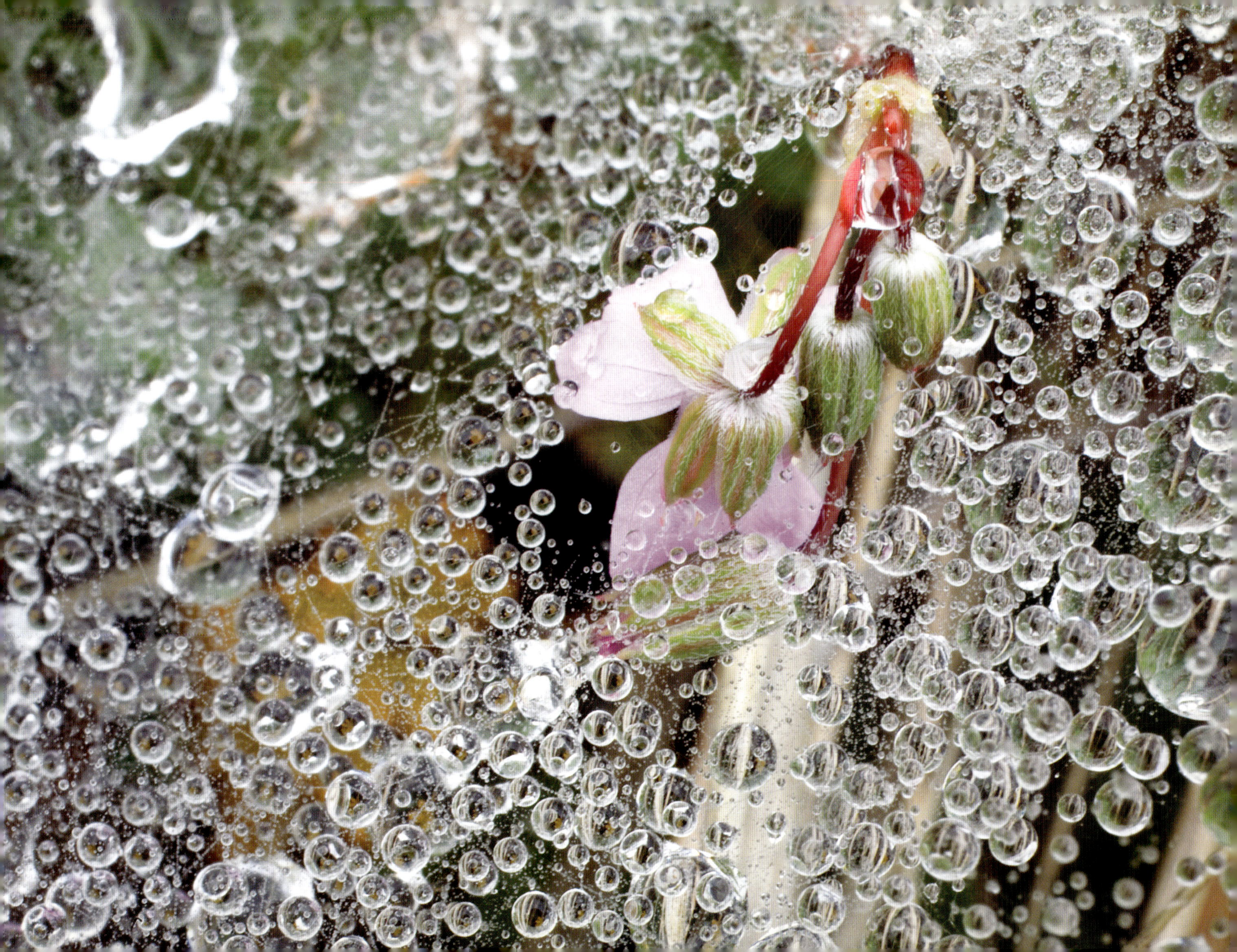

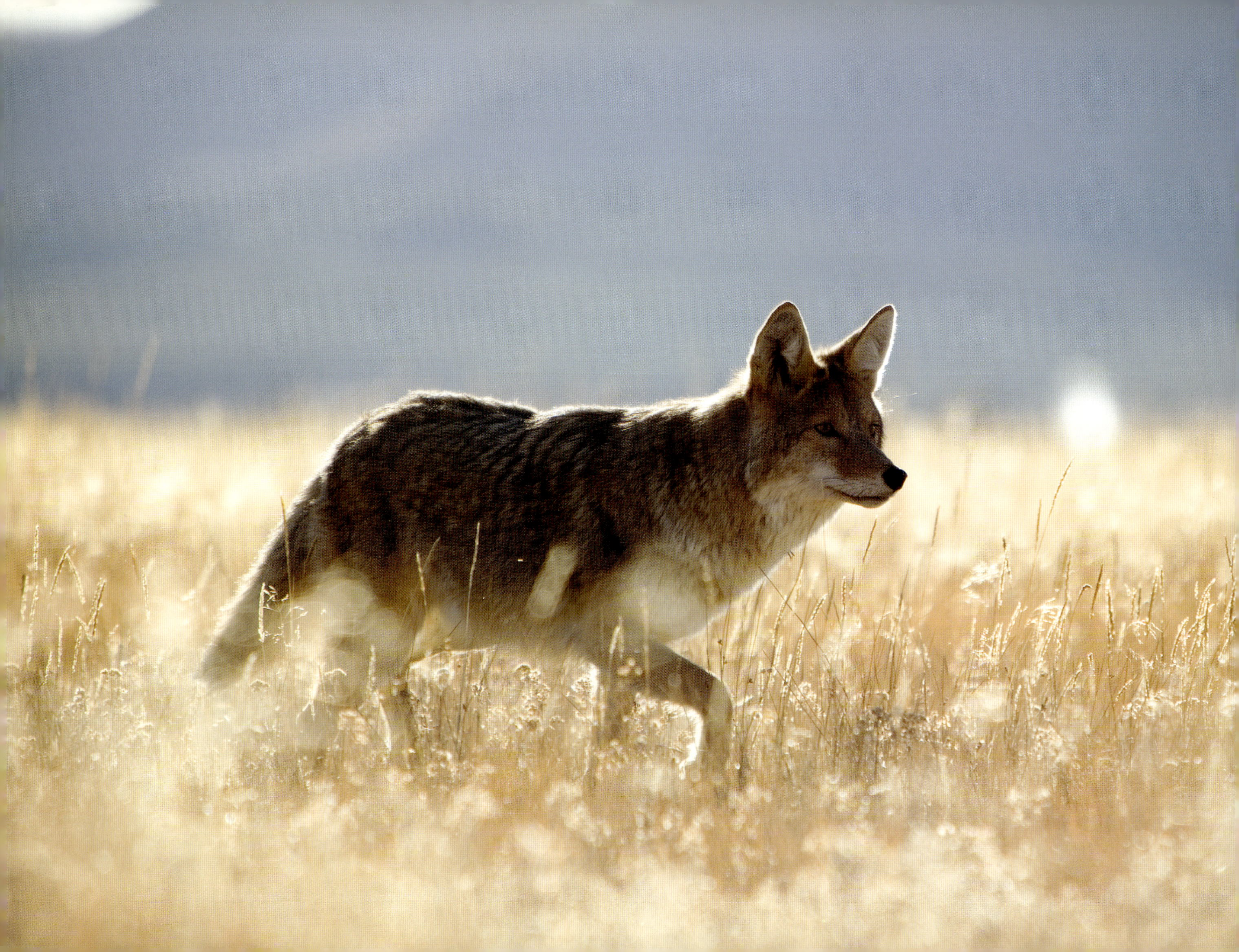

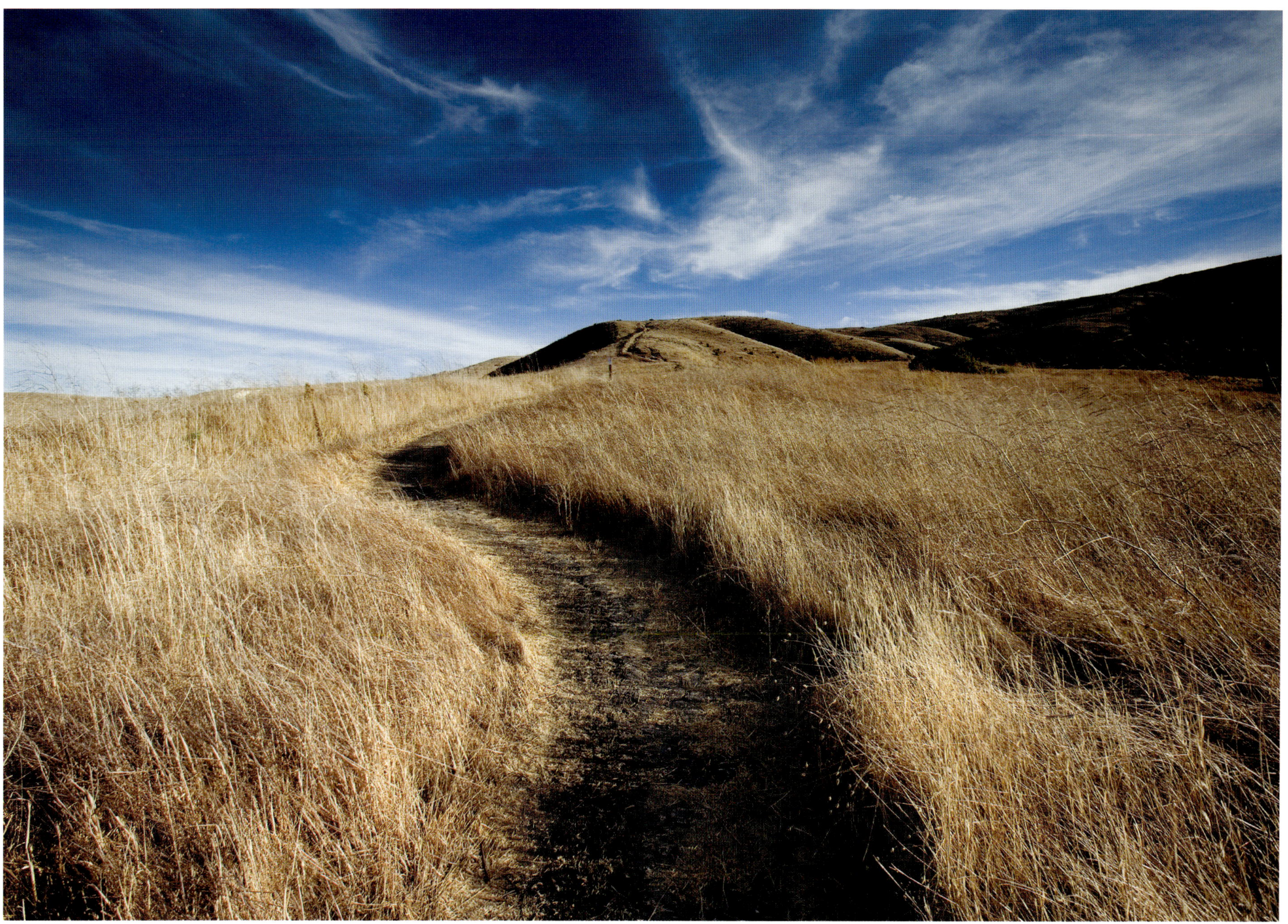

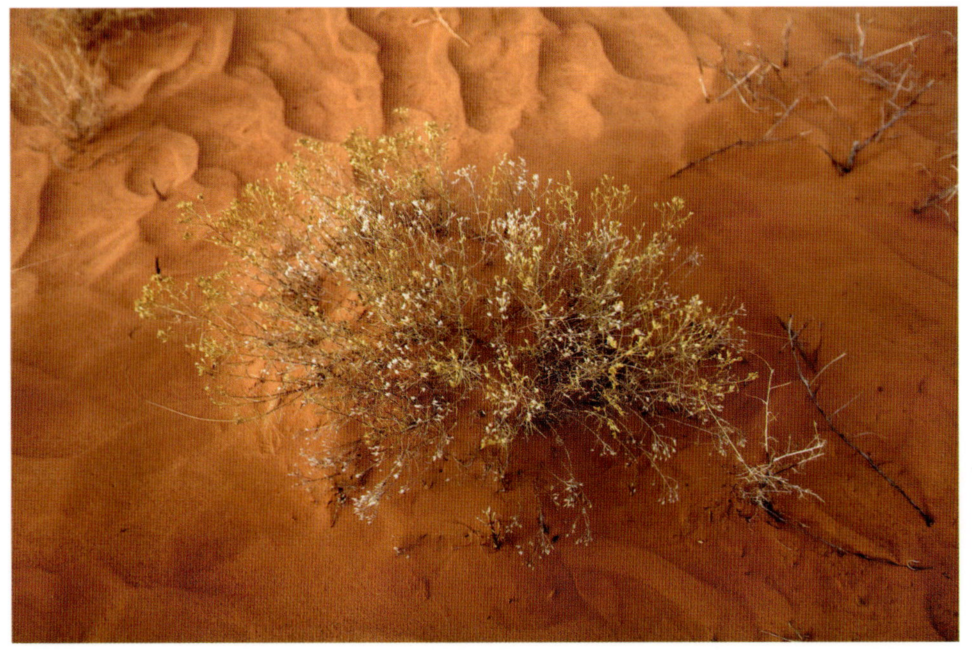

PAGE 74: **Yellowstone National Park; Wyoming, Montana, Idaho**
A coyote treks across an open field.

PAGE 75: **Channel Islands National Park, California**
The Scorpion Loop Trail.

LEFT: **Canyonlands National Park, Utah**
Detail of desert sand dune.

RIGHT: **Saguaro National Park, Arizona**
Saguaros bathed in evening light.

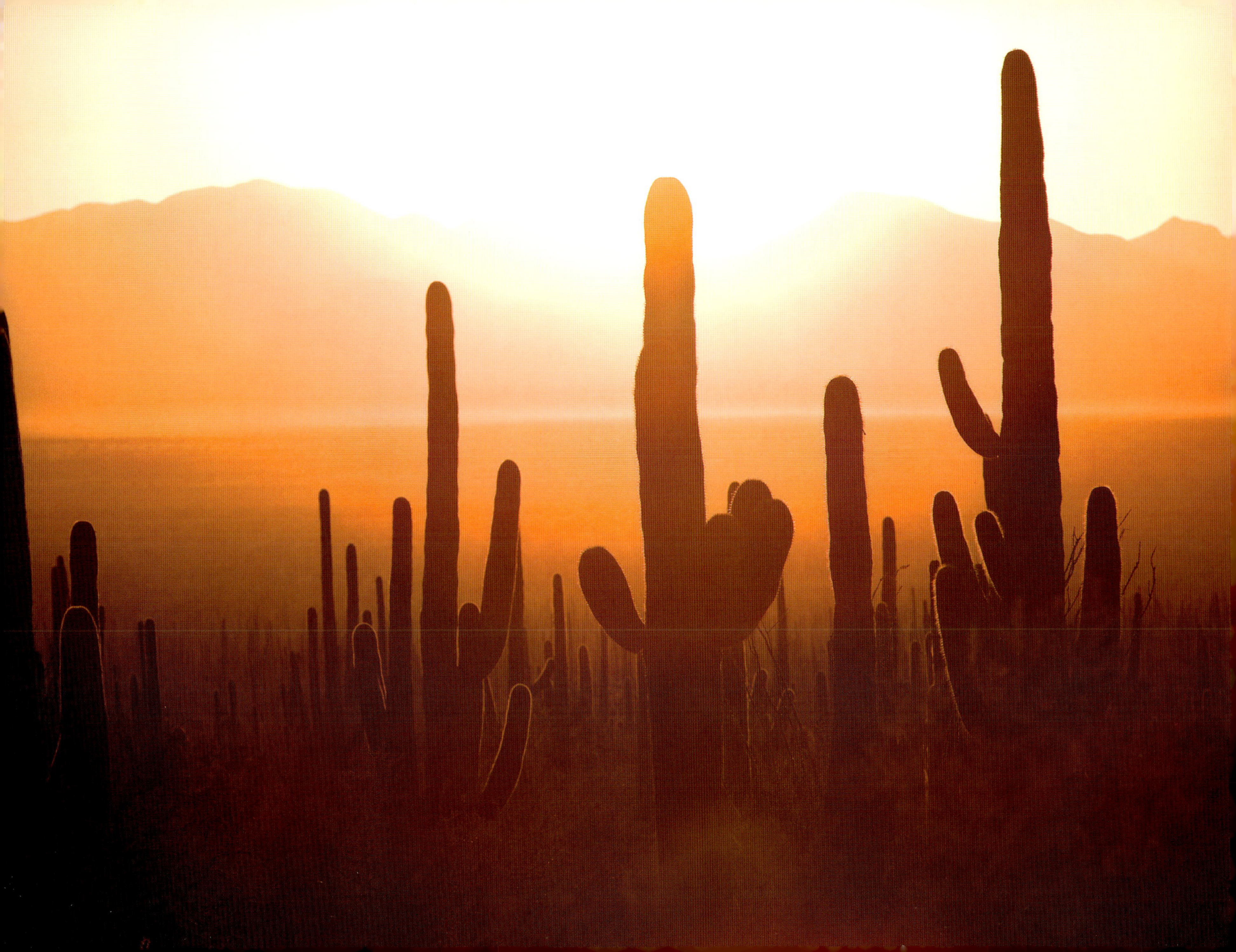

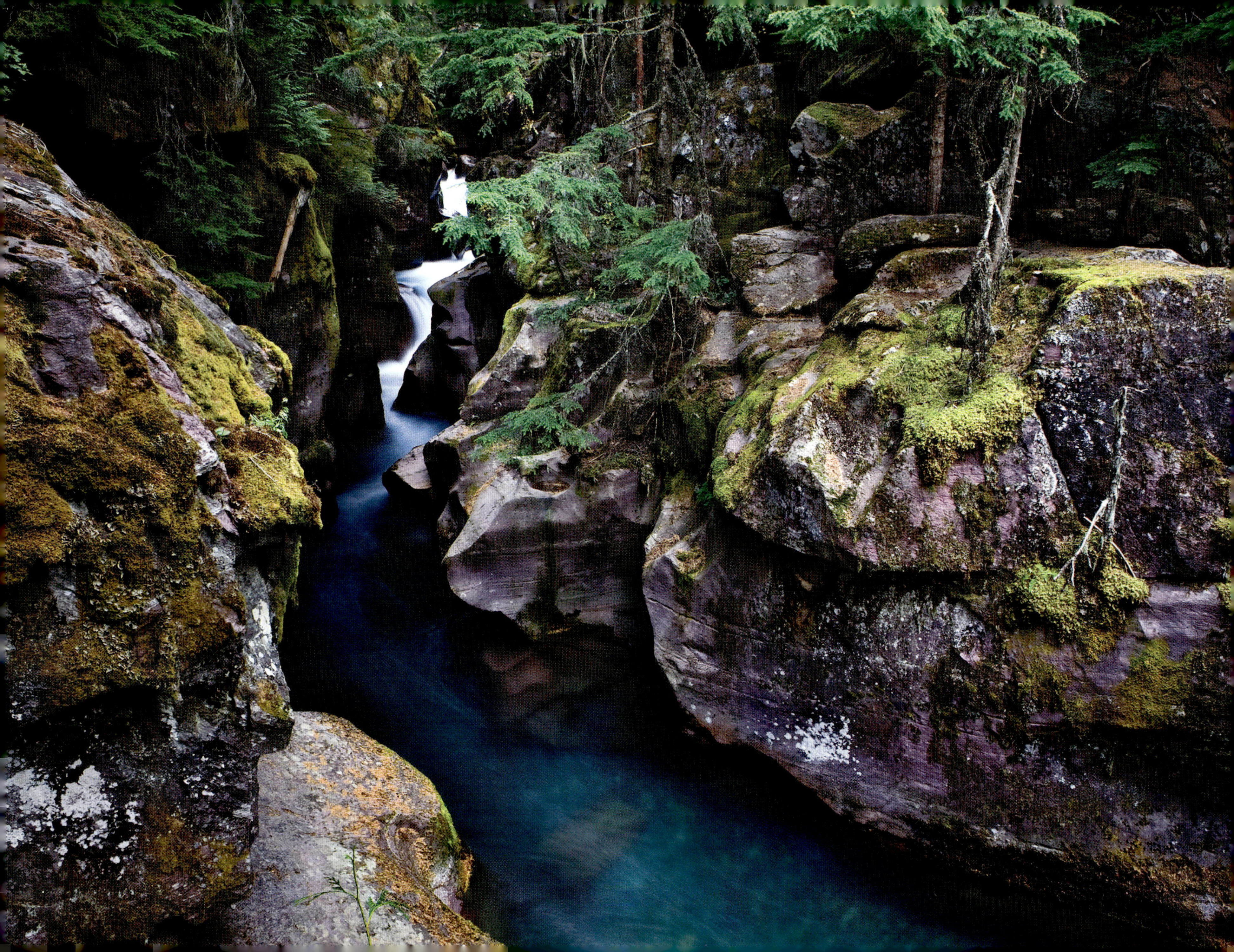

LEFT: **Glacier National Park, Montana**
Avalanche Creek: These turquoise waters are the result of glacial runoff that has worked its way down from the ancient blocks of ice that rest high above. Scenes like these are what I first think of when I imagine a national park. Far from being just another creek, its water glows an incredible blue color that I can't imagine occurring anywhere else in nature—except perhaps on the feathers of an exotic bird.

RIGHT: **Yellowstone National Park; Wyoming, Montana, Idaho**
Reflections of clouds are seen at Mammoth Hot Springs near Canary Spring. The landscape here is otherworldly. One of the greatest aspects of our national parks is that they are not only a reminder of the greatness all around us, but also of how alien our own planet can be and how much more there is to learn.

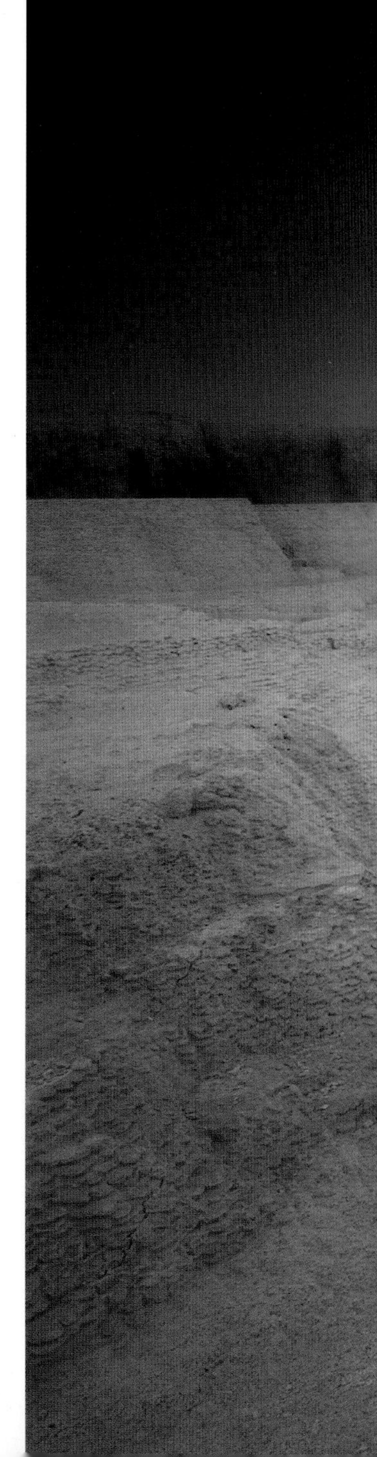

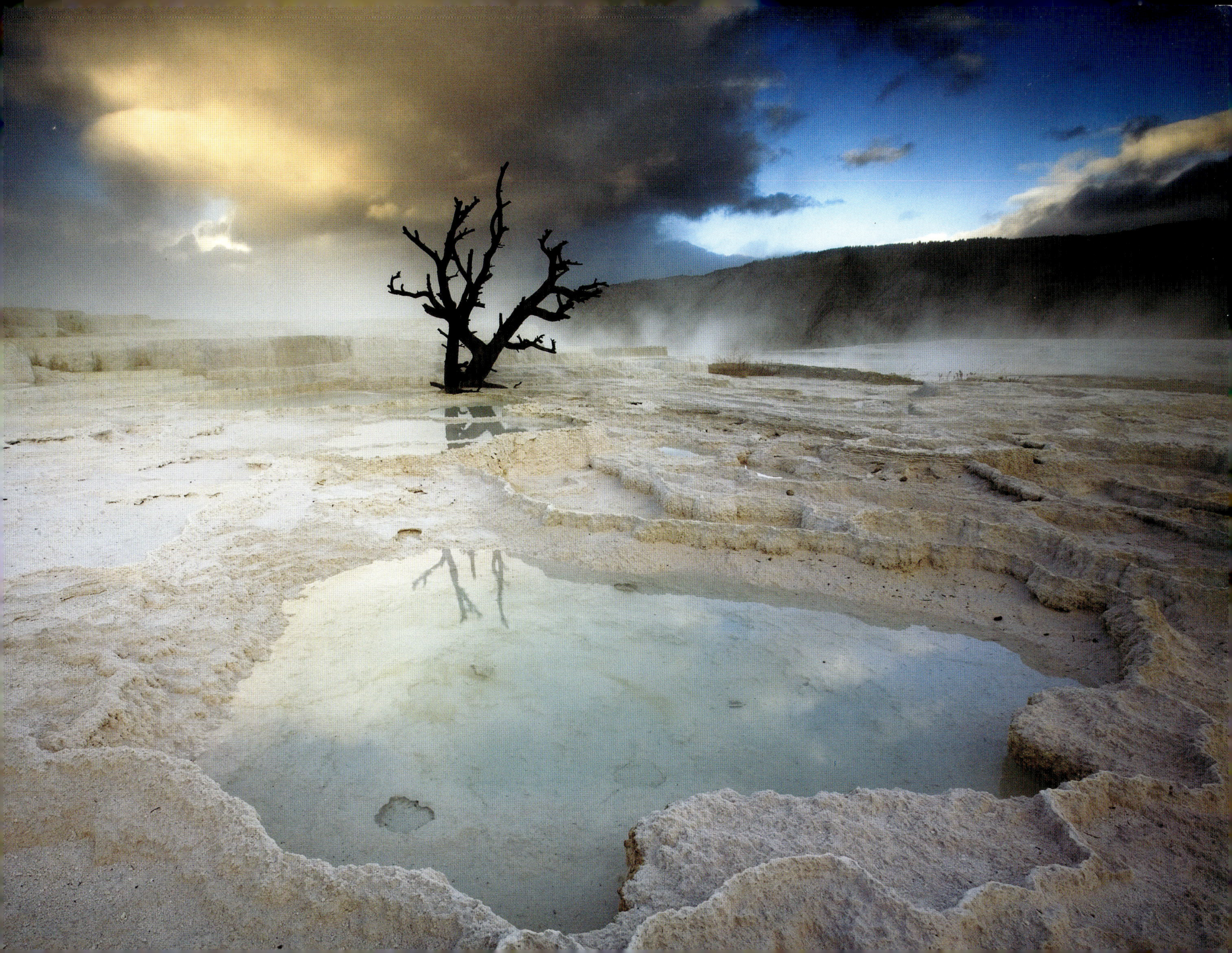

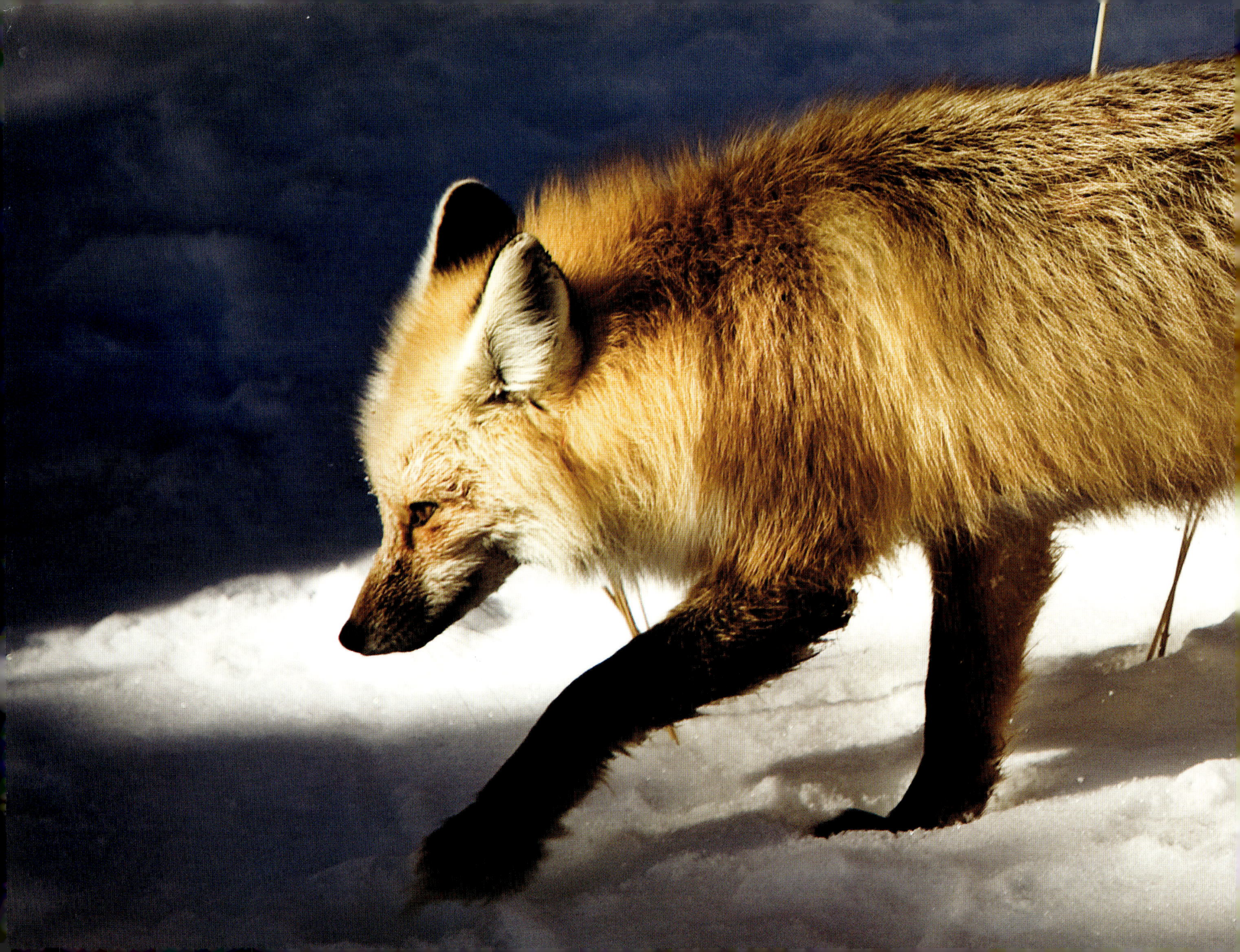

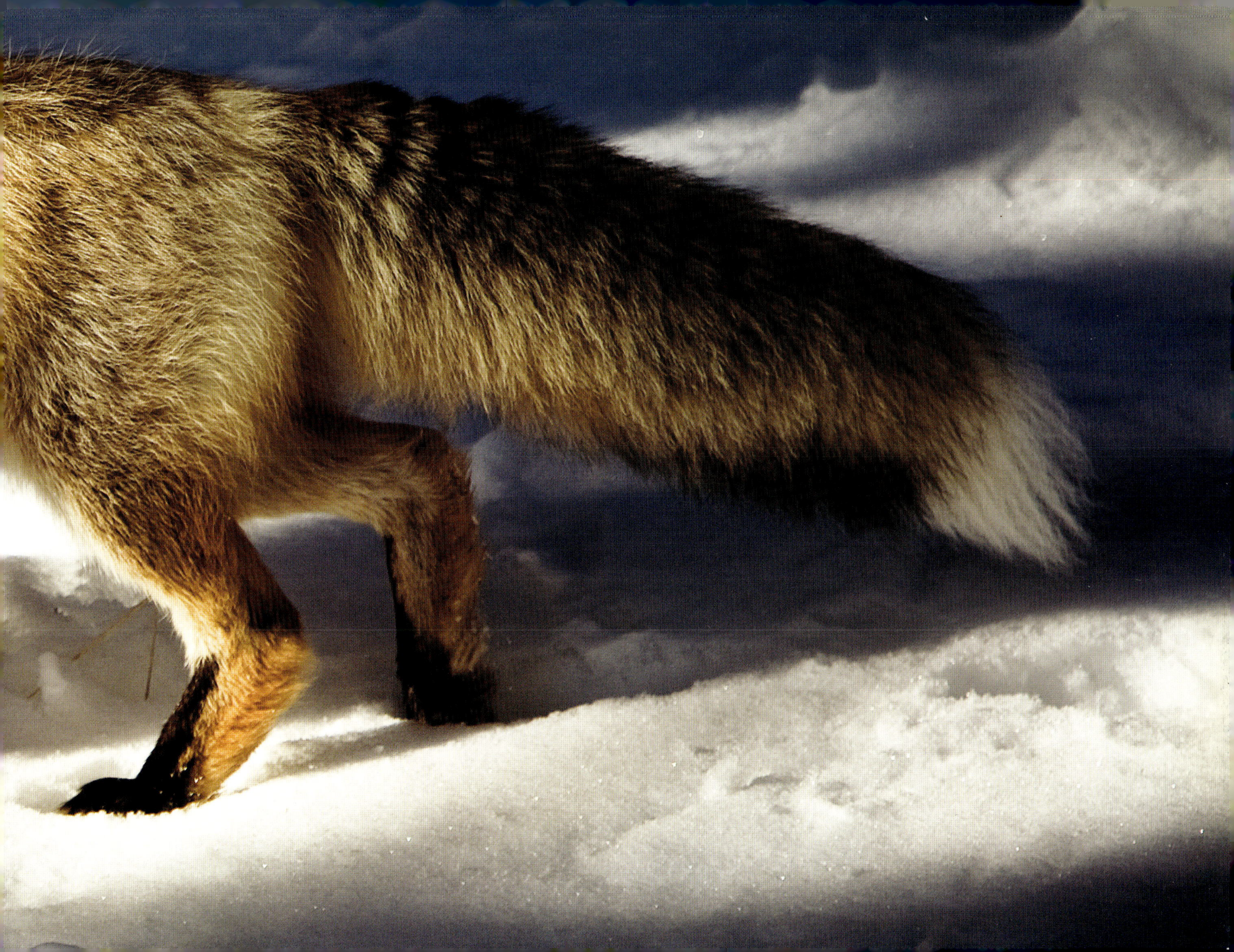

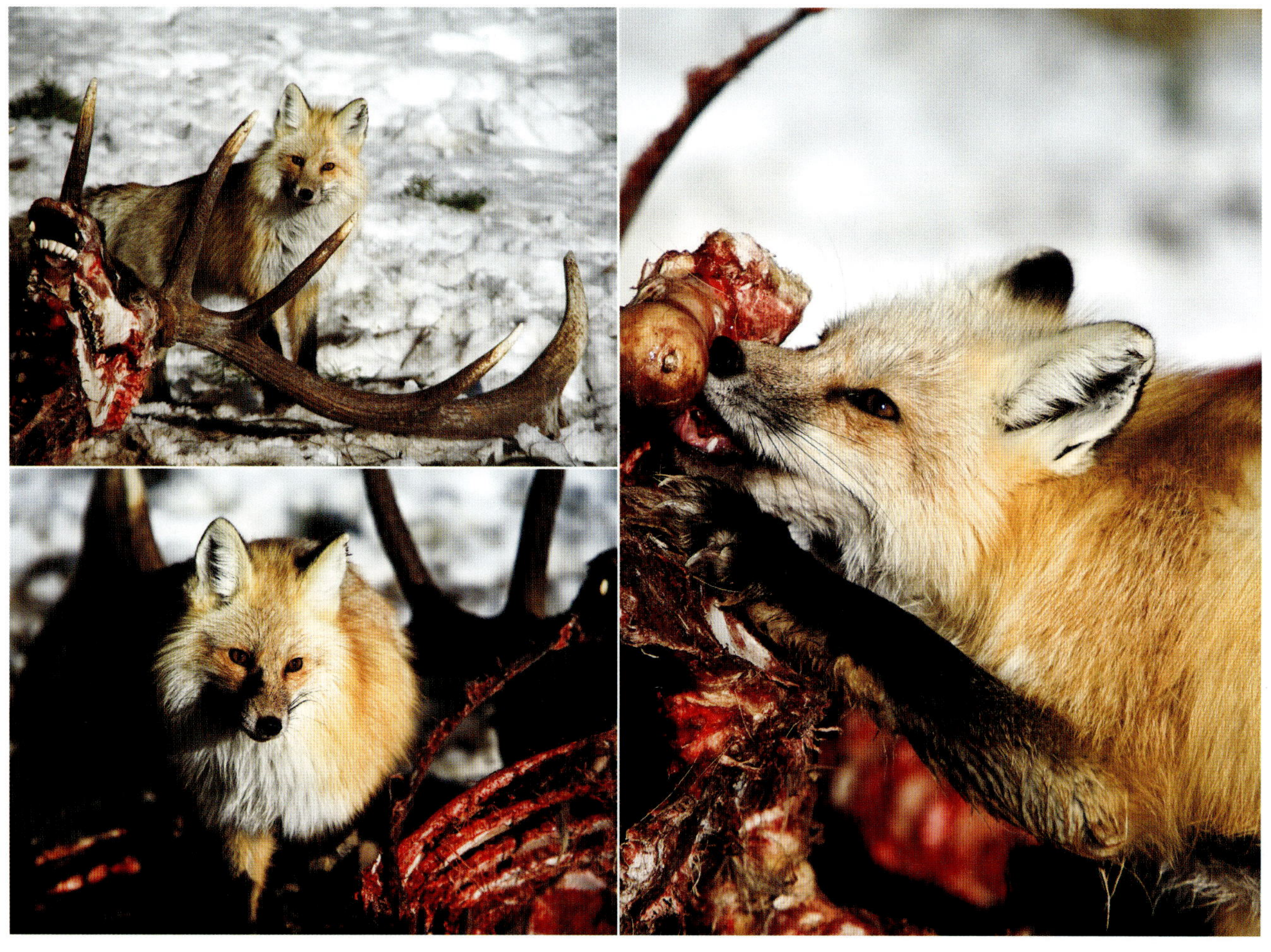

PAGES 82/83: **Yellowstone National Park; Wyoming, Montana, Idaho**
A red fox walks through the snow toward an elk in the backcountry of Lamar Valley. Evening light dances across the snow, highlighting the red fur. The fox is on the rebound in Yellowstone, its numbers closely tied to the successful reintroduction of the wolf.

LEFT: **Yellowstone National Park; Wyoming, Montana, Idaho**
A red fox feeding on the carcass of a bull elk in the backcountry of the Lamar Valley.

RIGHT: **Yosemite National Park, California**
Snow-covered trees in Yosemite Valley.

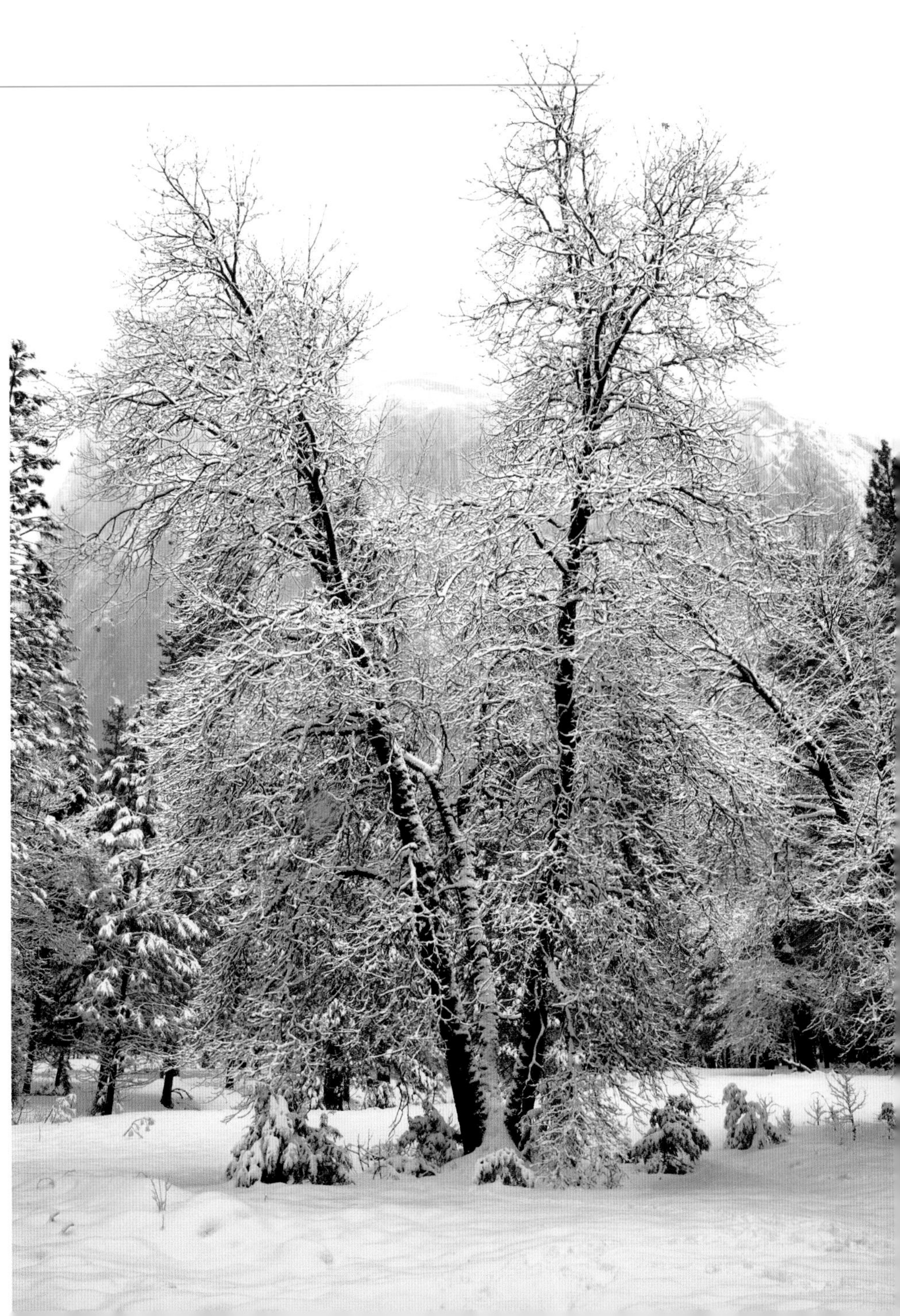

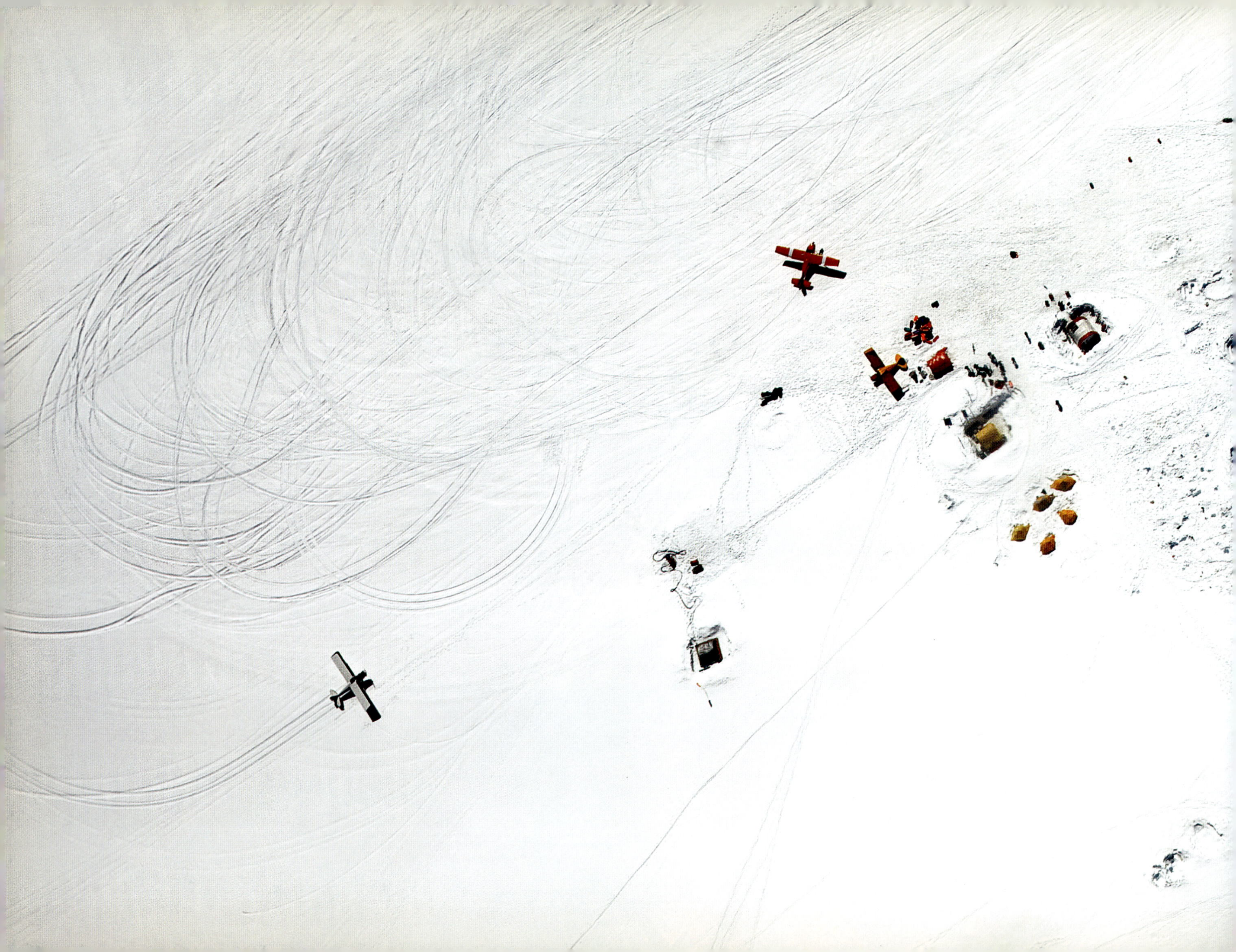

PAGE 86/87: **Denali National Park & Preserve, Alaska**
Looking straight down on the Kahiltna Glacier from a fixed-wing aircraft, the 7,200-foot base camp of Mount McKinley looks like it is made up of toy planes and tents. But it is no game—the Kahiltna Glacier is active, moving up to a foot per day, like a river in slow motion.

RIGHT: **Yosemite National Park, California**
Tunnel Overlook, one of the most famous views in all of the National Parks, which includes an overlook view of Yosemite Valley.

PAGE 90: **Yosemite National Park, California**
Portrait of a coyote.

PAGE 91: **Glacier National Park, Montana**
Grinnell Glacier and Upper Grinnell Lake—newly formed by the fast-receding glacier.

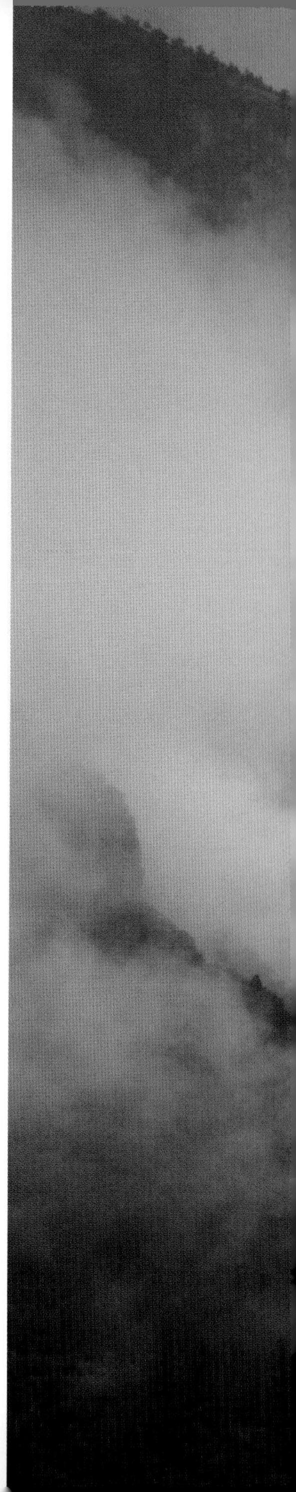

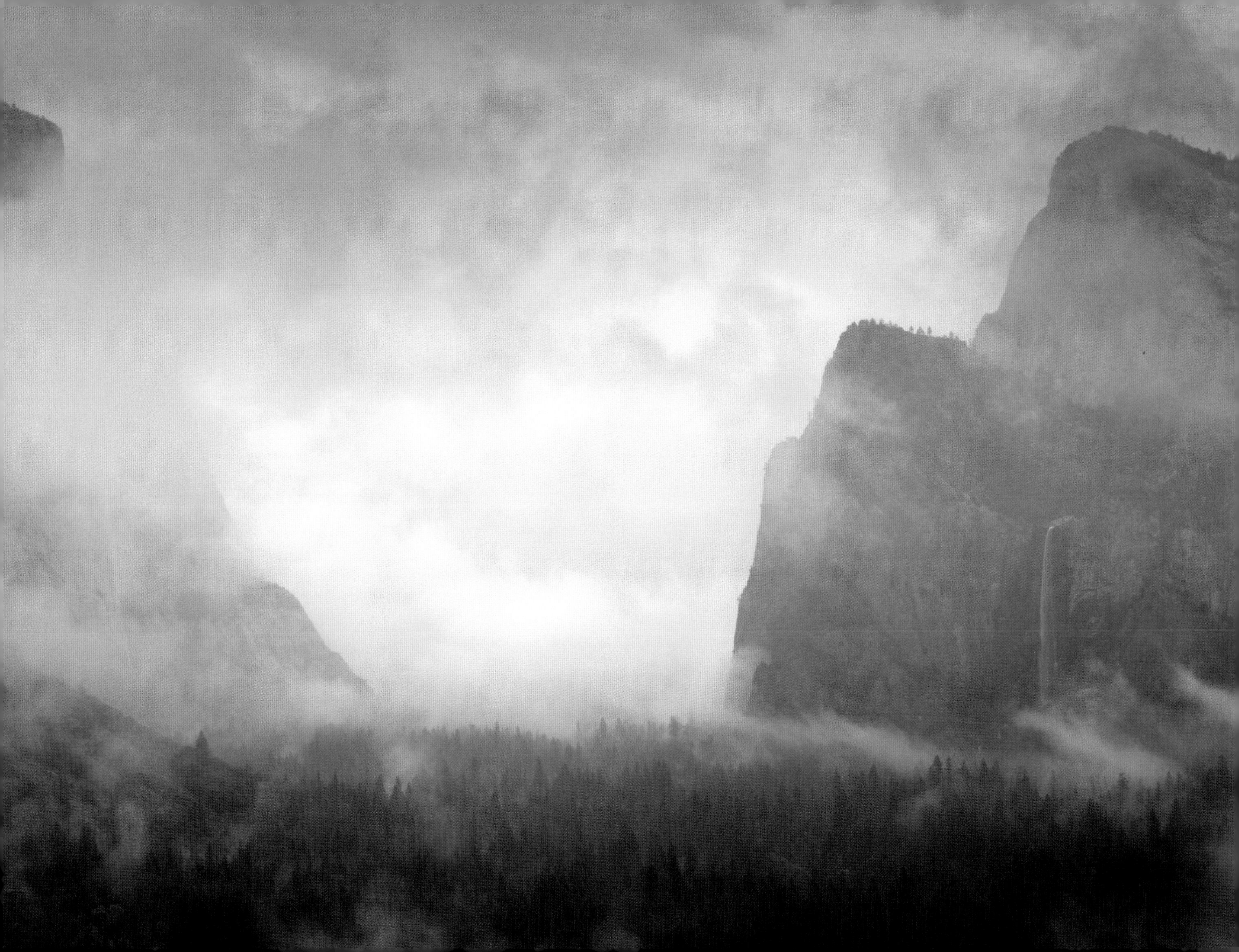

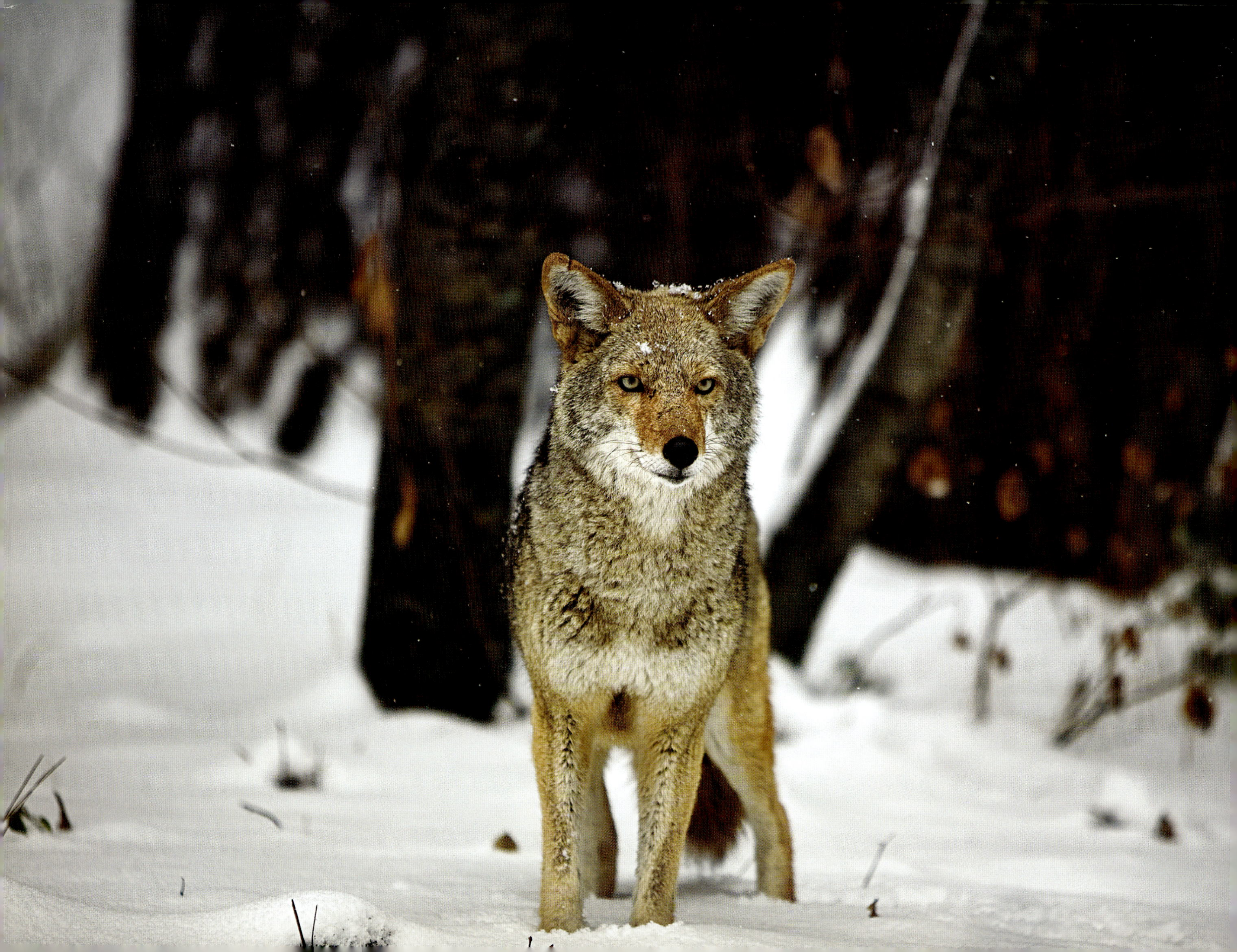

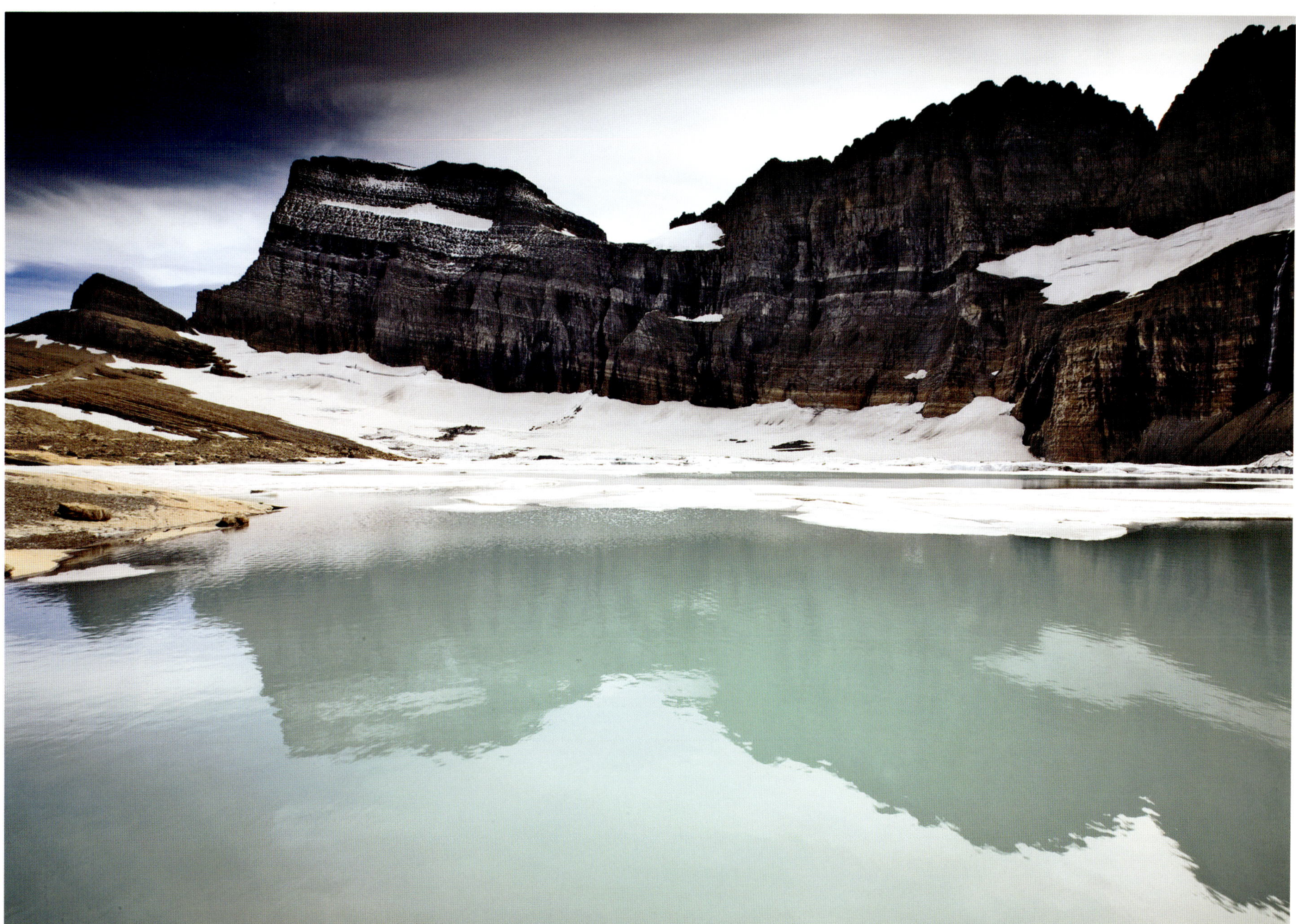

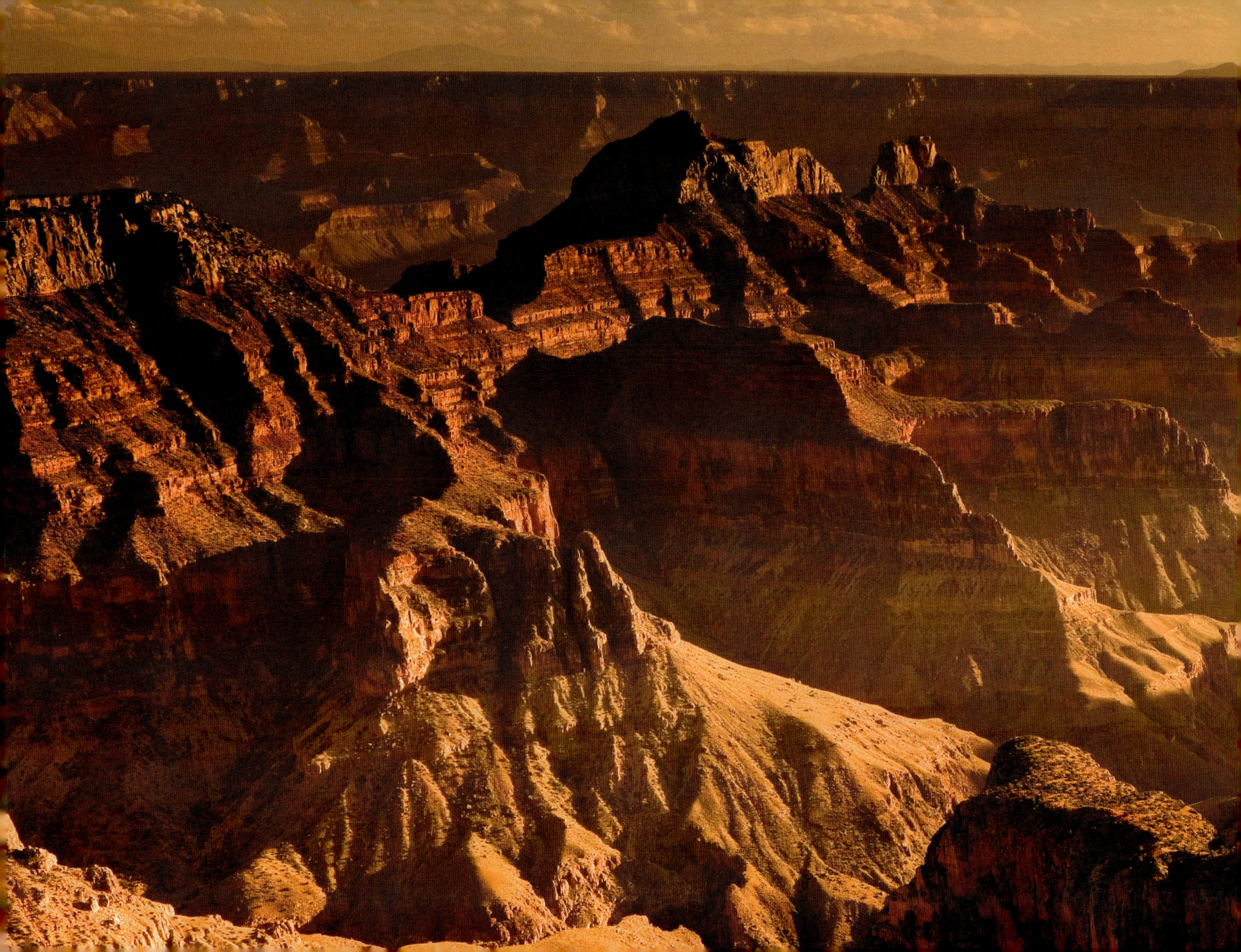

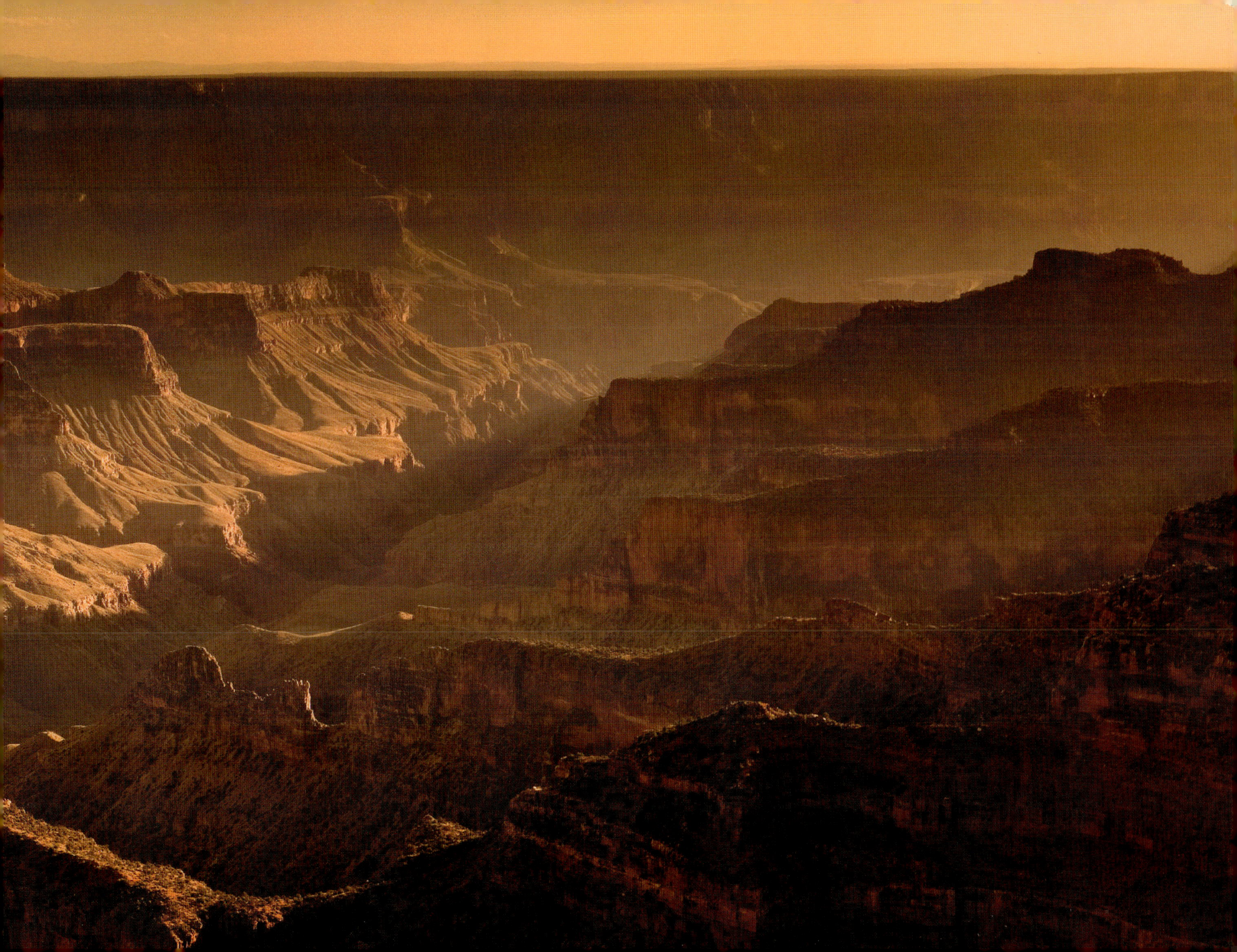

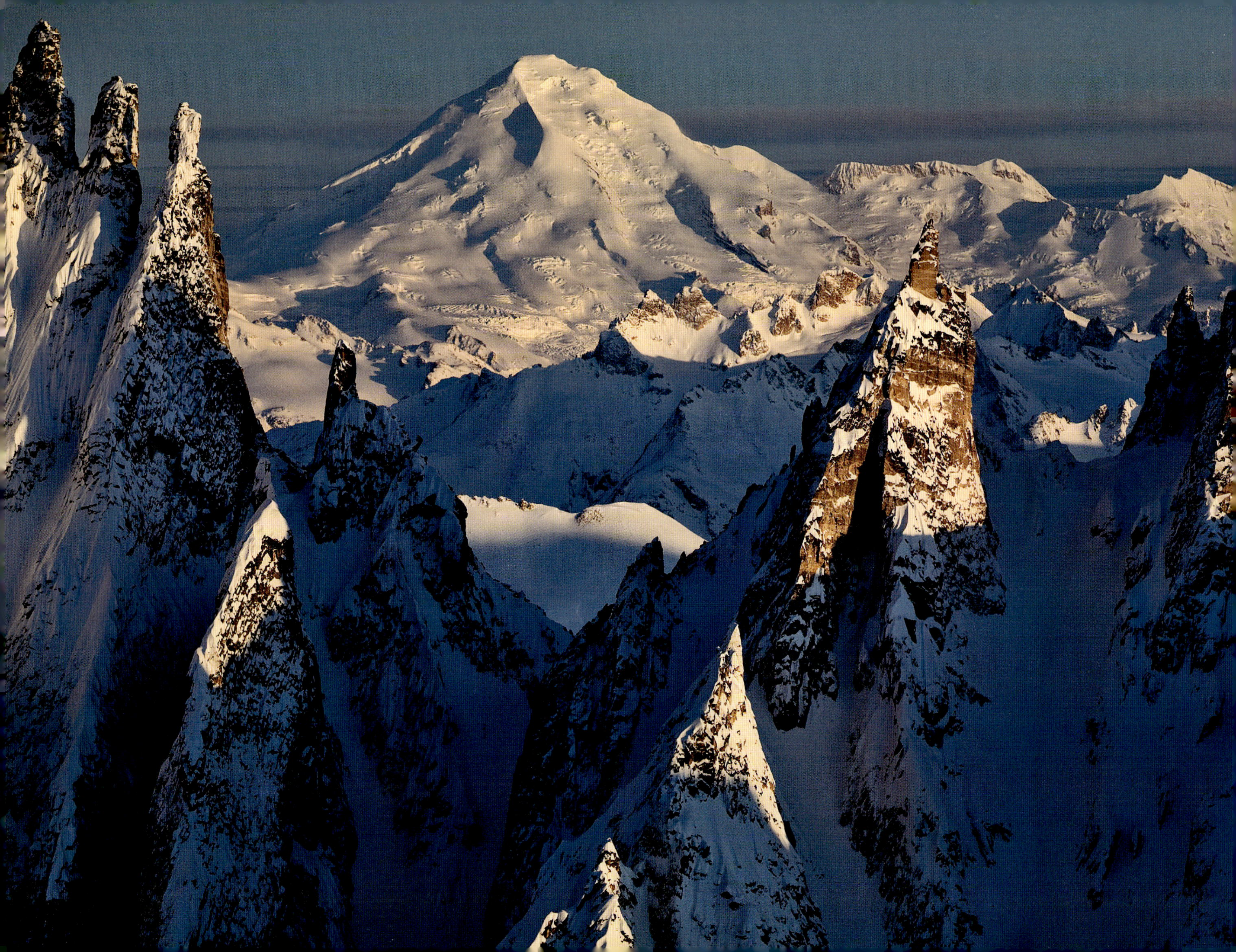

PAGES 92/93: **Grand Canyon National Park, Arizona**
Panoramic view looking into the North Rim of the Grand Canyon at sunset.

LEFT: **Lake Clark National Park & Preserve, Alaska**
Aerial views of the Aleutian Mountain Range and Chigmit Mountains at last light.

RIGHT: **Grand Teton National Park, Wyoming**
A scenic landscape at Jenny Lake.

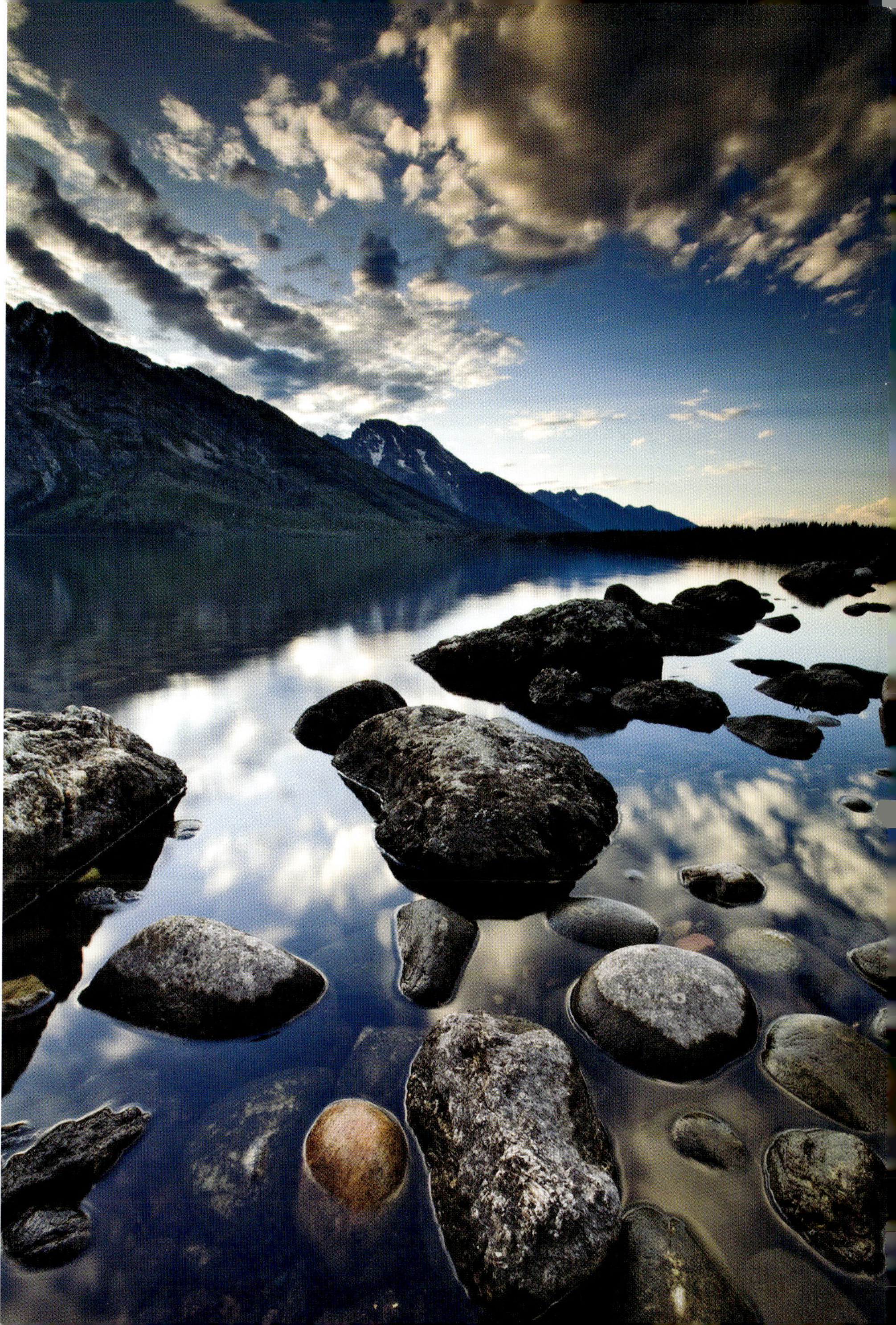

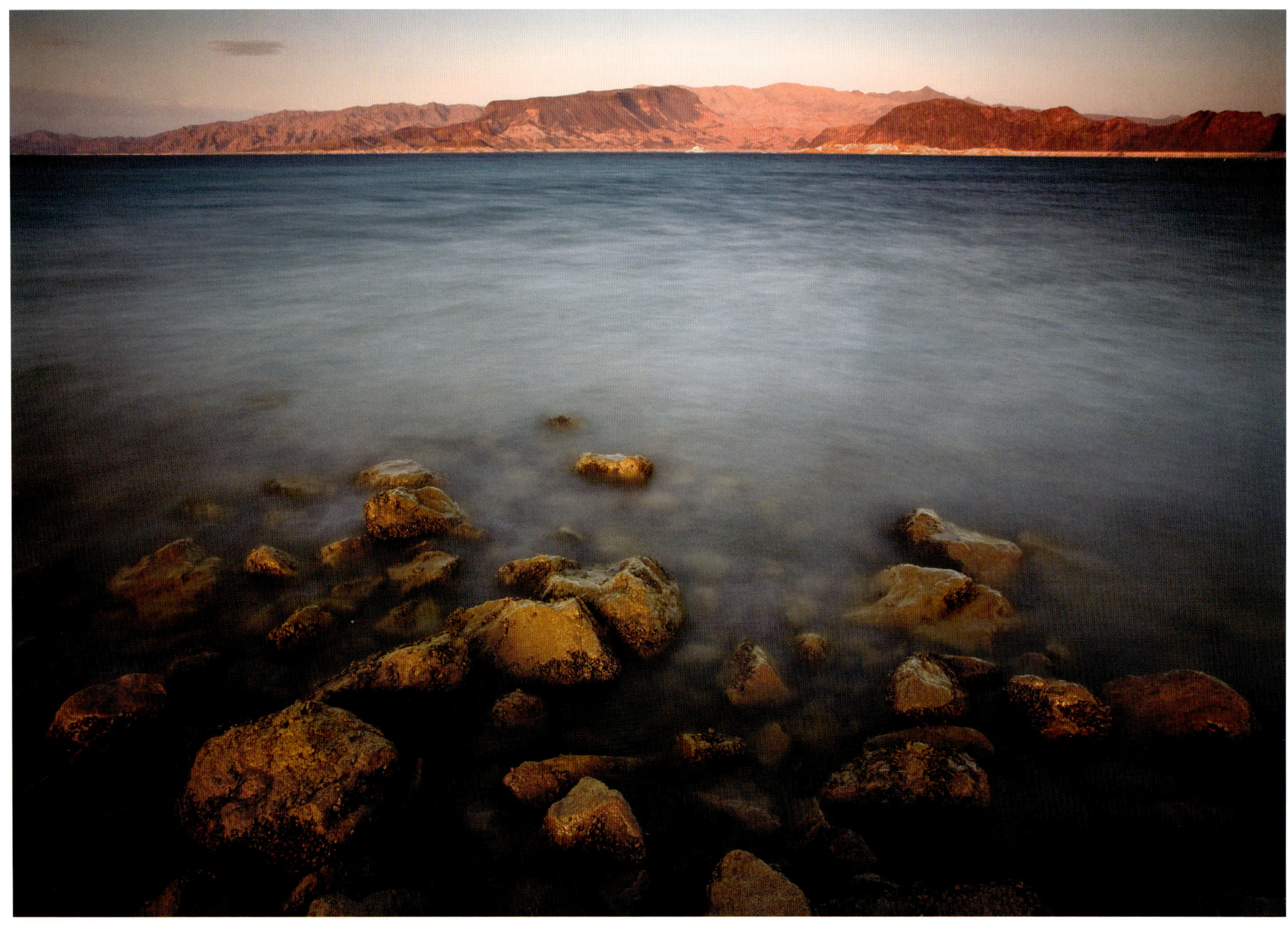

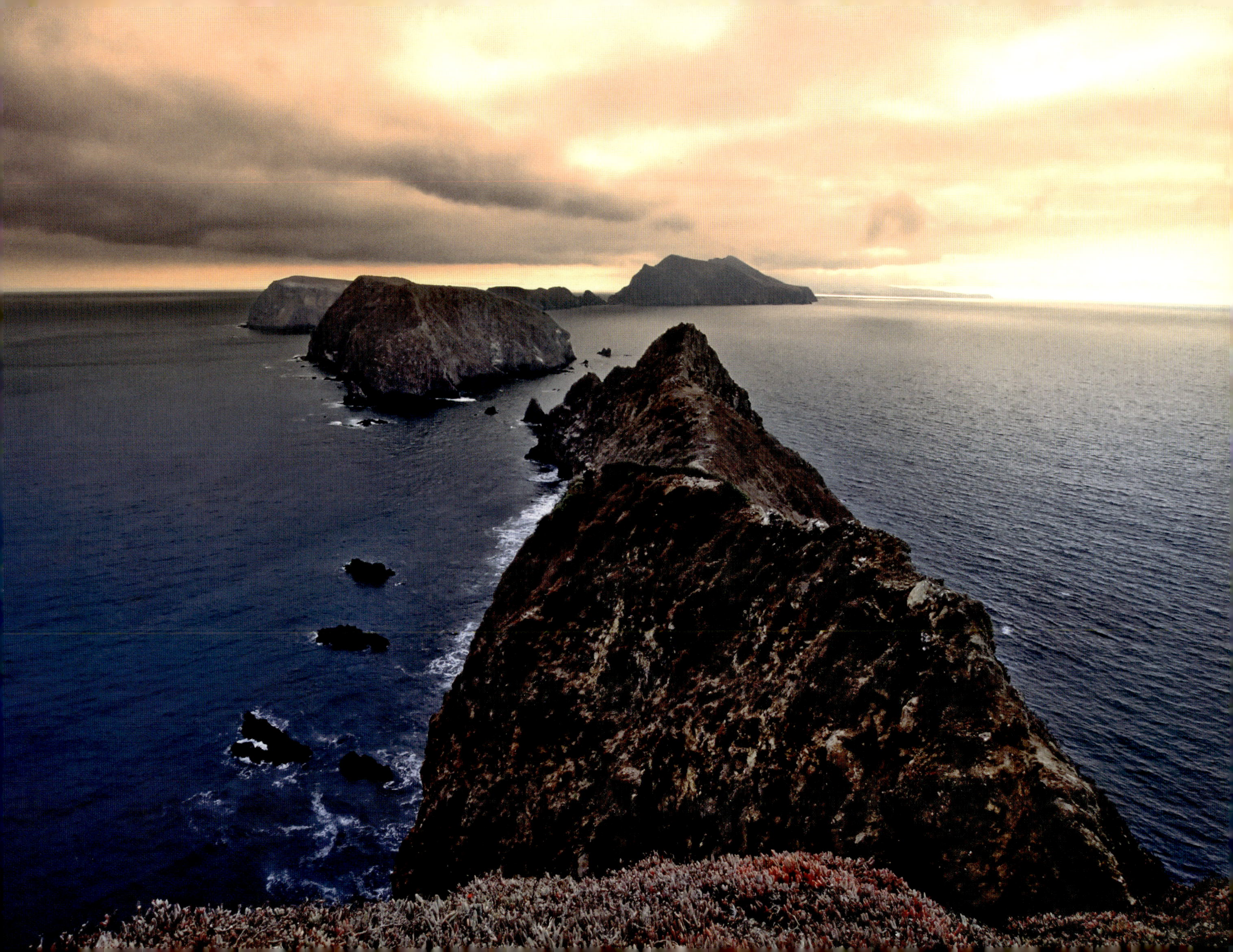

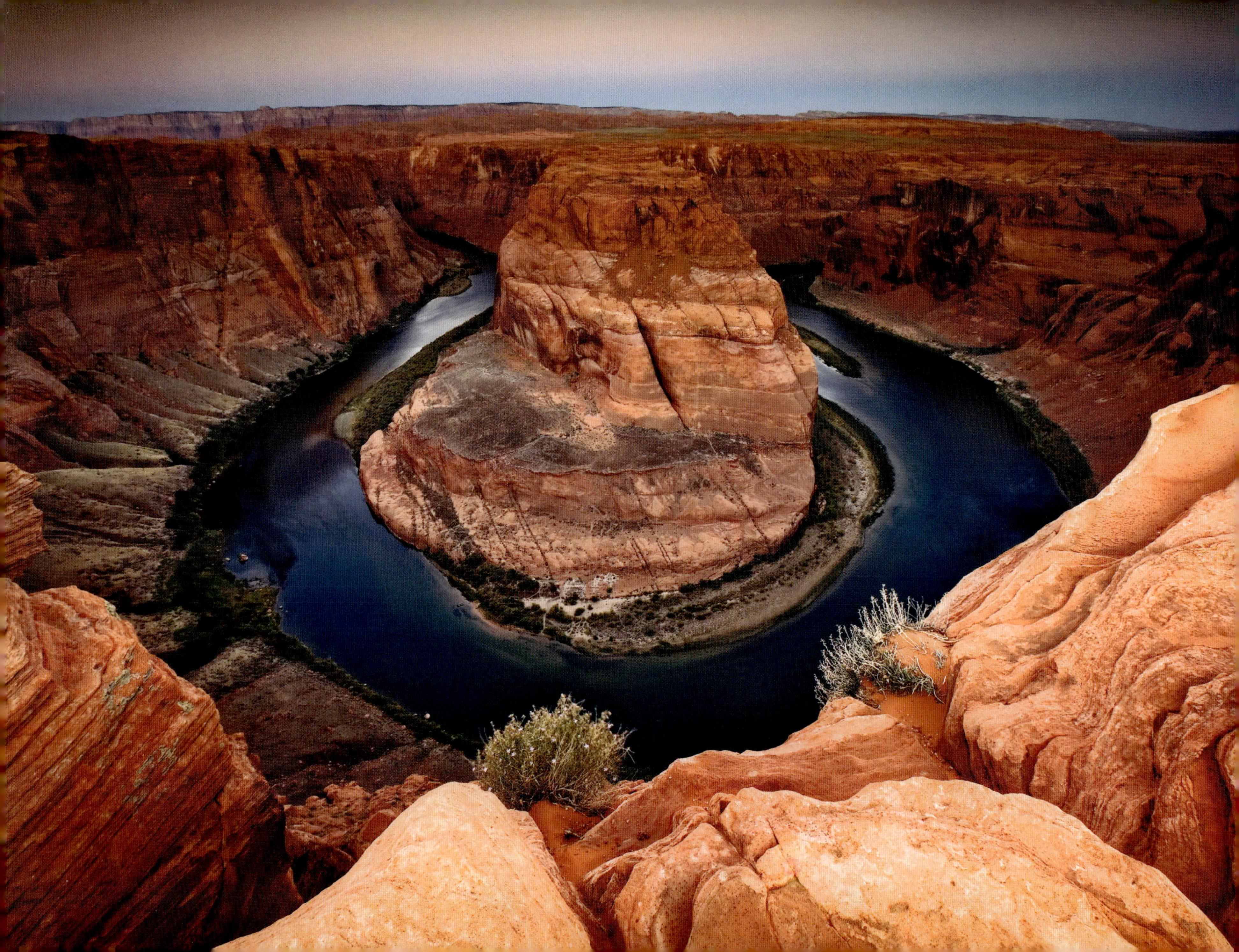

PAGE 96: **Lake Mead National Recreation Area, Nevada**
Lake Mead.

PAGE 97: **Channel Islands National Park, California**
Inspiration Point, Anacapa Island.

LEFT & RIGHT: **Glen Canyon National Recreation Area, Arizona**
Horseshoe Bend Overlook, only a few miles away from Glen Canyon Dam.

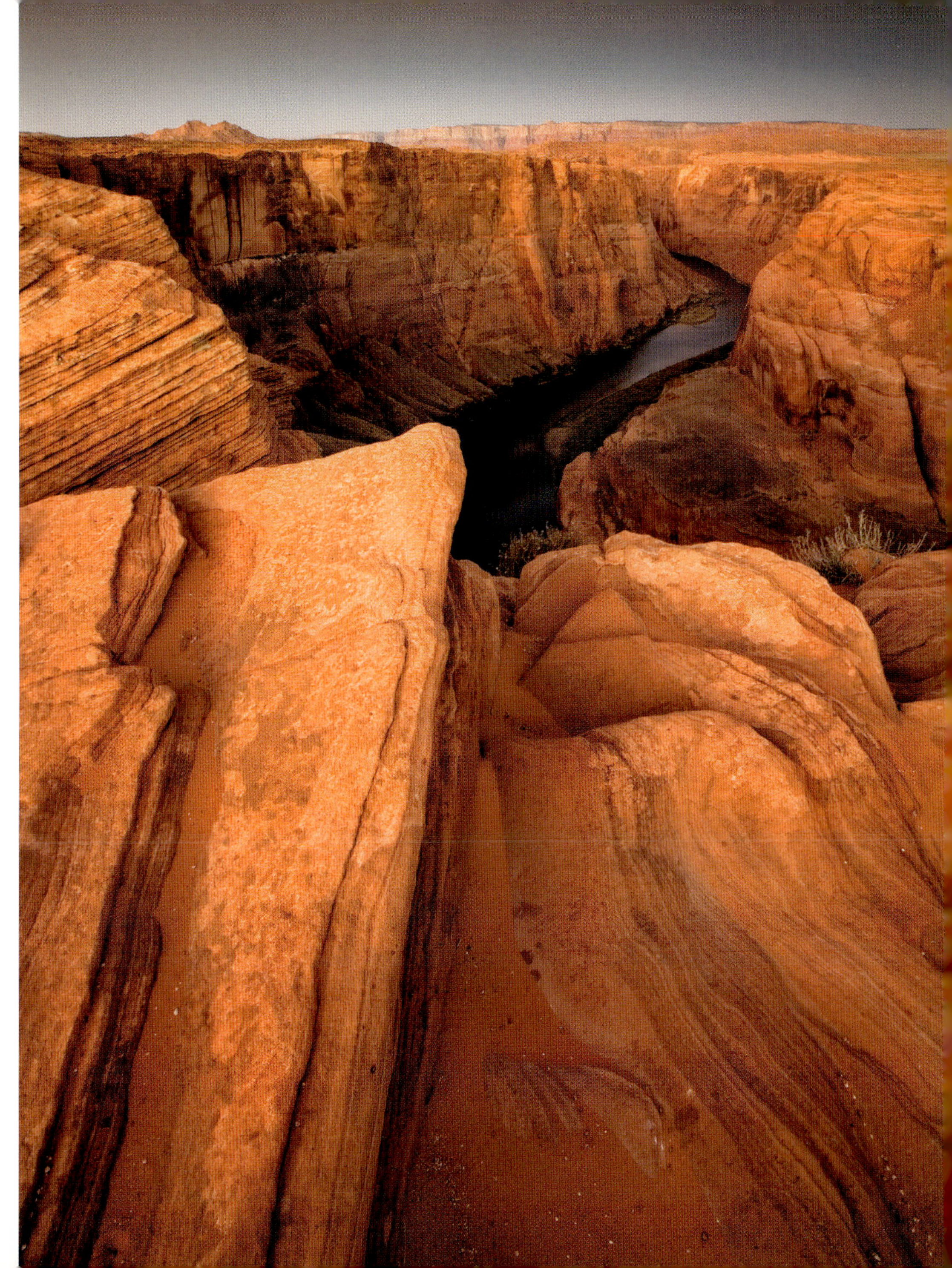

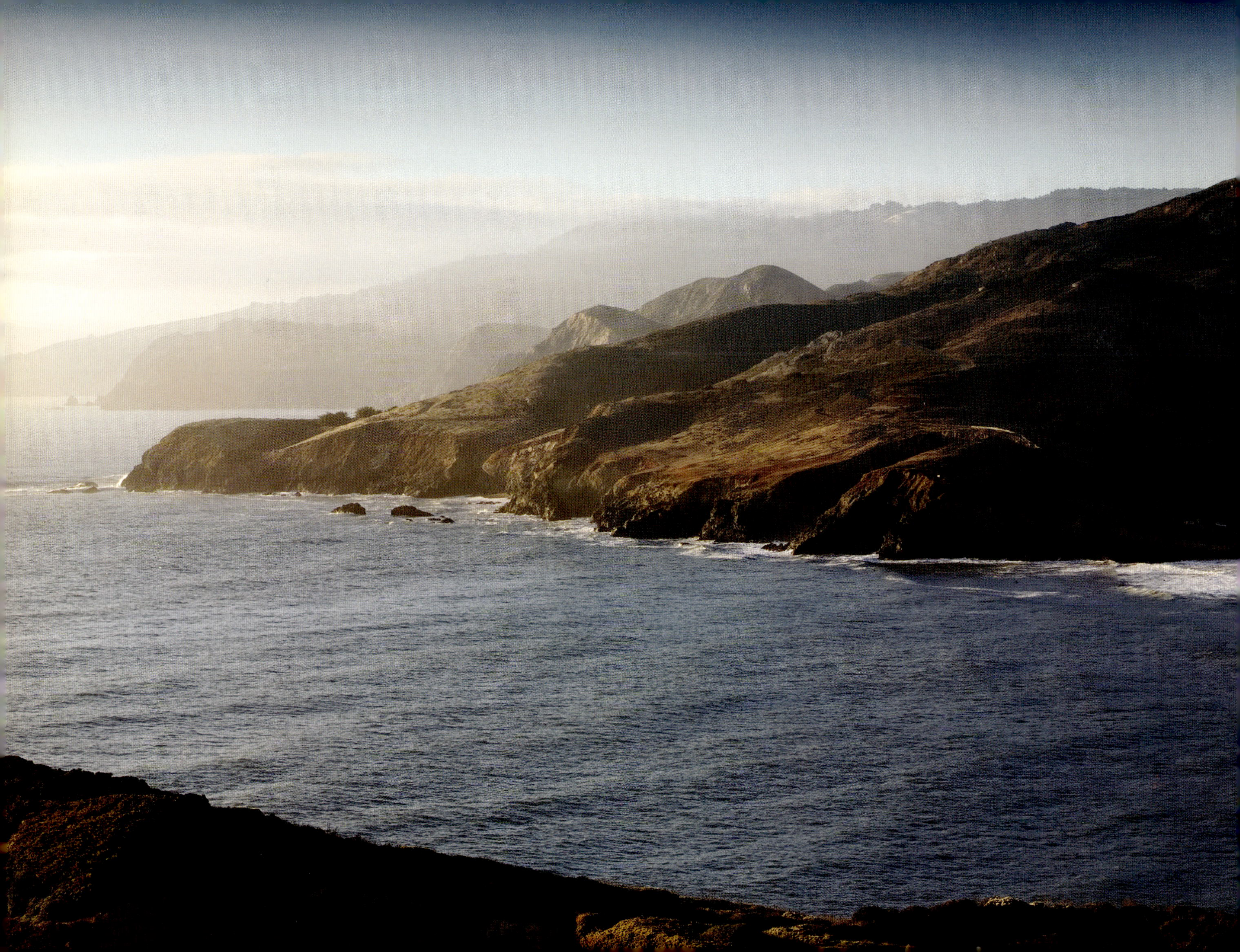

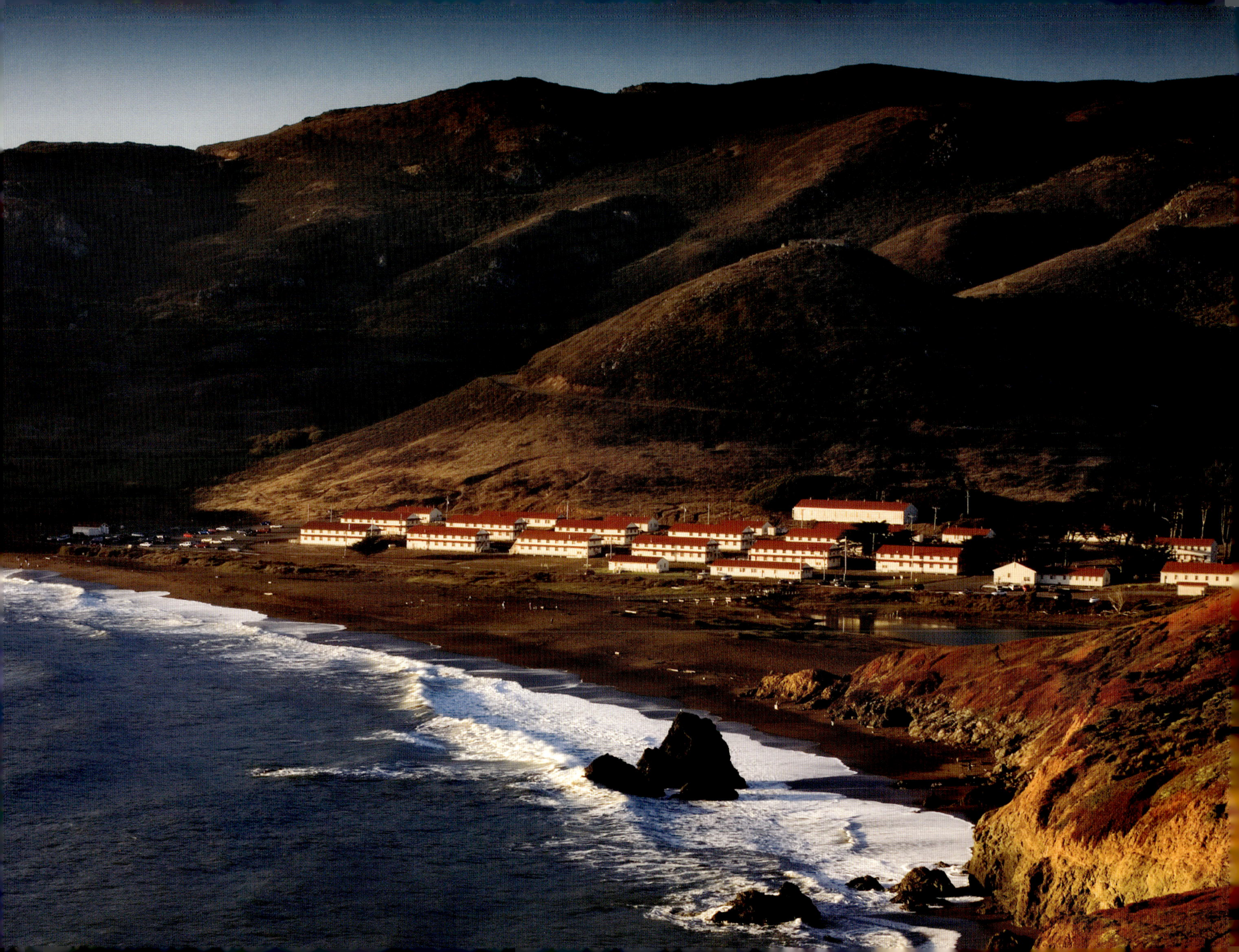

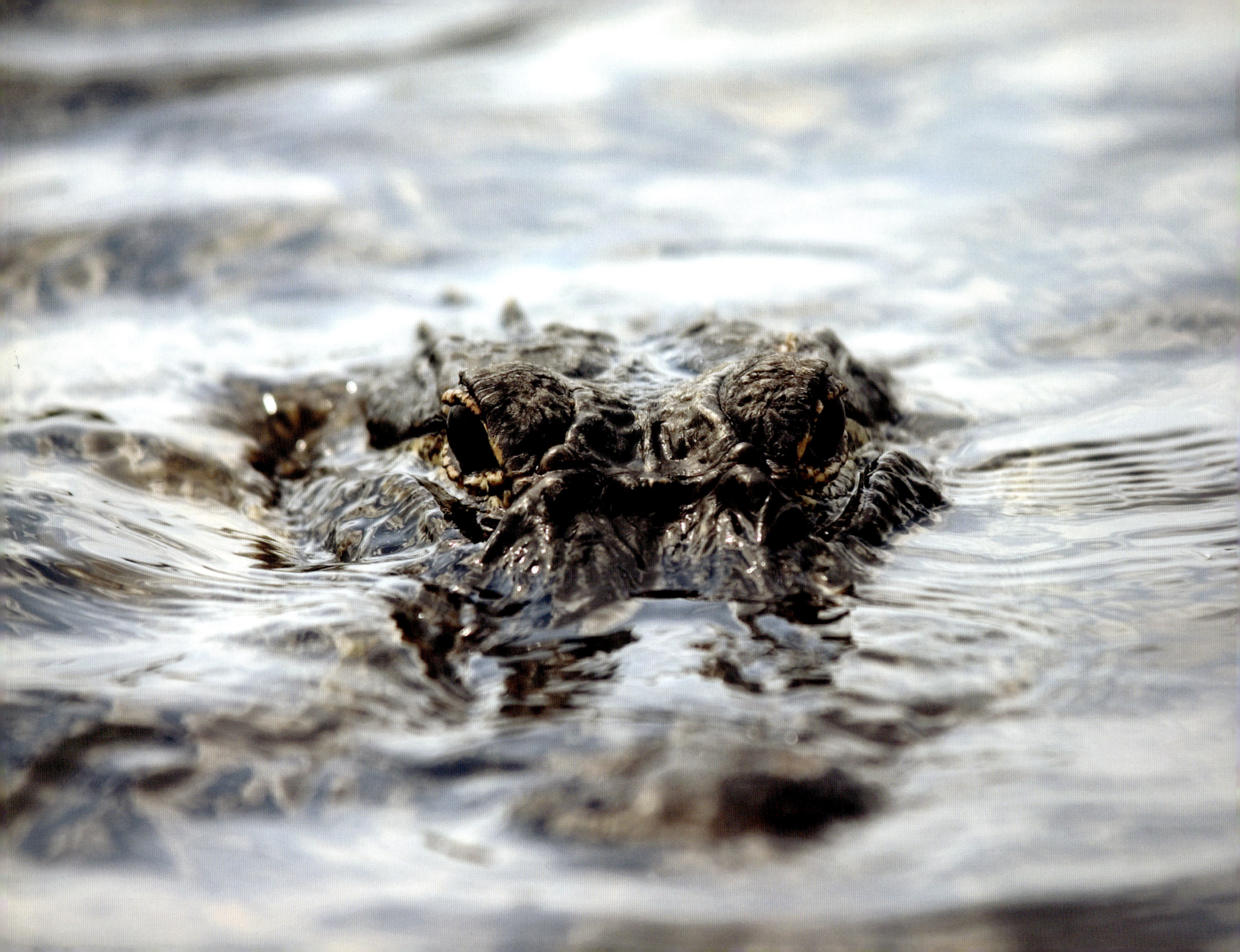

PAGES 100/101: **Golden Gate National Recreation Area, California**
View of the bay at the Marin Headlands, part of the Golden Gate National Recreation Area, the largest urban national park in the United States. The buildings are part of the historic Fort Cronkhite.

LEFT: **Everglades National Park, Florida**
An alligator swims through the waters of the Everglades.

RIGHT: **Grand Canyon National Park, Arizona**
Detail of an aspen "eye." So many of nature's designs reflect similar patterns. The "eye" of an aspen tree eerily resembles the folded and prehistoric eyes of the American alligator. Everything in nature has a connectivity in its design—much like the blood in our own veins resembles the flow and pattern of a river when viewed from above. Perhaps these subtle hints are reminders of our own roots and the importance of the natural world around us.

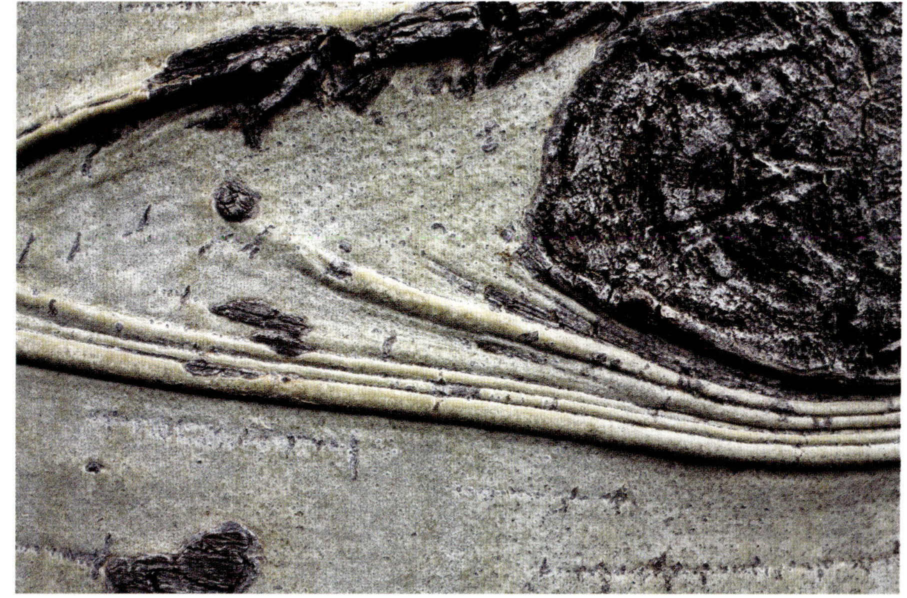

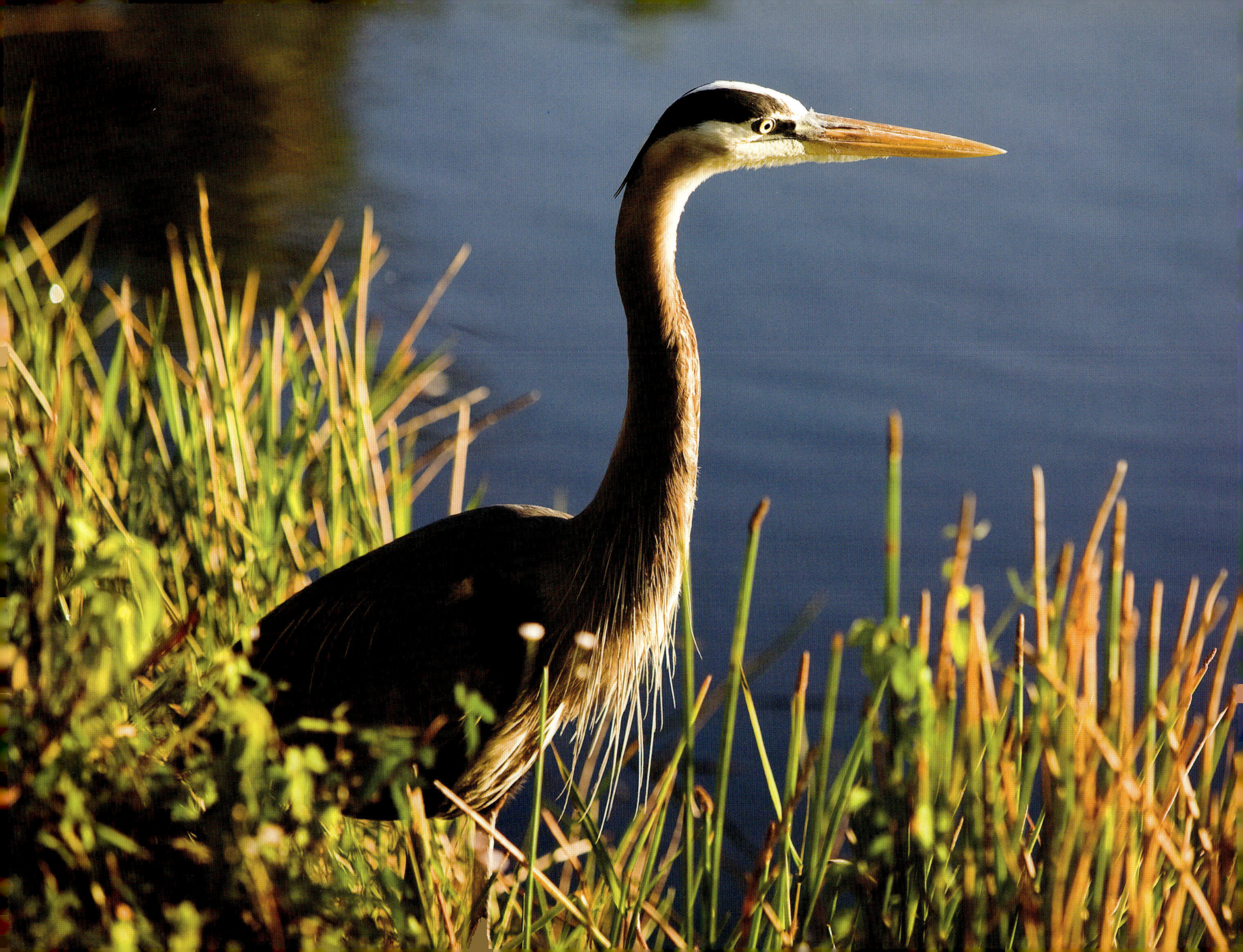

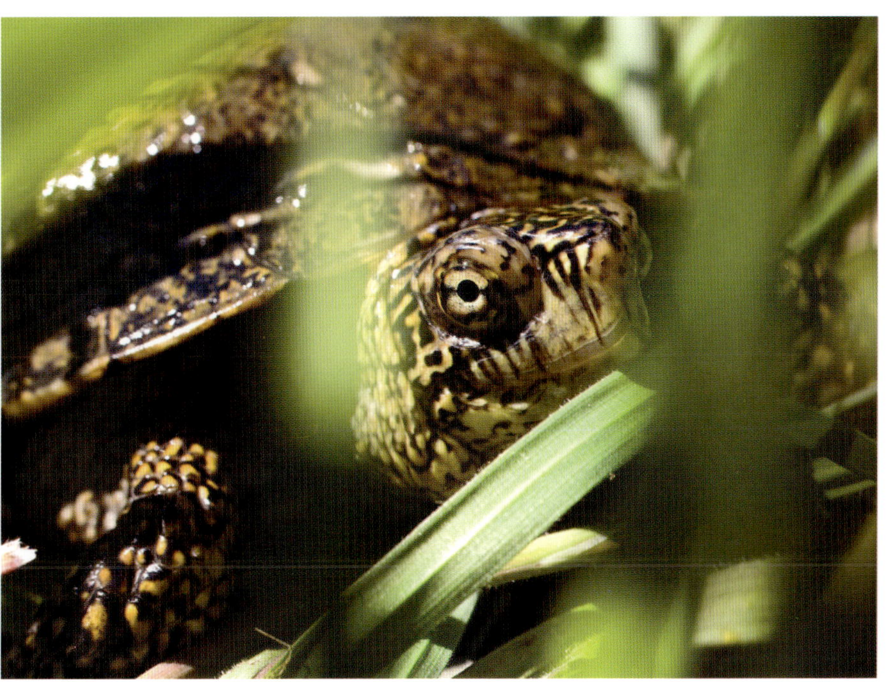

ABOVE: **Yosemite National Park, California**
A western pond turtle.

LEFT: **Everglades National Park, Florida**
A great blue heron.

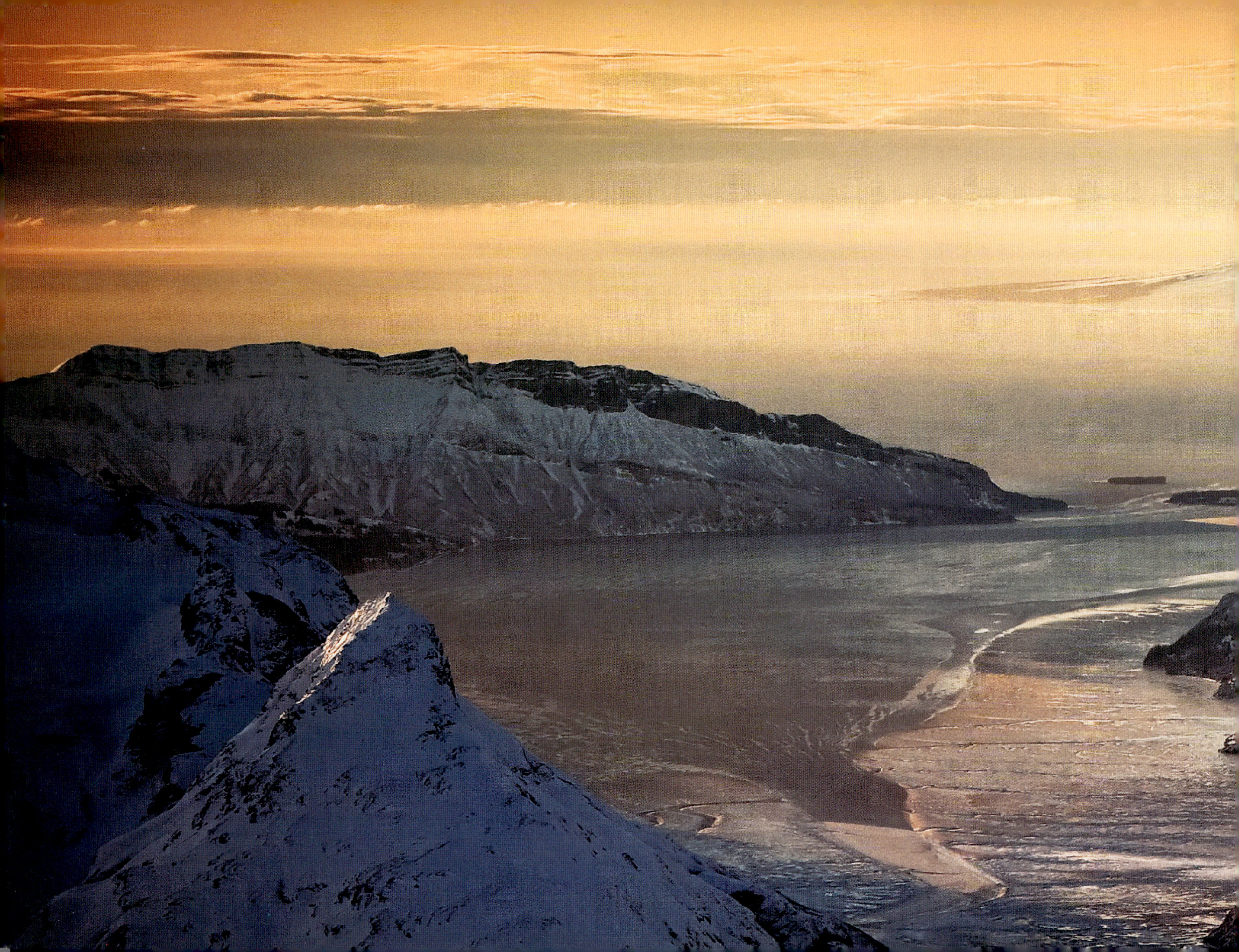

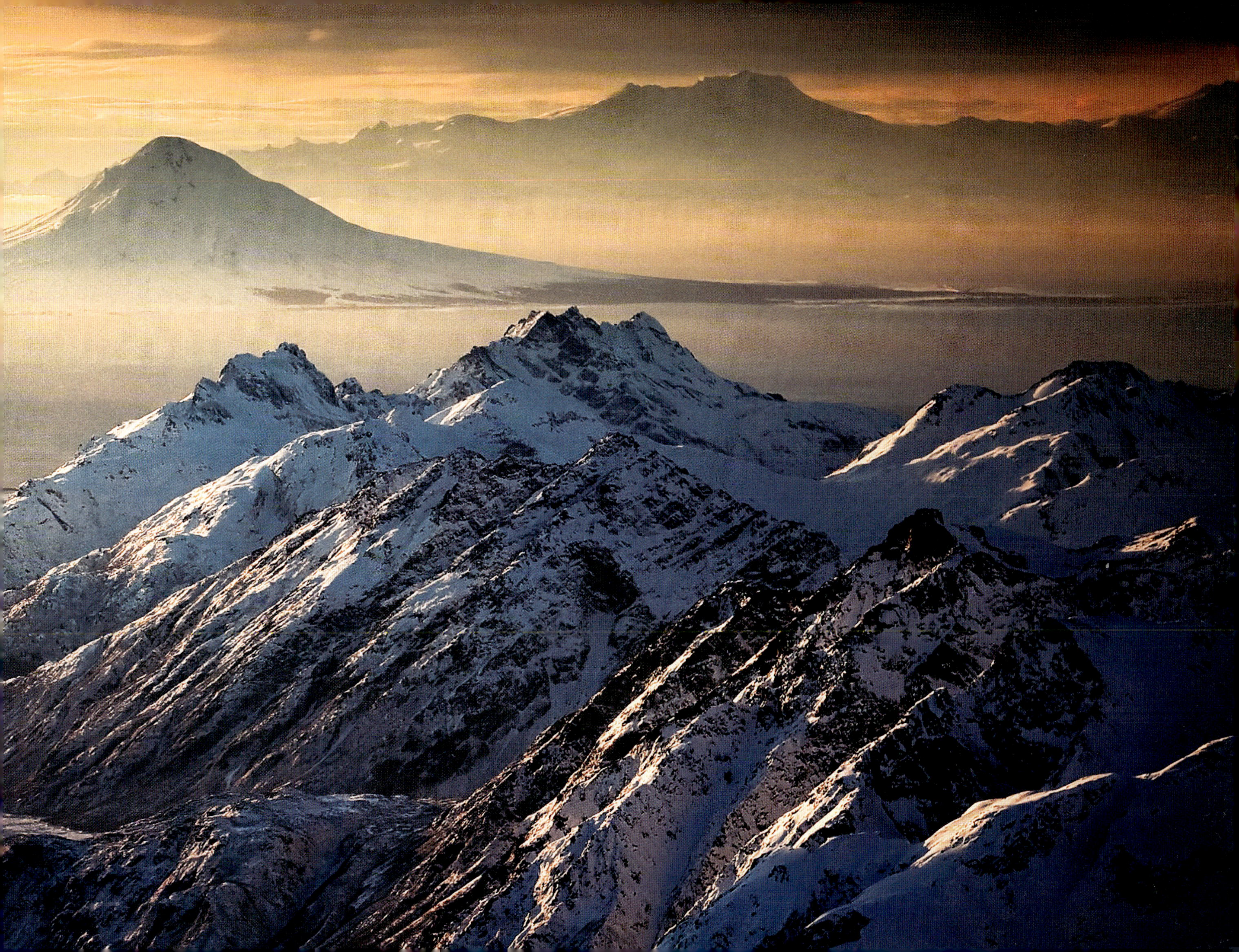

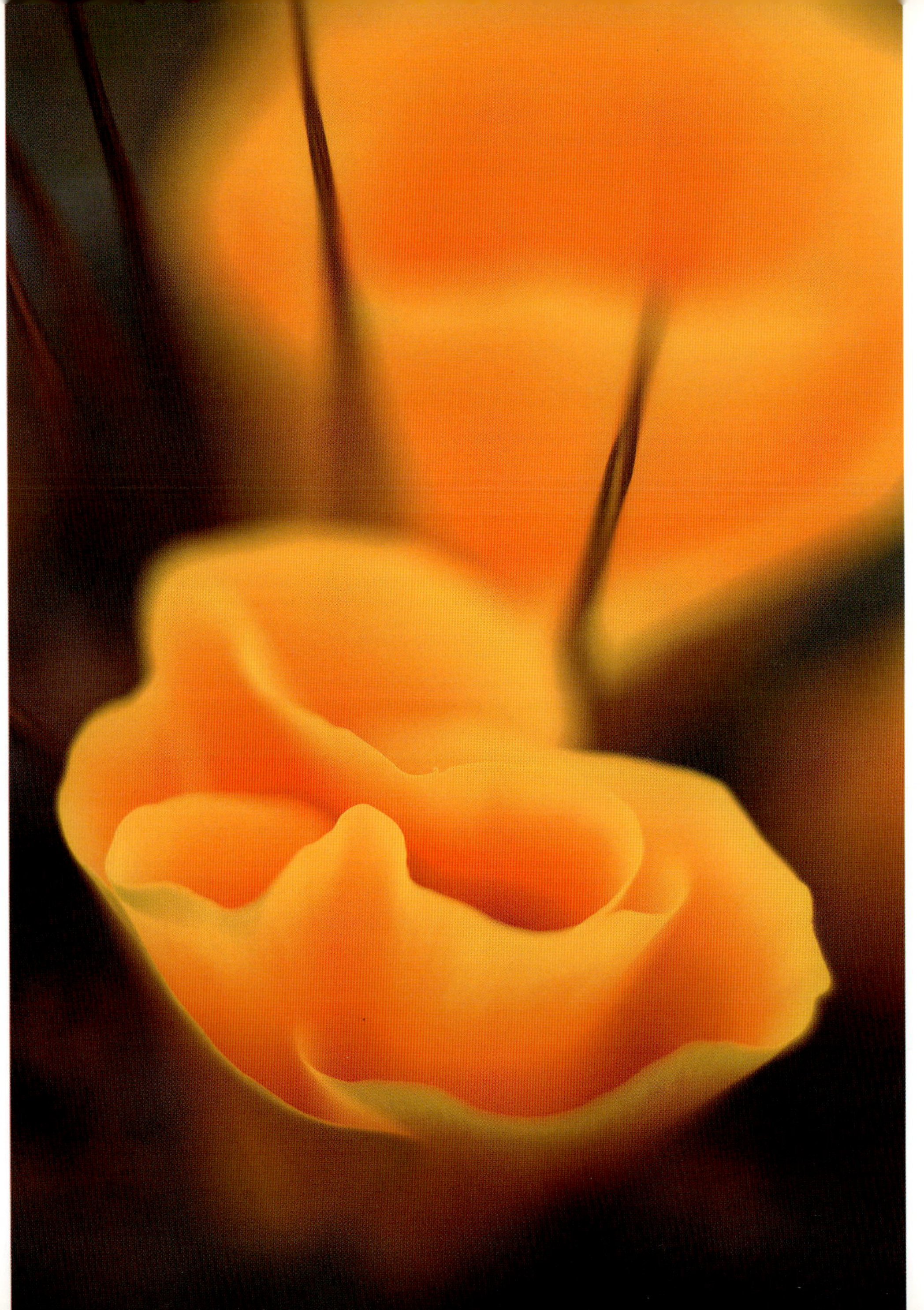

PAGES 106/107: **Lake Clark National Park & Preserve, Alaska**
Morning light on the Chigmit Mountains. In the distance is Mount Augustine—an active volcano and island in Cook Inlet.

LEFT & RIGHT: **Yosemite National Park, California**
A California poppy and a miniature lupine: Spring in California is an explosion of color and life. If there is enough rainfall in the late winter, spring flowers will carpet entire mountainsides.

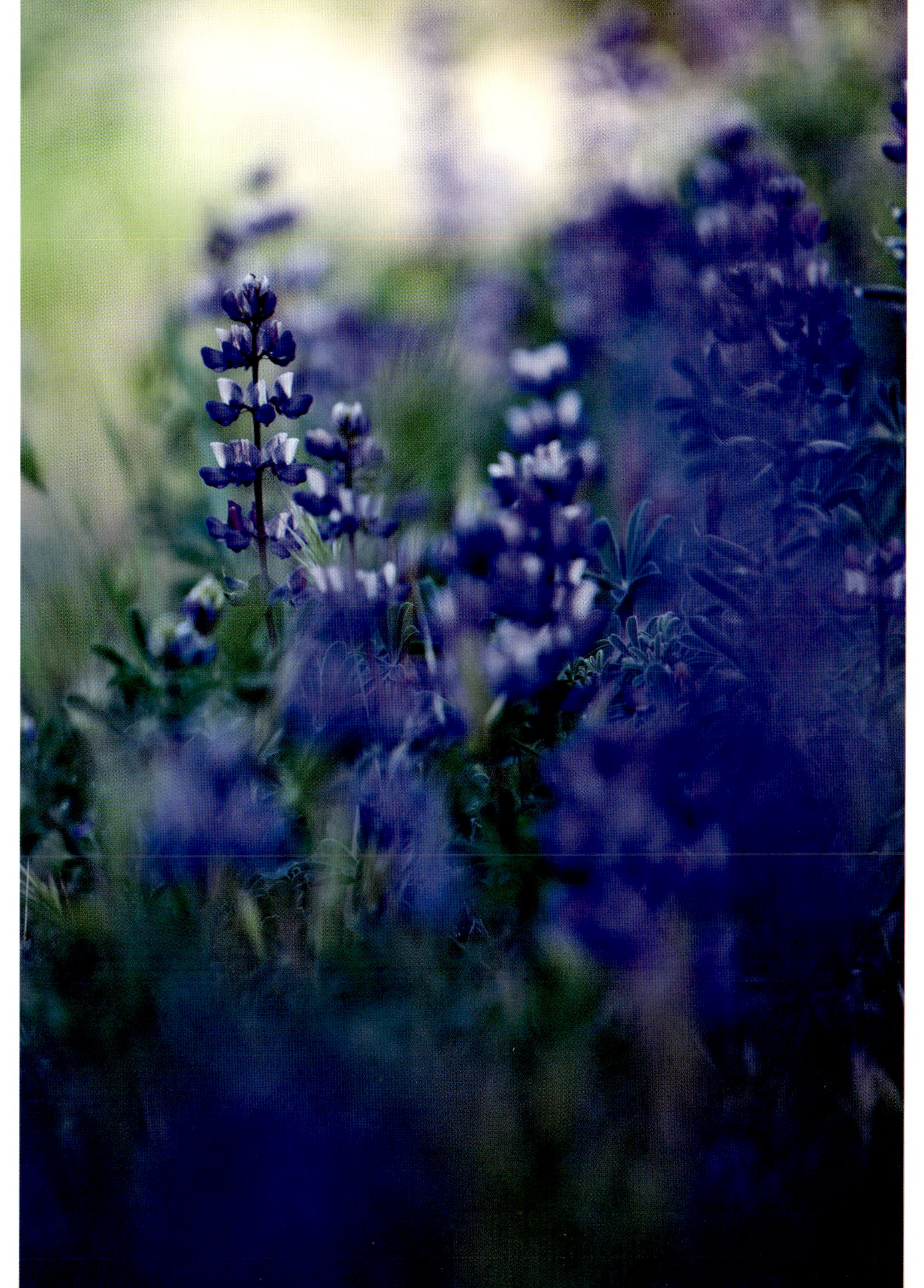

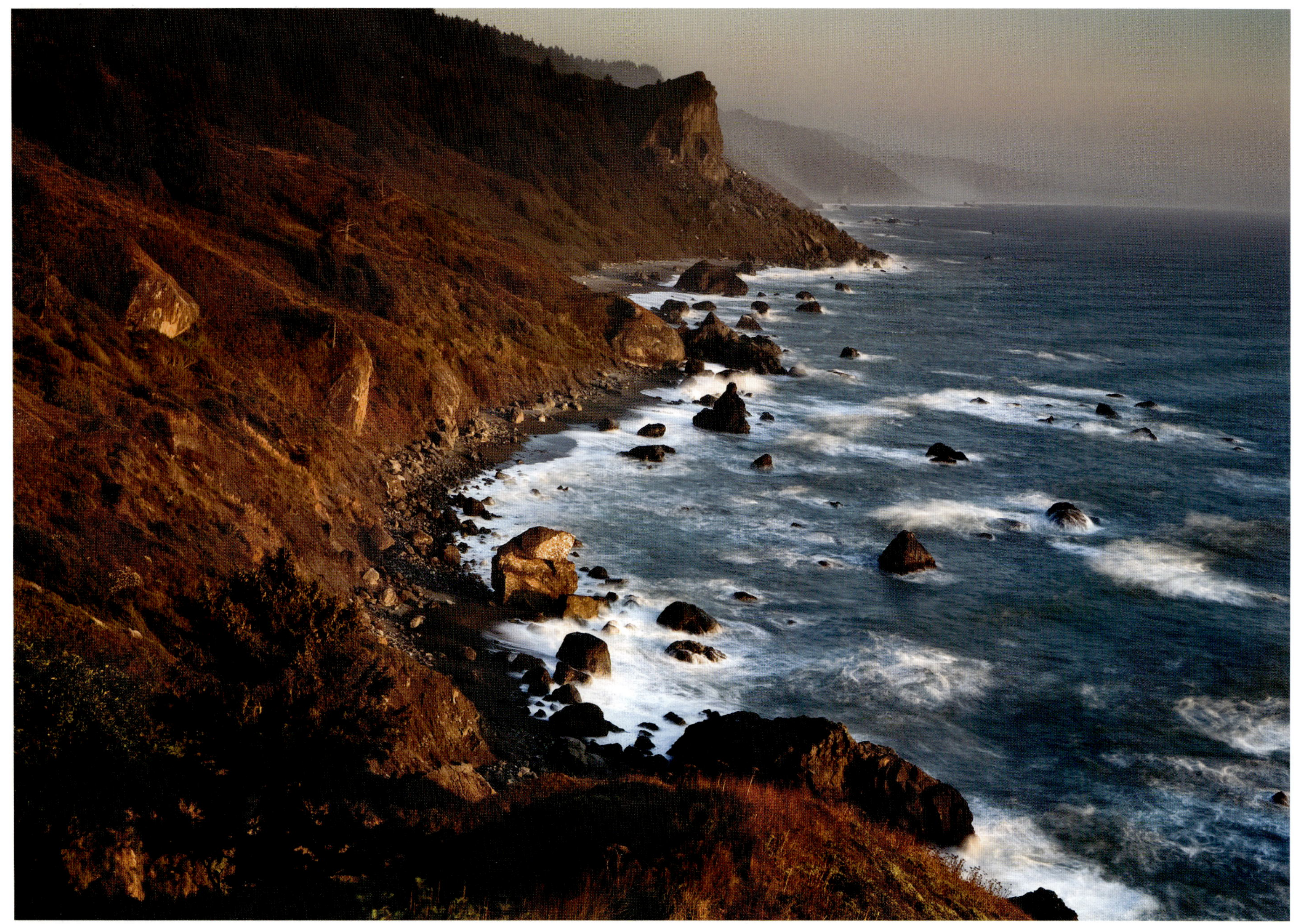

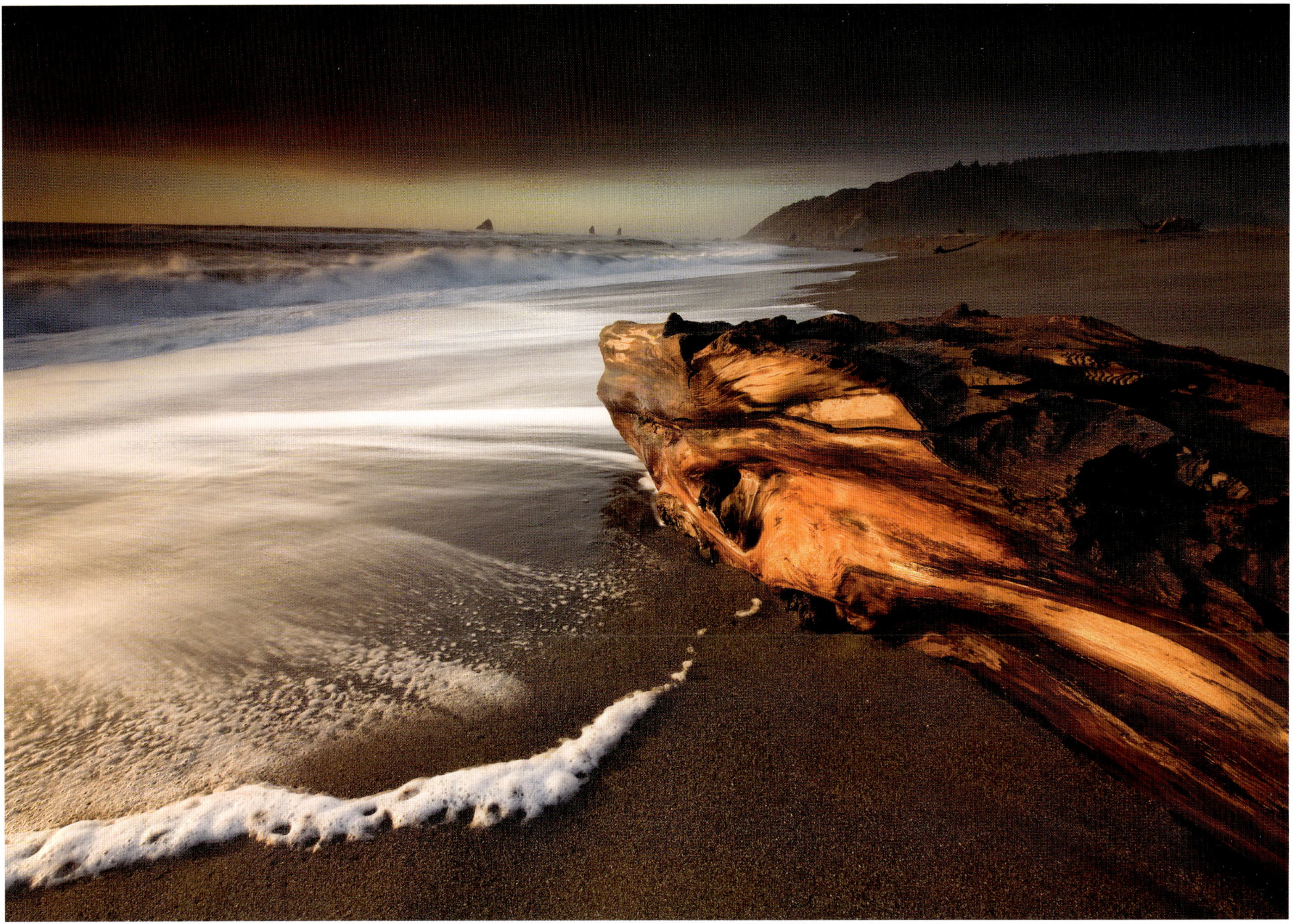

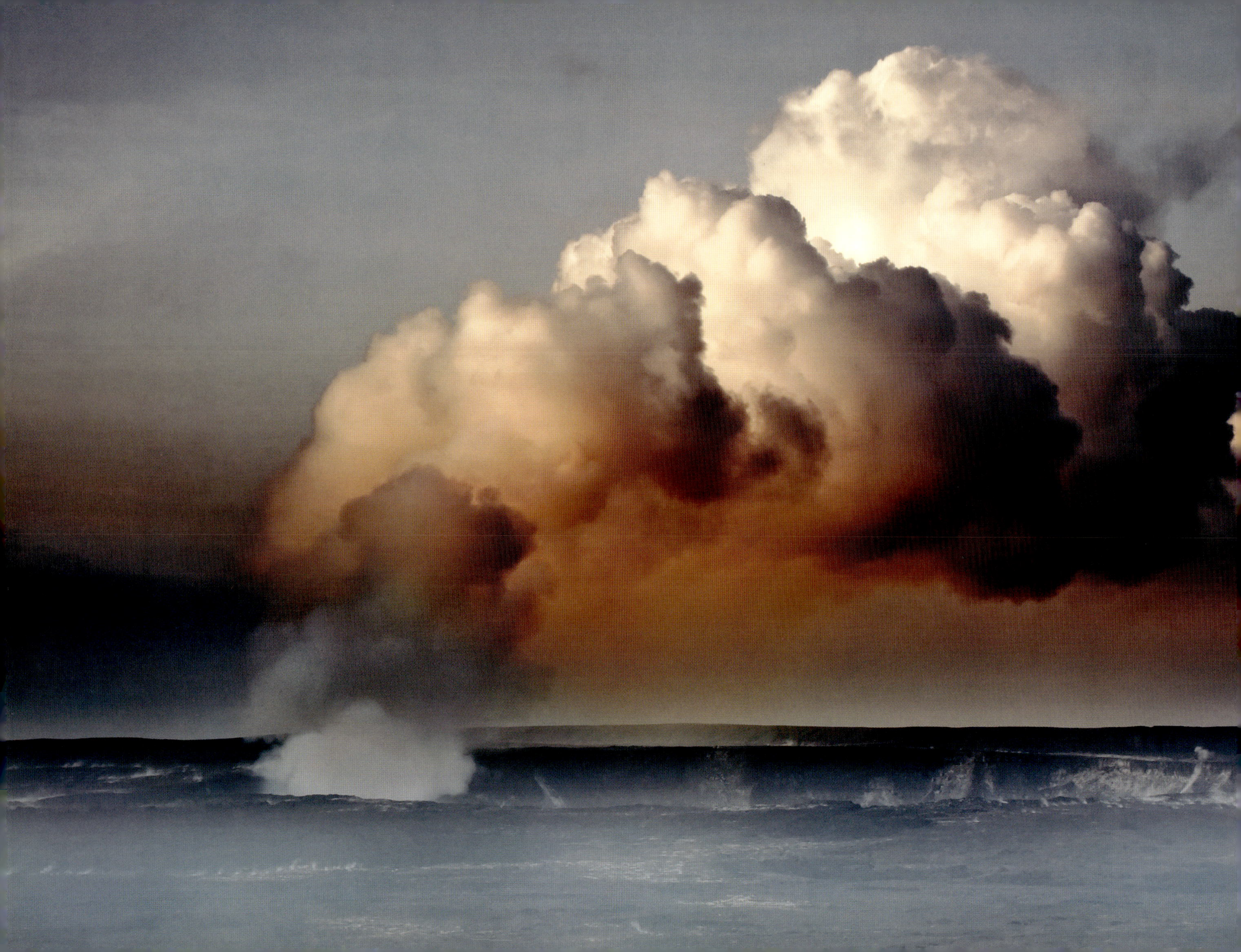

PAGES 110 & 111: **Redwood National and State Parks, California**
The northernmost end of Redwood National Park: The redwoods are a common stop for photographers in California. I hiked the same trails and saw these ancient giants reaching for the sky, but what moved me most wasn't the large patriarchs in the forest, but those scattered all along the Pacific Ocean. On the far end of the park, near Klamath, California, the forest truly meets the sea. There you find beaches that continue all the way to Oregon and into Washington, with massive, ocean-polished redwood beams everywhere.

LEFT: **Hawaii Volcanoes National Park, Hawaii**
A giant sulfur dioxide gas plume from Kilauea volcano is illuminated by the rising sun.

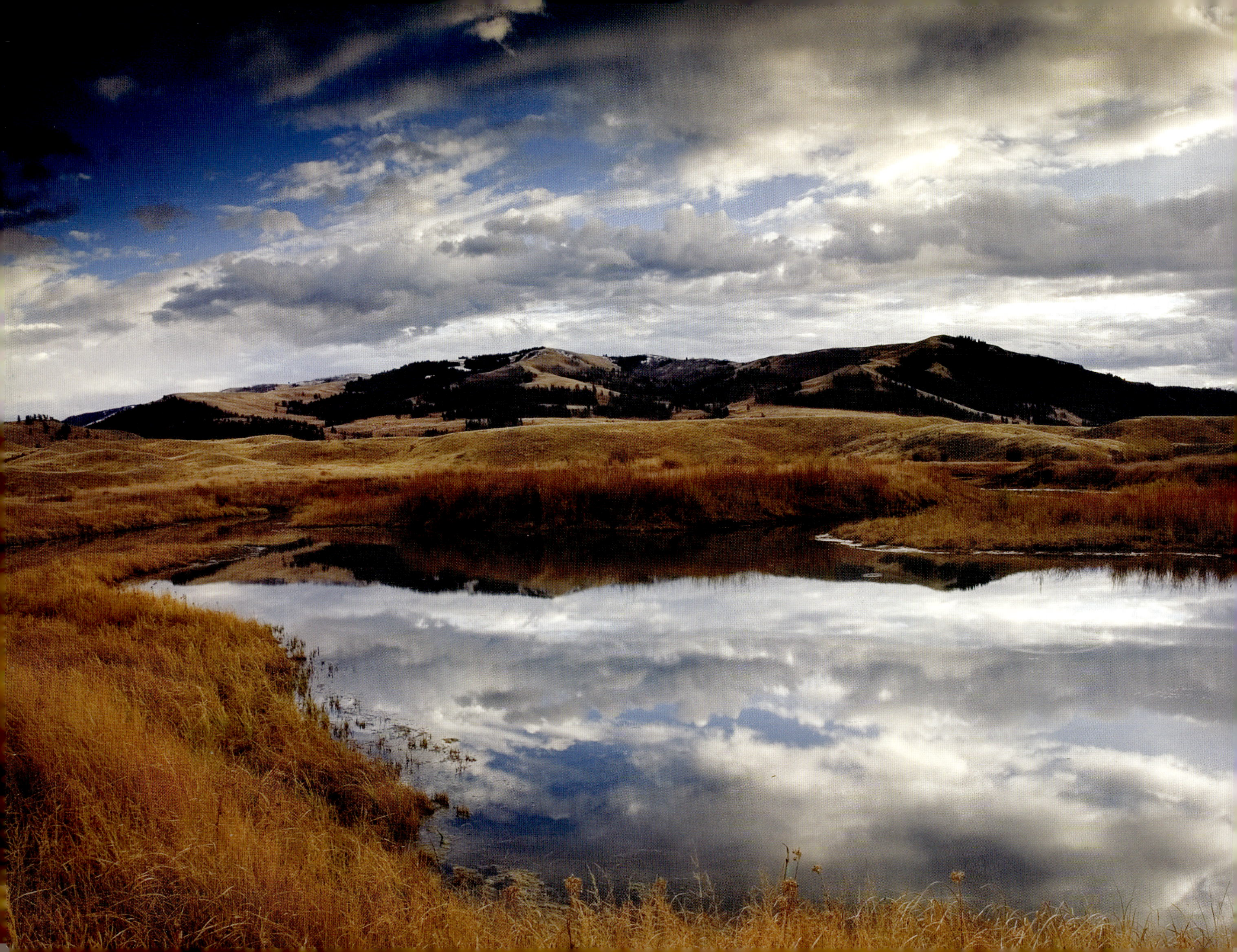

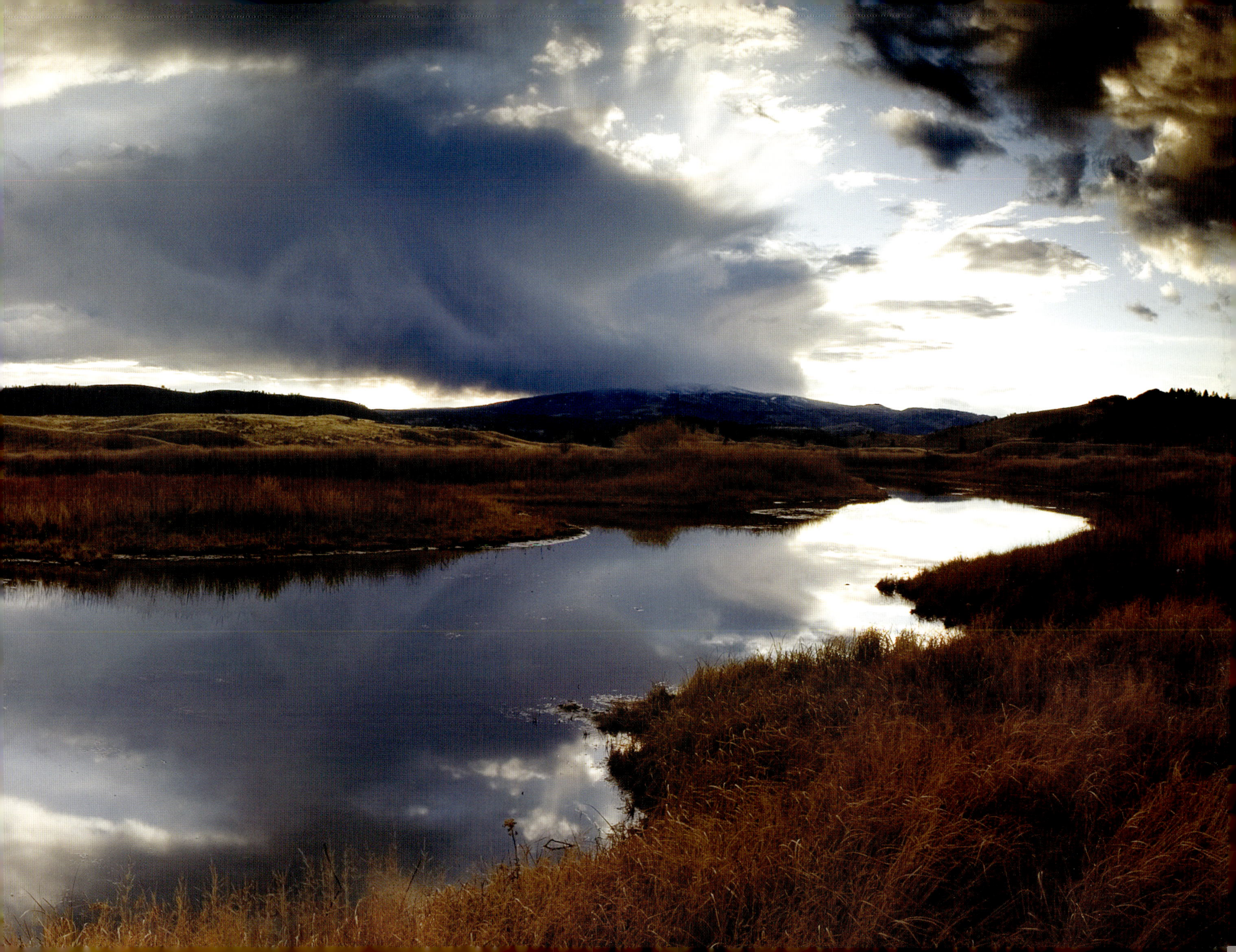

PAGES 114/115: **Yellowstone National Park; Wyoming, Montana, Idaho**
Panoramic of Slough Creek at sunset, near Lamar Valley.

RIGHT: **Olympic National Park, Washington**
Beach Number Two: The sun struggles to break through a thick marine layer lingering over the coast. Logs of fairy tale proportions are scattered everywhere, impeding any casual morning strolls except for those willing to get their feet wet in the cold surf.

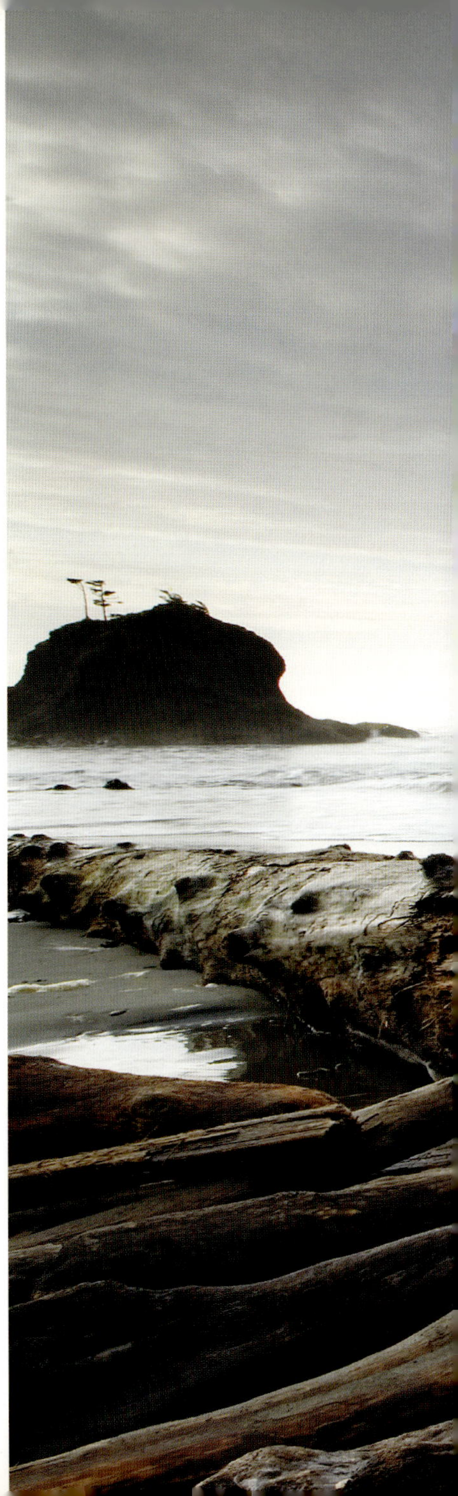

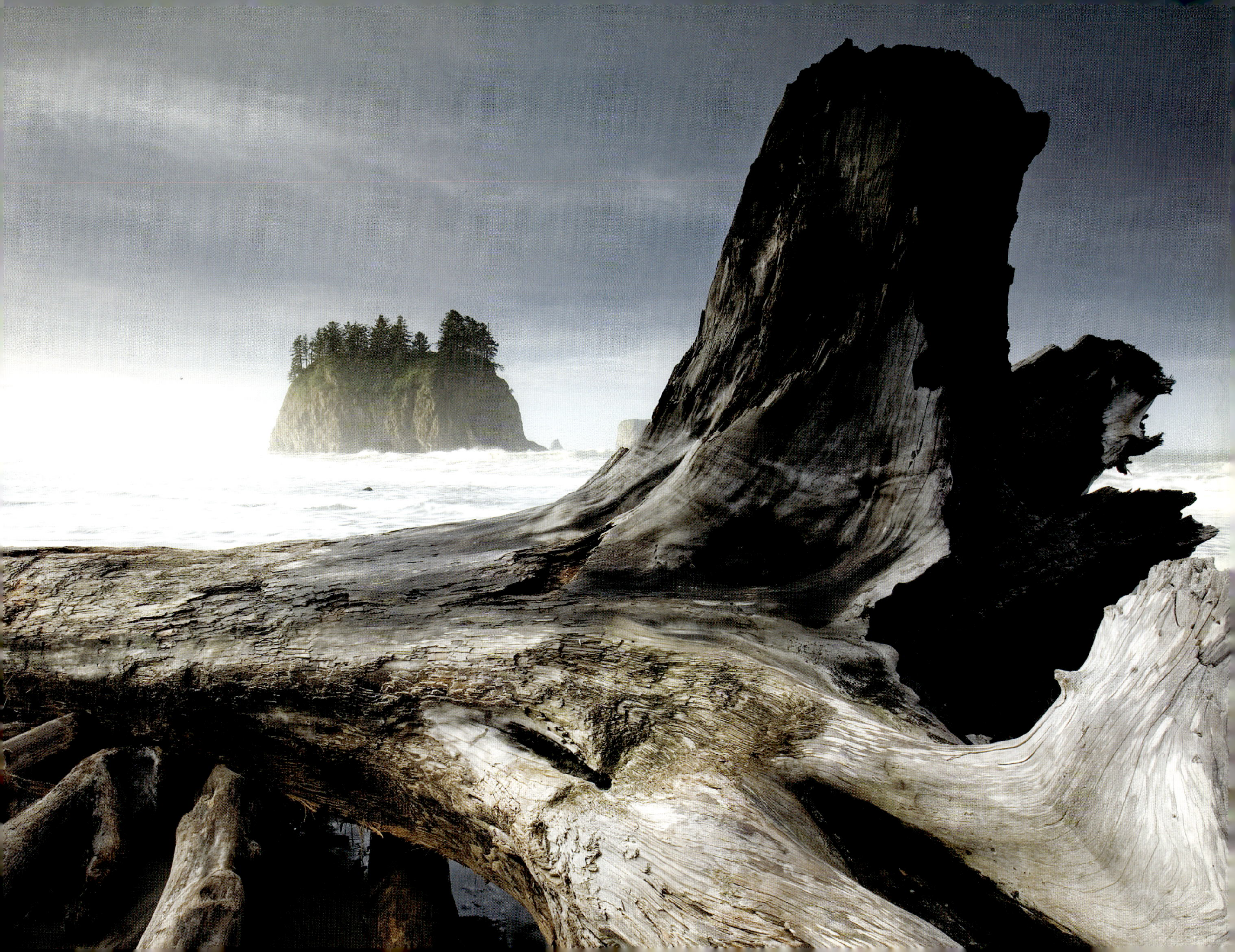

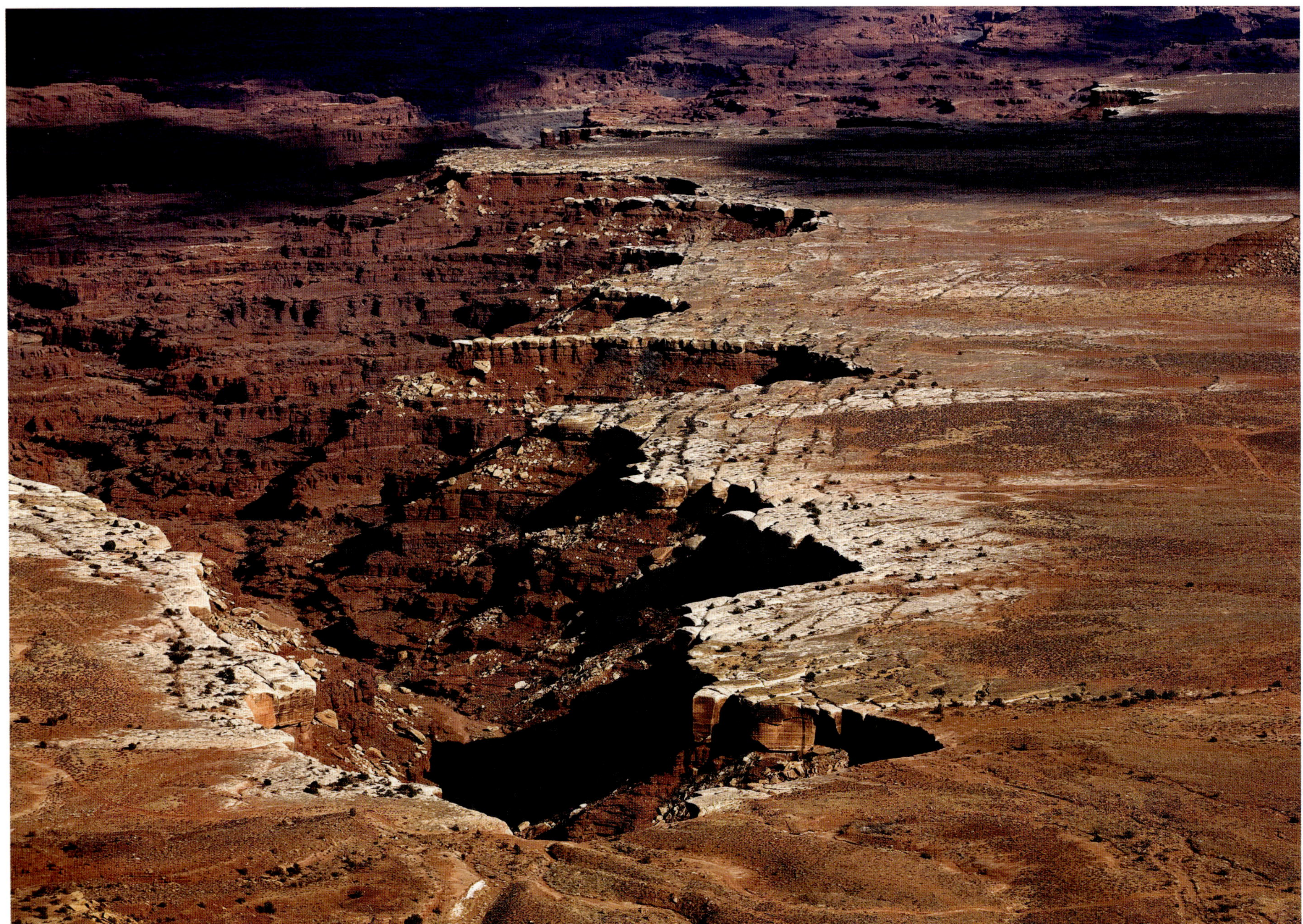

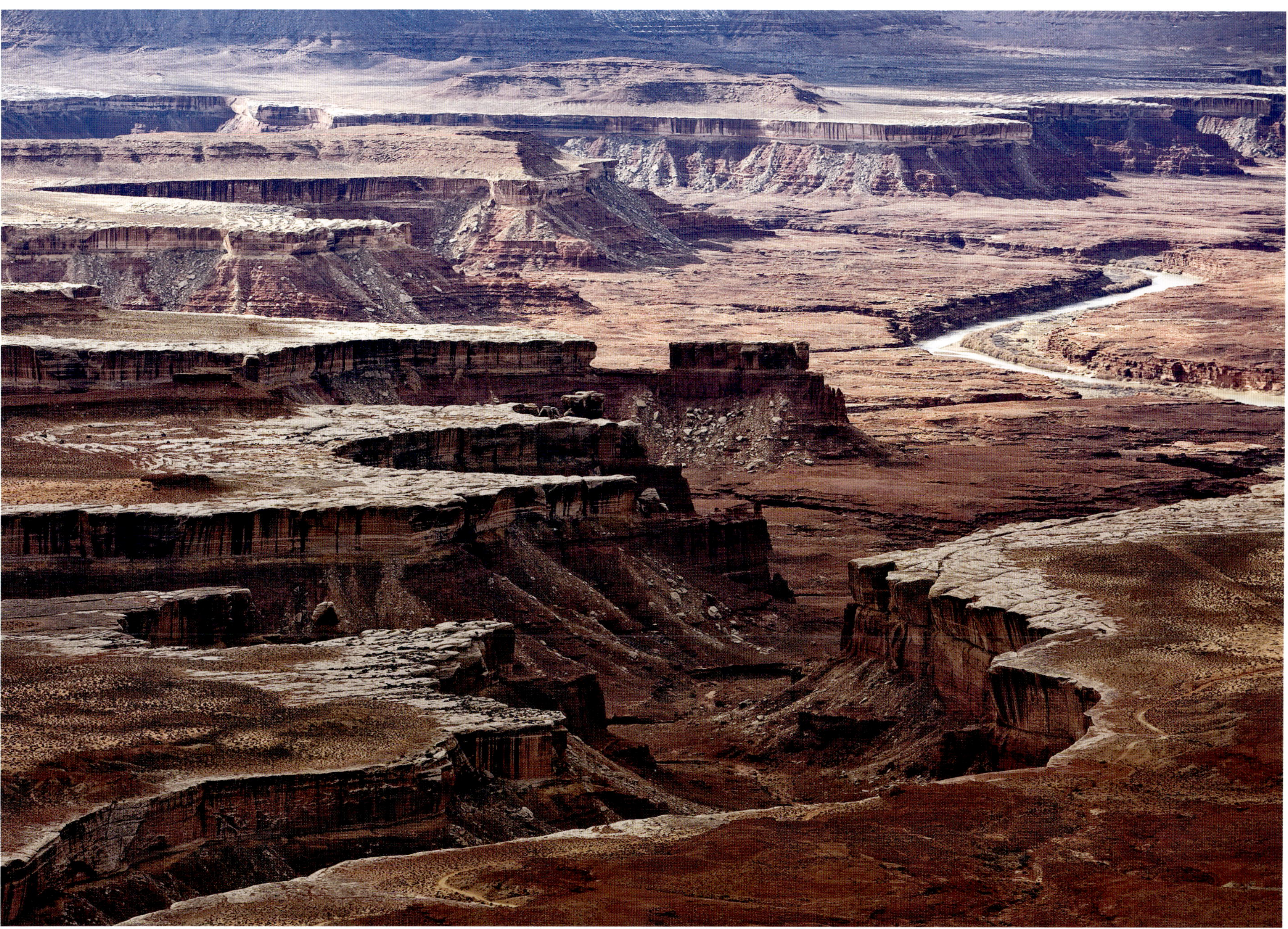

PAGES 118 & 119: **Canyonlands National Park, Utah**
A constantly evolving landscape shaped by wind and water.

ABOVE: **Yellowstone National Park; Wyoming, Montana, Idaho**
The moon rises above snow-covered hills in Lamar Valley.

RIGHT: **Denali National Park & Preserve, Alaska**
Mount Hunter with moon overhead.

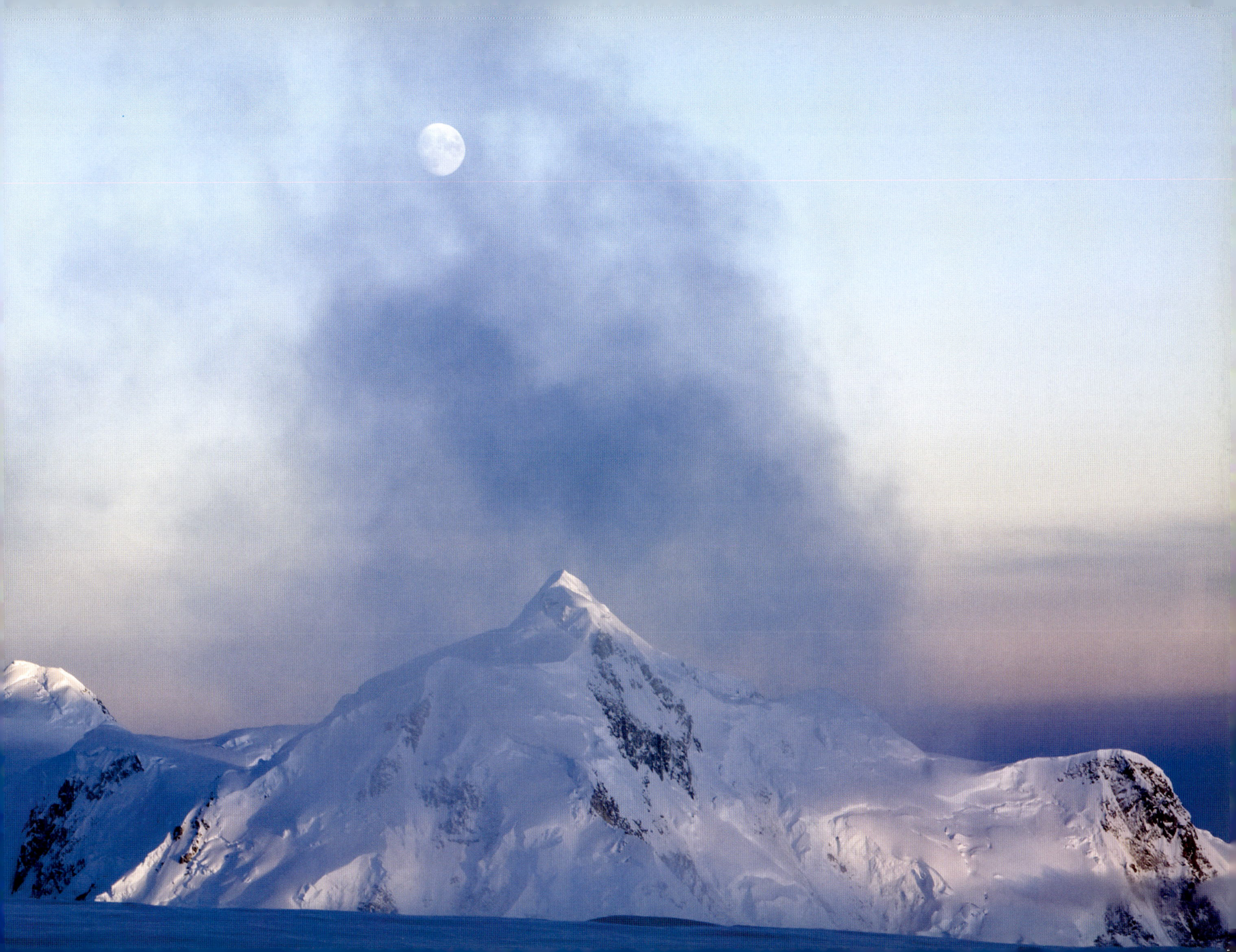

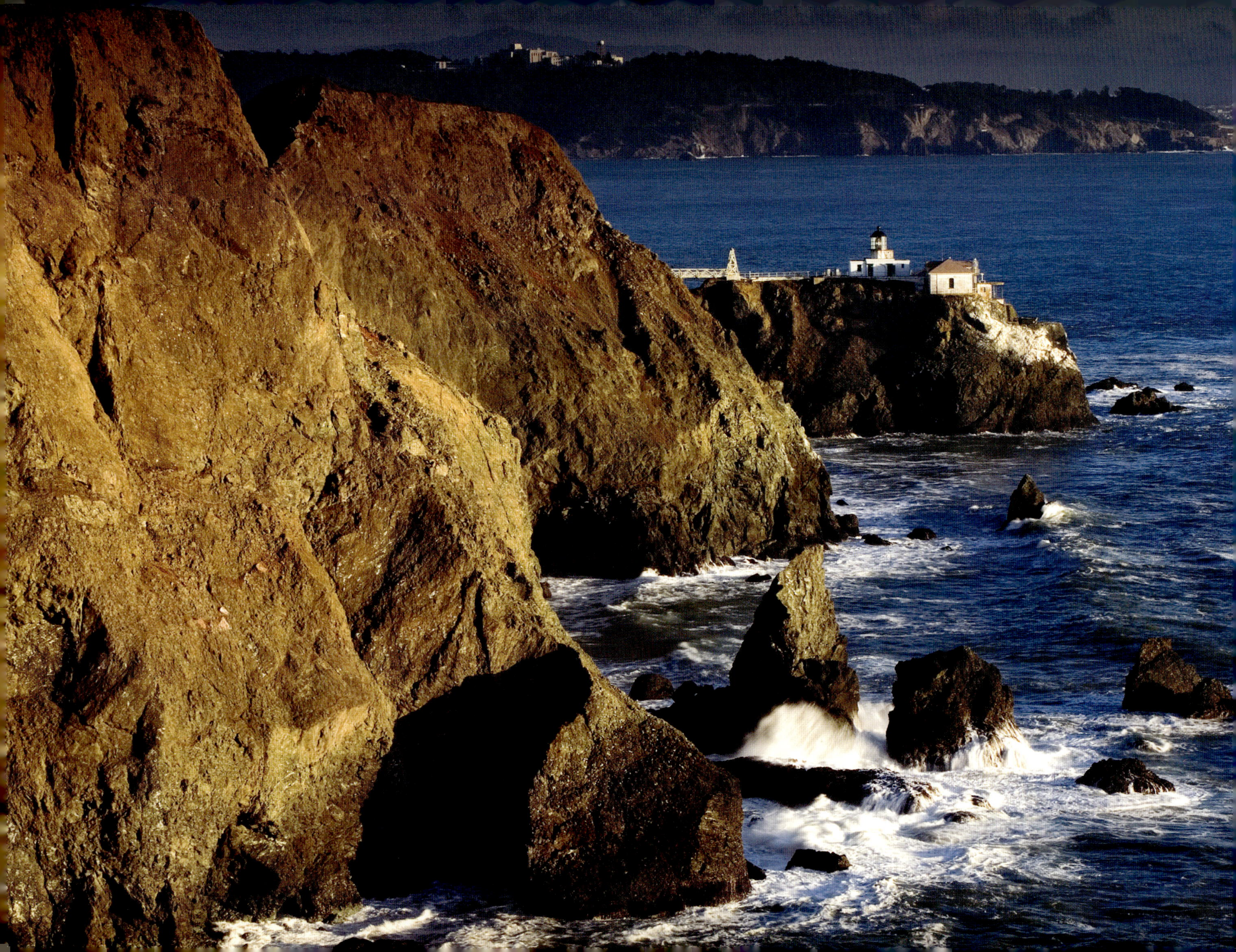

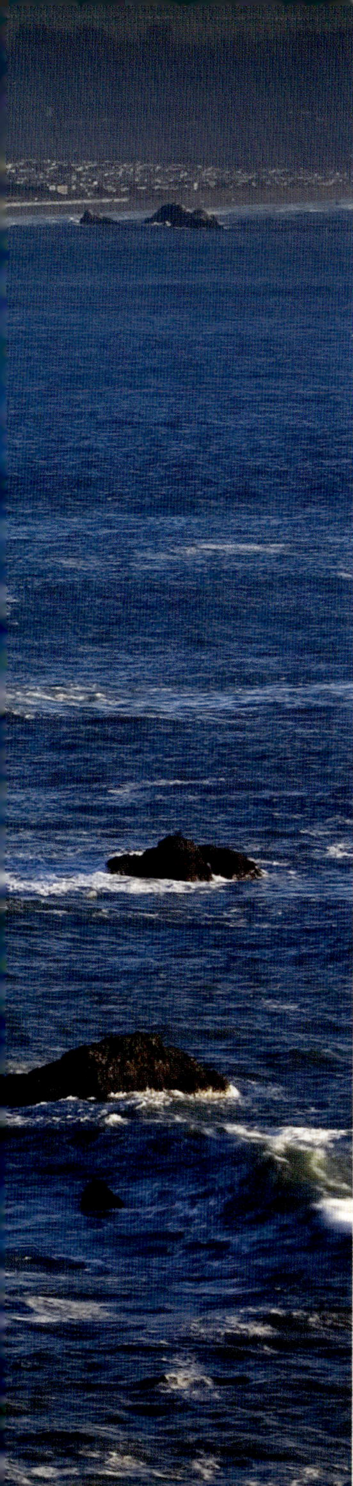

LEFT: **Golden Gate National Recreation Area, California**
Point Bonita sits at the tip of the San Francisco Bay in the Marin Headlands. The Golden Gate National Recreation Area is home to historic landscapes ranging from lighthouses to dairy ranches.

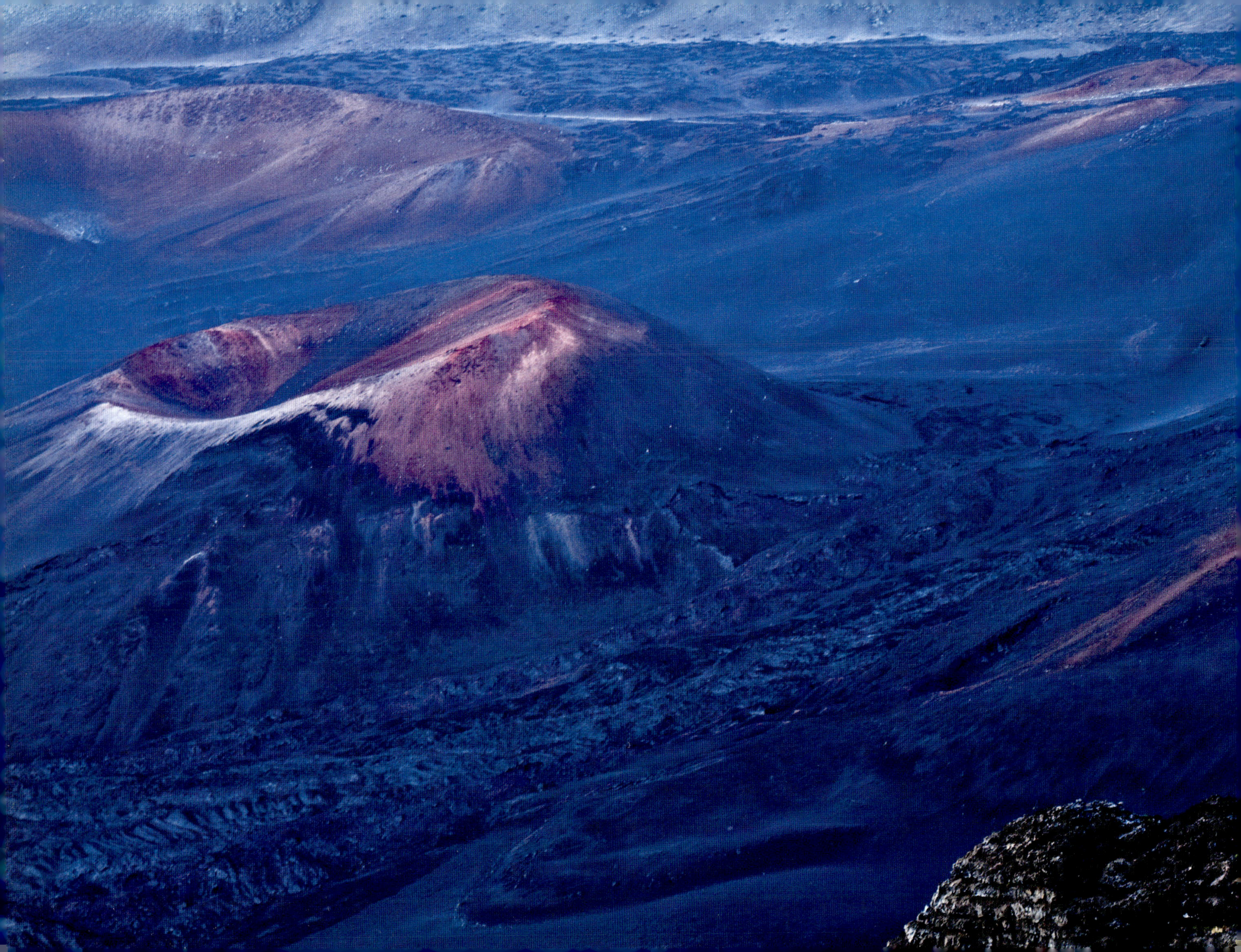

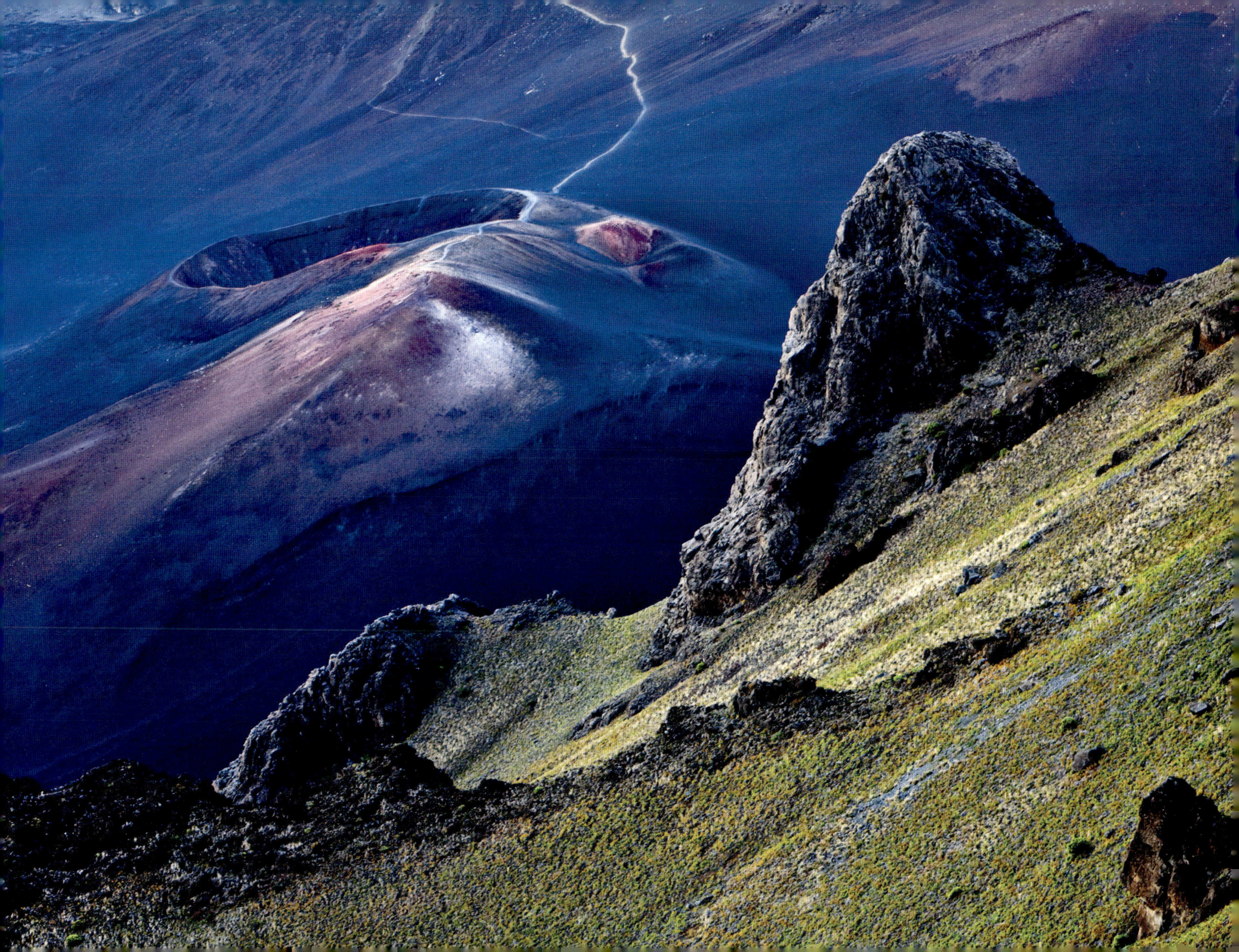

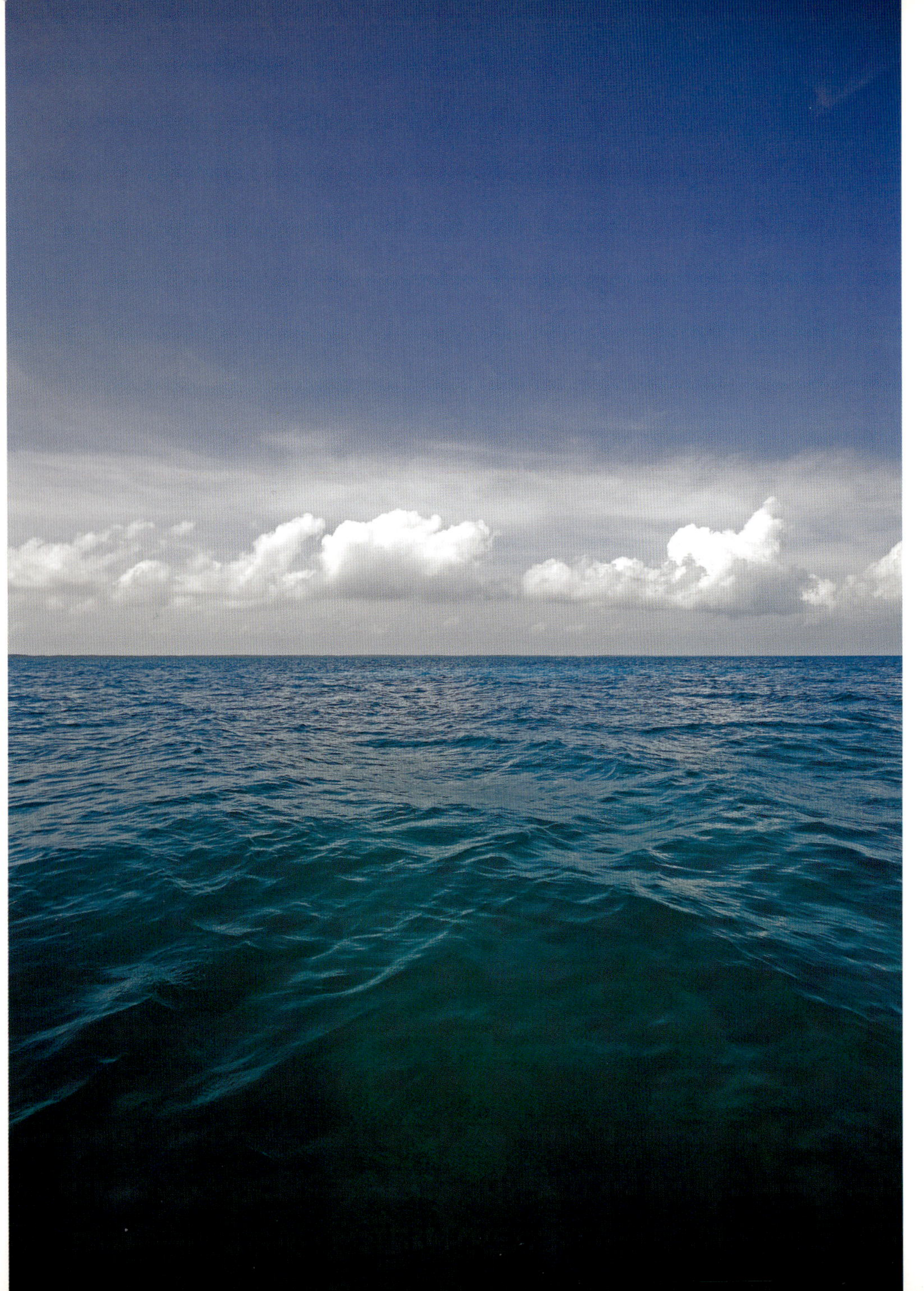

PAGES 124/125: **Haleakala National Park, Hawaii**
The view looking into the crater of Haleakala, a massive volcano that makes up three-quarters of the island of Maui, is both barren and desolate but also a wondrous palette of color.

LEFT: **Biscayne National Park, Florida**
Above the surface.

RIGHT: **Channel Islands National Park, California**
Kelp forests in the marine sanctuary: I always go back to my default description of the national parks—they are like fairty tales gone awry. How else can you describe hundred-foot-high stalks growing from the bottom of the ocean?

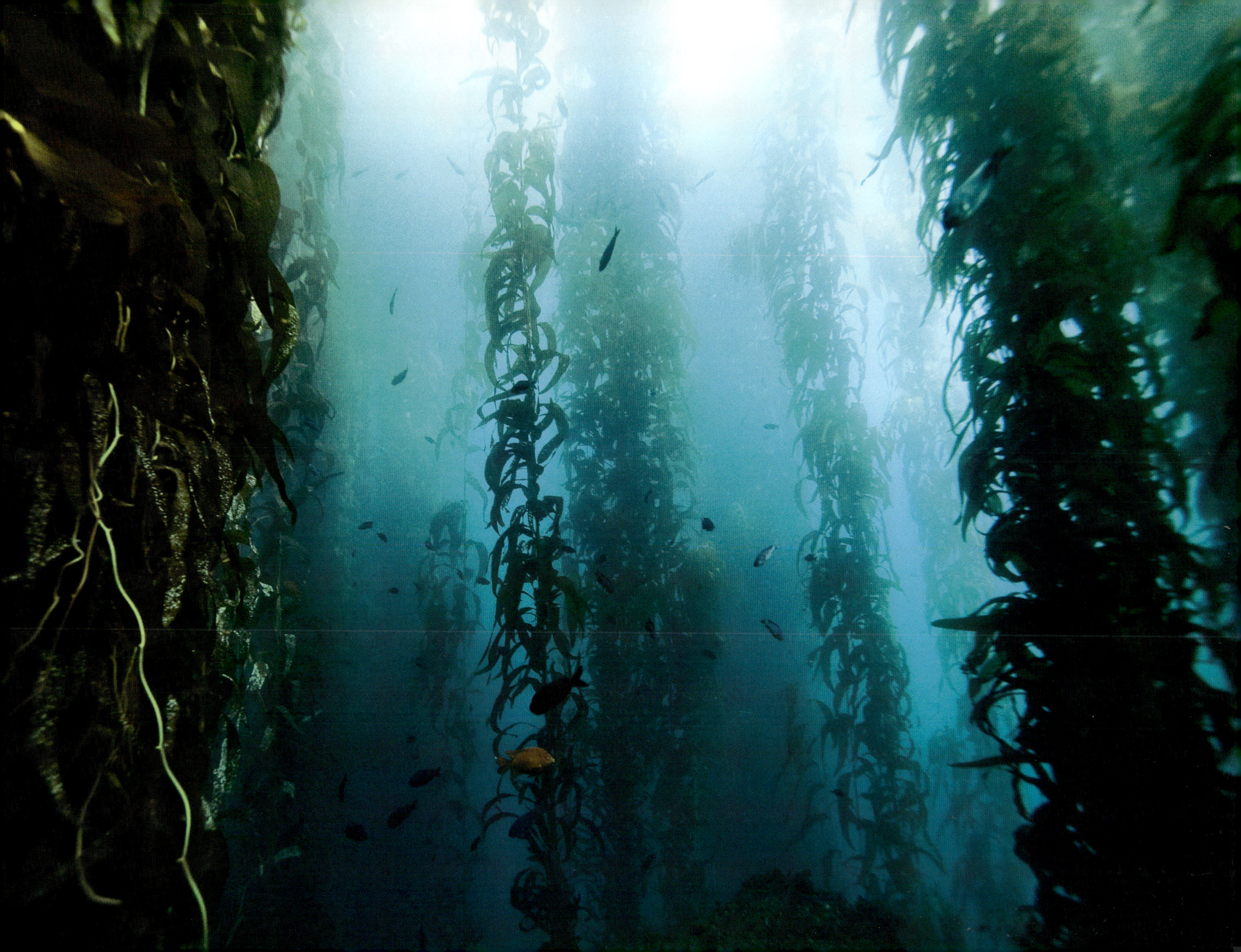

RIGHT: **Glacier National Park, Montana**
The sun breaks through the clouds illuminating Bear Valley.

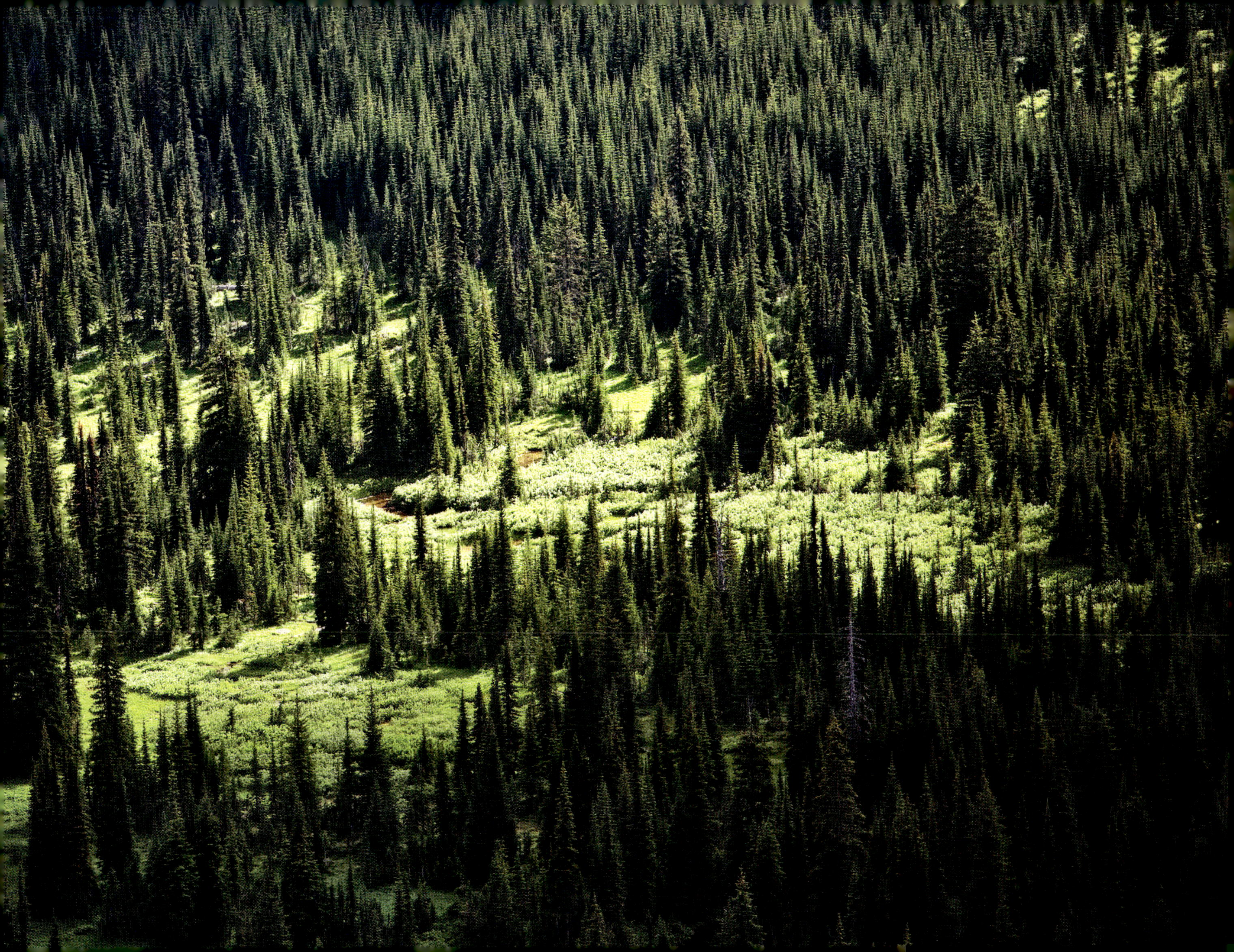

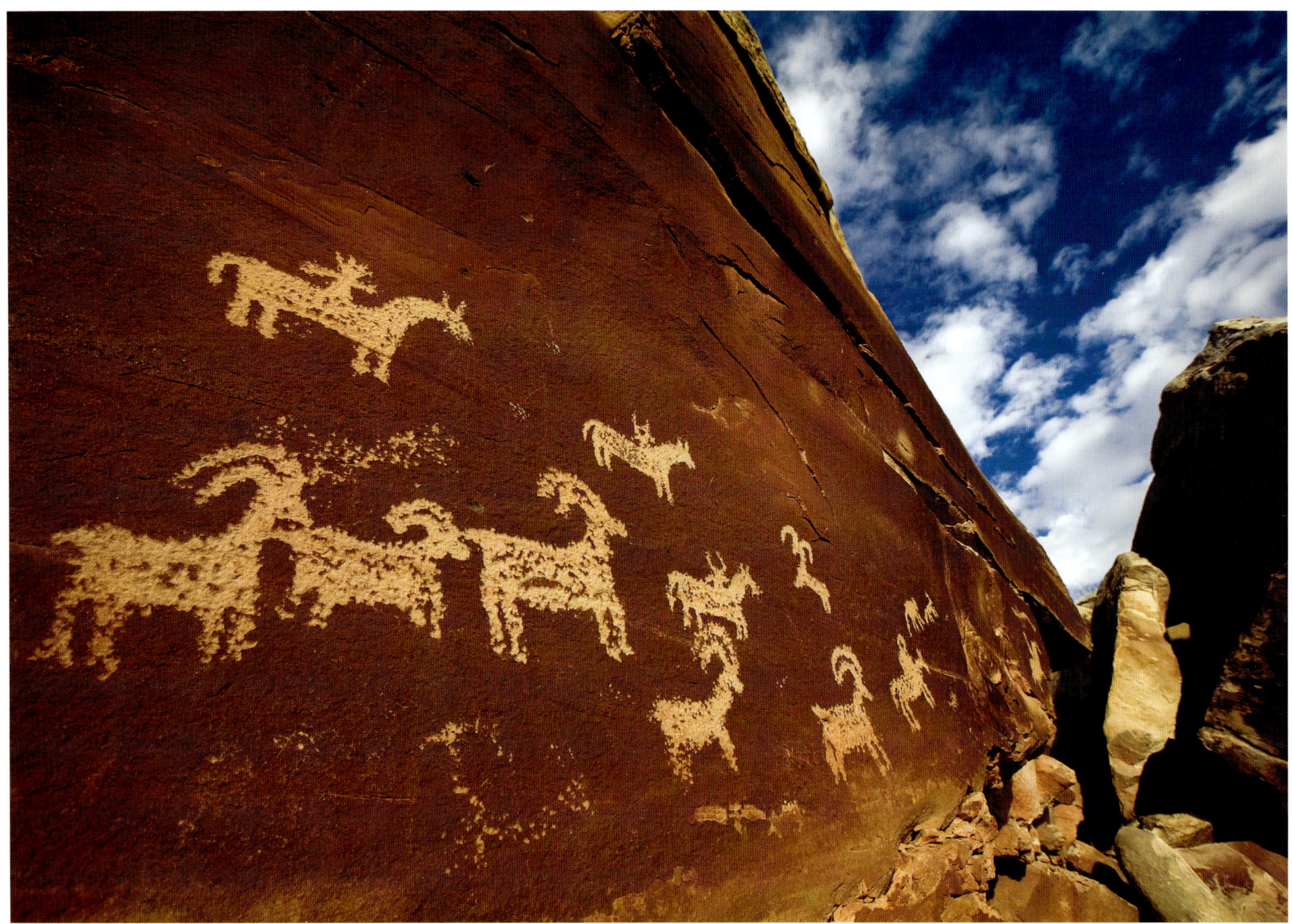

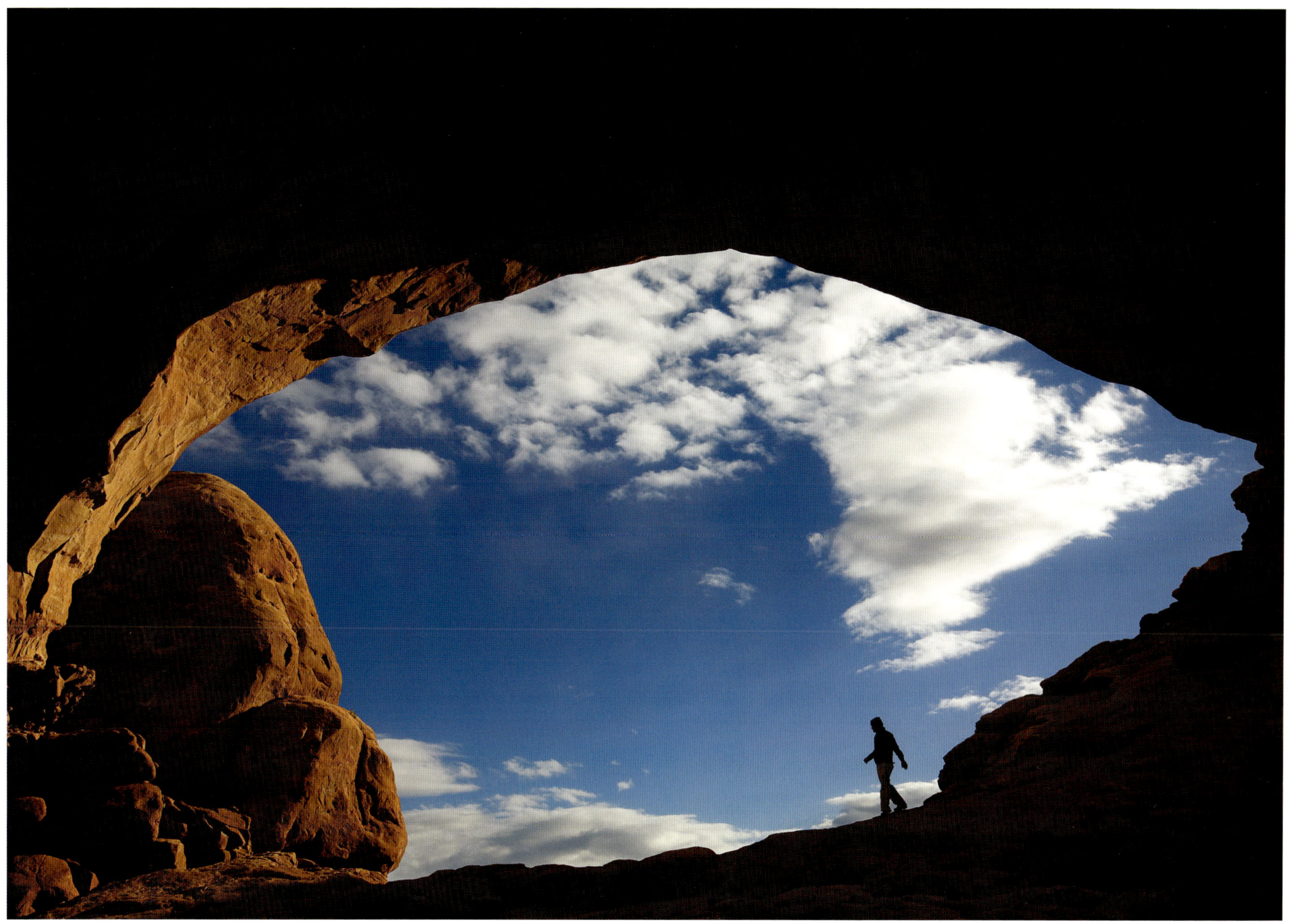

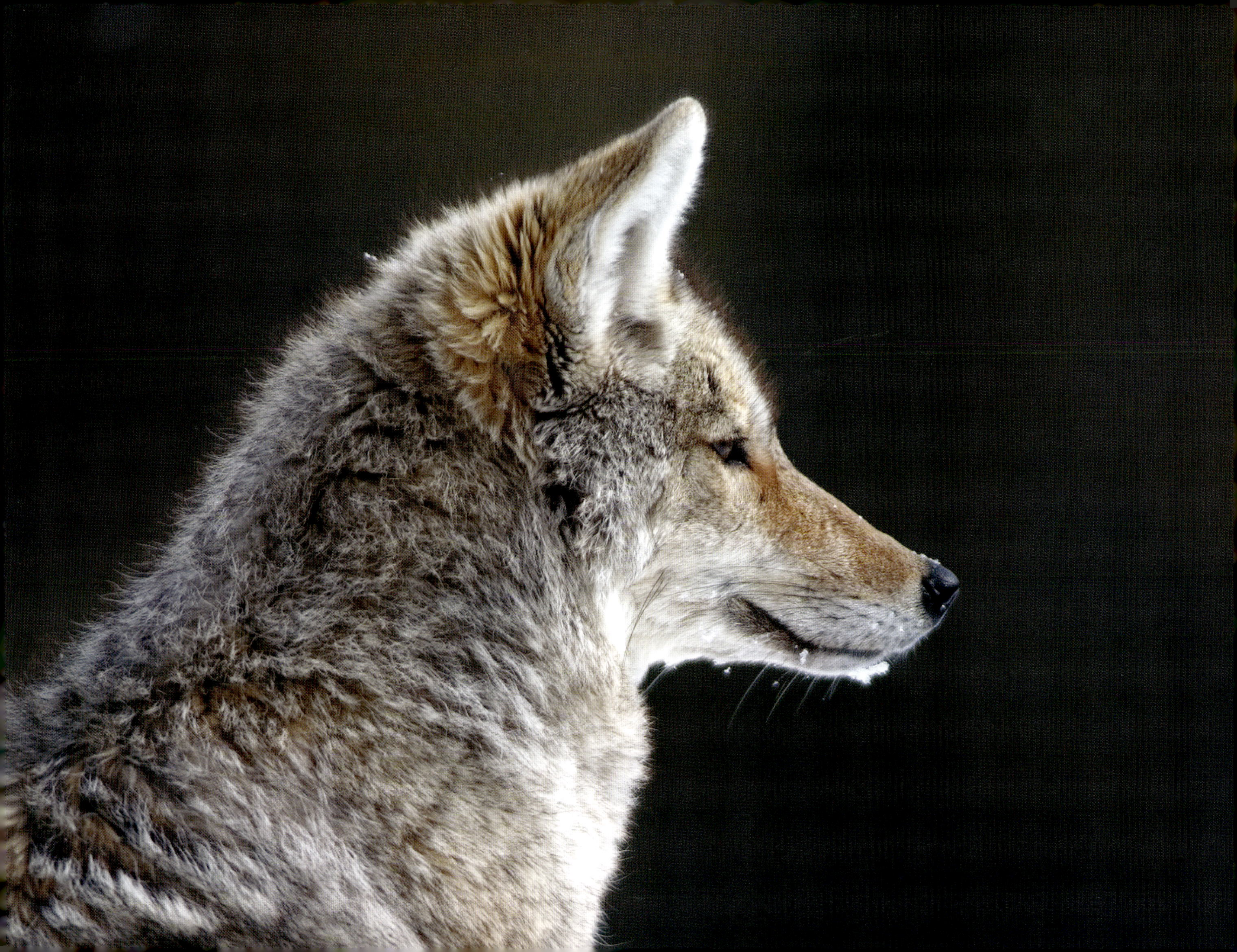

PAGE 130: **Arches National Park, Utah**
Petroglyphs.

PAGE 131: **Arches National Park, Utah**
Window Rock: The formations in Arches National Park are so unique and occur with such frequency in this part of the country that it is truly a one-of-a-kind experience to visit and witness these wonders. Here, geology merges with circumstance—a perfect combination to create stunning rock monuments that will remain an iconic part of this changing landscape.

LEFT: **Yellowstone National Park; Wyoming, Montana, Idaho**
A coyote in Yellowstone: It seems that with the success of the wolf and the recovery of the red fox, the coyote gets a slack reputation in Yellowstone. They are considered by most ranchers to be nothing more than vermin, while many Yellowstone visitors mistake them for wolves. Despite their sagging reputation, they remain a vital component to the success of Yellowstone's ecosystem, and, in my opinion, they are beautiful creatures that work hard to make a living in a wintry landscape. It's been said that when all else on this planet has failed, few creatures will remain. One that is certain to continue to roam is the cunning and resilient coyote.

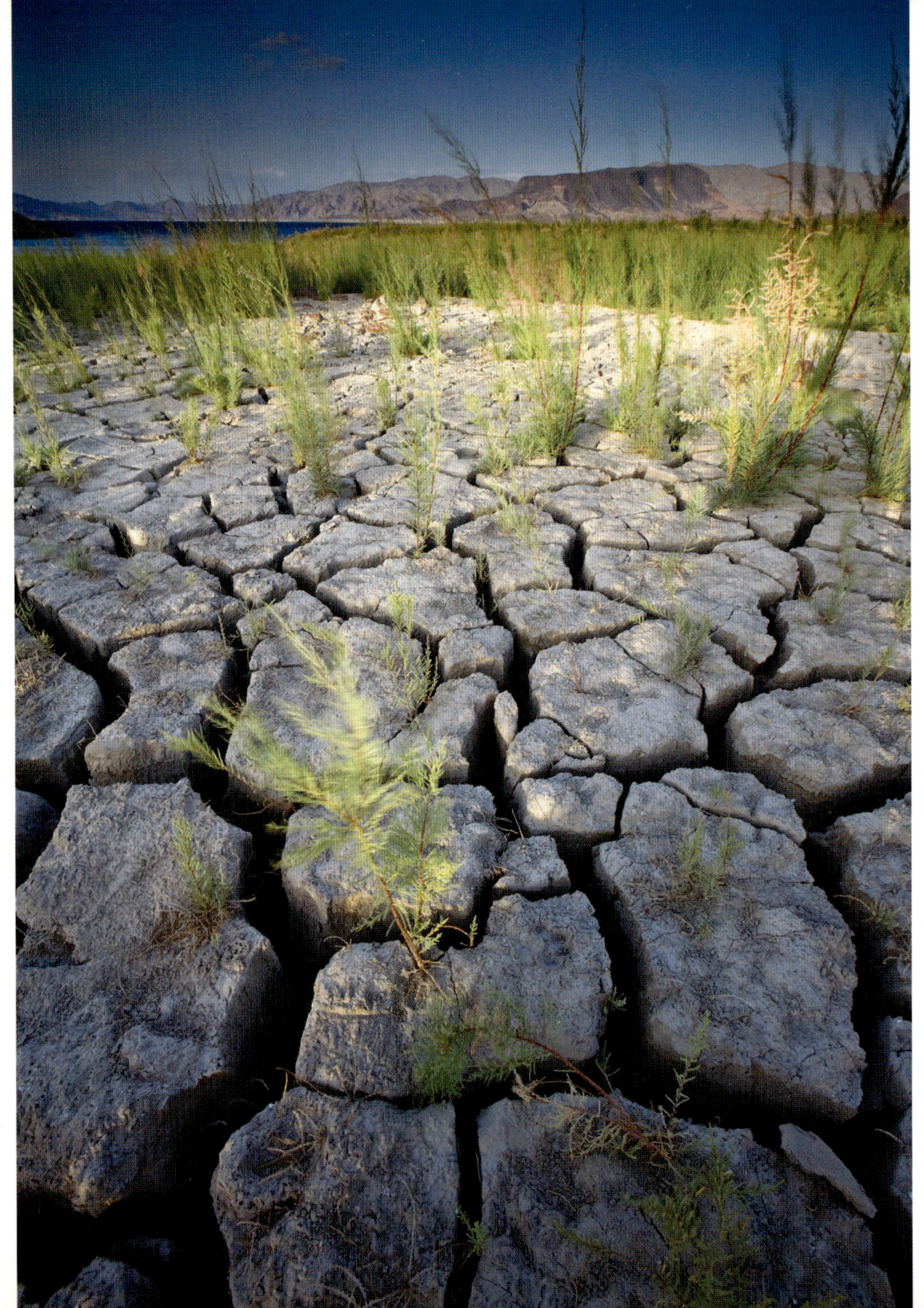

LEFT: **Lake Mead National Recreation Area, Nevada**
A dried lake bed.

RIGHT: **Lake Mead National Recreation Area, Nevada**
An aerial view during a drought at Lake Mead

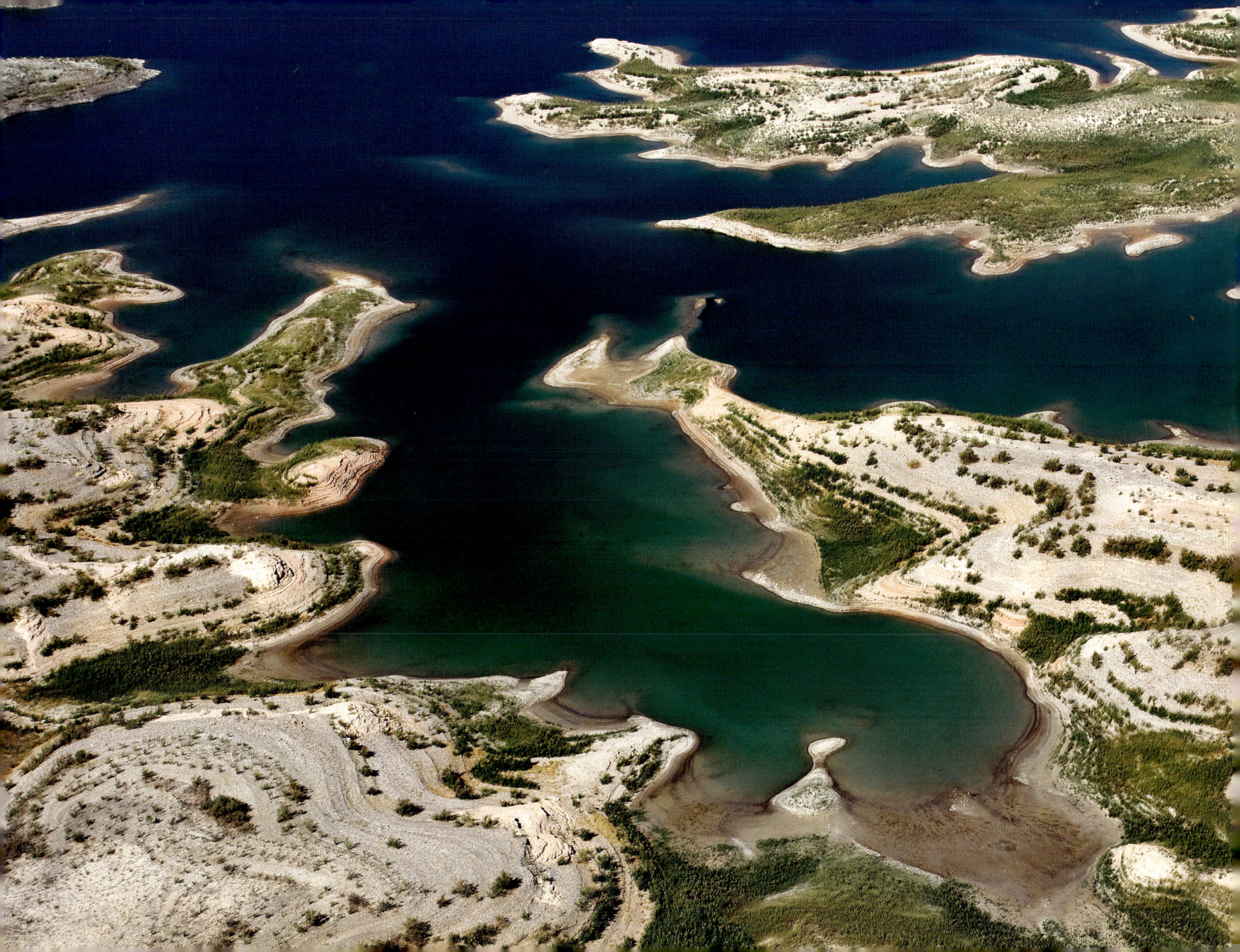

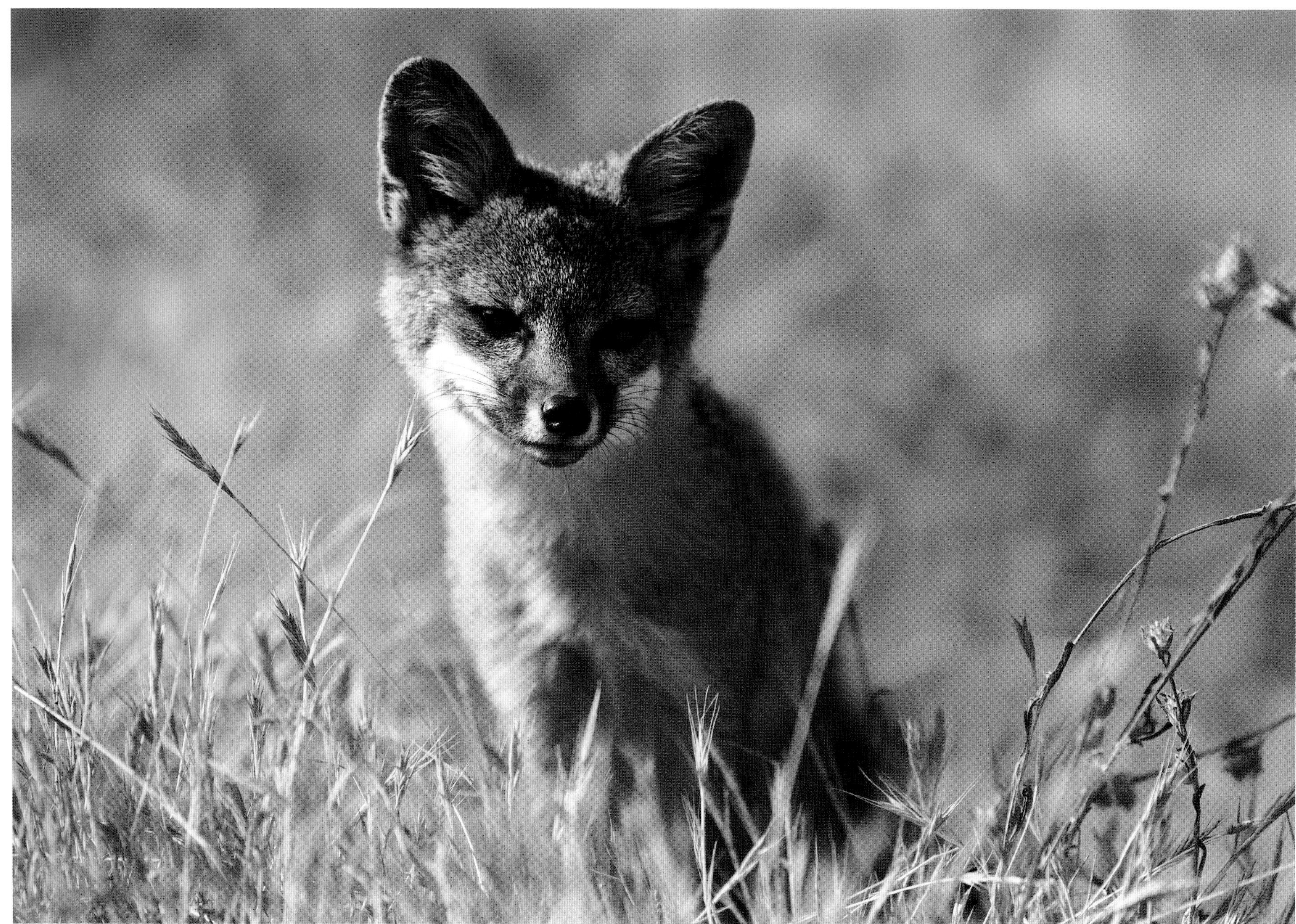

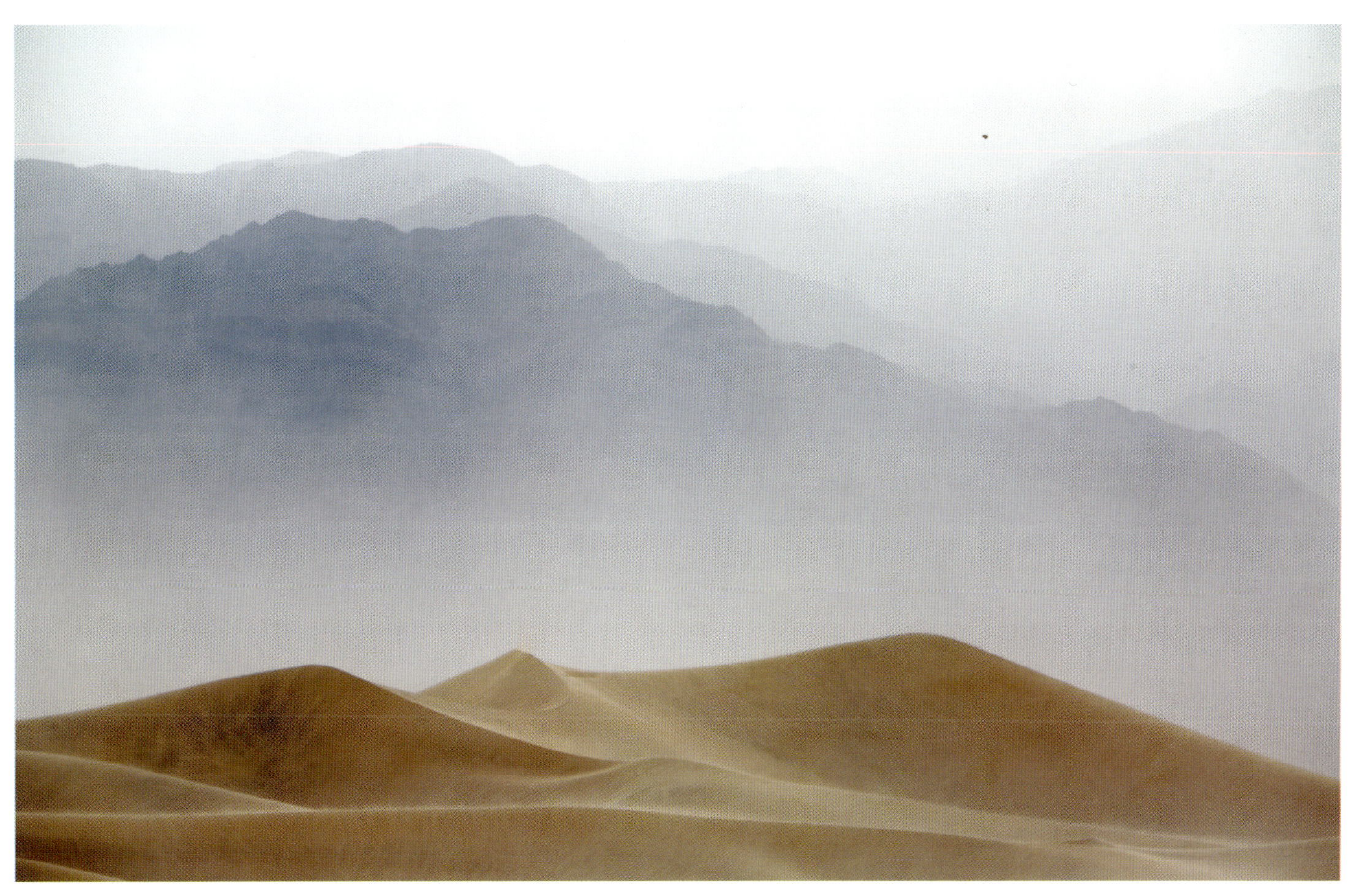

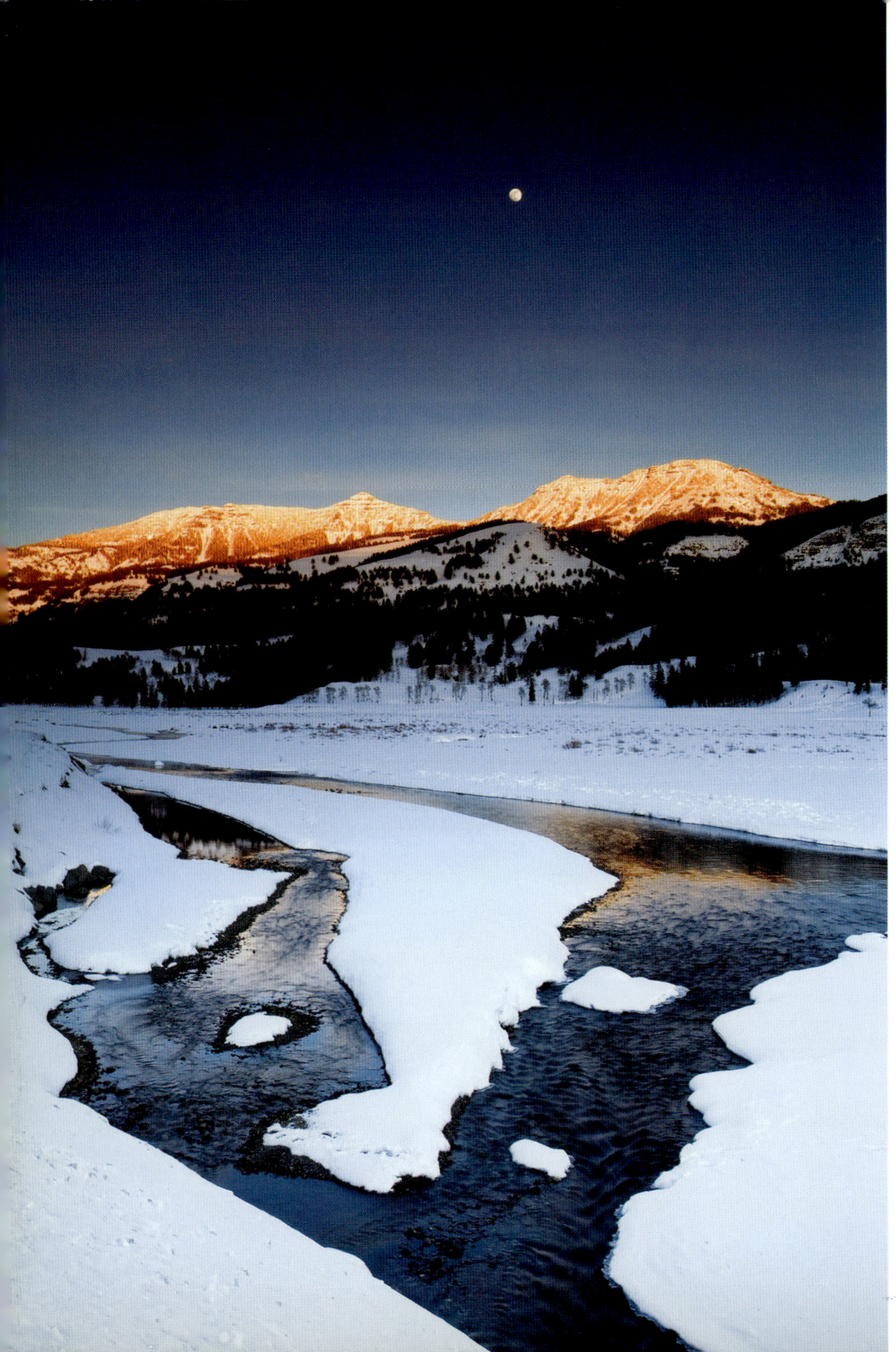

PAGE 136: **Channel Islands National Park, California**
The Santa Cruz Island fox.

PAGE 137: **Death Valley National Park, California**
A sandstorm obscures the mountains at Stovepipe Wells Sand Dunes.

LEFT: **Yellowstone National Park; Wyoming, Montana, Idaho**
The Lamar River in Lamar Valley at sunset.

RIGHT: **Big Bend National Park, Texas**
An agave, or century plant, in front of the Chisos Mountains at sunset. The Chisos Mountains are considered "sky islands" because of their geographical isolation.

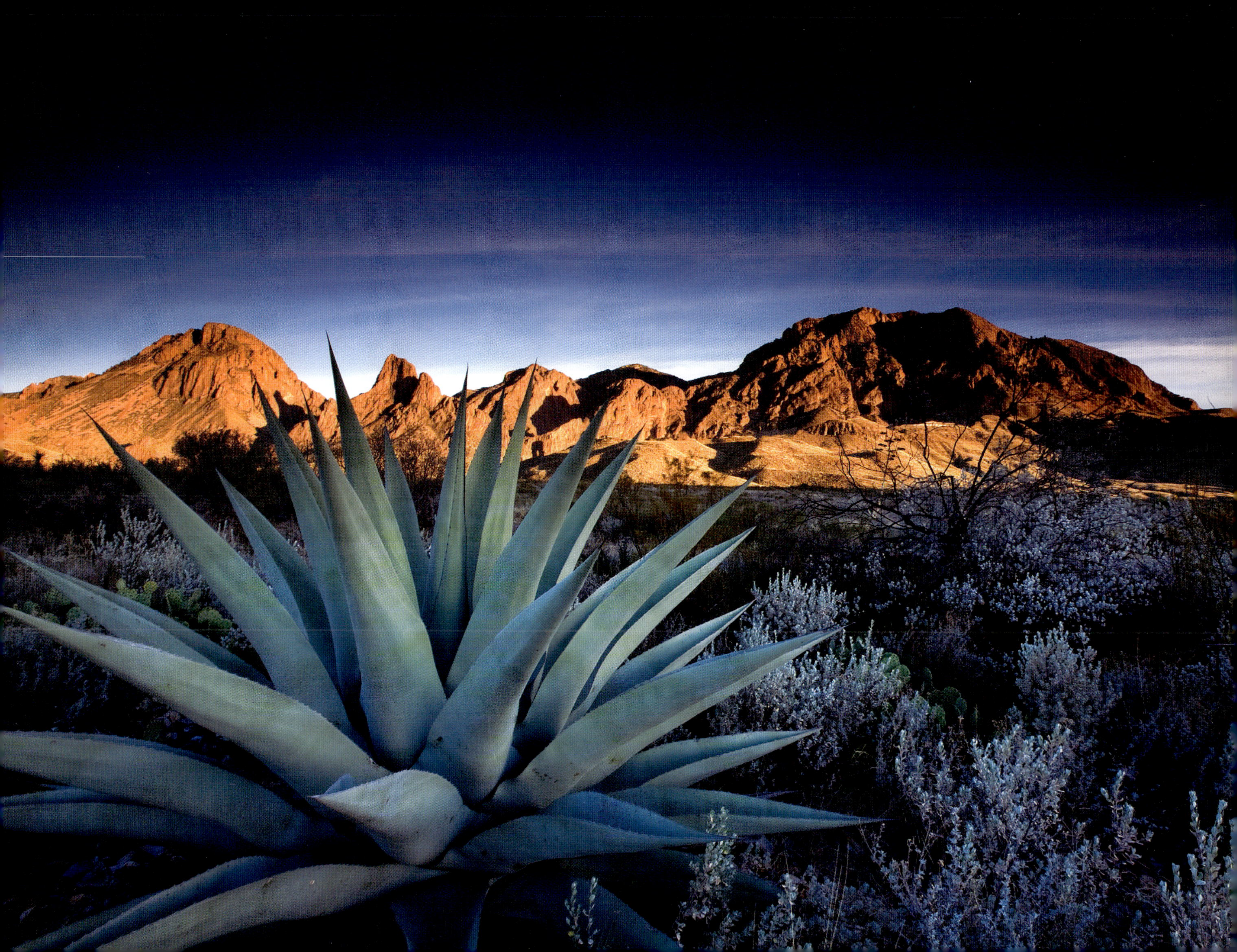

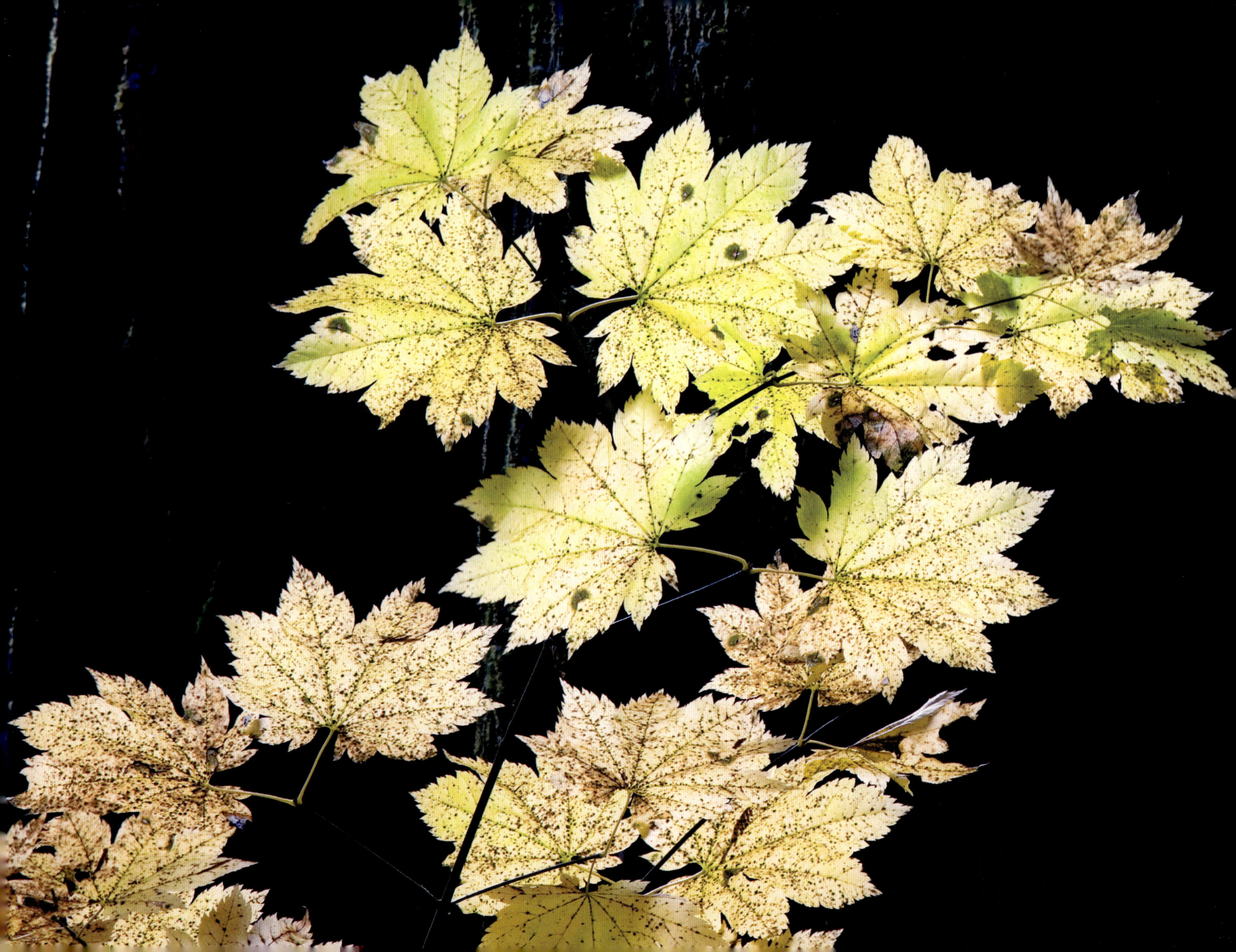

LEFT & RIGHT: **Mount Rainier National Park, Washington**
Details of autumn leaves against the giant trees in the Grove of the Patriarchs.

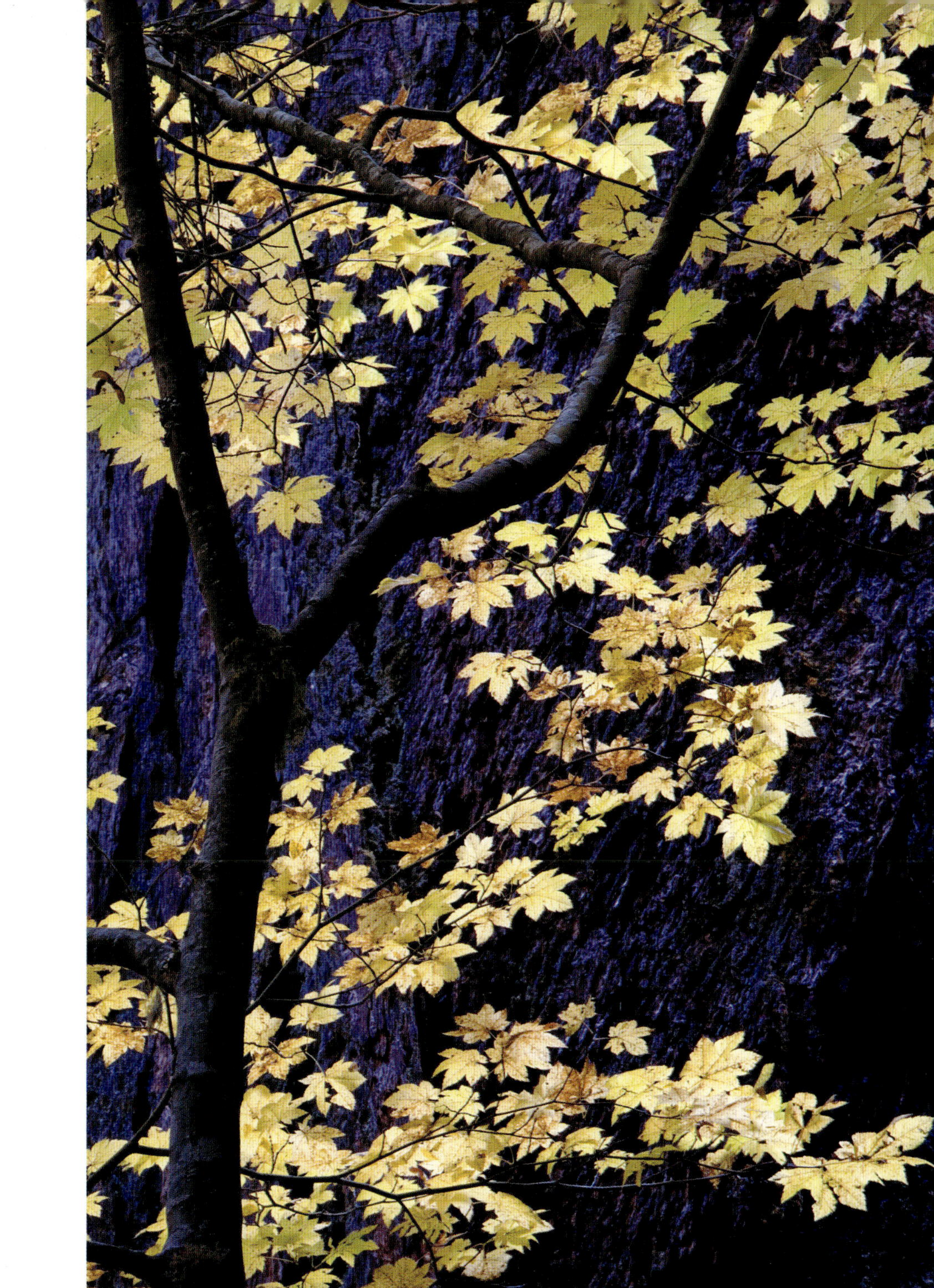

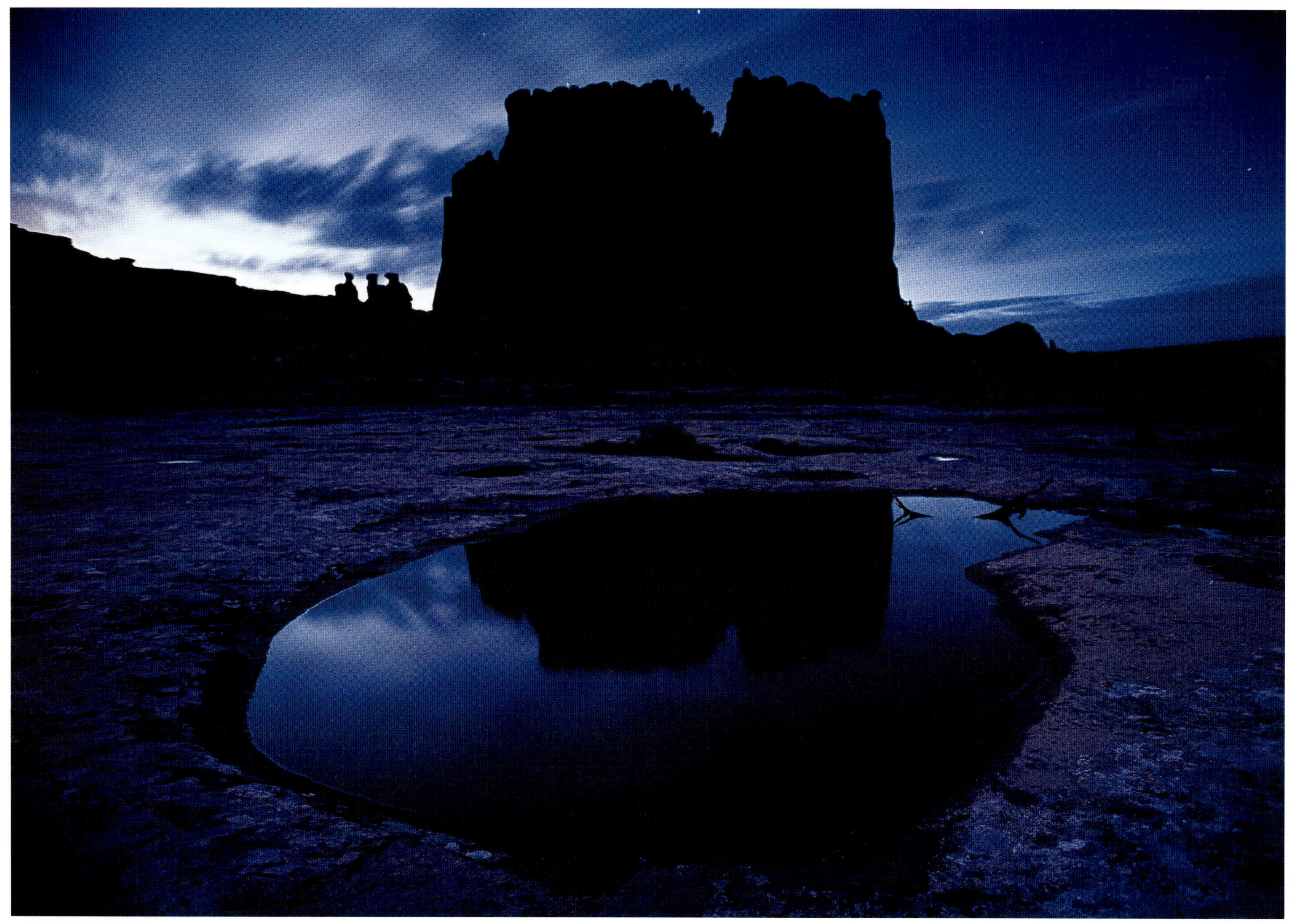

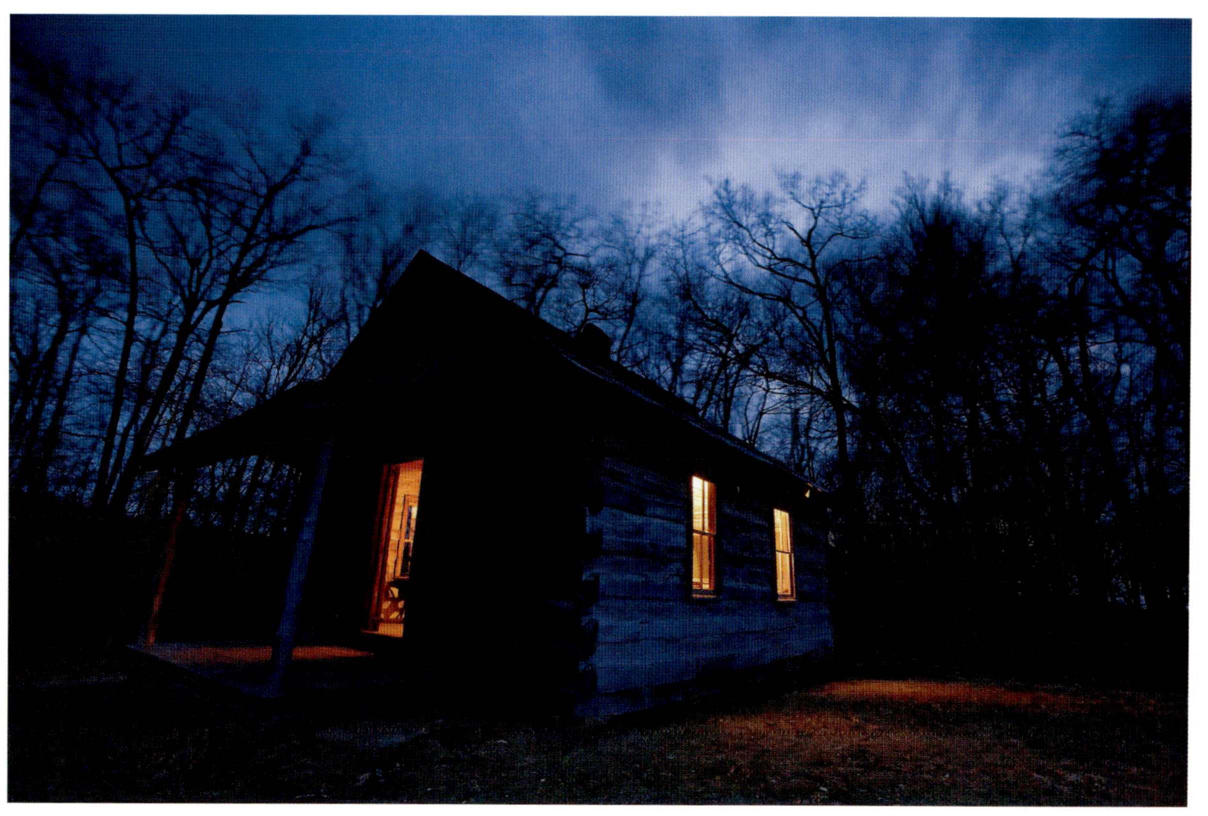

ABOVE: **Cumberland Gap National Historical Park; Kentucky, Tennessee, Virginia**
Historic Hensley Settlement schoolhouse — artificially lit by interior strobes.

LEFT: **Arches National Park, Utah**
Courthouse Towers reflected in a pool of water.

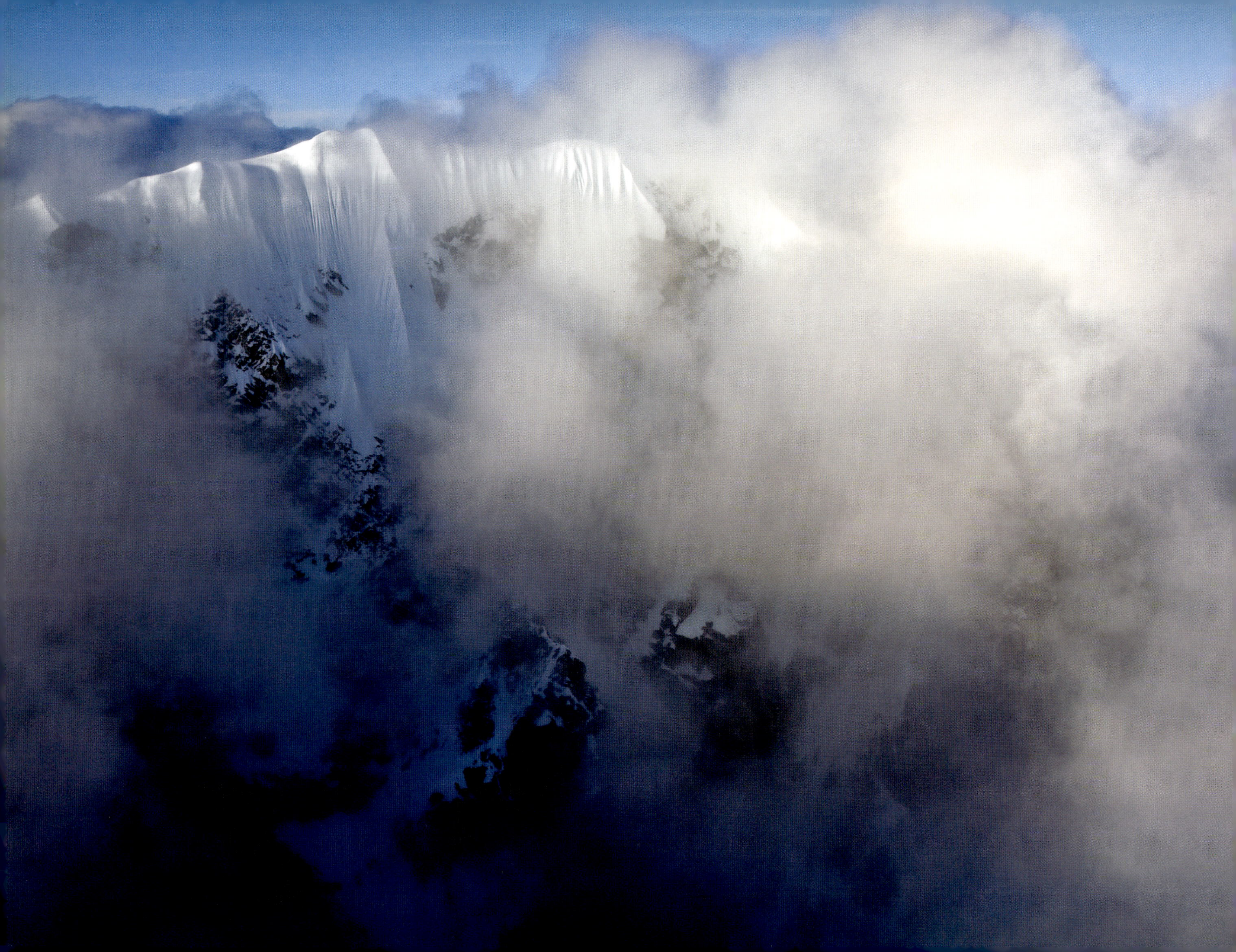

LEFT: **Denali National Park & Preserve, Alaska**
Flying over the heart of the Alaska Range in a Lama high-altitude helicopter, I had a view of this prehistoric landscape that few ever get to experience. Like an embryonic capsule, snow still covers entire mountains, only occasionally peeling off the sides in a massive avalanche and revealing—perhaps for the first time—the rocky mountains beneath.

RIGHT: **Rocky Mountain National Park, Colorado**
A frozen lake.

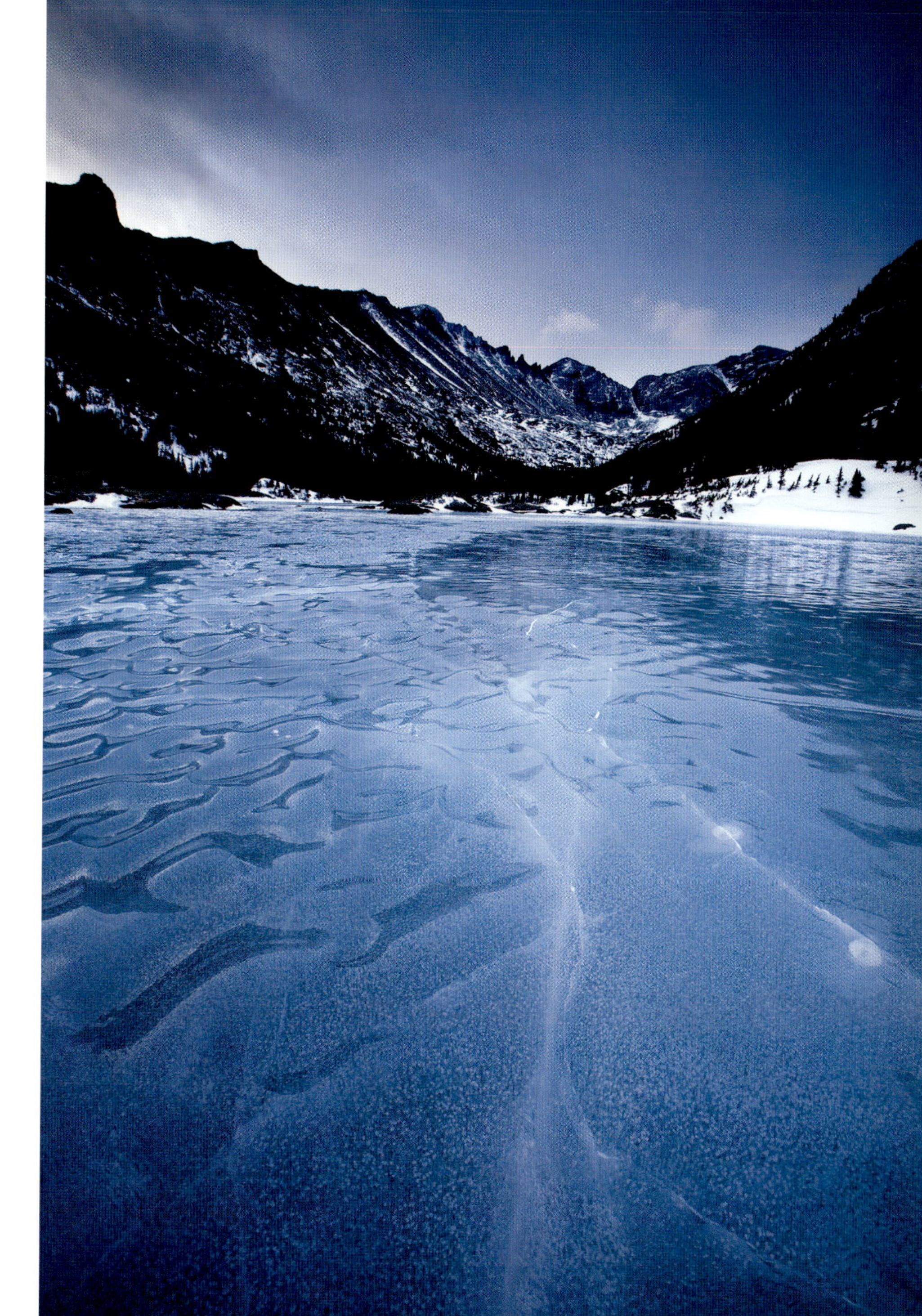

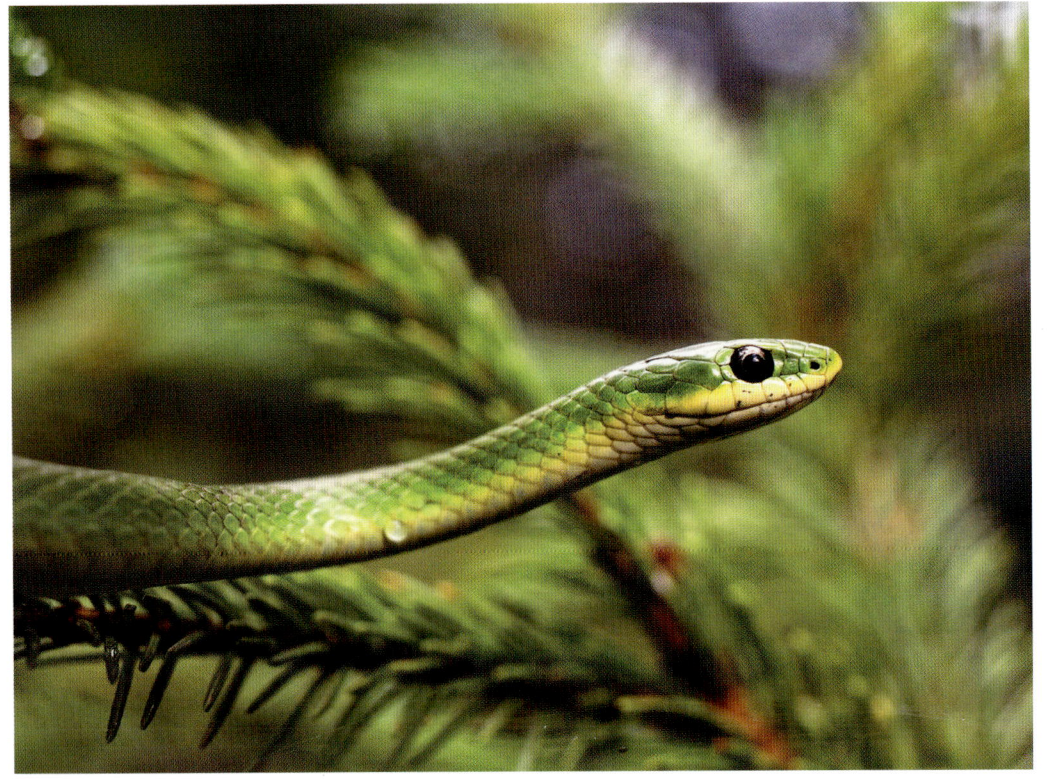

ABOVE: **Acadia National Park, Maine**
A smooth green snake weaves among pine boughs near the Otter Cliffs area.

RIGHT: **Hawaii Volcanoes National Park, Hawaii**
A tropical rain forest near the Thurston Lava Tube.

PAGES 148/149: **Craters of the Moon National Monument & Preserve, Idaho**
An otherworldly landscape, this monument has a rather humorous story for its inception. It was proclaimed on May 2, 1924, by U.S. president Calvin Coolidge that Craters of the Moon National Monument shall be created to "preserve the unusual and weird volcanic formations."

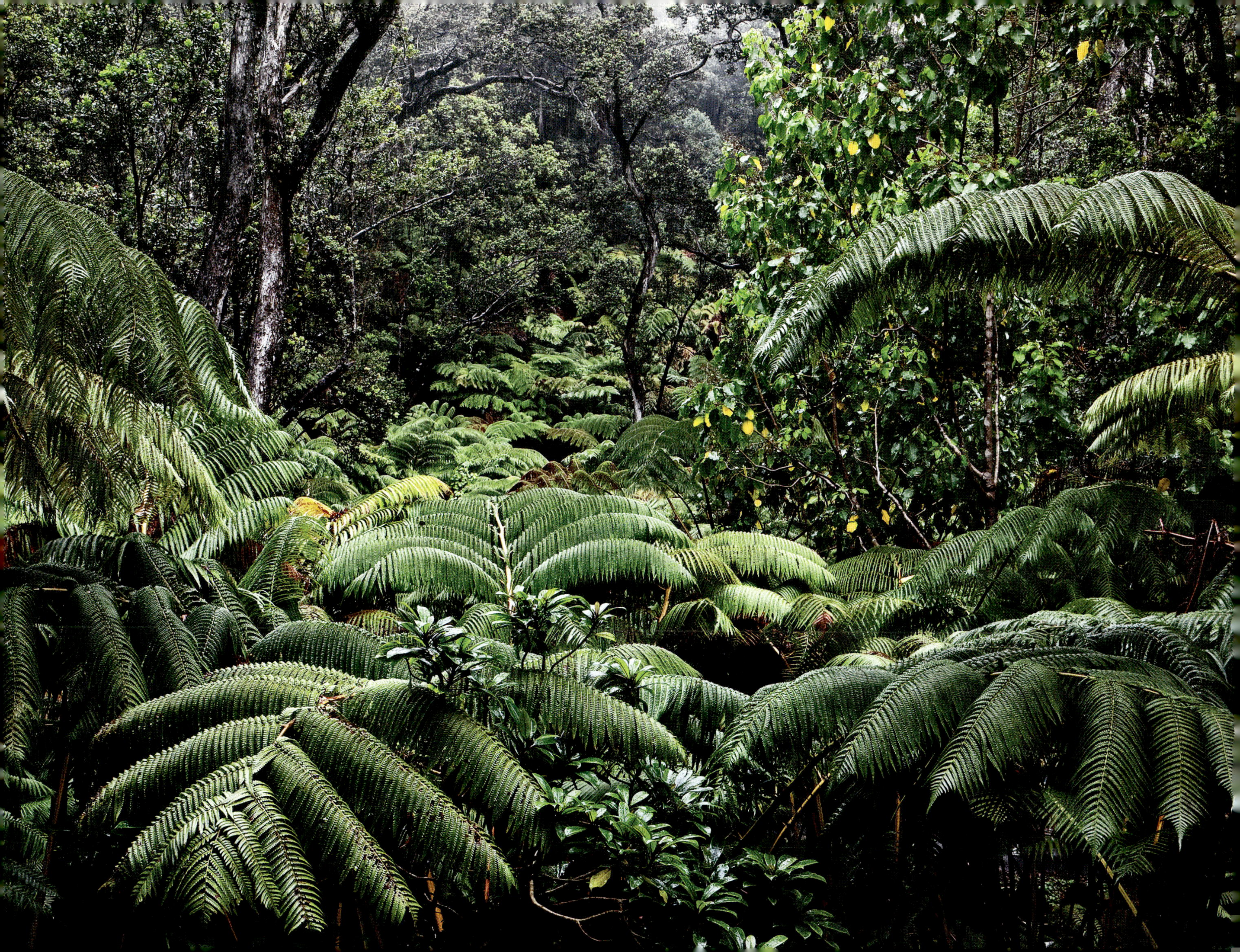

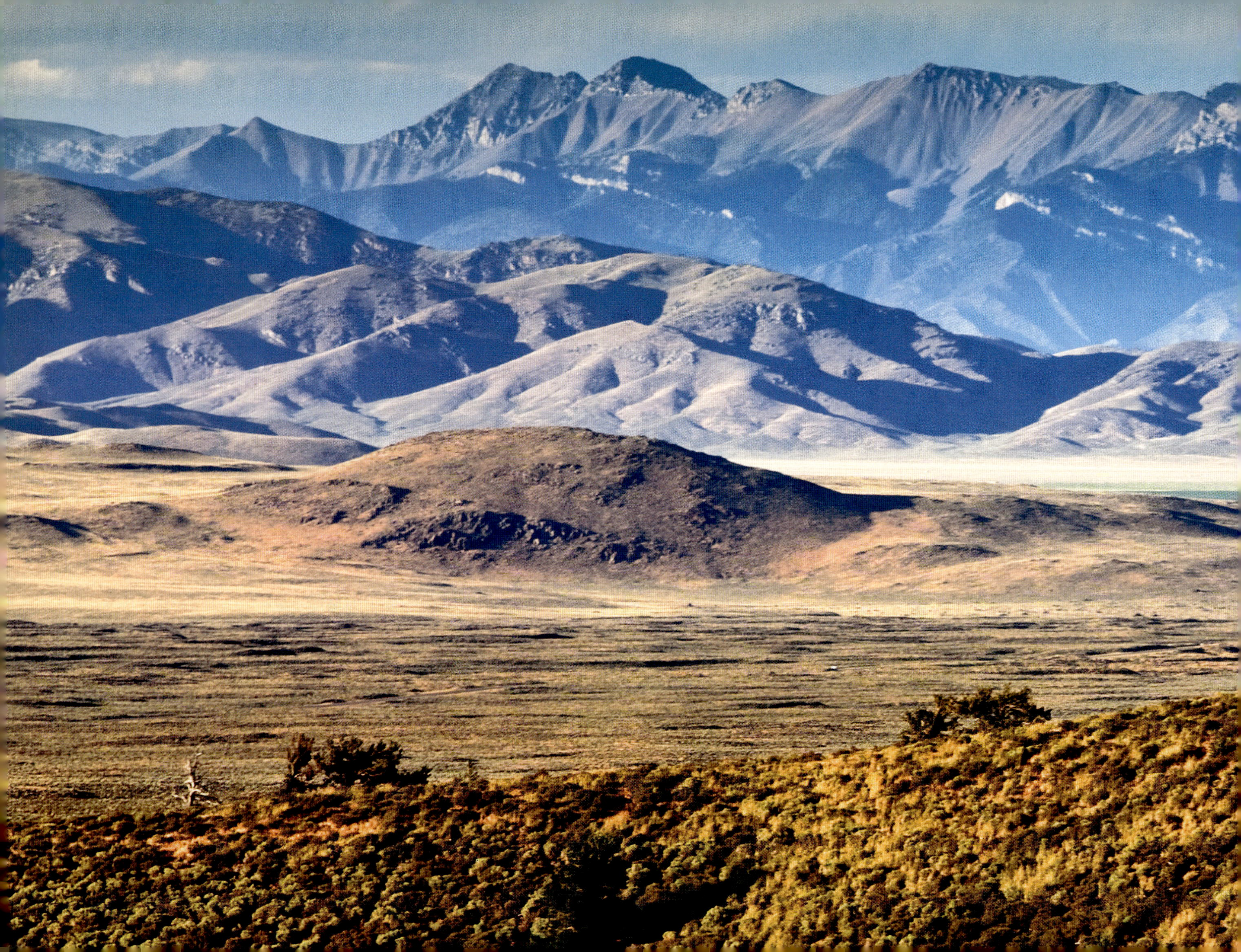

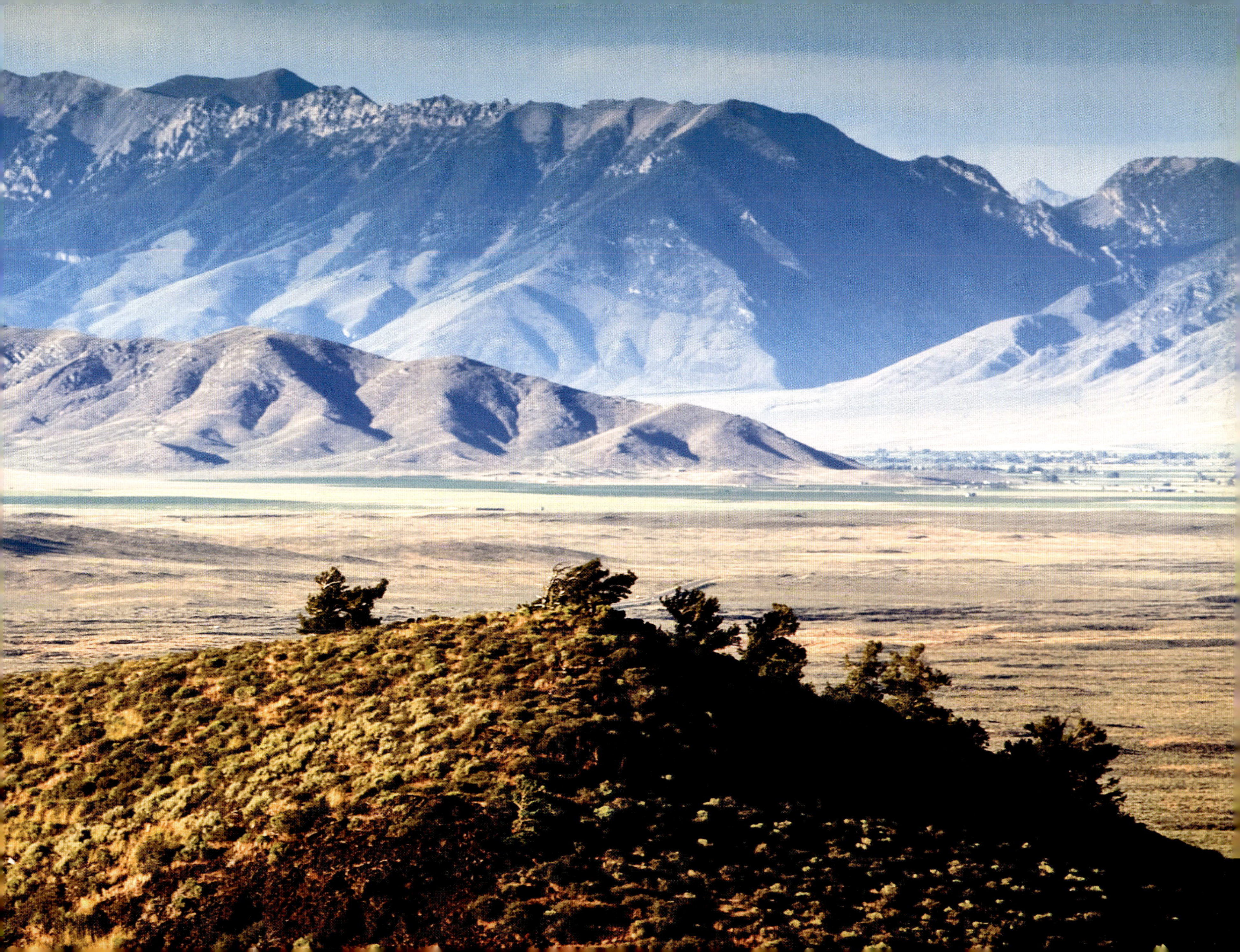

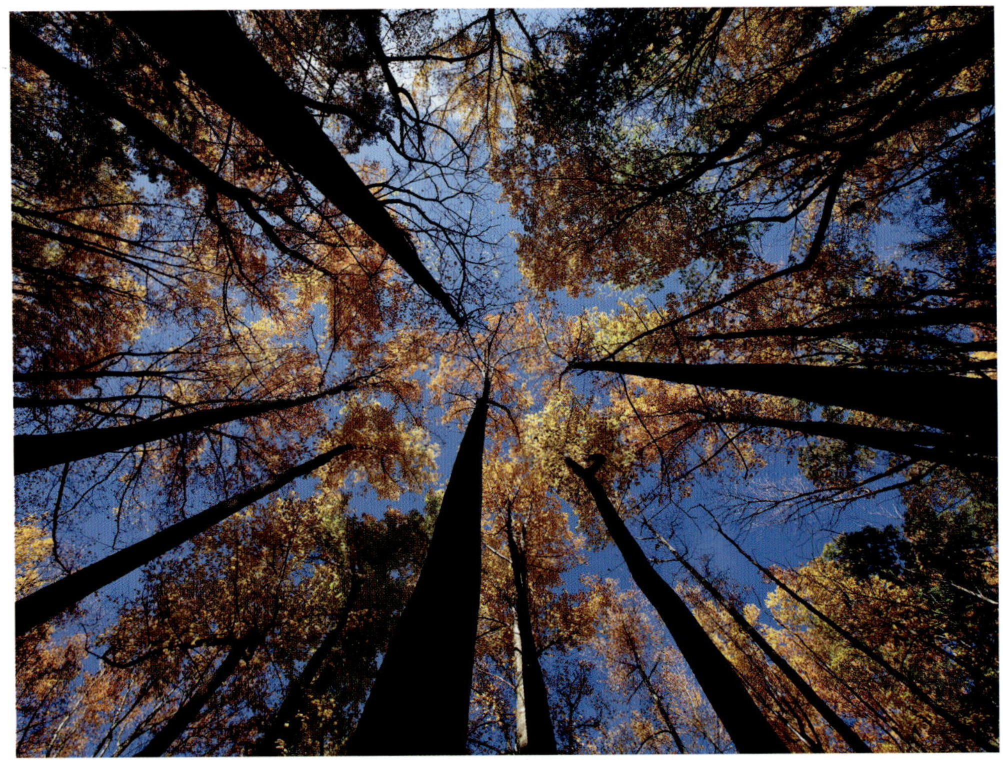

ABOVE: **Great Smoky Mountains National Park, Tennessee**
Looking up through the hardwood forest near Cades Cove.

RIGHT: **Great Smoky Mountains National Park, Tennessee**
This image taken during the last days of autumn in the Smokies reminds me of a classic American pastoral painting. Often influenced by painters, I relish in moments like this where a magical light becomes the brush that paints the scene for my camera.

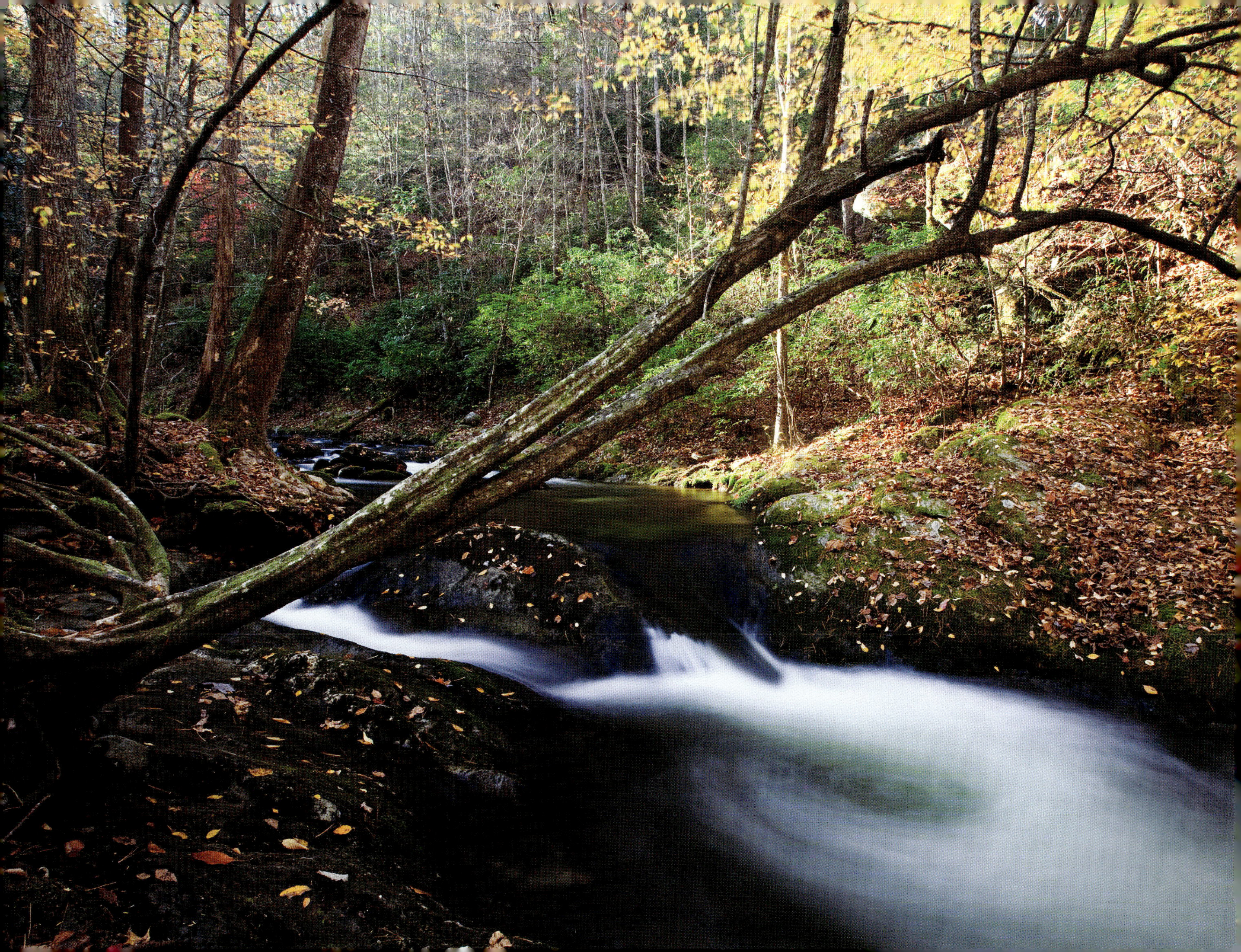

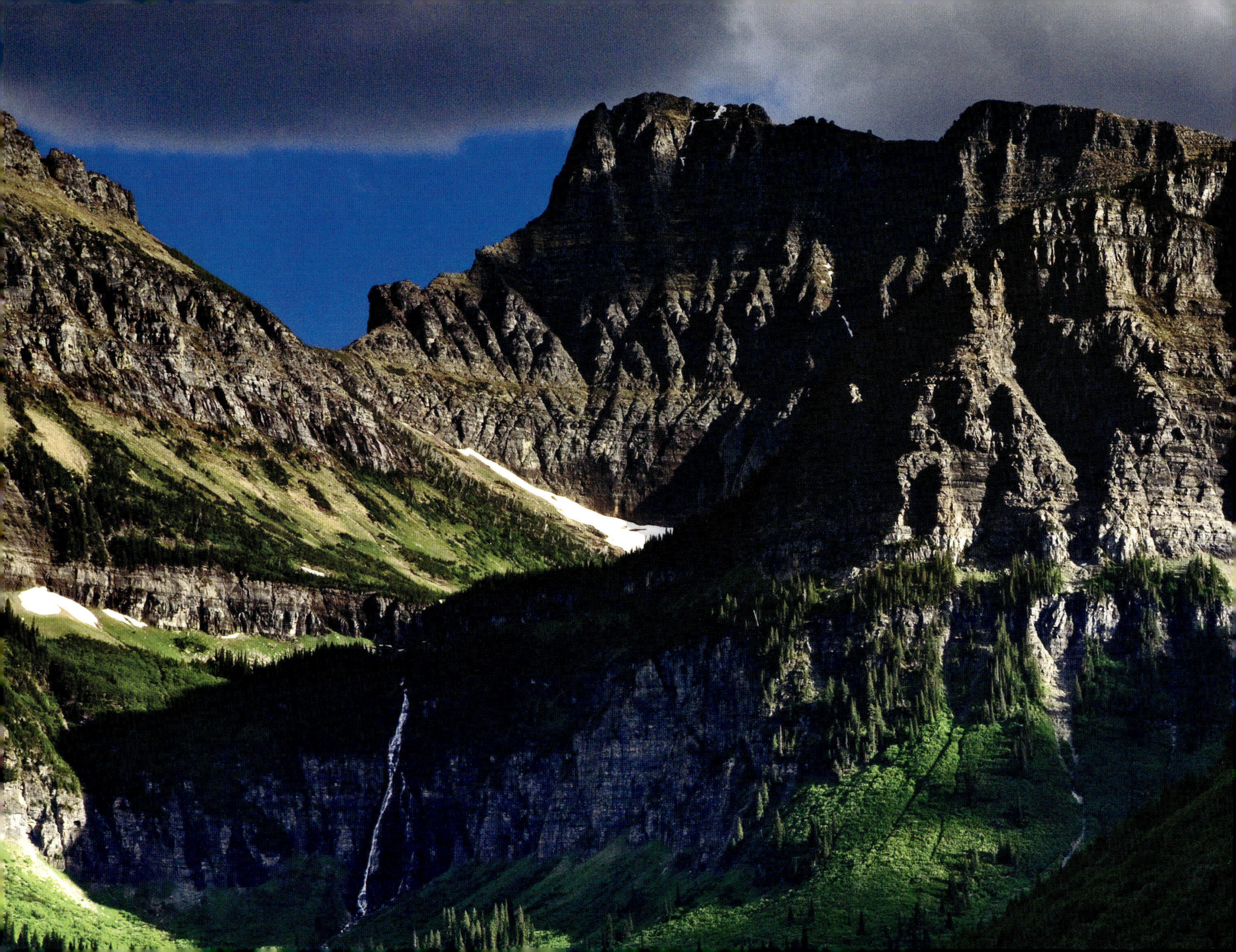

LEFT: **Glacier National Park, Montana**
The view from Going-to-the-Sun road near Logan Pass.

RIGHT: **Yosemite National Park, California**
Winter on the Merced River with Half Dome in the background: Yosemite is a park full of iconic views. As a photographer visiting the park, I find it beautiful and inspiring, but realize that there are few angles on its landscape that haven't been photographed many times over. The greatest challenge for me is to step outside the postcards and brochures and all the images we've come to appreciate the place for, and think of a new way to express the feelings I get from being there. This image was taken on one of the quietest days I've ever experienced in the park—all the roads coming in were closed because of snow, and so, for a day, I had one of America's oldest and most cherished national parks almost entirely to myself. I feel that this image captures that.

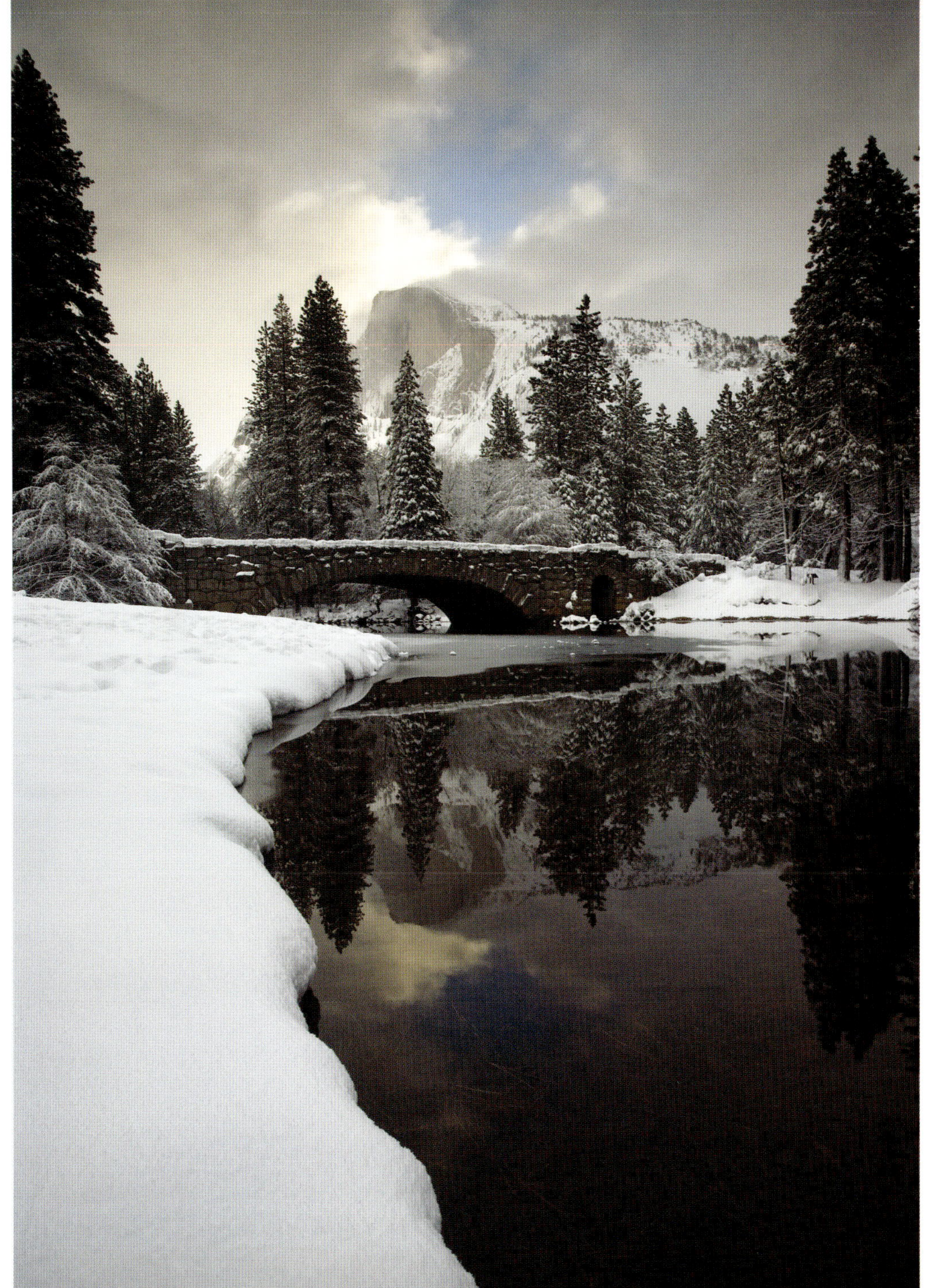

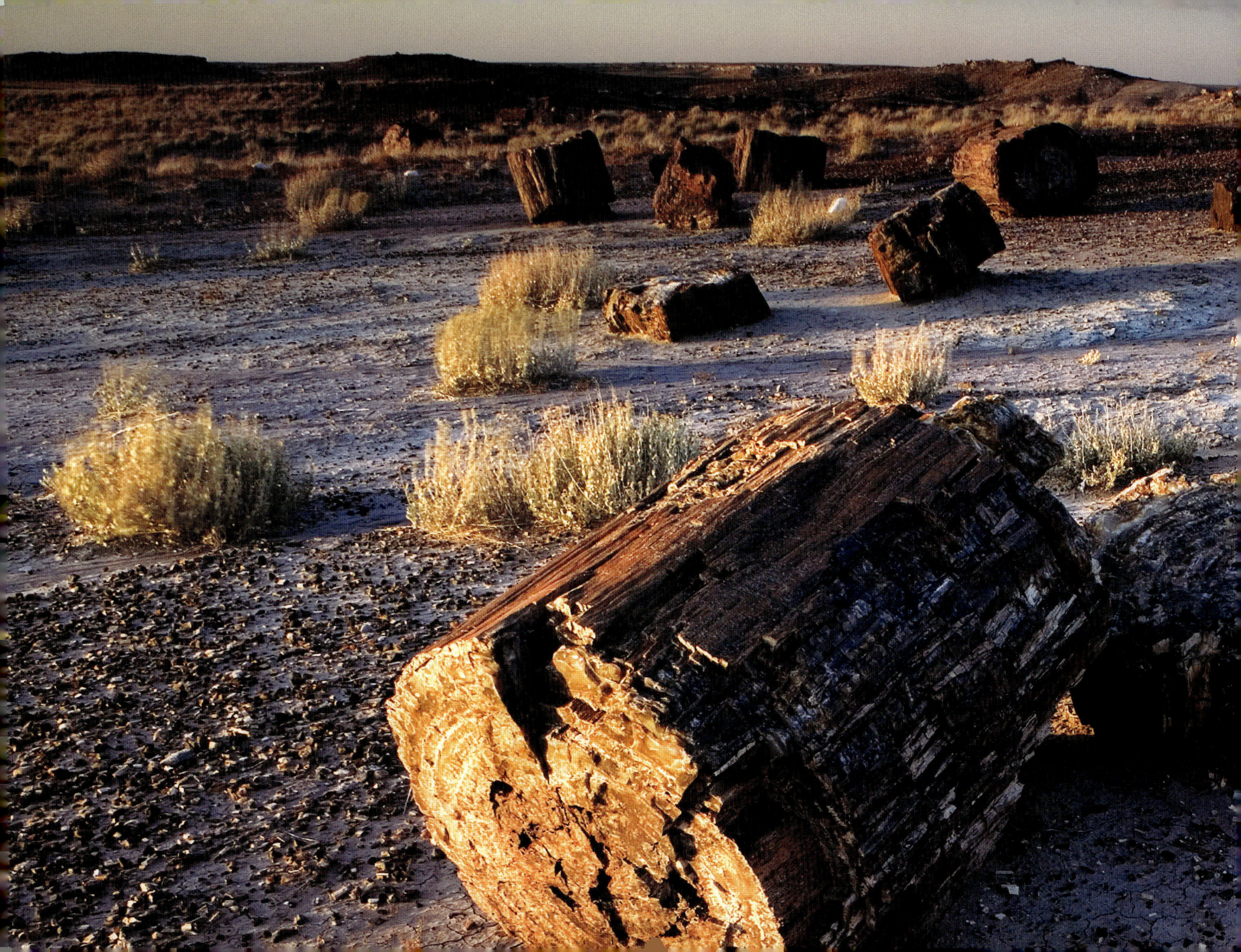

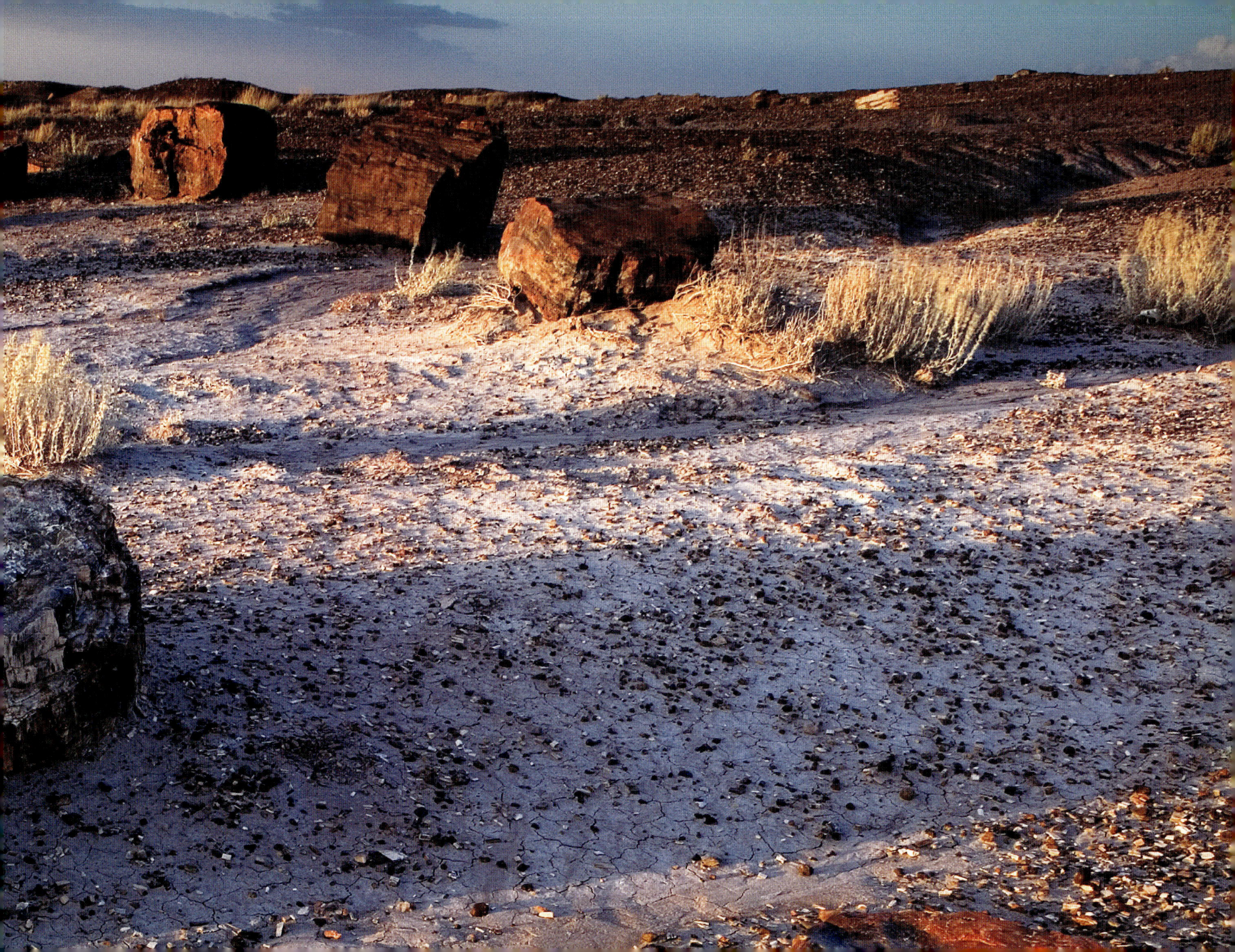

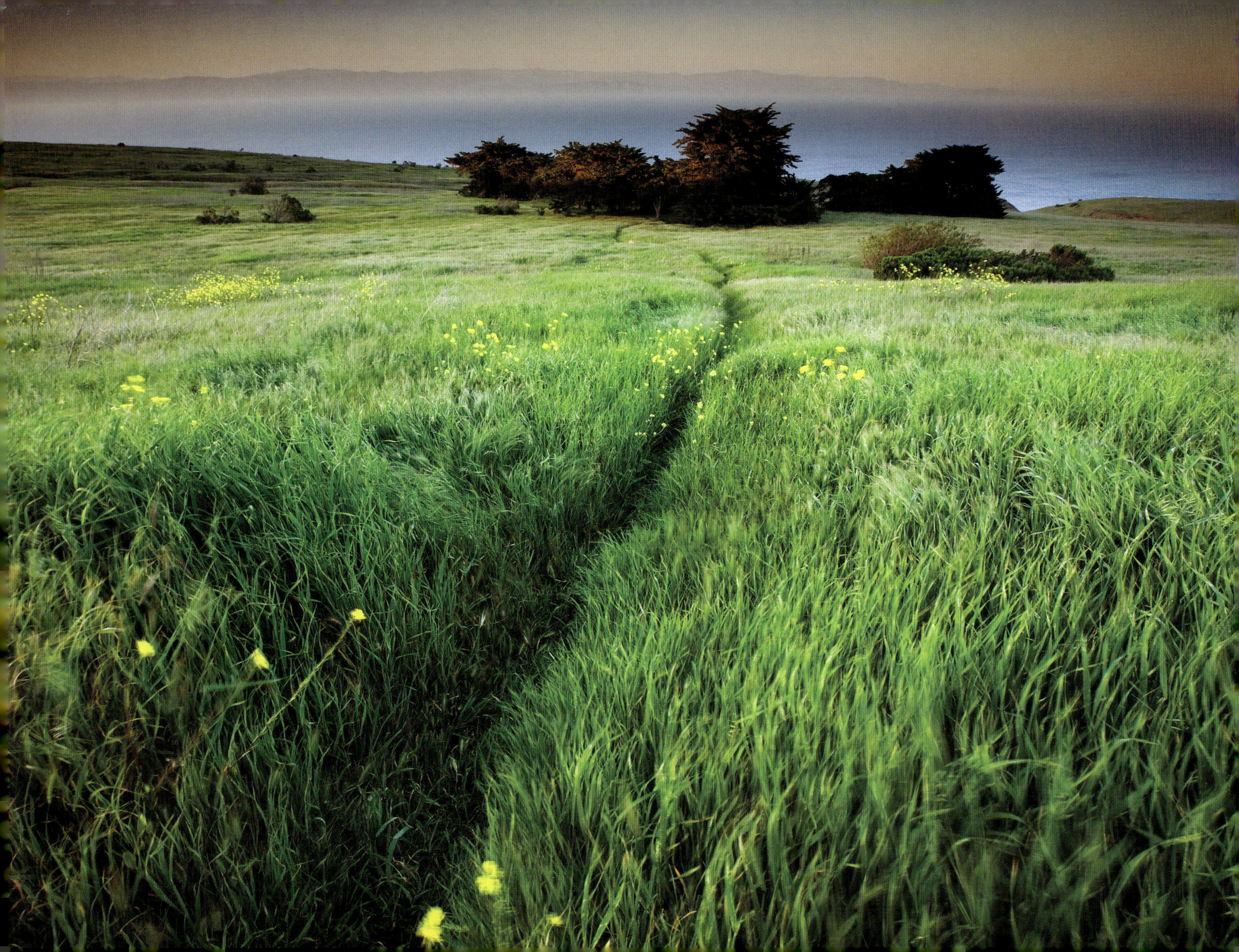

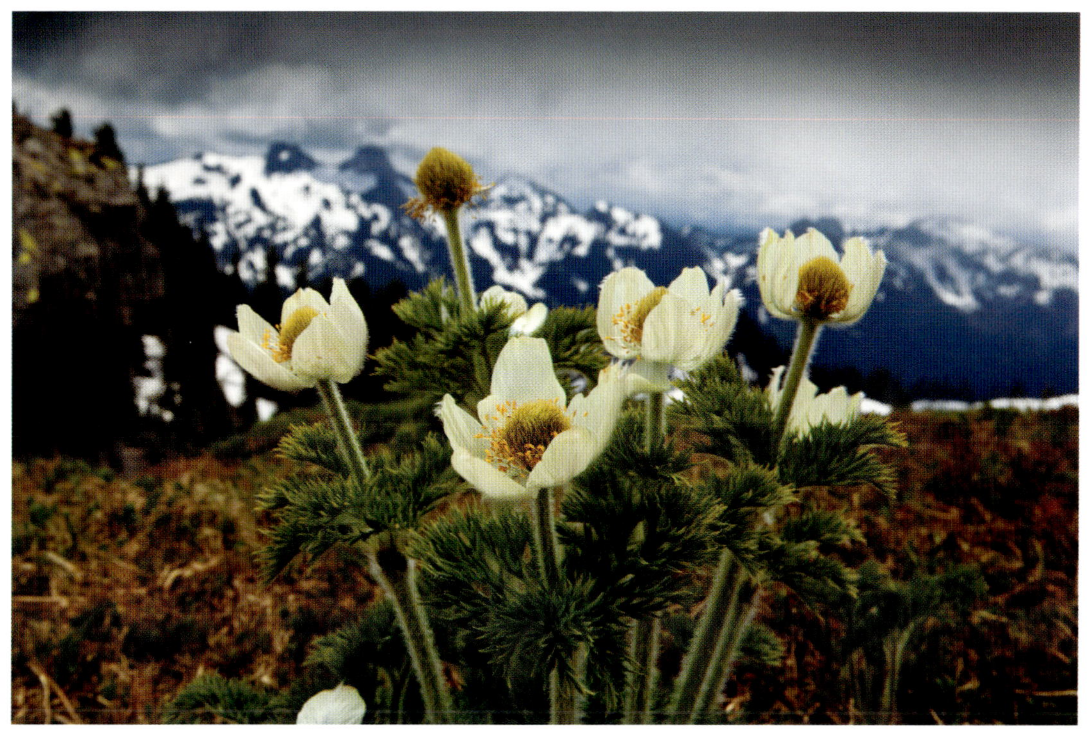

PAGES 154/155: **Petrified Forest National Park, Arizona**
Petrified trees, which are 225 million years old, are scattered across the landscape.

ABOVE: **Mount Rainier National Park, Washington**
Wildflowers in bloom.

LEFT: **Channel Island National Park, California**
A scenic landscape on Santa Cruz Island.

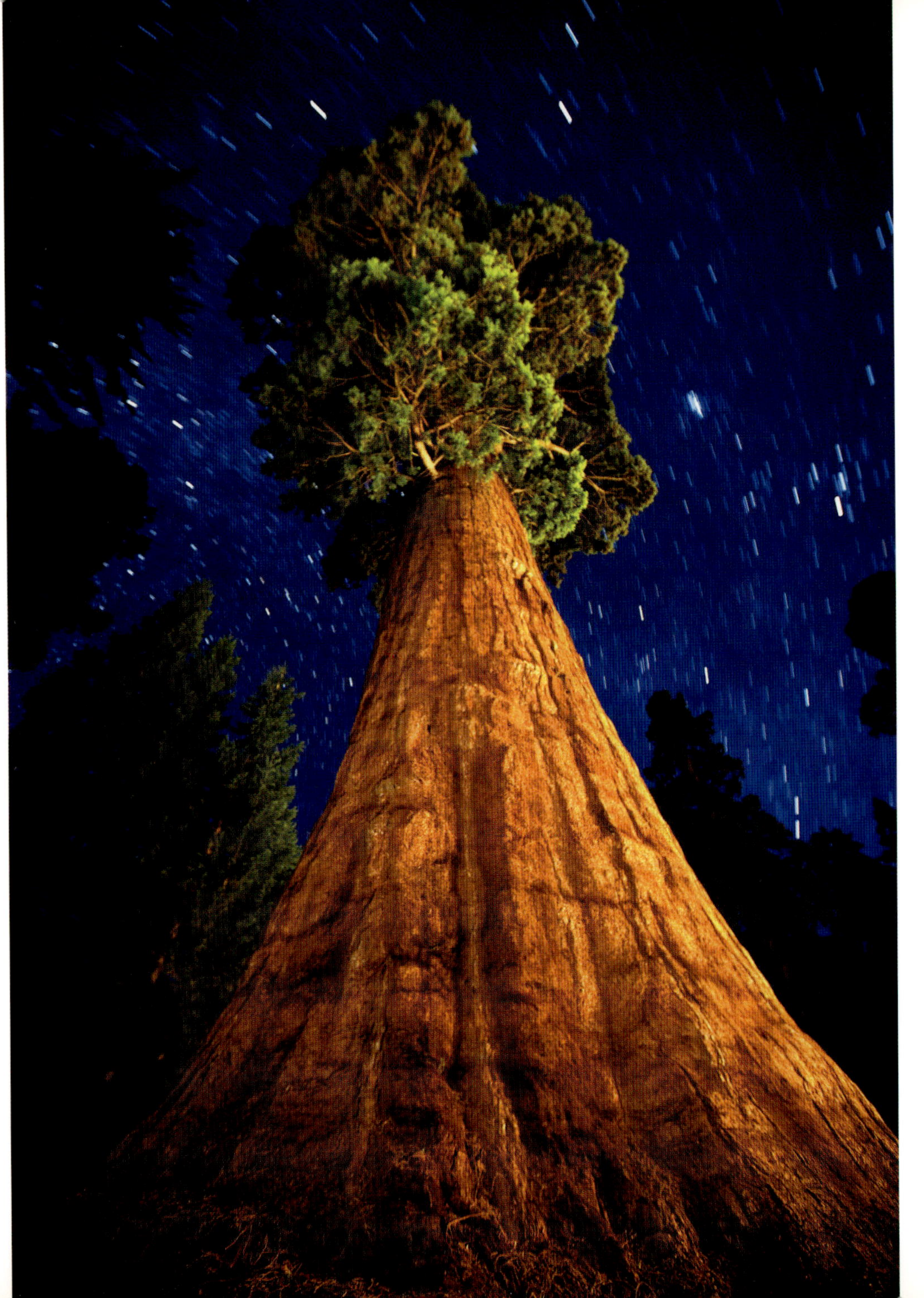

LEFT: **Sequoia & Kings Canyon National Parks, California**
A giant sequoia against the backdrop of a starry night sky.

RIGHT: **Arches National Park, Utah**
Balanced Rock at last light.

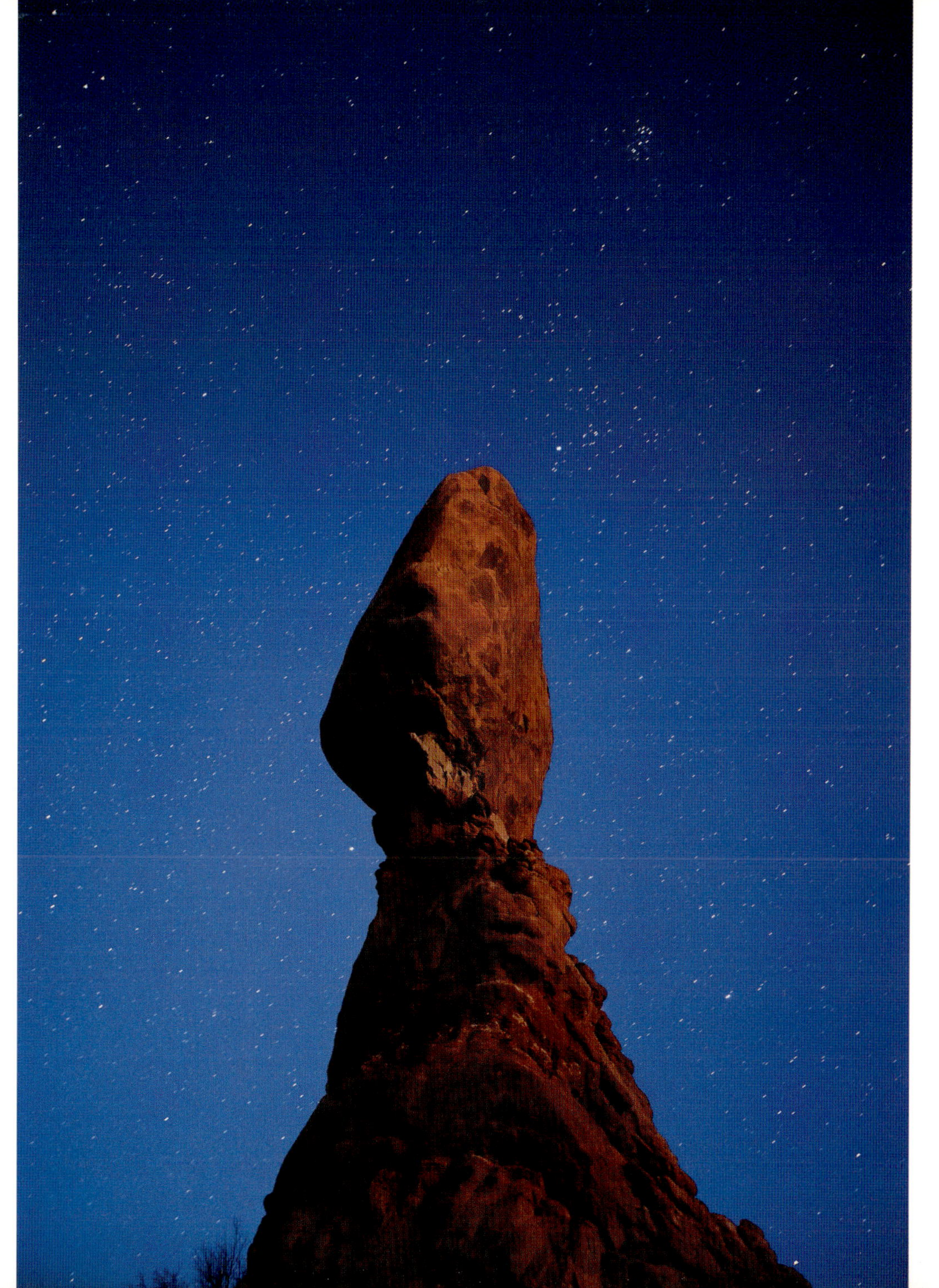

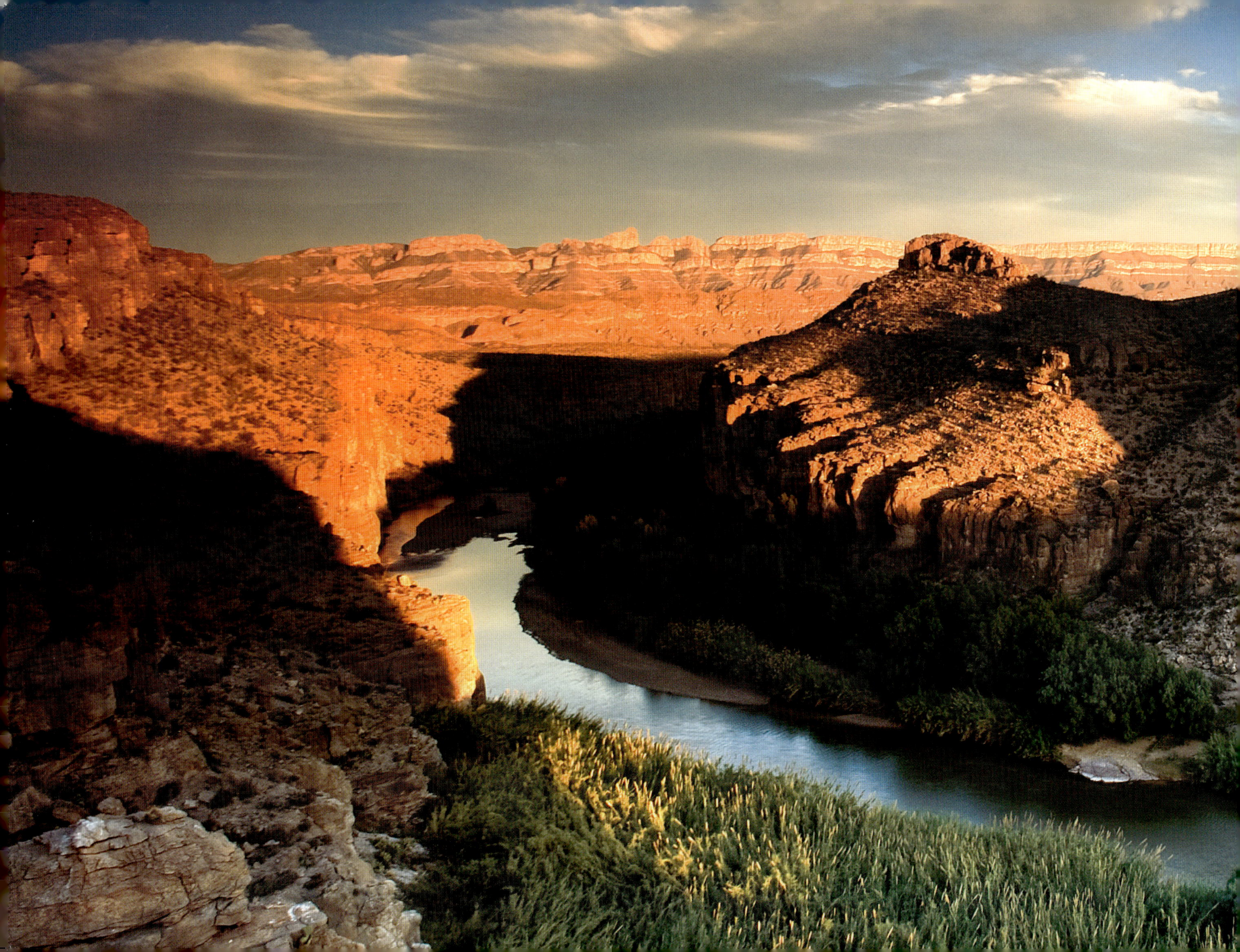

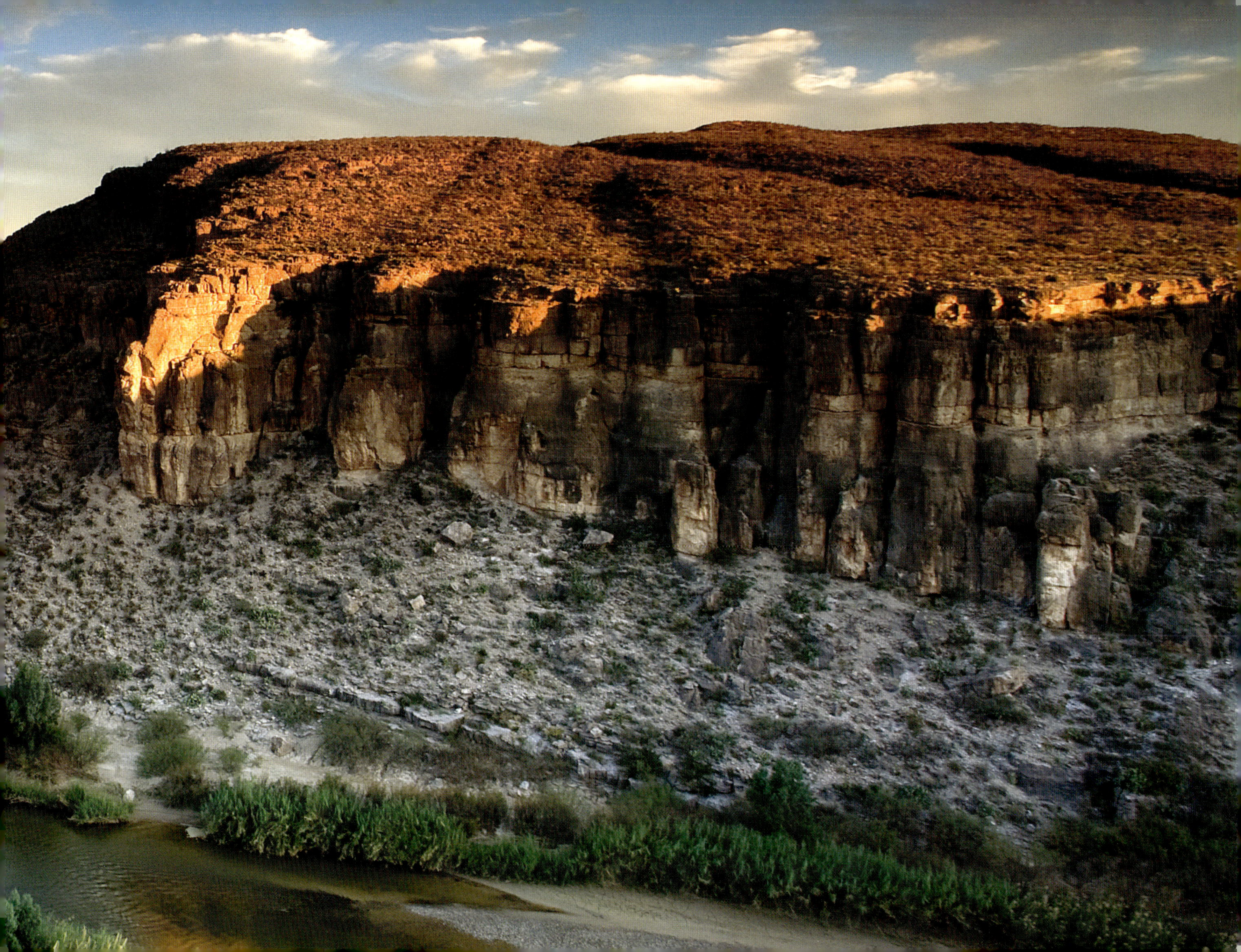

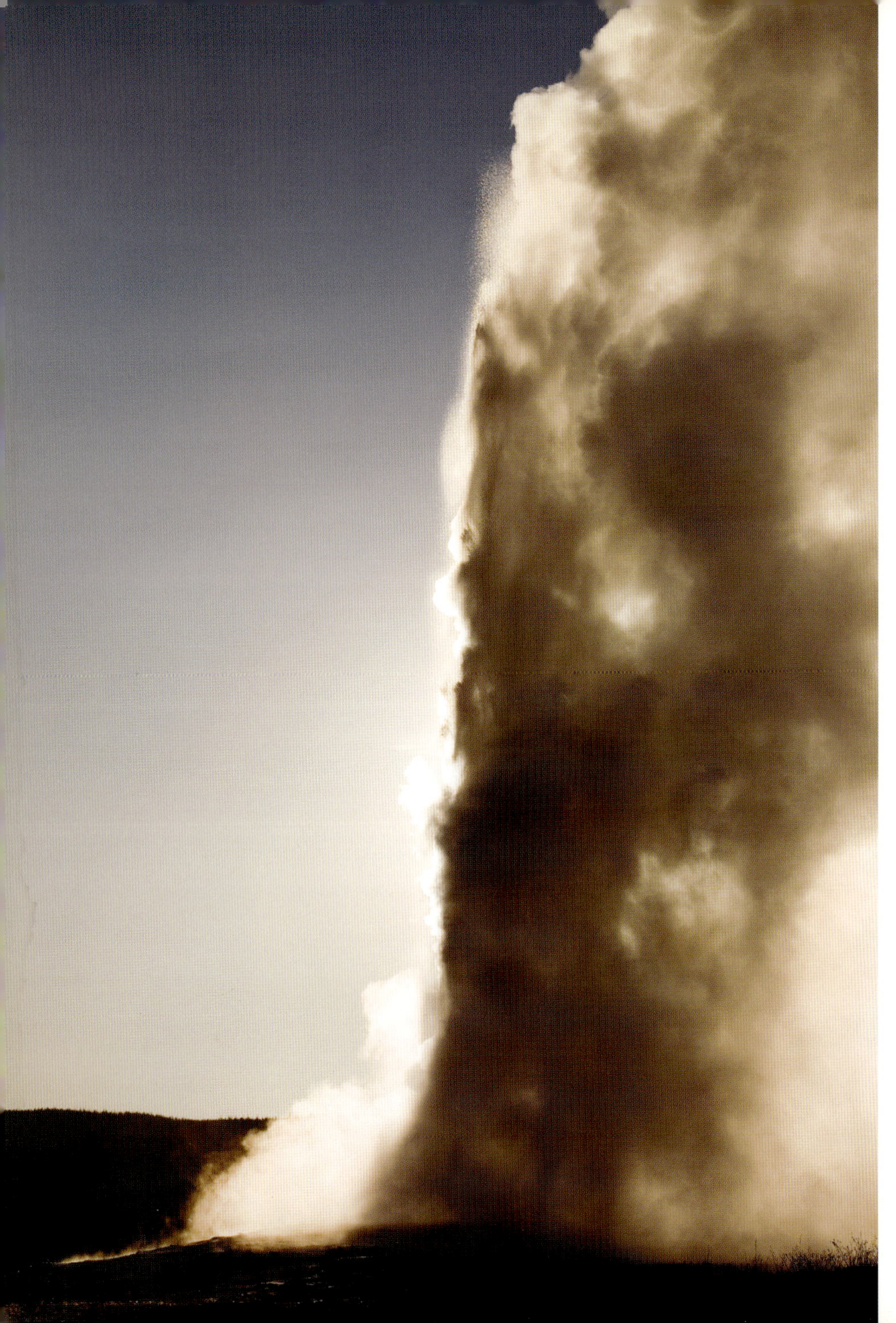

PAGES 160/161: RIGHT: **Big Bend National Park, Texas**
View of the Rio Grande, which separates Mexico (on the right) from the United States (on the left). In the distance, the Sierra del Carmen Mountains are visible.

LEFT: **Yellowstone National Park; Wyoming, Montana, Idaho**
Last light on Old Faithful.

RIGHT: **Golden Gate National Recreation Area, California**
A man looks out over the Pacific from the Marin Headlands with Point Bonita Lighthouse in the background.

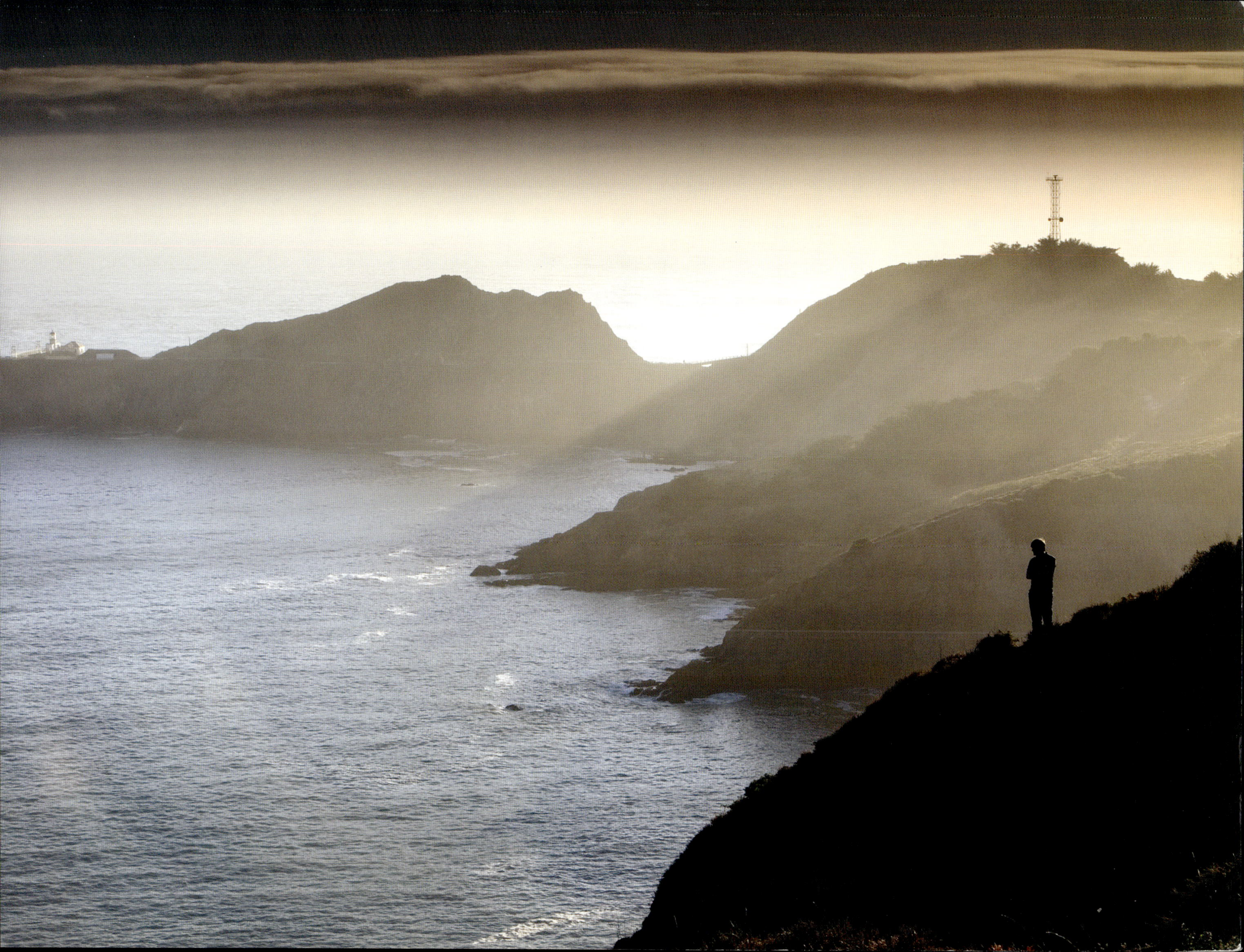

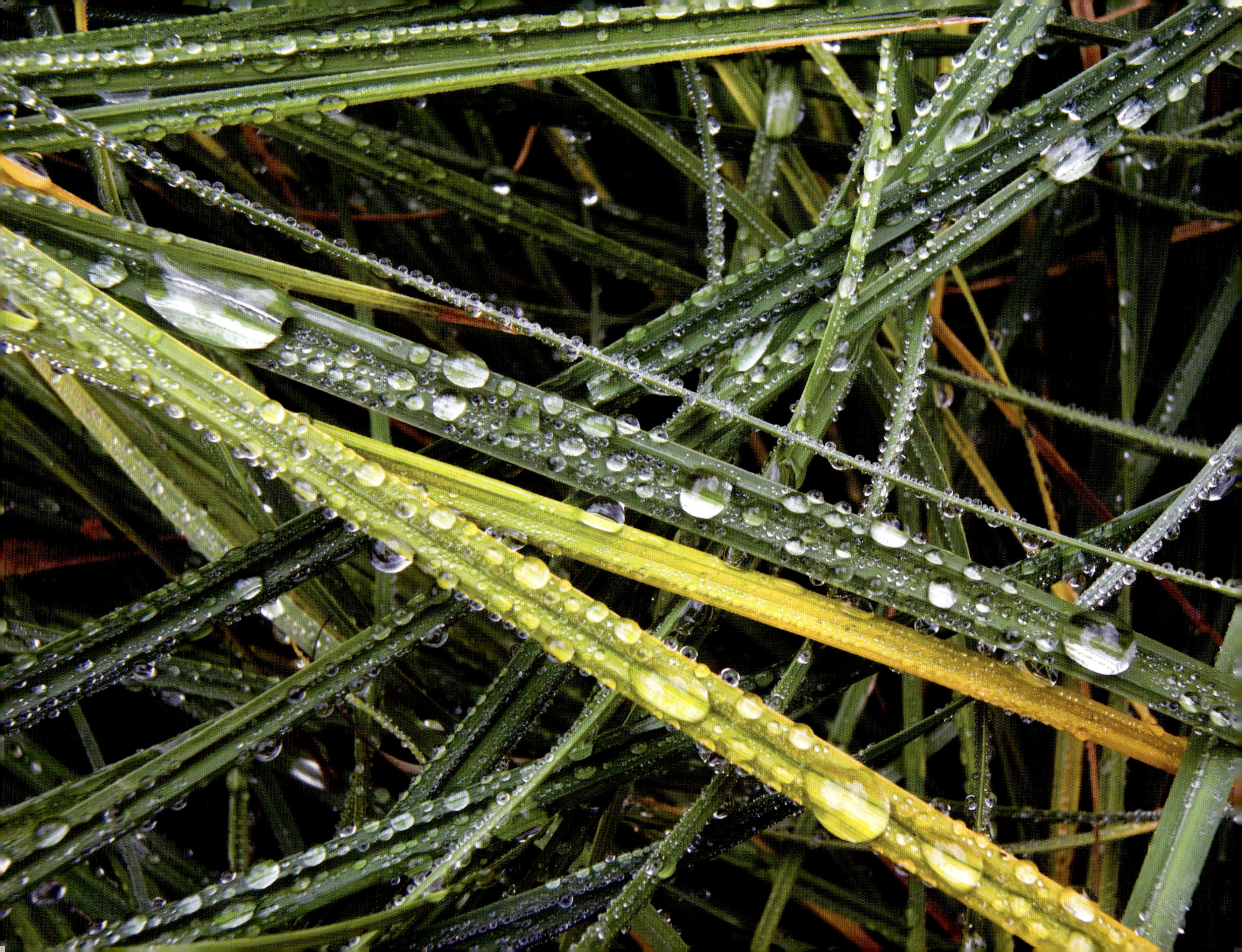

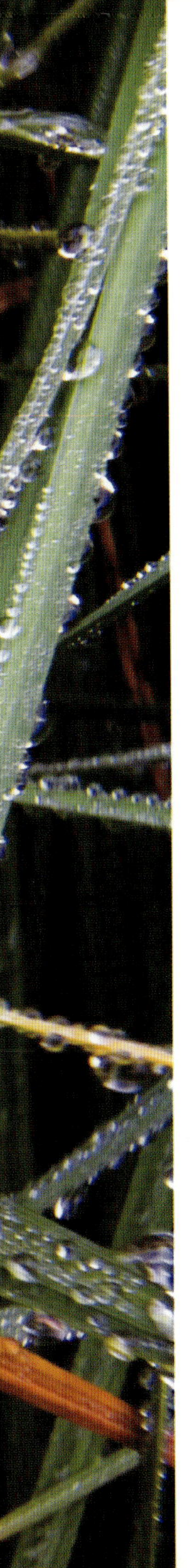

LEFT: **Yosemite National Park, California**
Blades of grass glisten with water drops after a light rain.

RIGHT: **Yosemite National Park, California**
A fiddleneck glows in the warm sun.

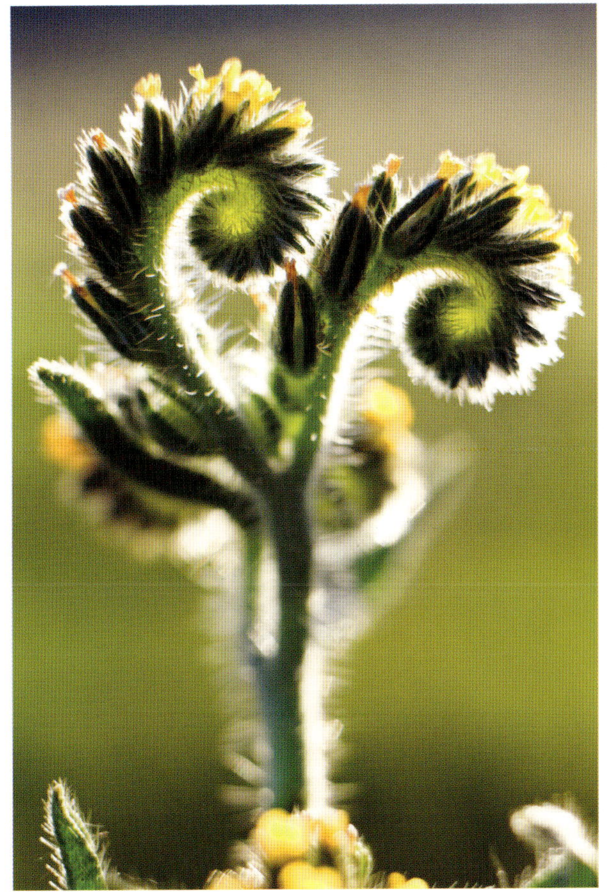

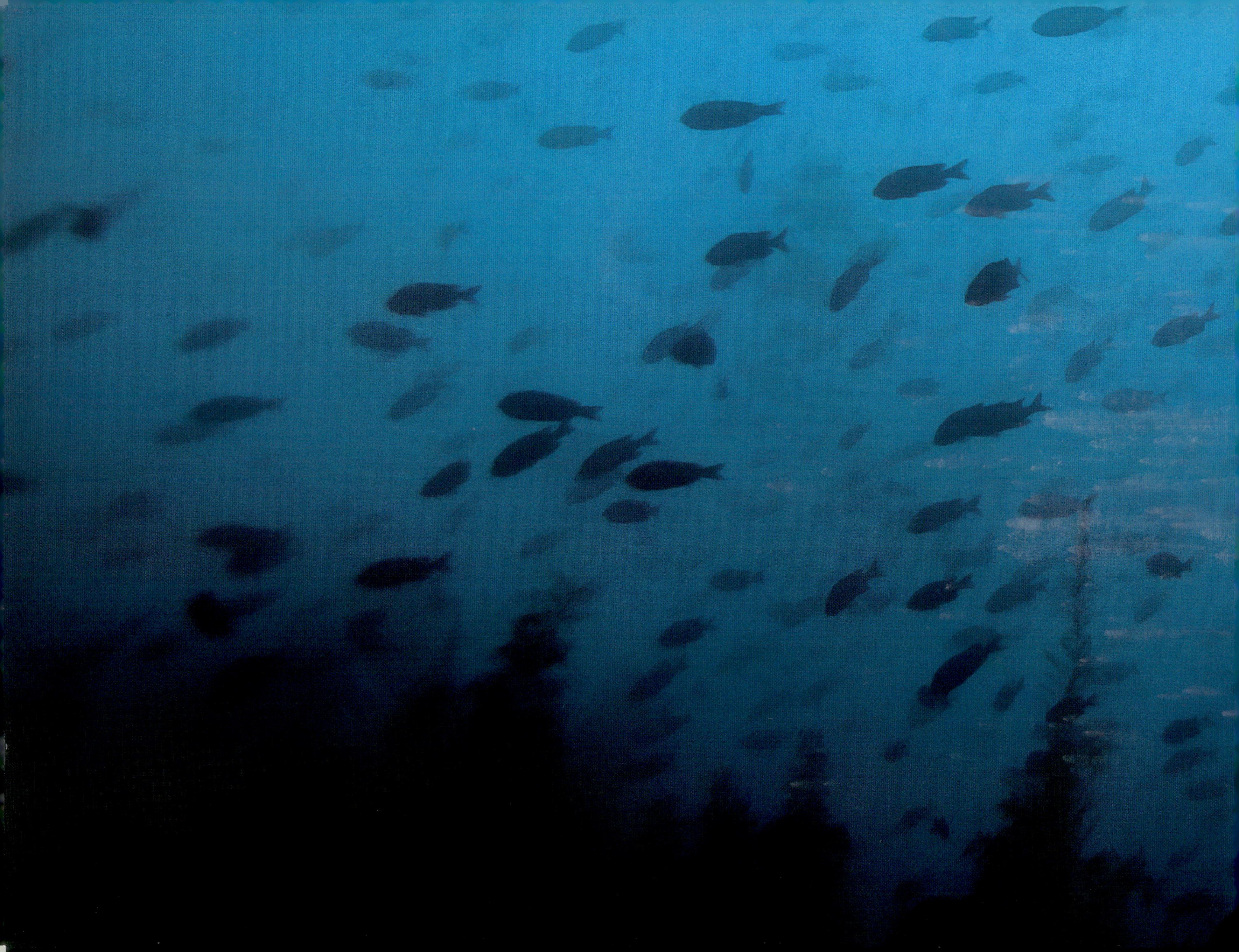

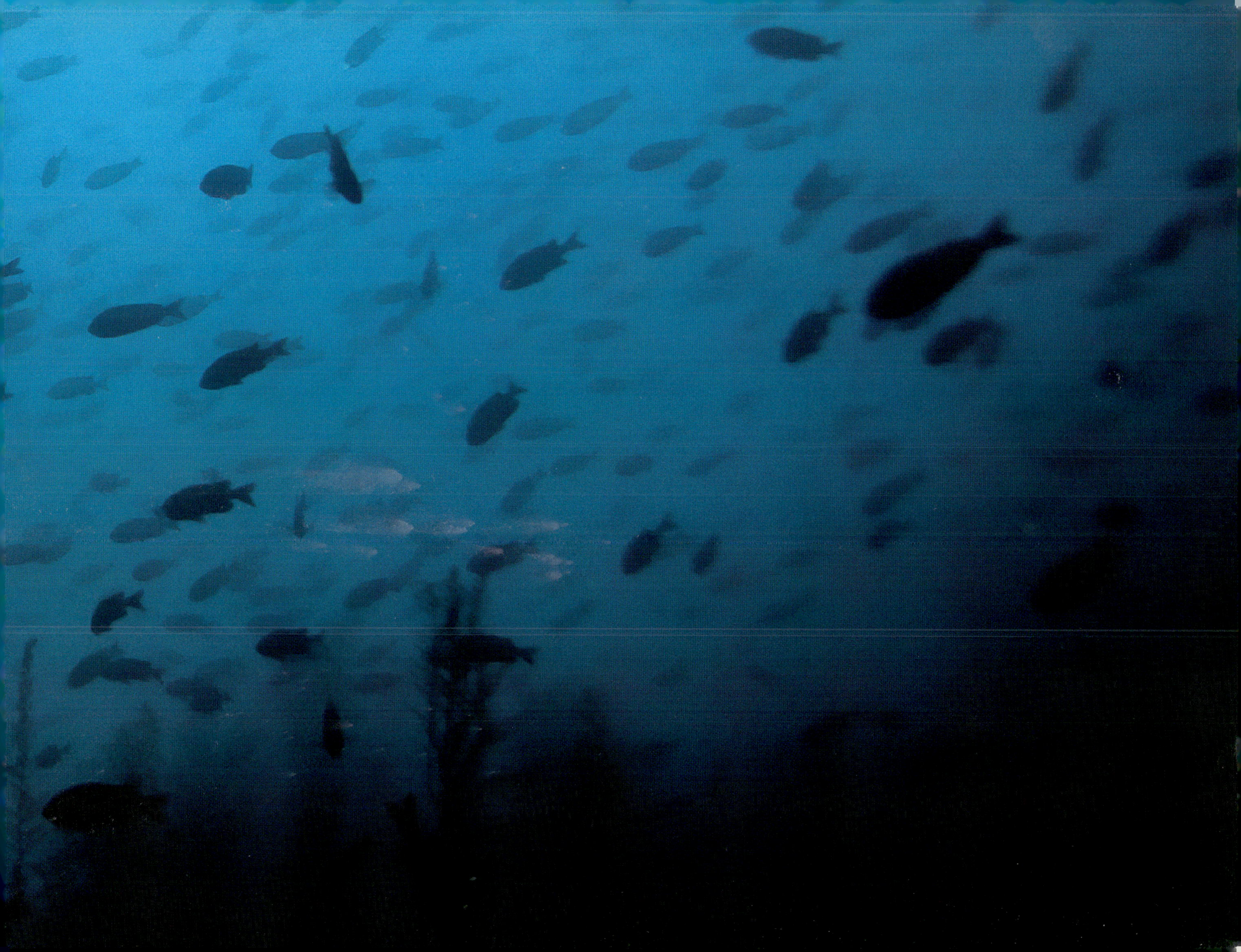

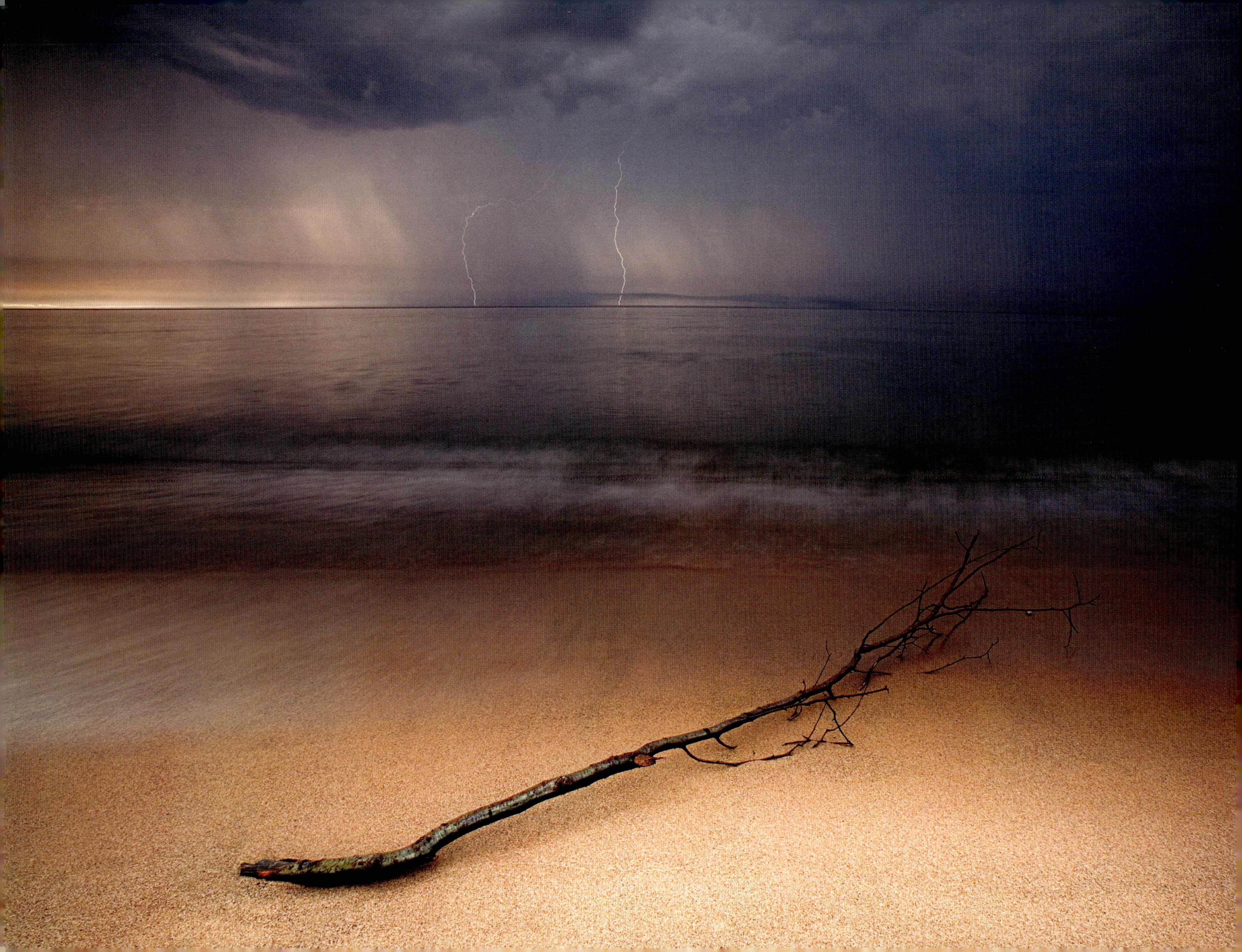

PAGES 166/167: **Channel Islands National Park, California**
Fish are abundant in the clear waters of the marine sanctuary.

LEFT: **Apostle Islands National Lakeshore, Wisconsin**
Lightning dances across the horizon of Lake Superior.

RIGHT: **Mount Rainier National Park, Washington**
Detail of mushrooms growing under a log in the moisture-rich forests of the park.

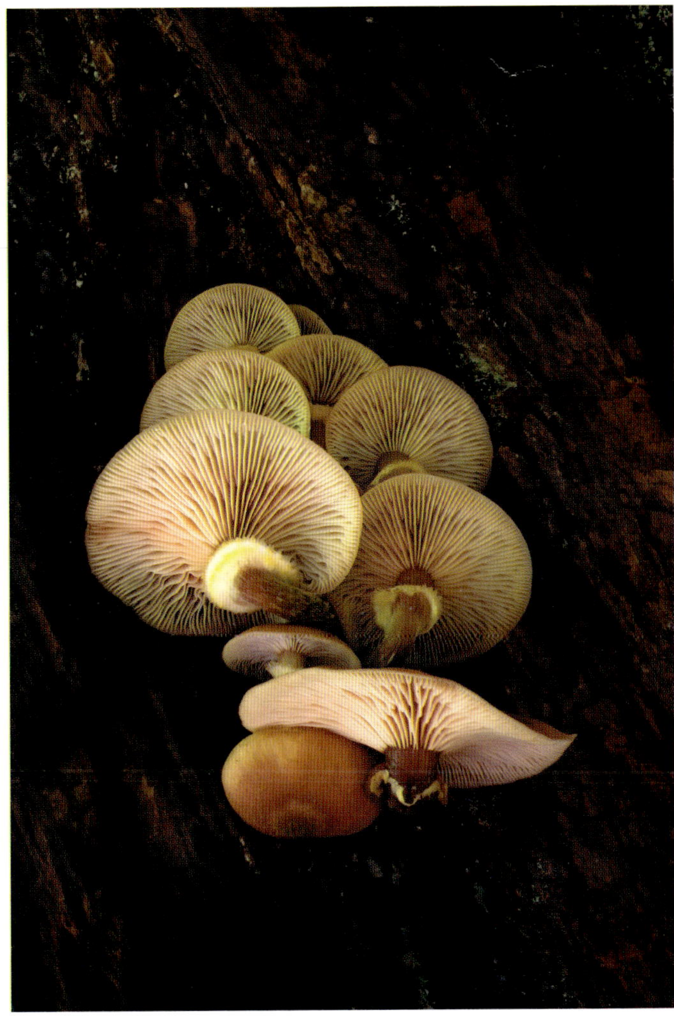

RIGHT: **Glacier National Park, Montana**
Wildflowers.

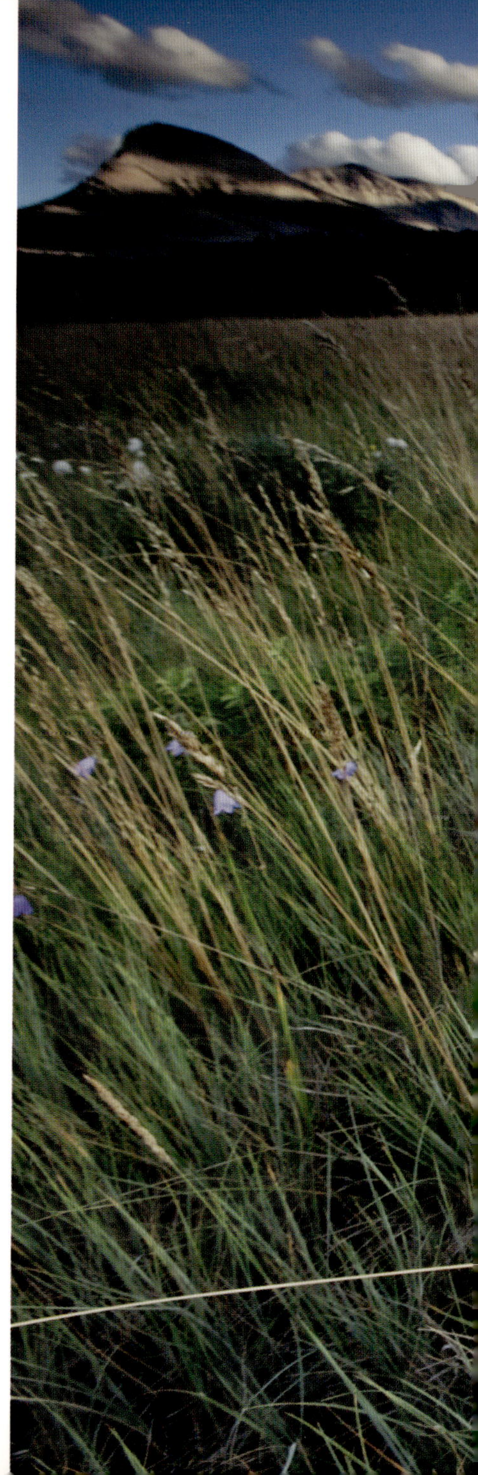

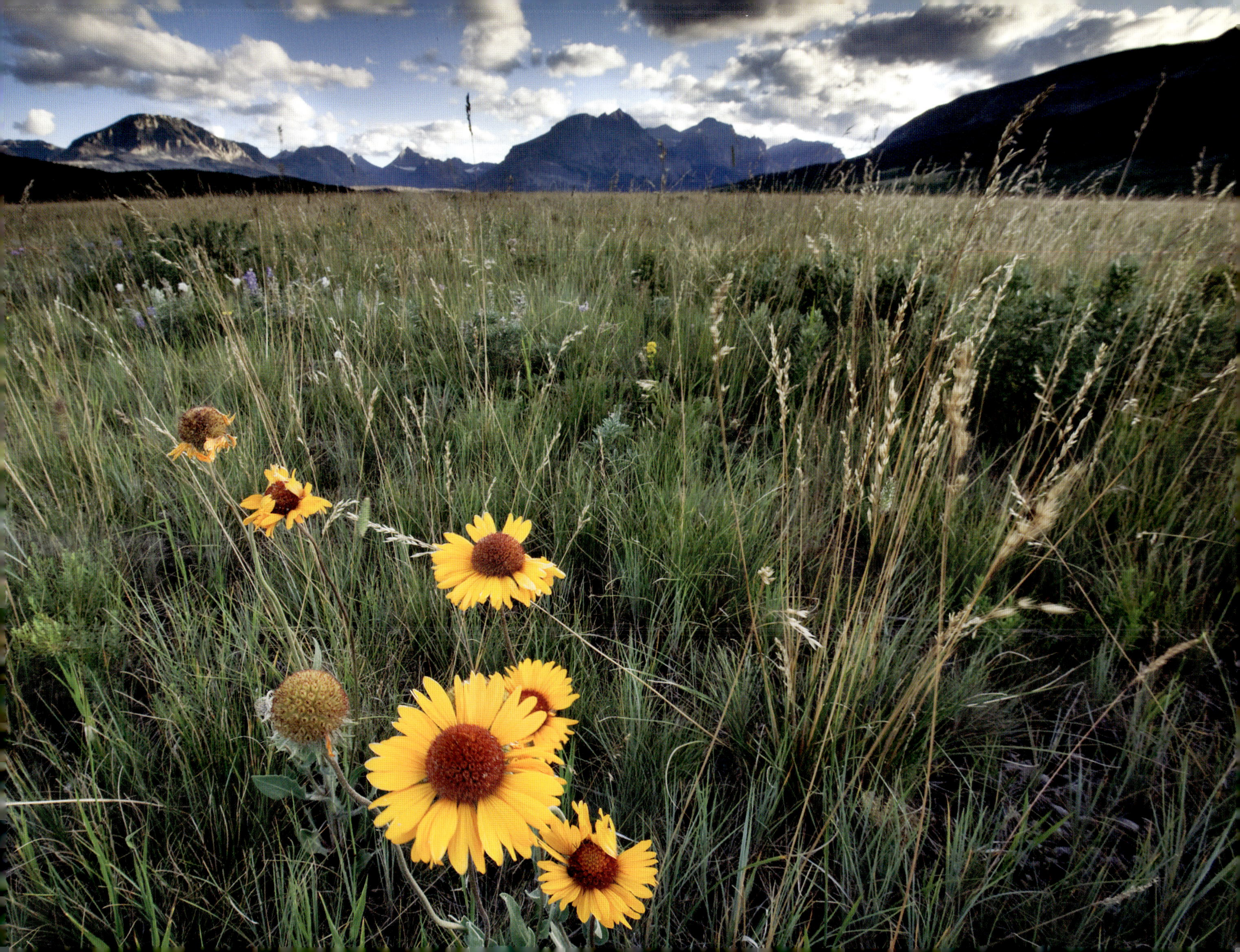

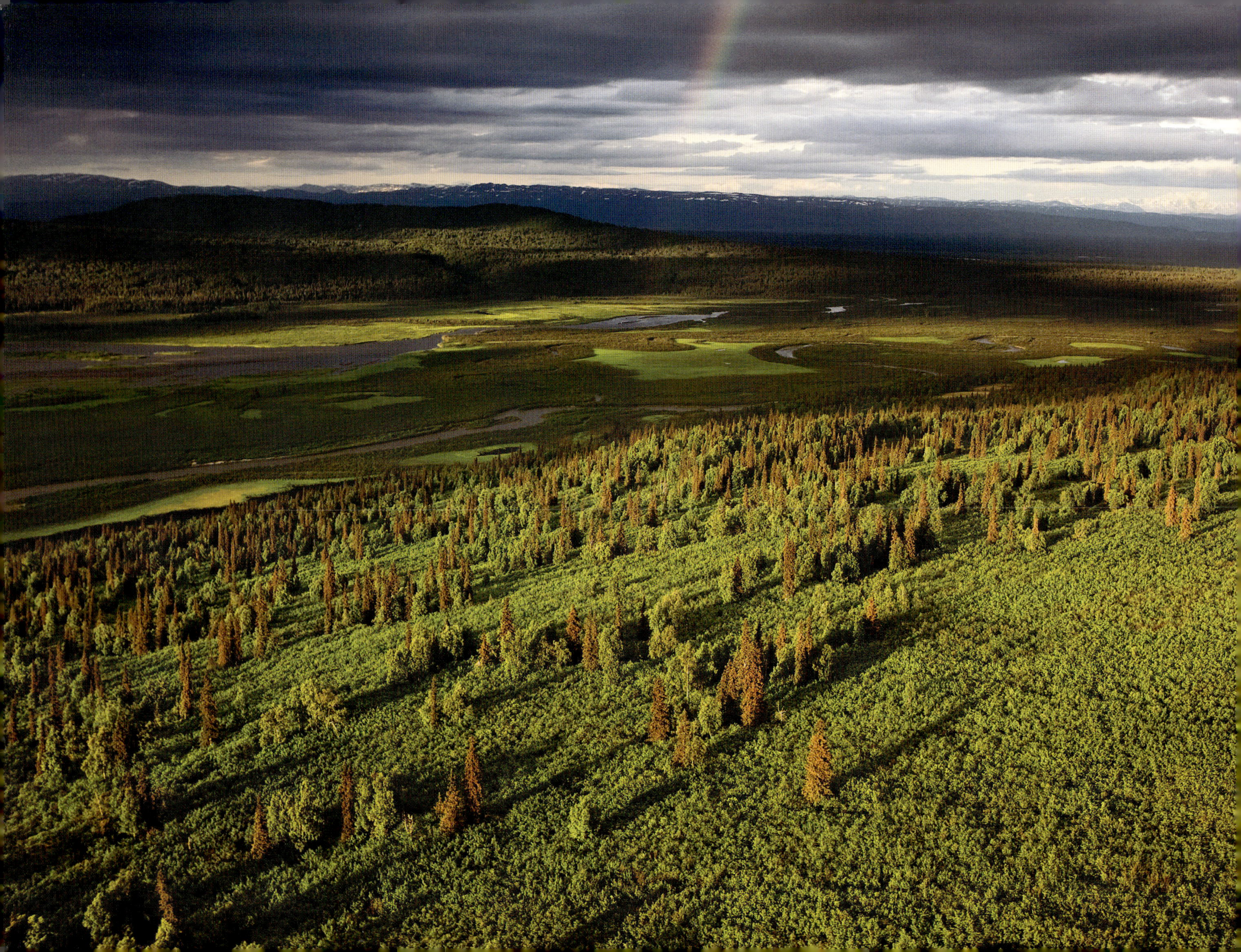

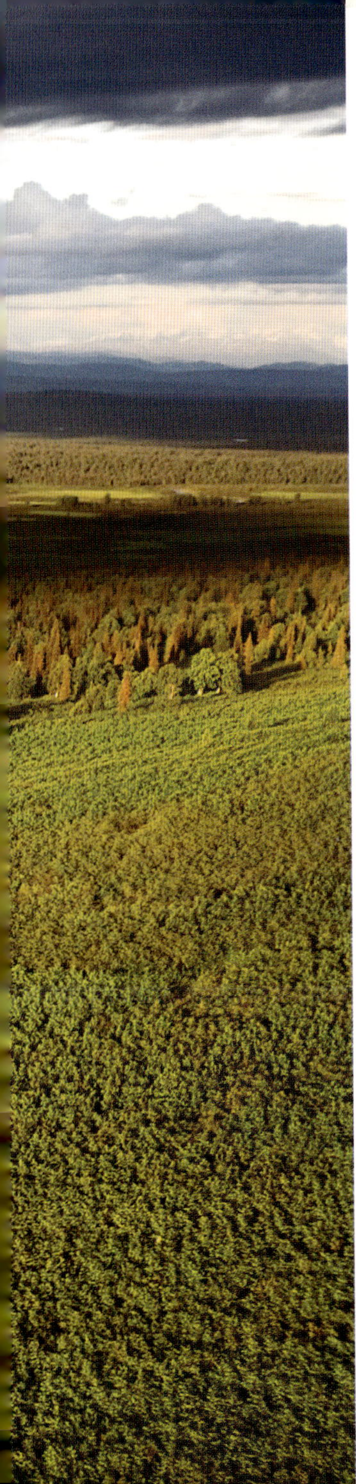

LEFT: **Denali National Park & Preserve, Alaska**

Alaska is not like the rest of the United States, nor are its national parks like those found in the lower forty-eight states. While places like Yellowstone are rugged and remote, its wildness pales in comparison to that of Denali. This place is the epitome of wilderness—it is the American West as it was a thousand years ago. Salmon still clog the rivers, bears roam the plains, and mountains are still being born. It is, therefore, imperative that we always remember this and recognize it so that we can take the lead in protecting these rare places forever, as less and less of them exist with each passing day. We need to remember that our national parks should not be the only safe havens, but that they should be seen as examples of effective conservation. This model needs to extend beyond the boundaries of our Denalis and Yellowstones and into the heart of every wild land.

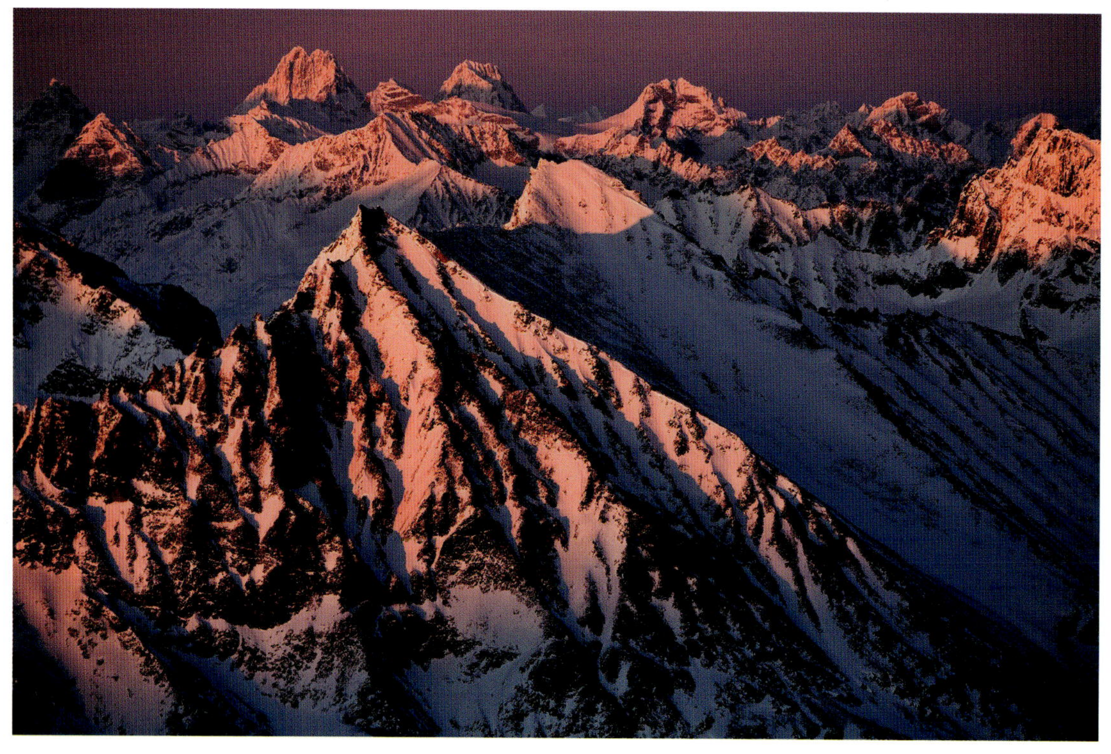

ABOVE: **Lake Clark National Park & Preserve, Alaska**
Aerial views of the Aleutian Mountain Range and the Chigmit Mountains at last light.

RIGHT: **Death Valley National Park, California**
A dry lake bed bathed in sunset light. I was driving into the park, and it was nearing dark. As a photographer, sunset is, for me, an adrenaline rush of colorful, contrasting light. But by the time I had reached this dry lake bed, the sun had already moved behind the mountains. I thought I had missed the best part of the day, but as is often the case, the best part of the day for me came later—in this case more than an hour after sunset. The ambient, warm light cast incredible pinks and reds across an otherwise pale, brown landscape.

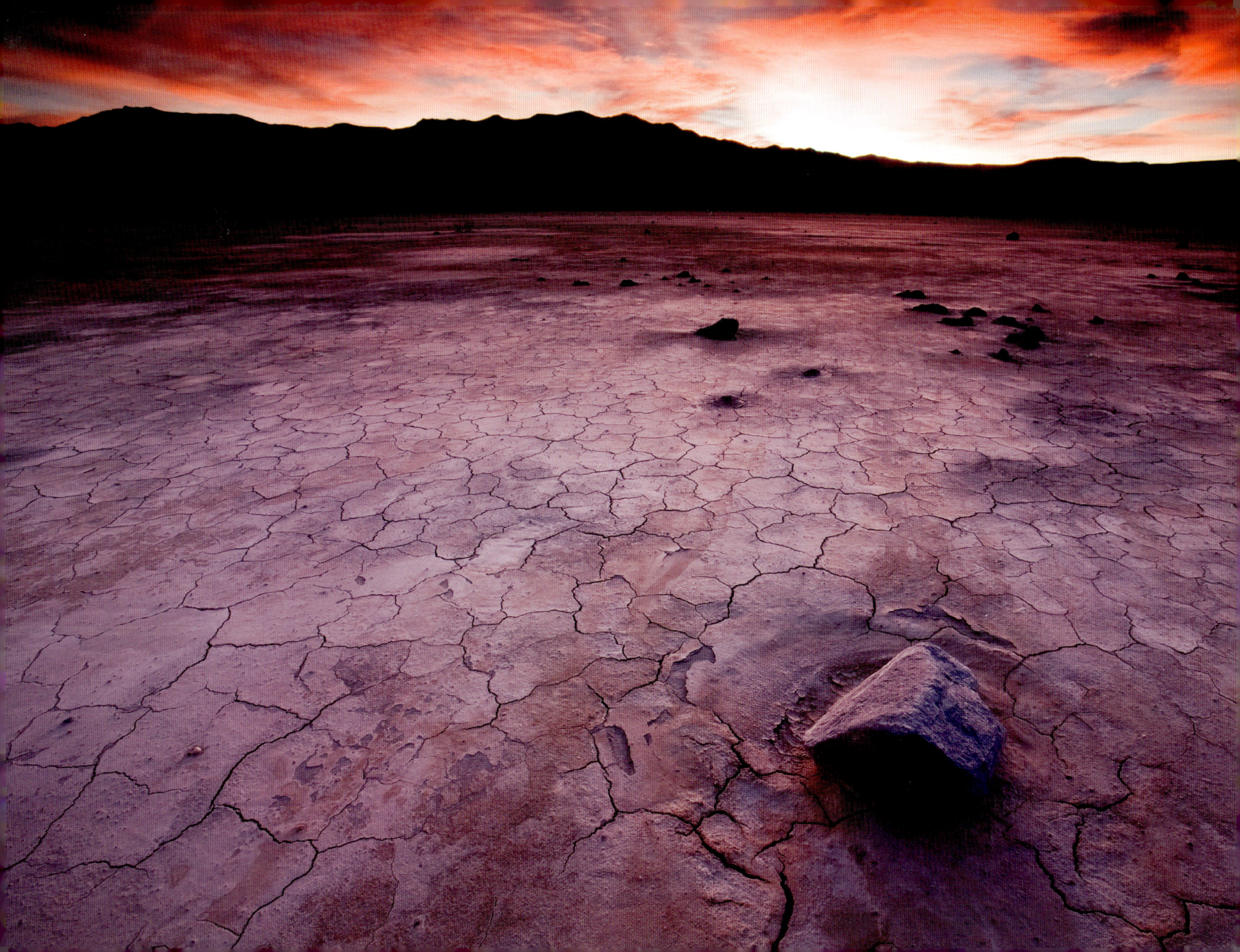

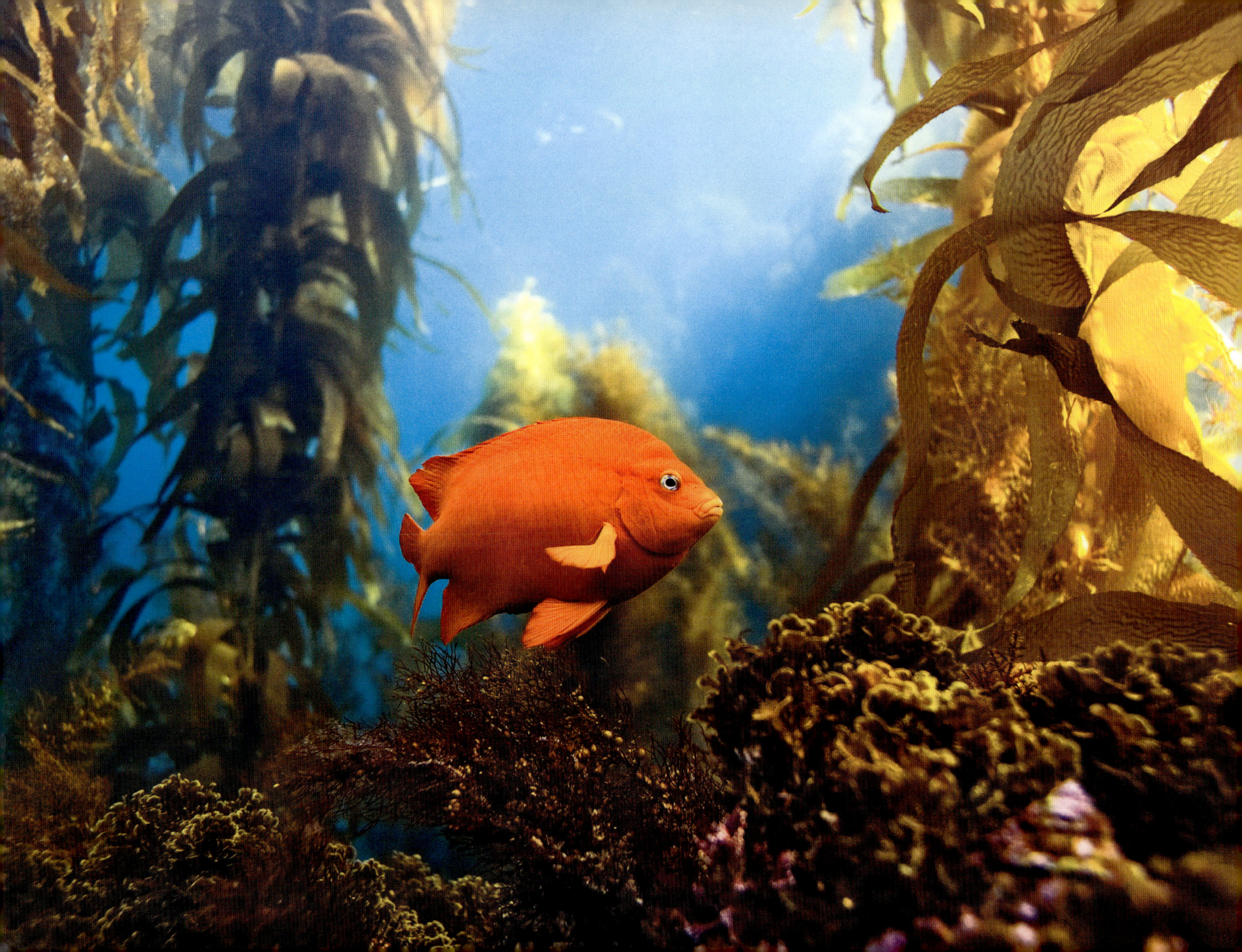

LEFT: **Channel Islands National Park, California**
A garibaldi swimming in the Channel Islands Marine Sanctuary.

RIGHT: **Channel Islands National Park, California**
A giant kelp forest is part of the marine sanctuary of Santa Cruz Island.

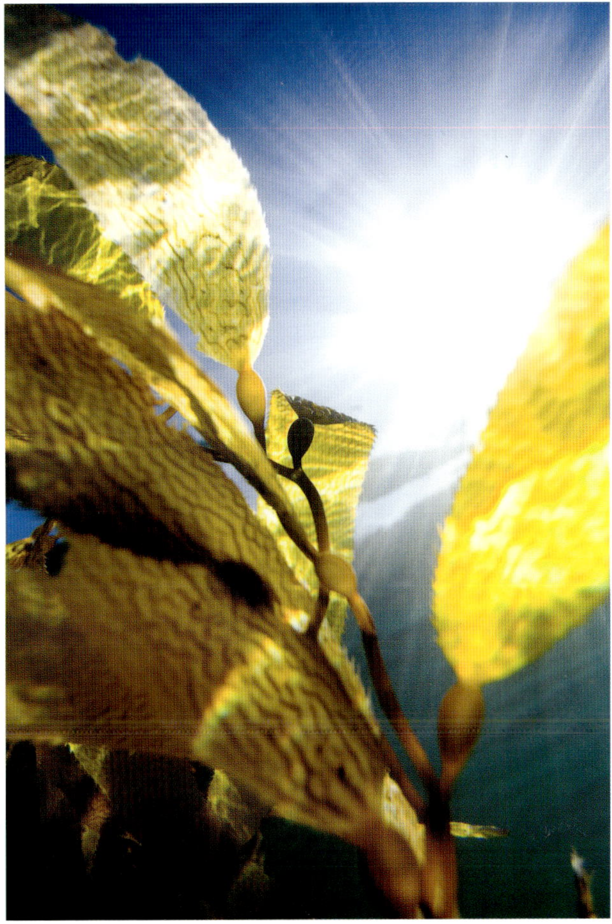

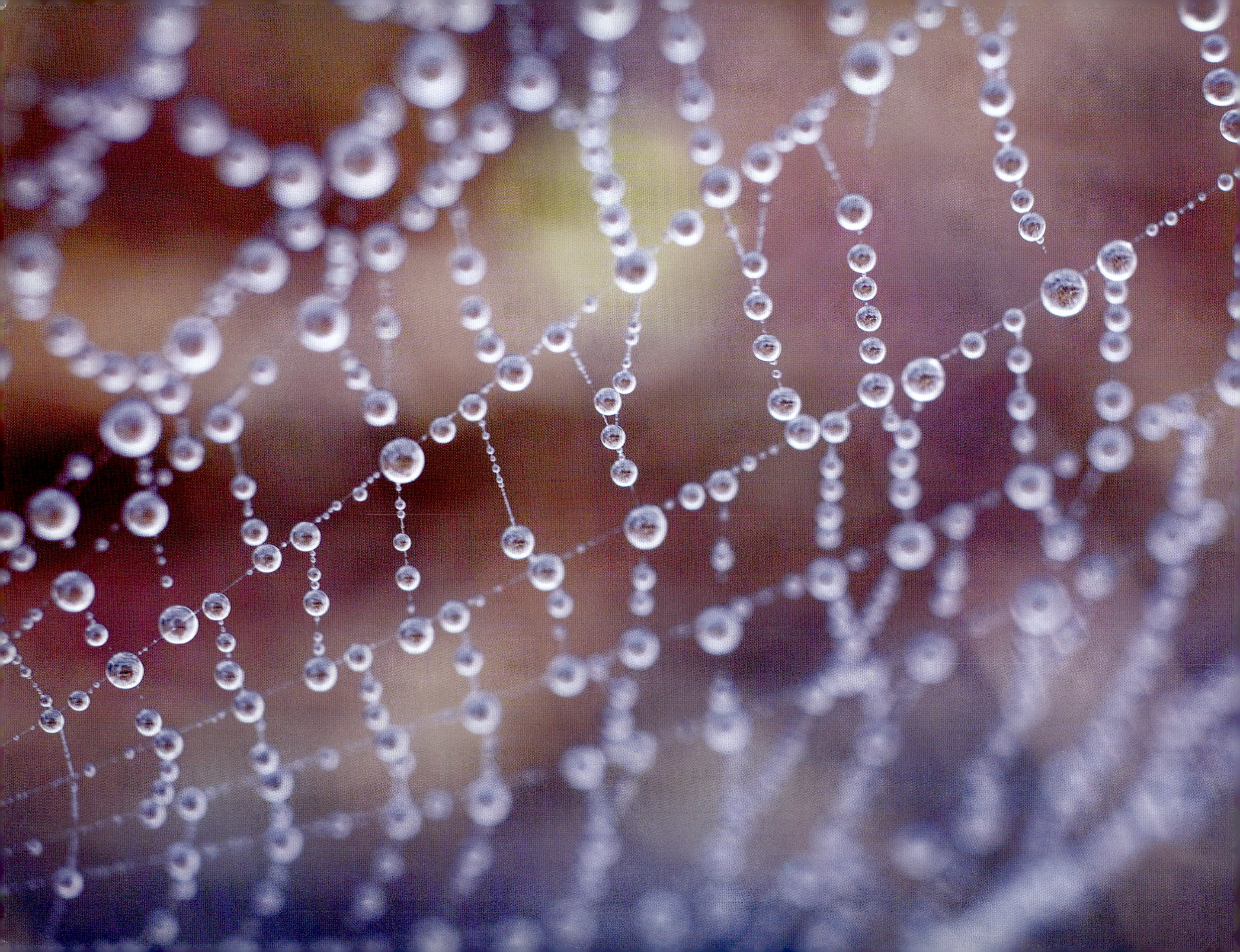

LEFT: **Channel Islands National Park, California**
Moisture from morning fog clings to a spider web on Santa Cruz Island.

RIGHT: **Channel Islands National Park, California**
Detail of a Santa Cruz Island morning glory.

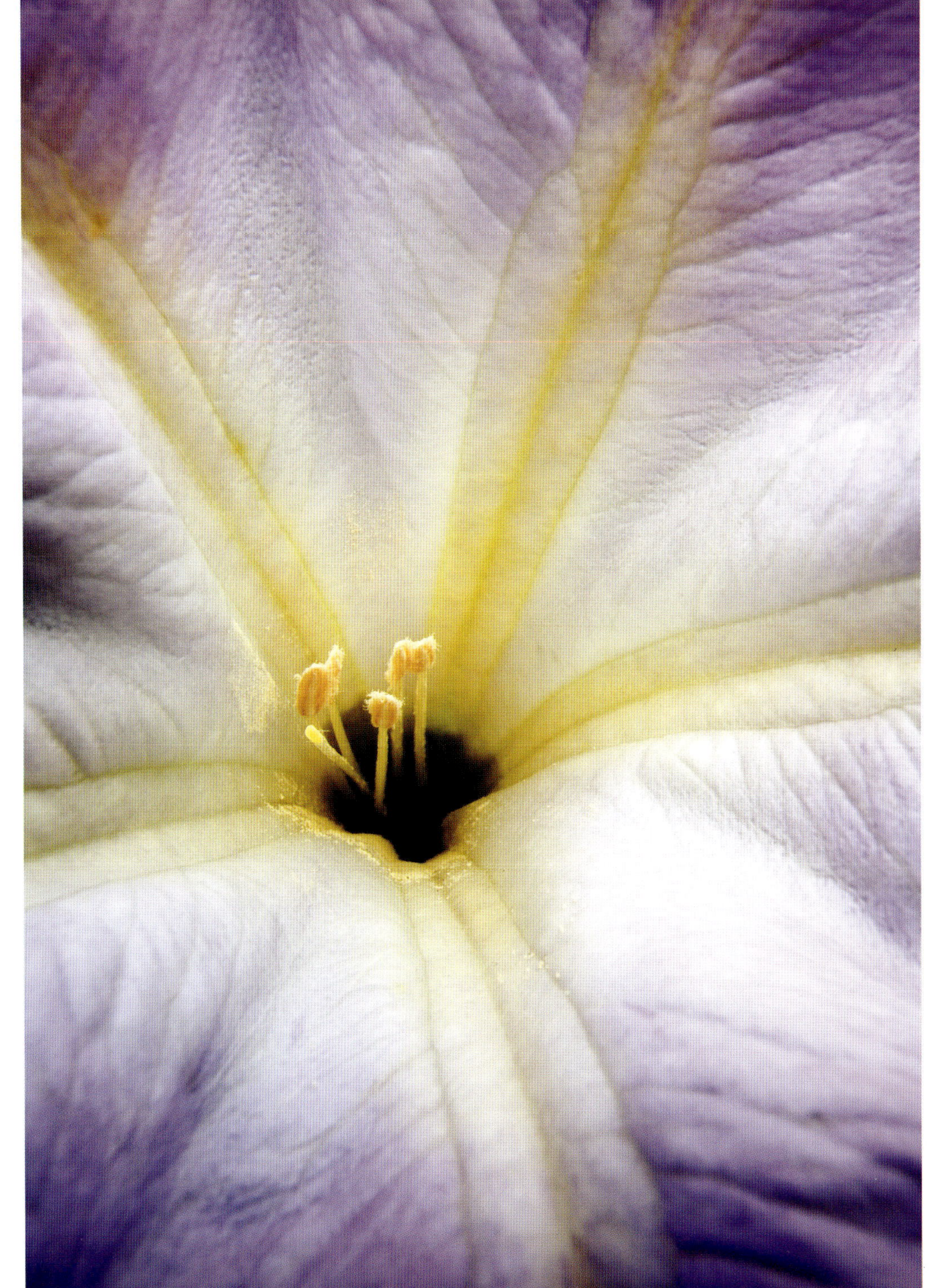

RIGHT: **Grand Teton National Park, Wyoming**
The sun peeks through storm clouds over the Snake River.

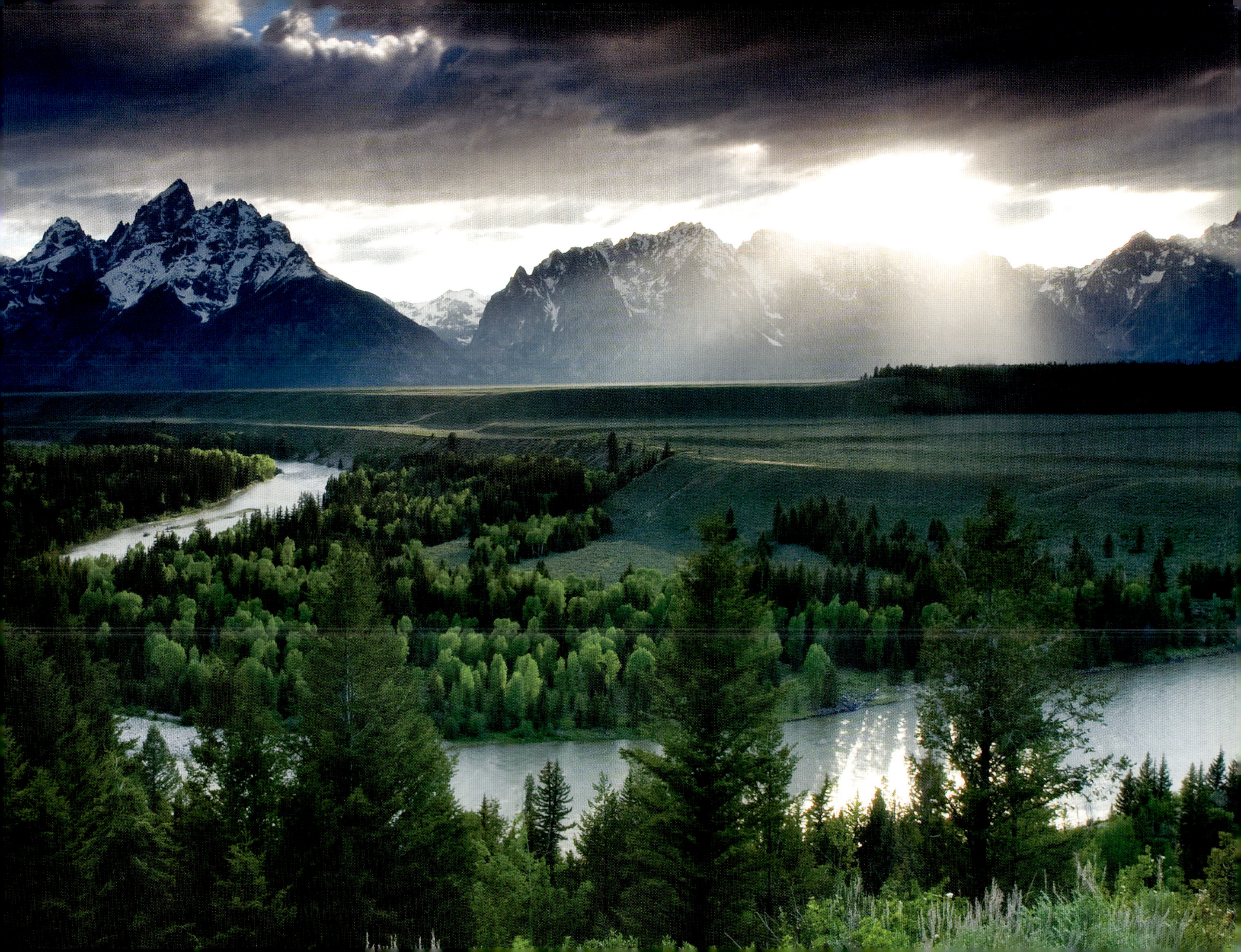

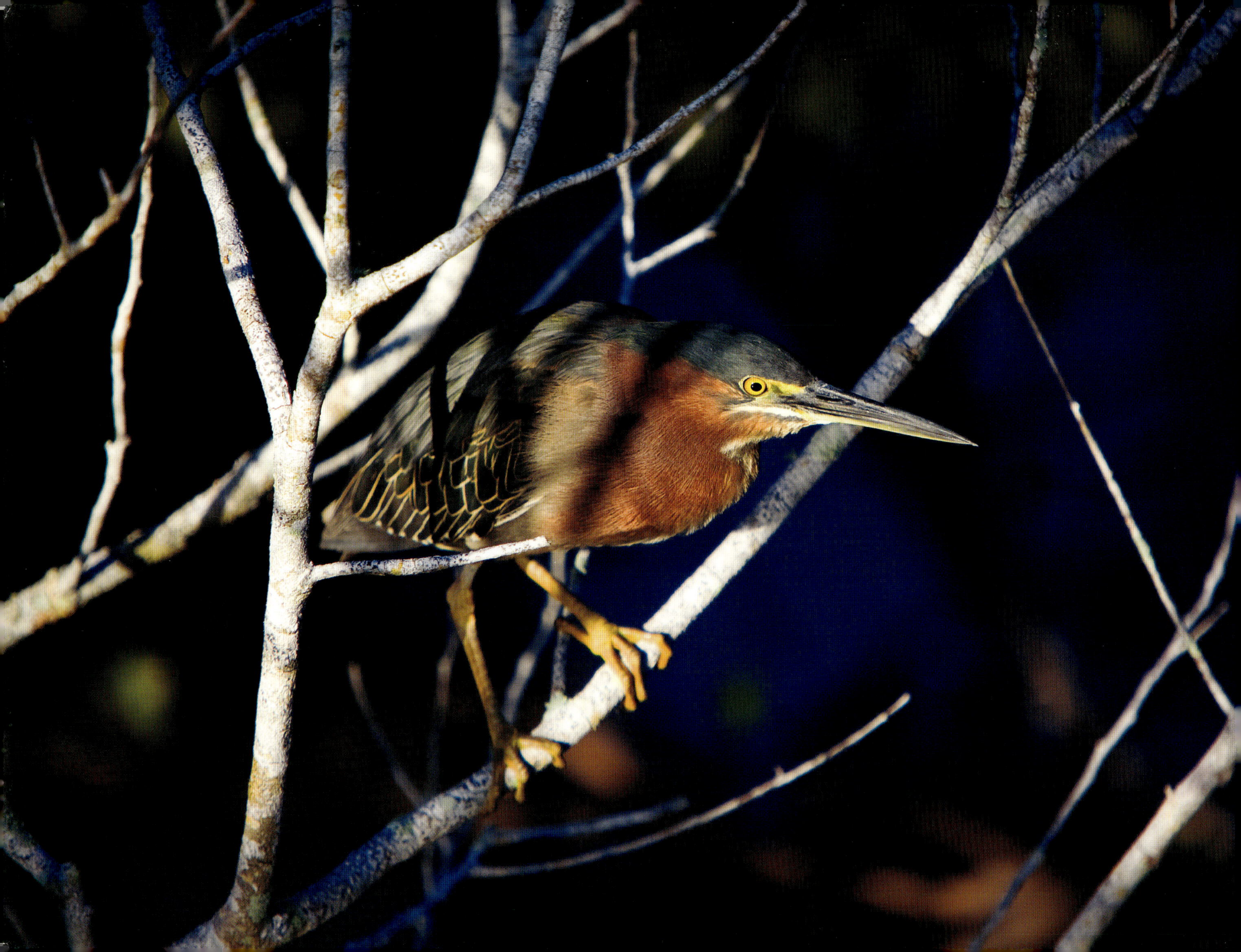

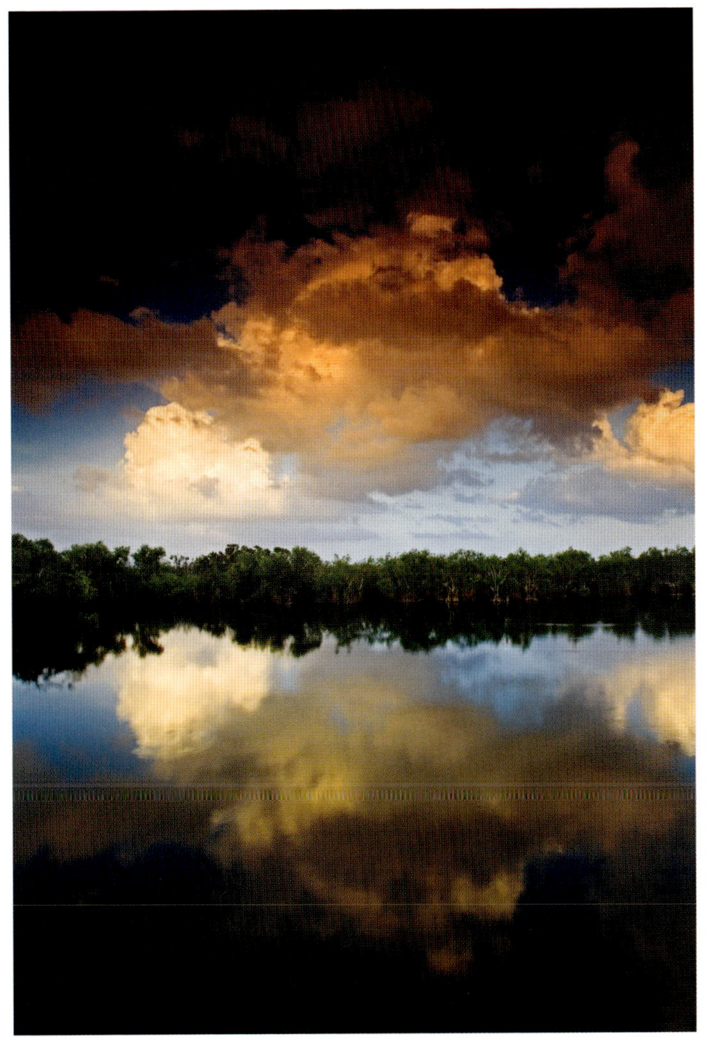

LEFT: **Everglades National Park, Florida**
A green heron keeps a watchful lookout.

RIGHT: **Everglades National Park, Florida**
Storm clouds gather over the wetlands and mangrove swamps.

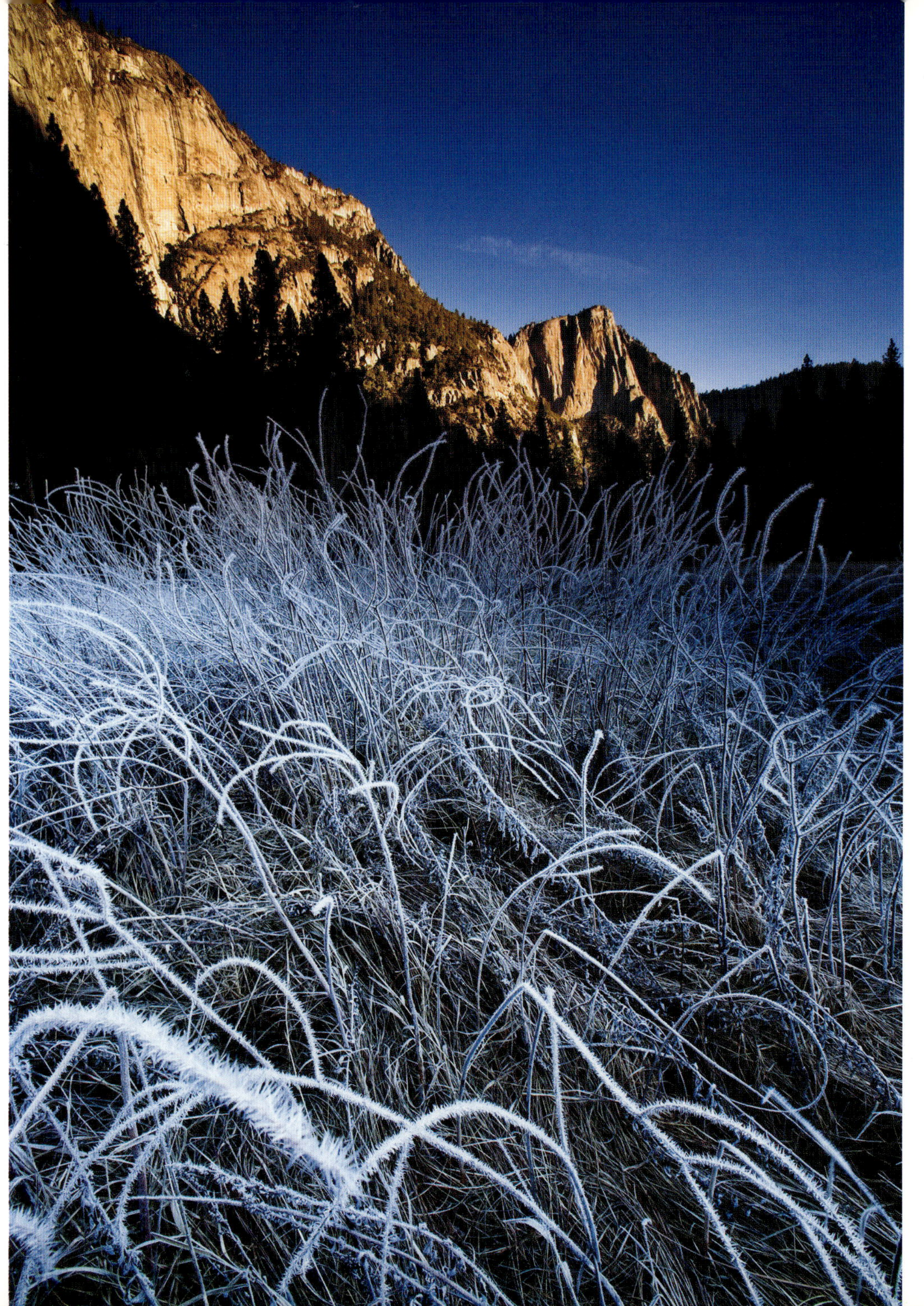

LEFT: **Yosemite National Park, California**
Frozen stems of meadow grass just before the morning sun hits them.

RIGHT: **Yosemite National Park, California**
Veiny details on a leaf frozen in morning dew.

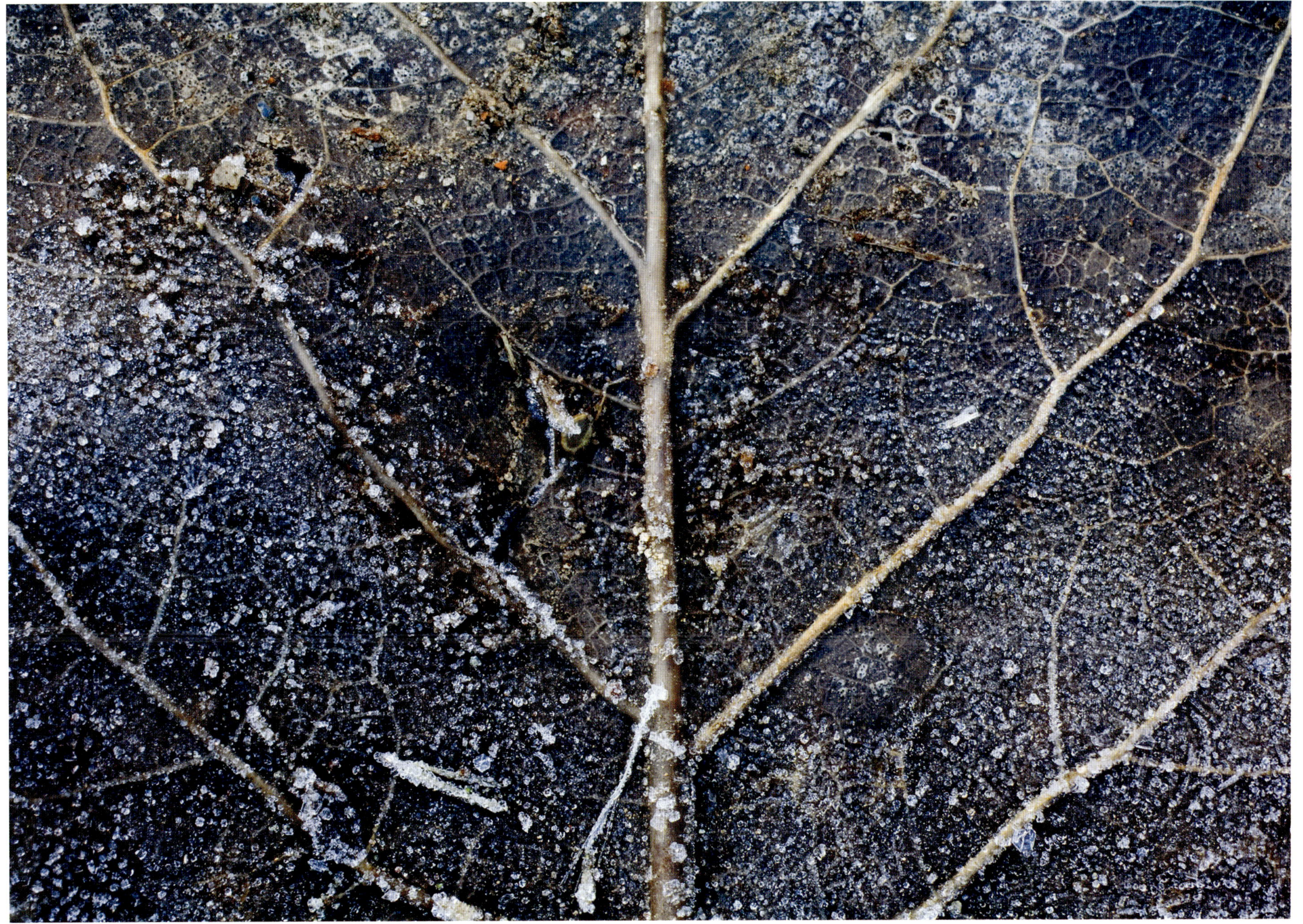

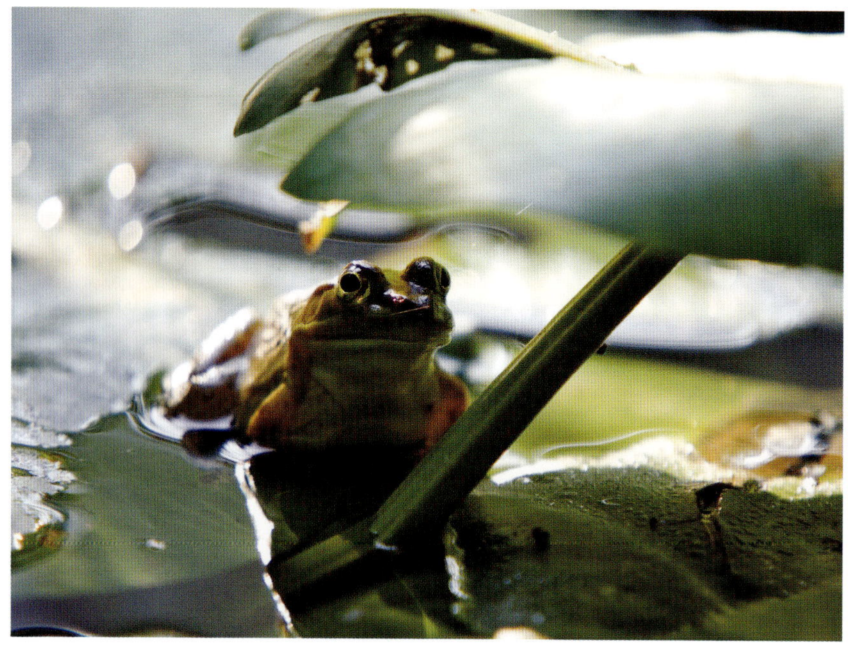

ABOVE: **Acadia National Park, Maine**
A bullfrog sits on and under lily pads.

RIGHT: **Acadia National Park, Maine**
Spring rains and wildflowers.

PAGE 188: **Denali National Park & Preserve, Alaska**
Sunrise mixes with breaking clouds deep within the heart of the Alaska Range.

PAGE 189: **Yosemite National Park, California**
Snow mounds.

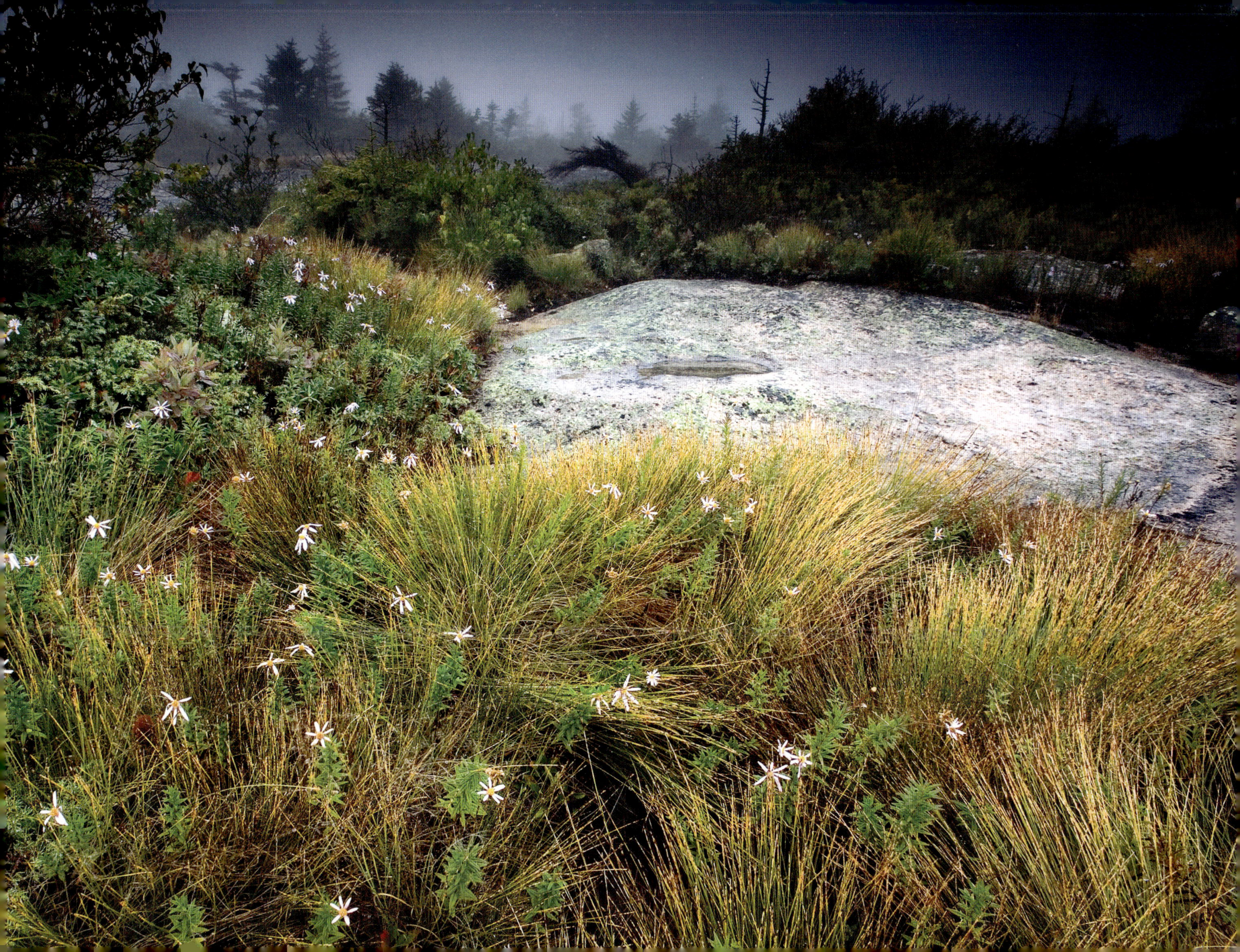

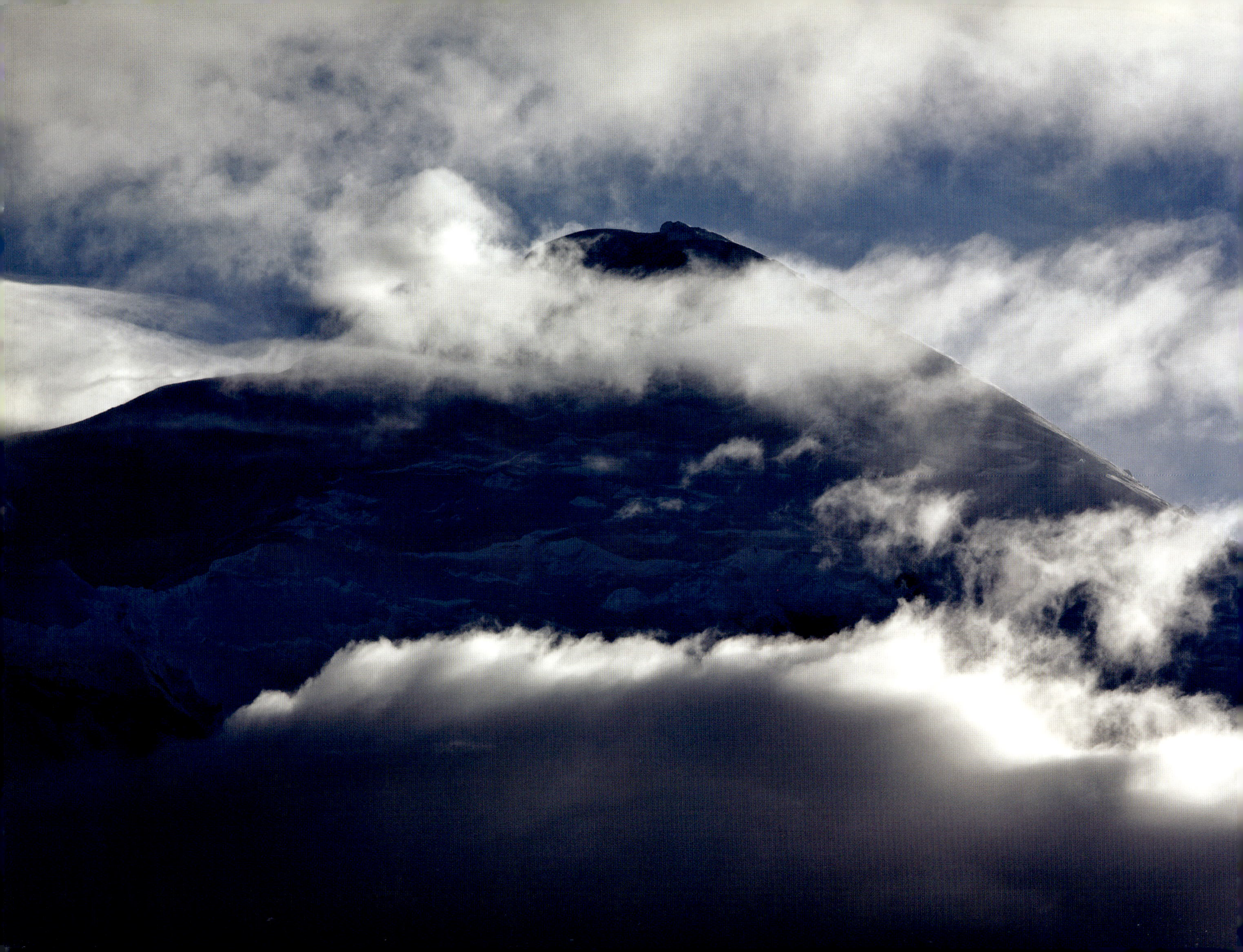

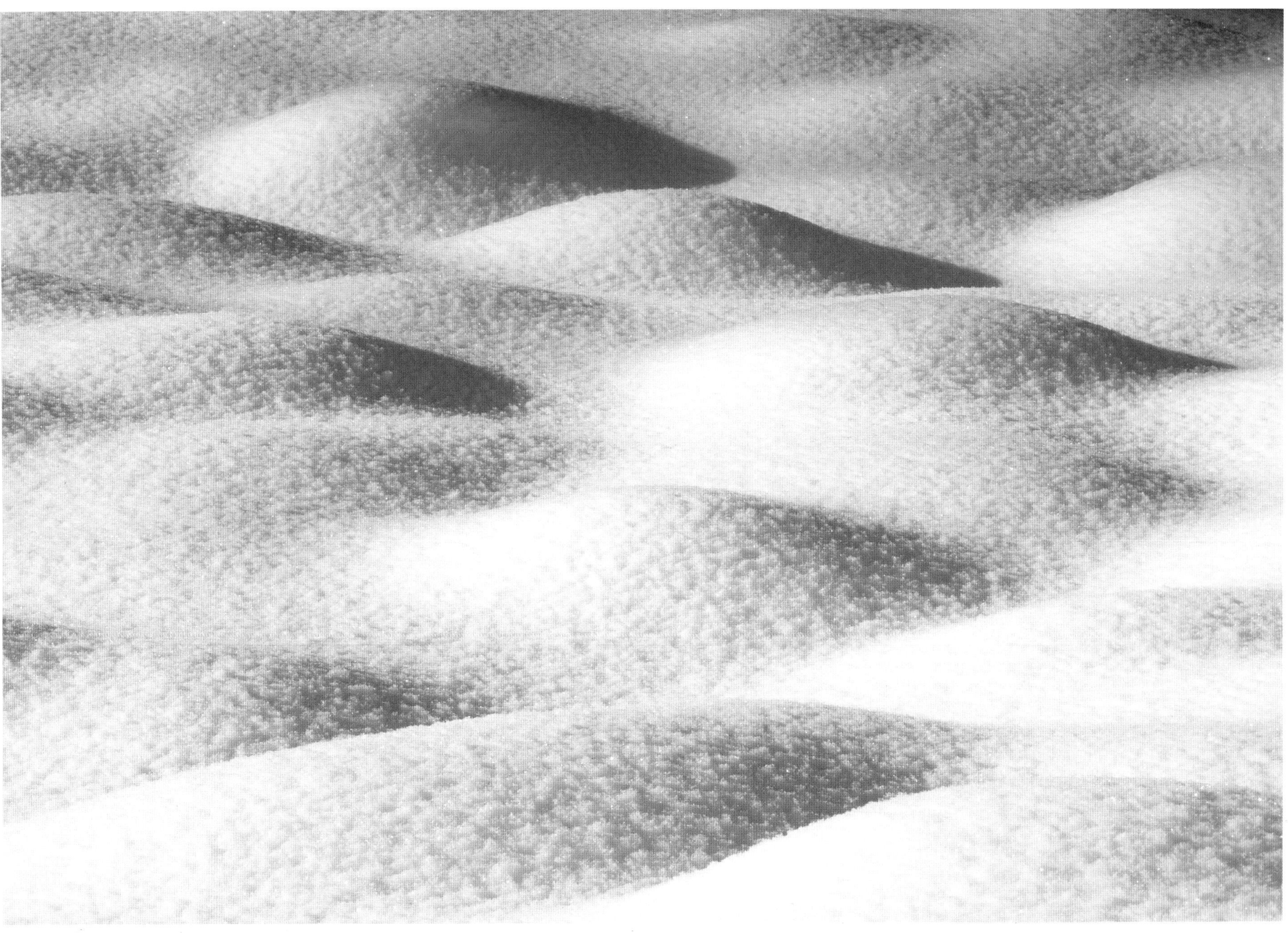

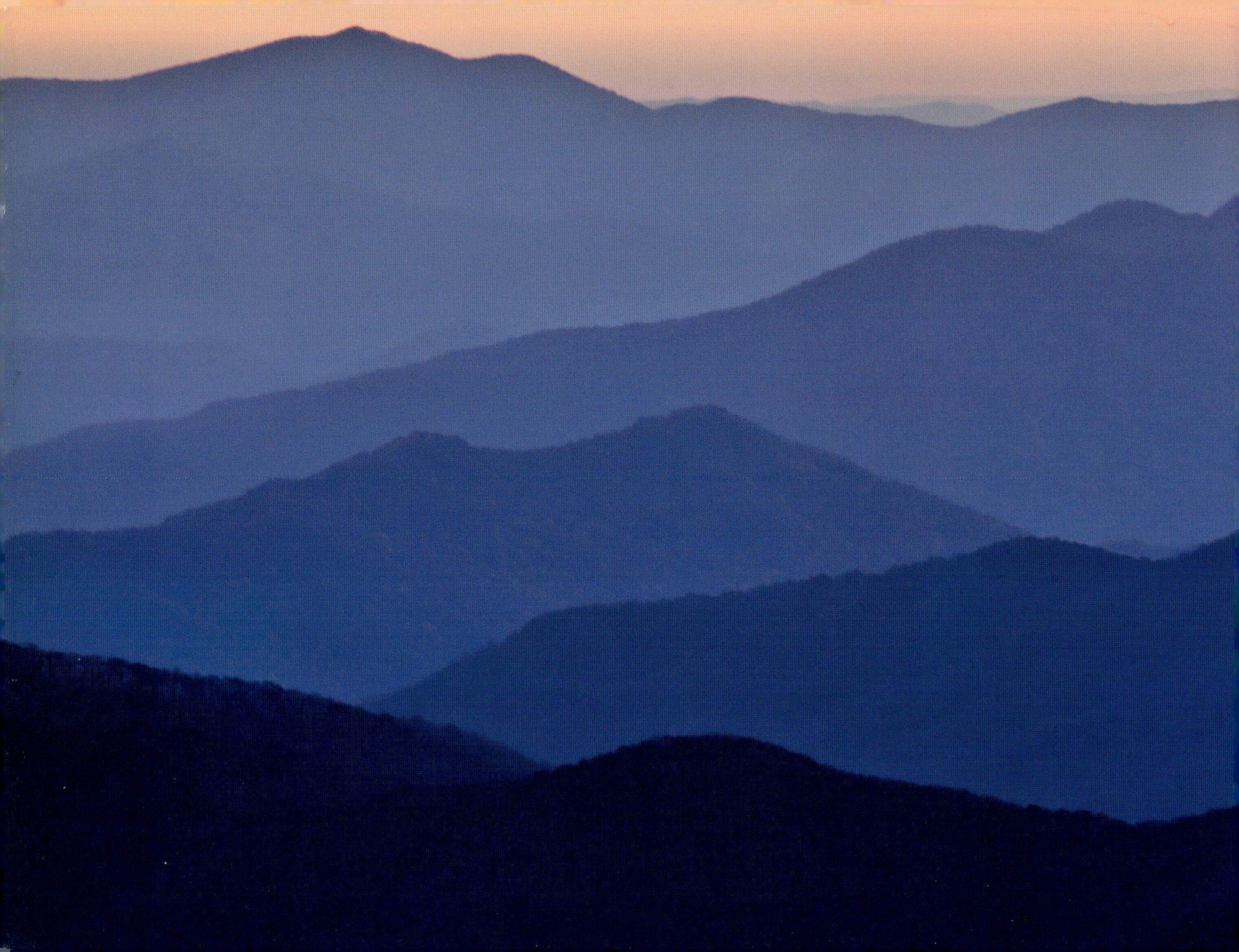

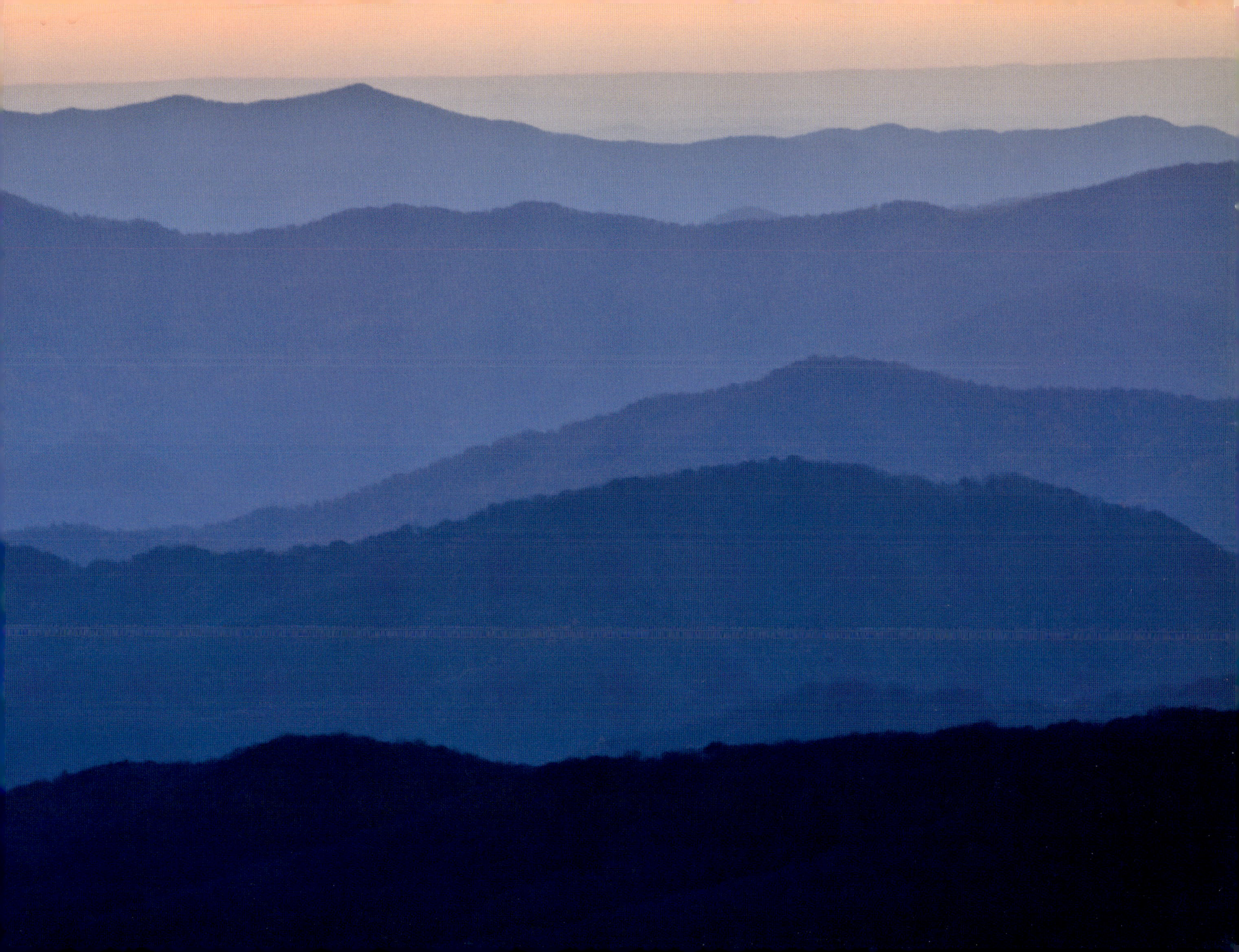

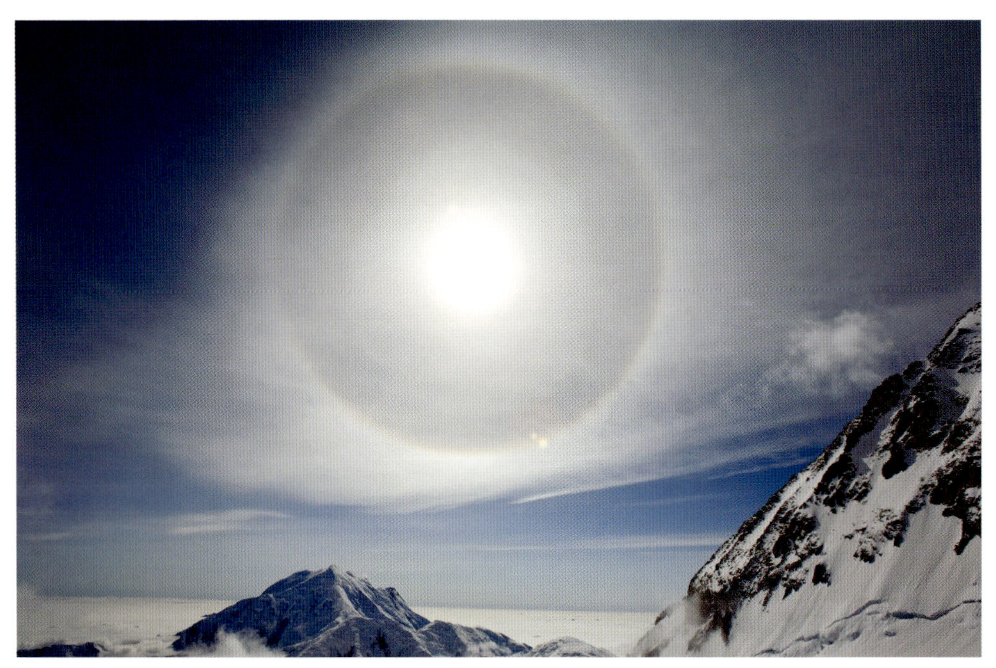

PAGES 190/191: **Great Smoky Mountains National Park, Tennessee**
Perhaps one of the most iconic views of all national parks, this sunset view of the layered mountains from the top of Clingman's Dome is a favorite for photographers and nature revelers alike. The Smokies get their name from the veil of fog that forms as a result of warm, humid air from the Gulf of Mexico that cools rapidly in the mountains. In addition to holding the title for most visited national park, these mountains are also a UNESCO World Heritage Site.

LEFT: **Denali National Park & Preserve, Alaska**
Mount Foraker.

RIGHT: **Denali National Park & Preserve, Alaska**
The view from Mount McKinley base camp at 14,200 feet.

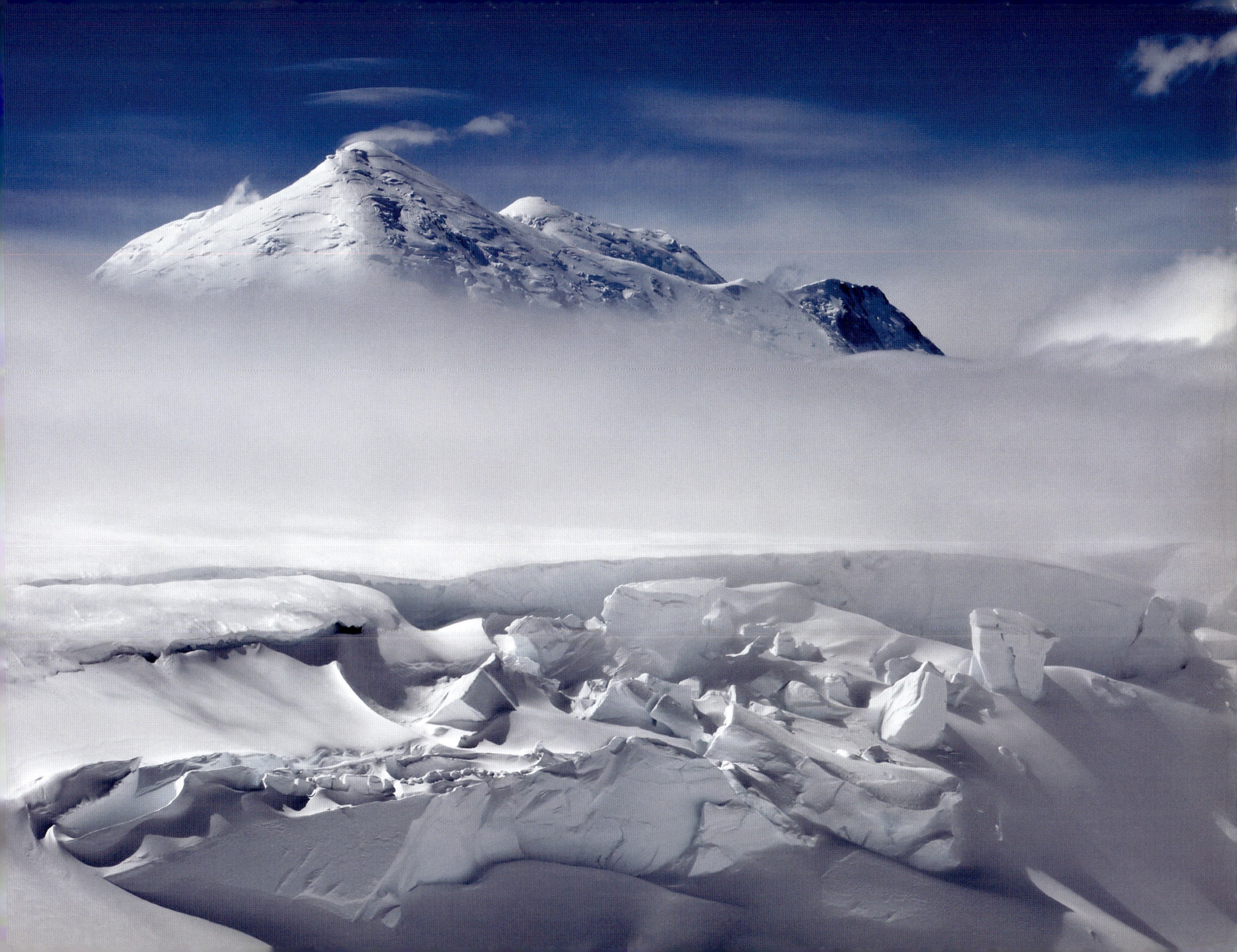

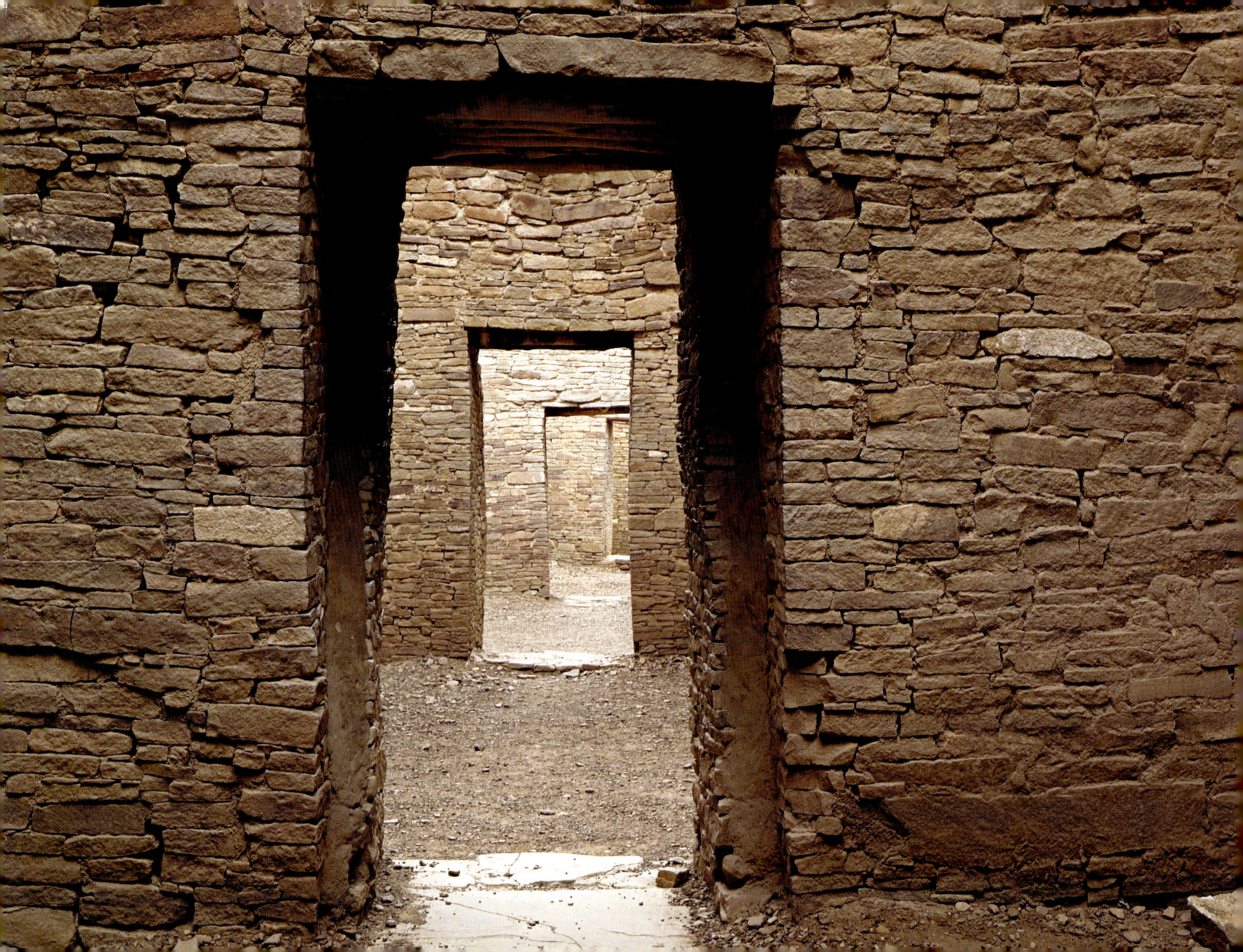

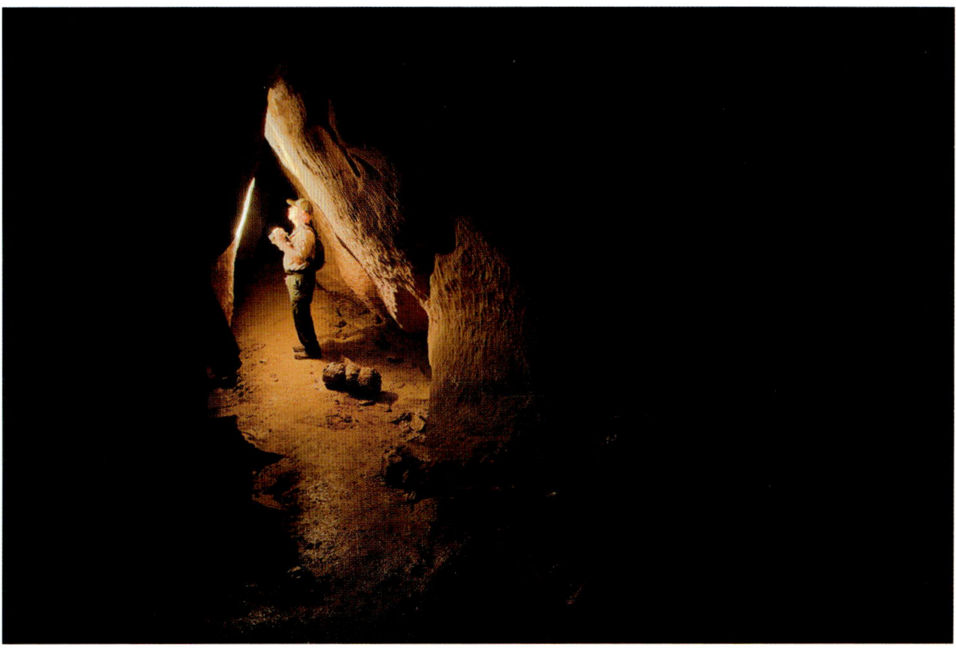

ABOVE: **Cumberland Gap National Historical Park; Kentucky, Tennessee, Virginia**
A National Park Service ranger illuminates the caves.

LEFT: **Chaco Culture National Historical Park, New Mexico**
Doorways in Pueblo Bonito, the largest and best-known Great House inside the historic site. This mysterious and enigmatic site was built by ancestral Puebloans from AD 828 through 1126.

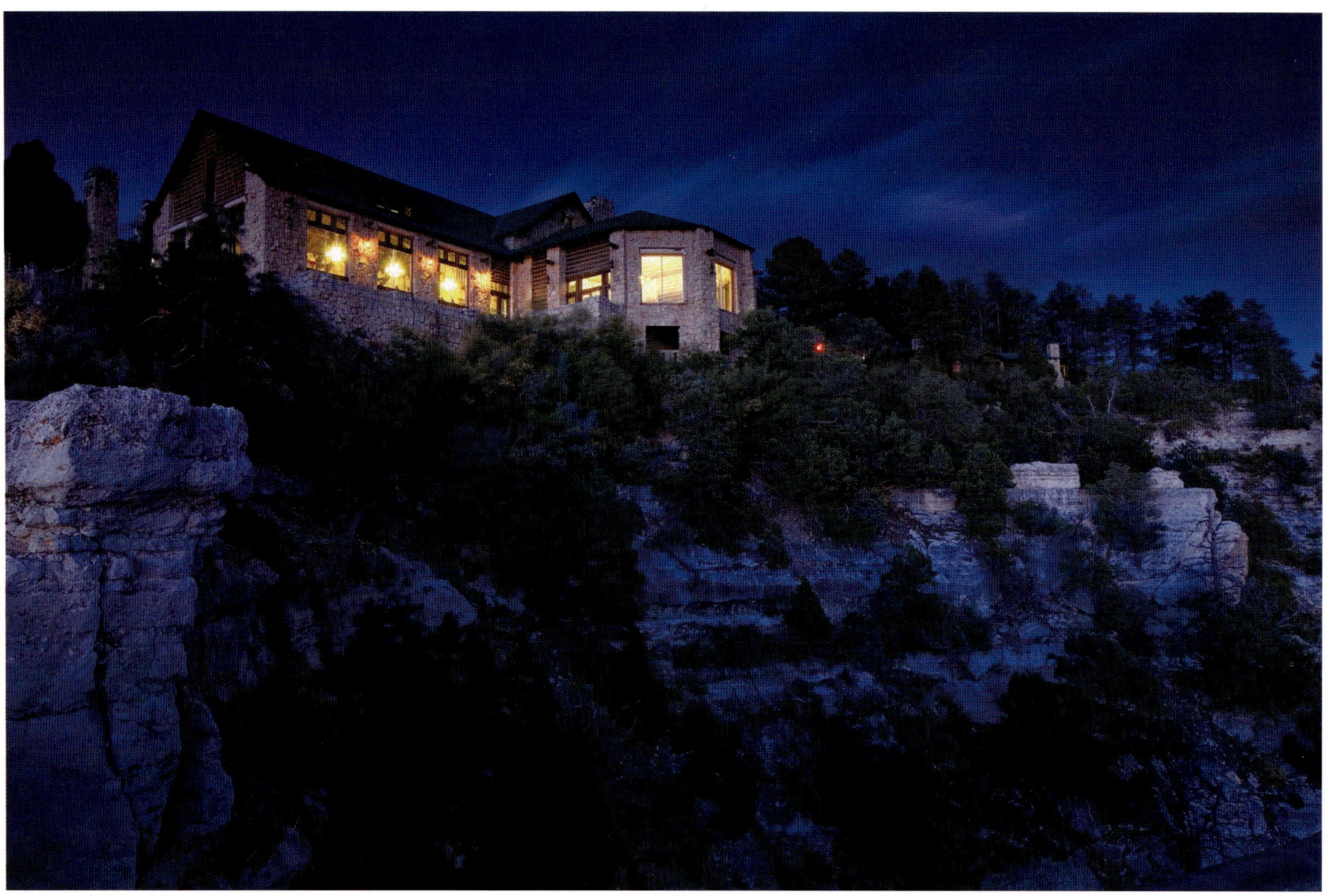

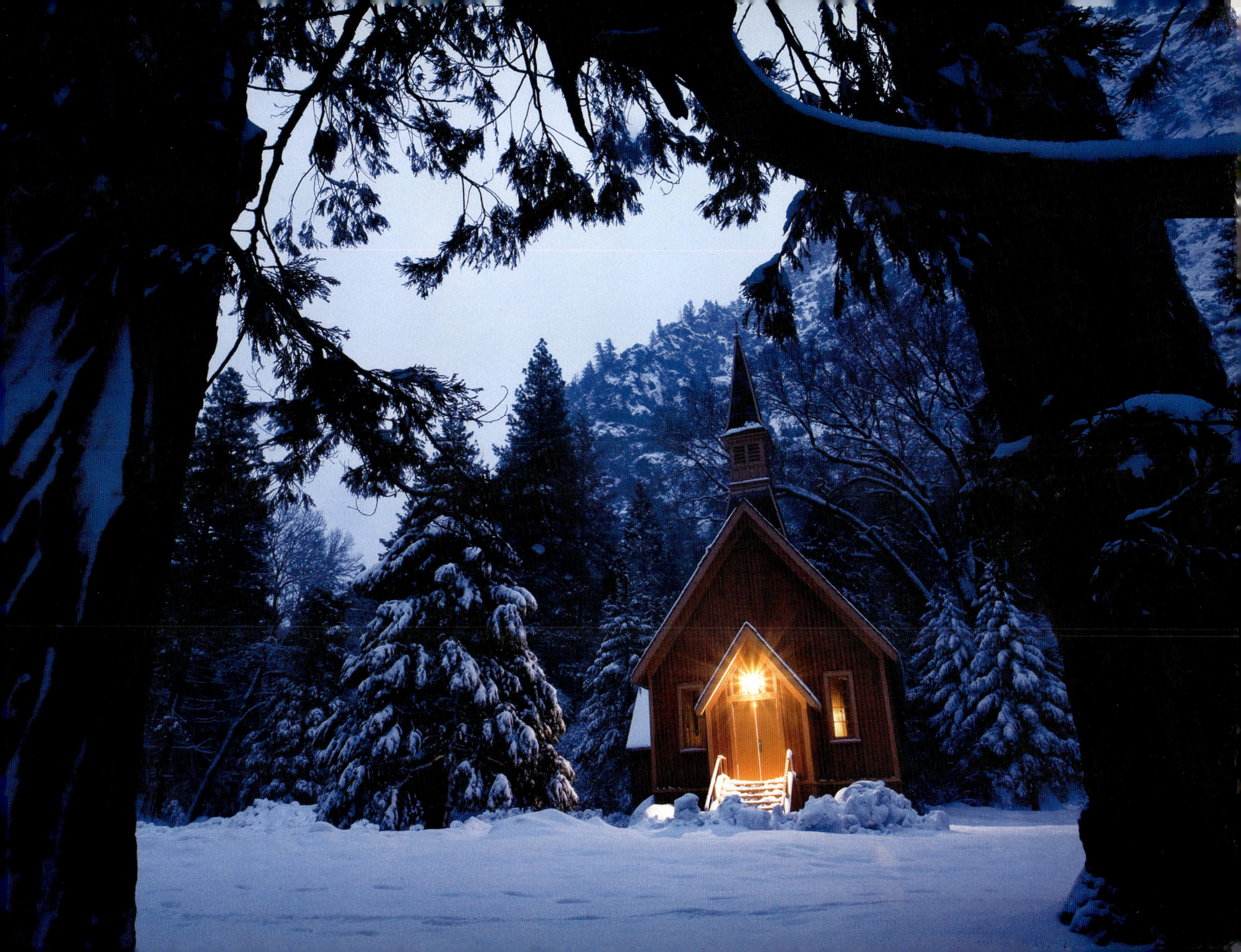

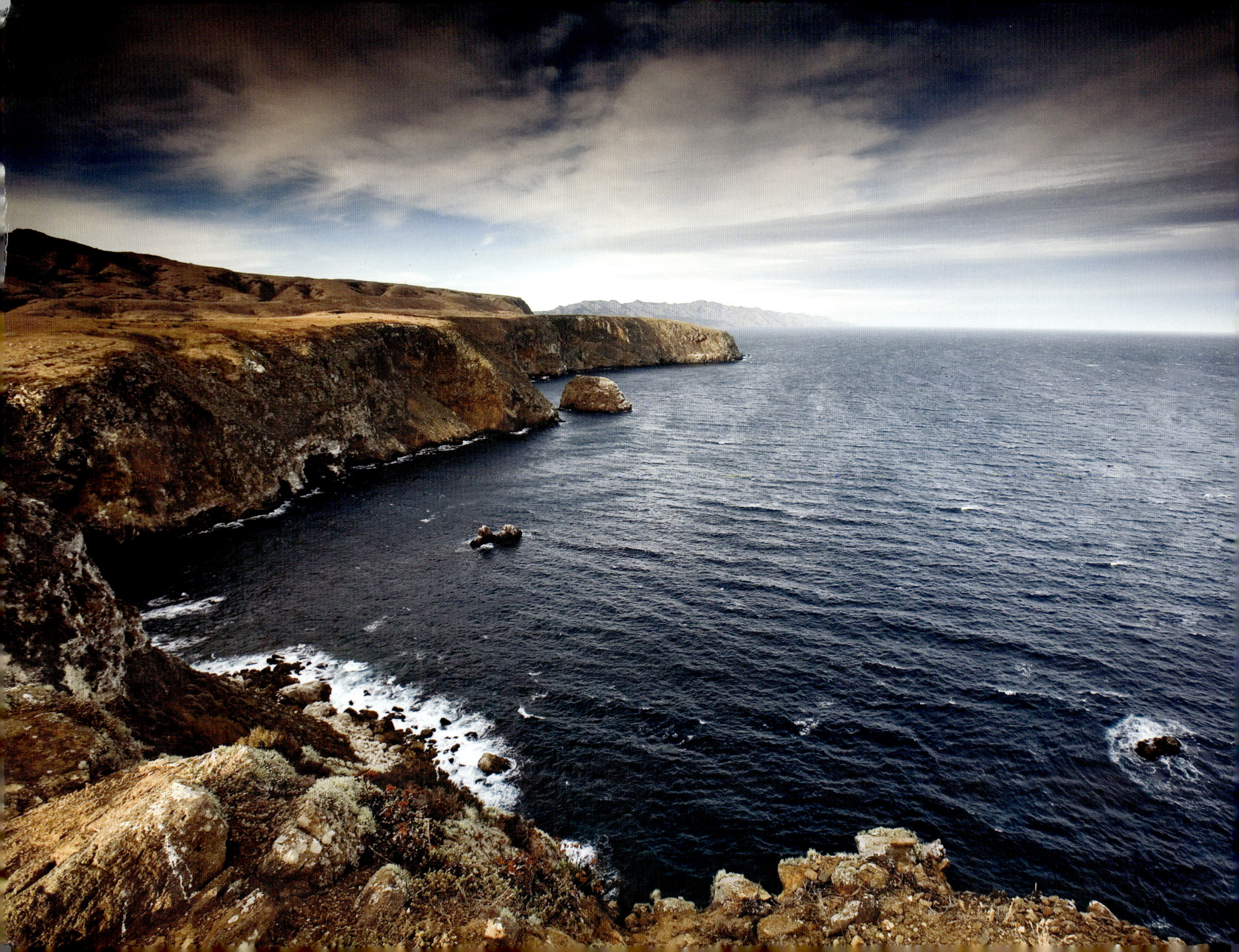

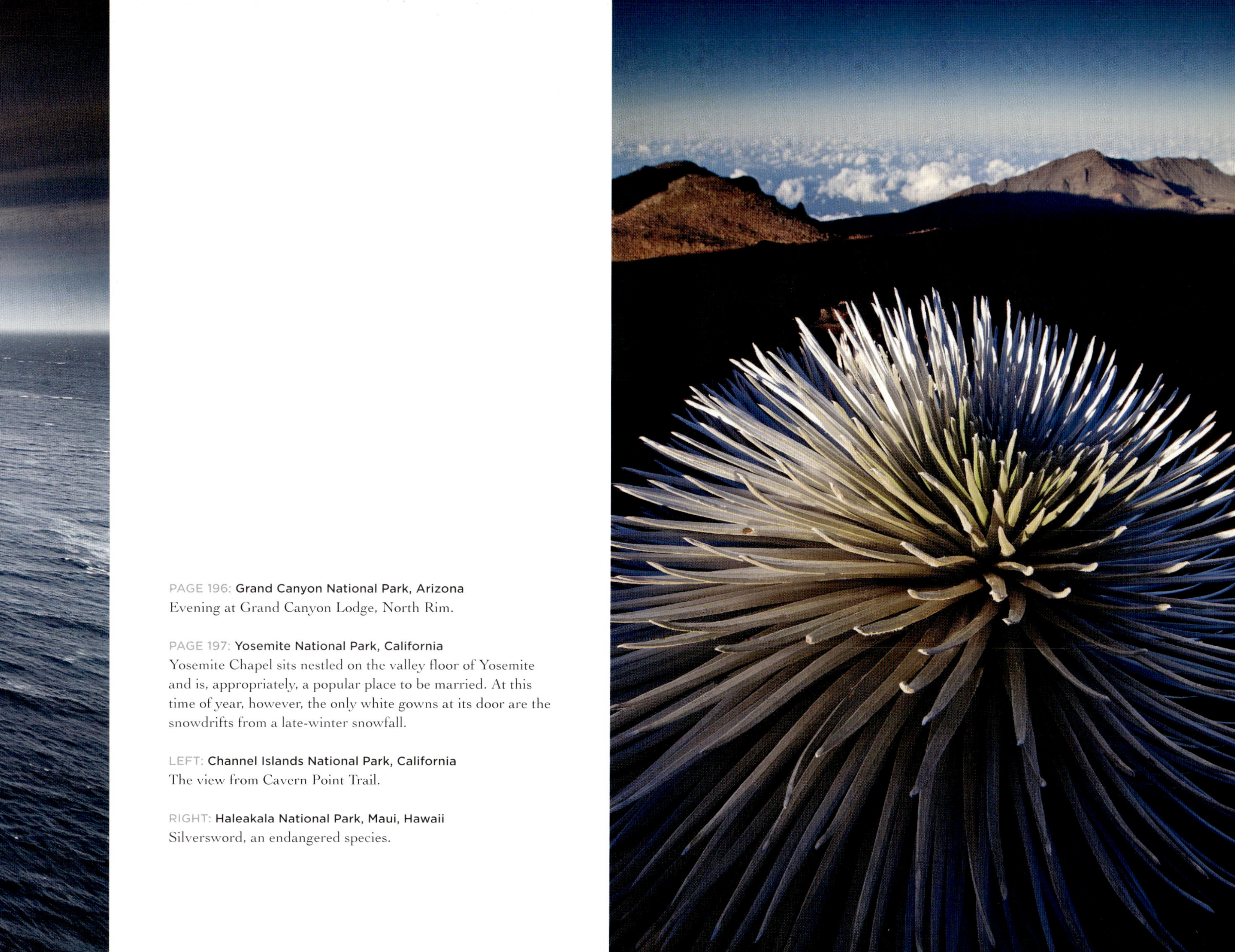

PAGE 196: **Grand Canyon National Park, Arizona**
Evening at Grand Canyon Lodge, North Rim.

PAGE 197: **Yosemite National Park, California**
Yosemite Chapel sits nestled on the valley floor of Yosemite and is, appropriately, a popular place to be married. At this time of year, however, the only white gowns at its door are the snowdrifts from a late-winter snowfall.

LEFT: **Channel Islands National Park, California**
The view from Cavern Point Trail.

RIGHT: **Haleakala National Park, Maui, Hawaii**
Silversword, an endangered species.

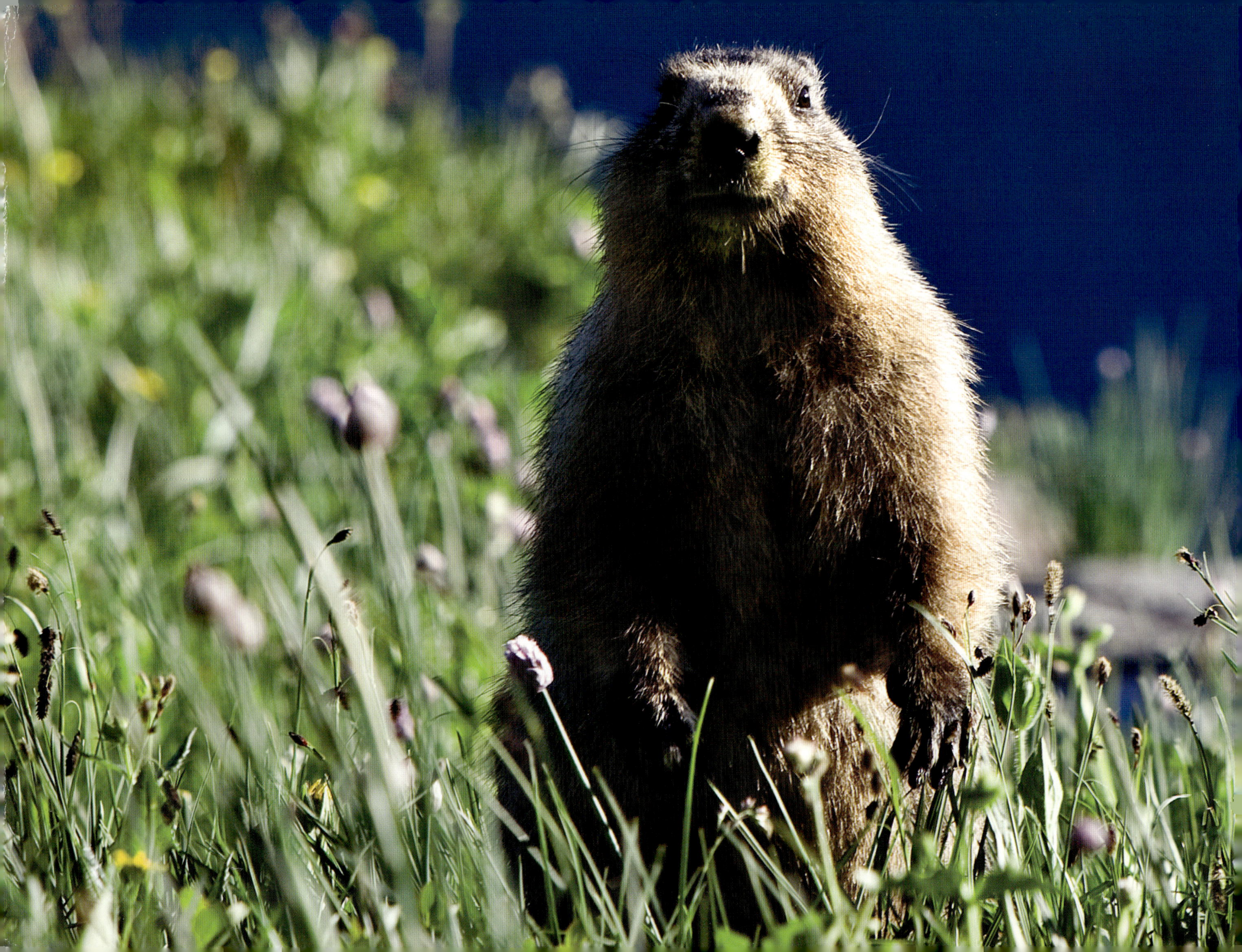

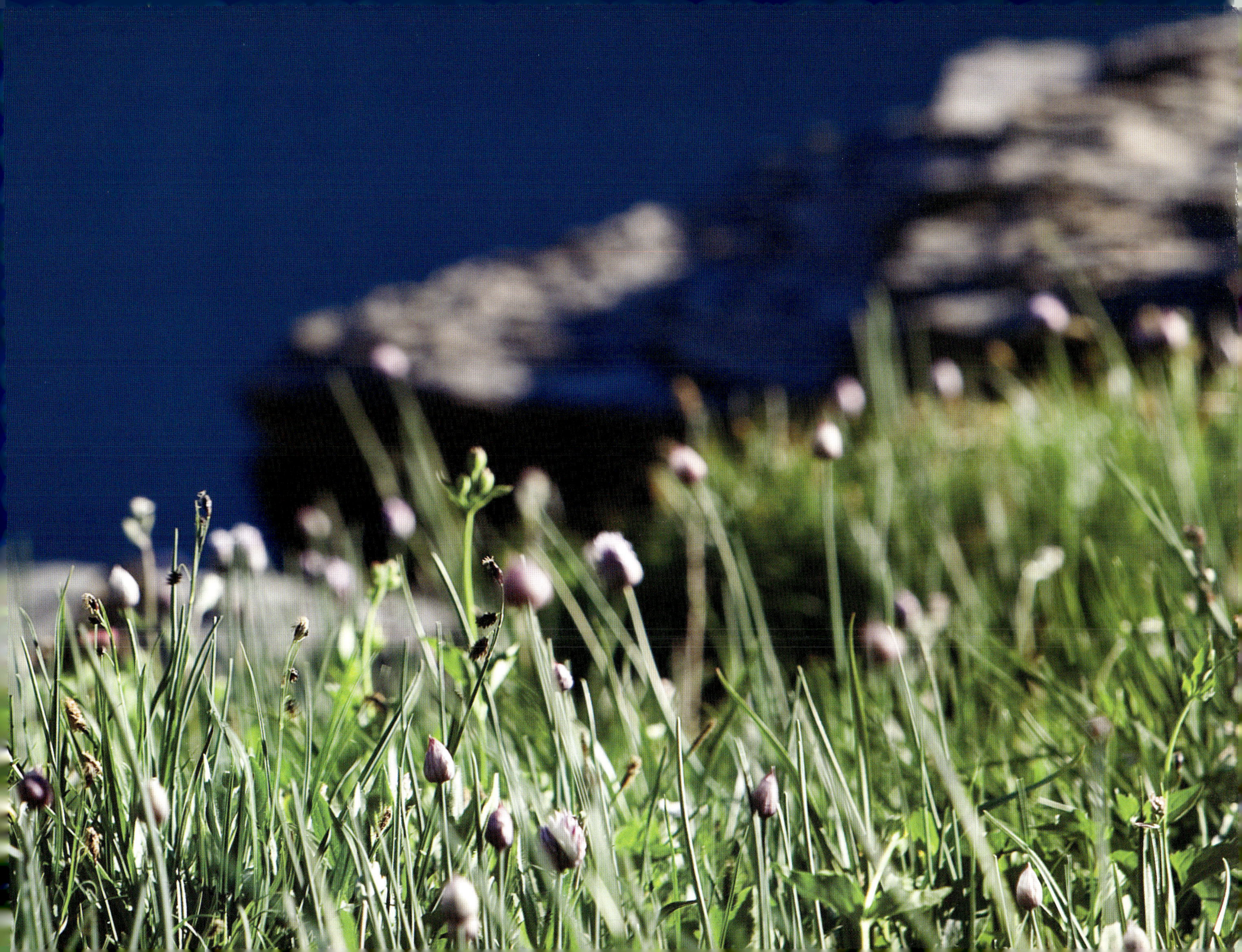

PAGES 200/201: **Glacier National Park, Montana**
A hoary marmot near Logan Pass.

RIGHT: **Acadia National Park, Maine**
Bar Harbor, Maine: The town of Bar Harbor and its relationship to Acadia National Park are unique. The park itself has a layout that spreads out and around like fingers, wrapping itself around the little town of Bar Harbor and creating a popular and classic town for tourists to visit. While the town itself is not technically inside the park, it is surrounded on all sides by it. This relationship allows visitors access to such popular novelties as easy-to-rent kayaks and homemade ice cream.

PAGES 204/205: **Acadia National Park, Maine**
Sunset on Cadillac Mountain: From the summit, you can see little lights from the town of Bar Harbor as the sweeping forests wind and wend their way down to the coast. Acadia was the first national park east of the Mississippi River and protects forty-seven thousand acres of ocean, forests, lakes, and mountains.

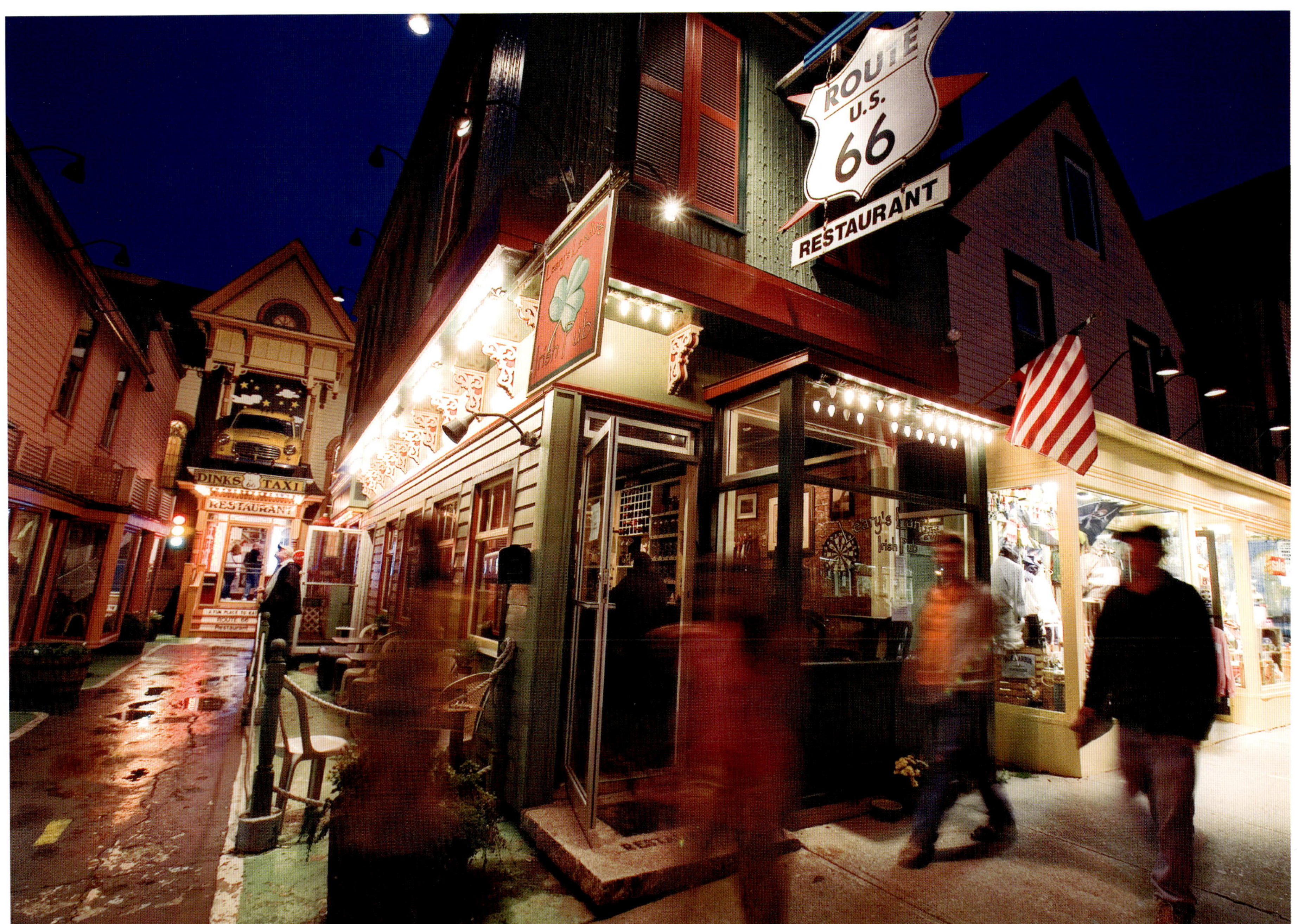
ROUTE
U.S.
66
RESTAURANT
DINKS TAXI
RESTAURANT
Irish Pub

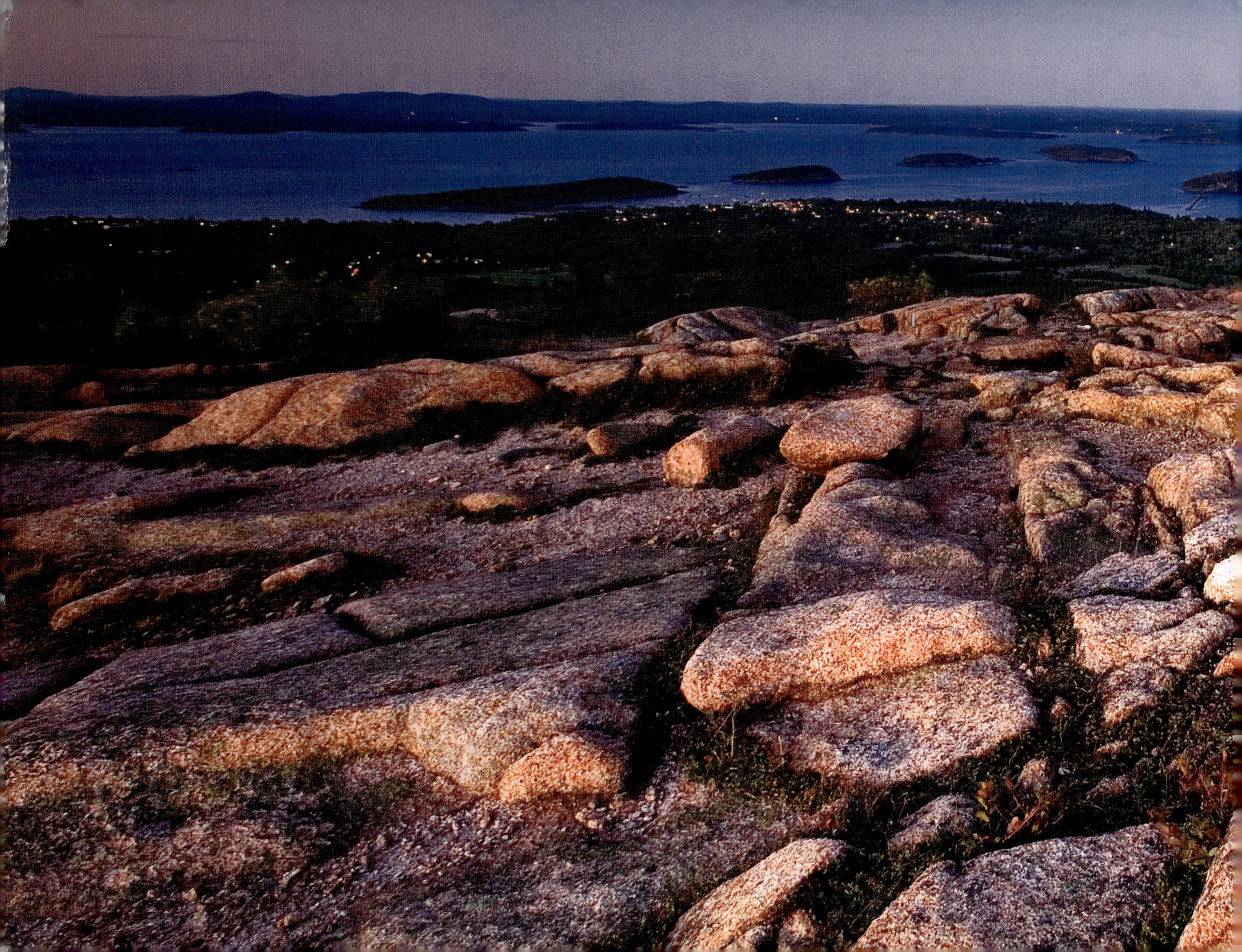

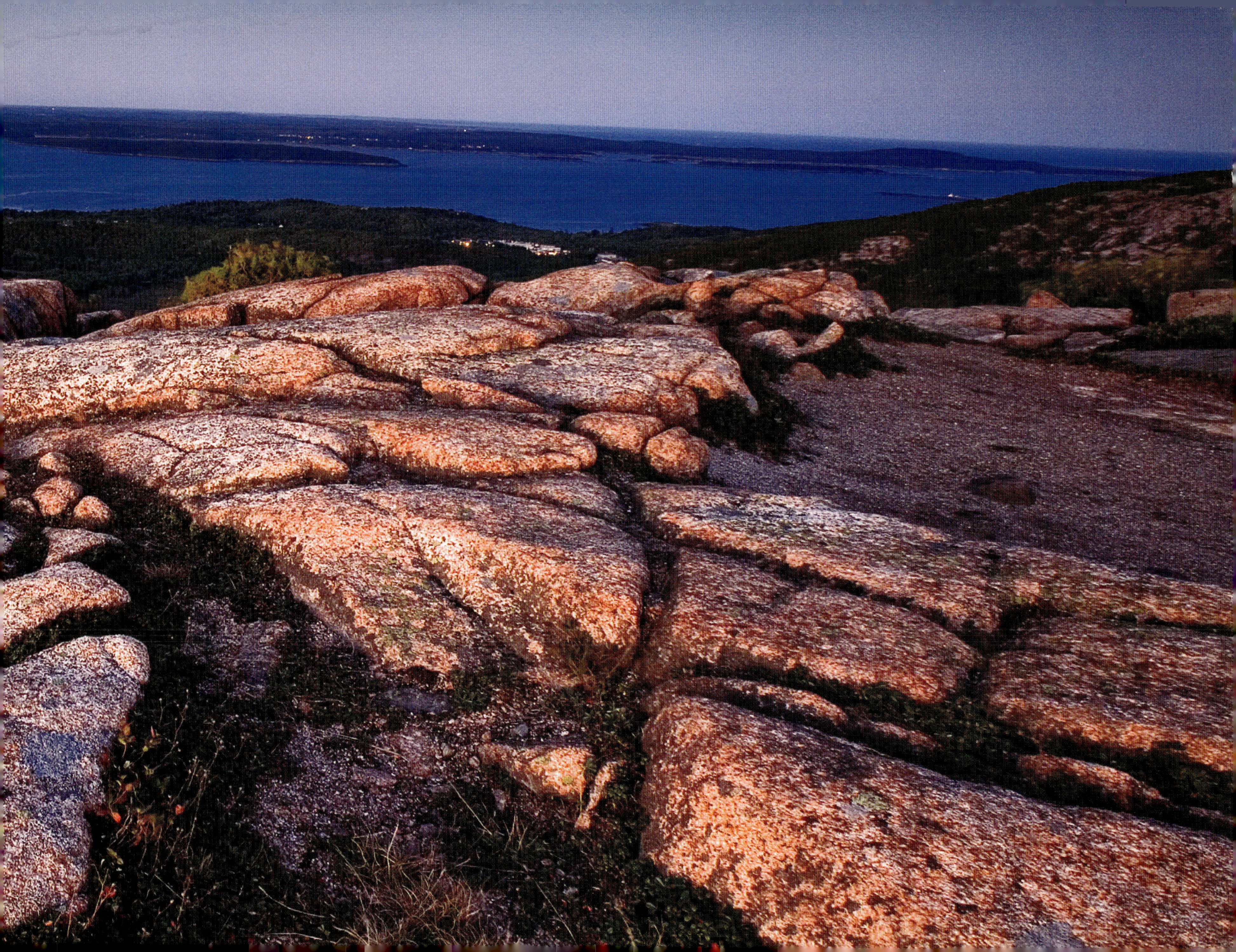

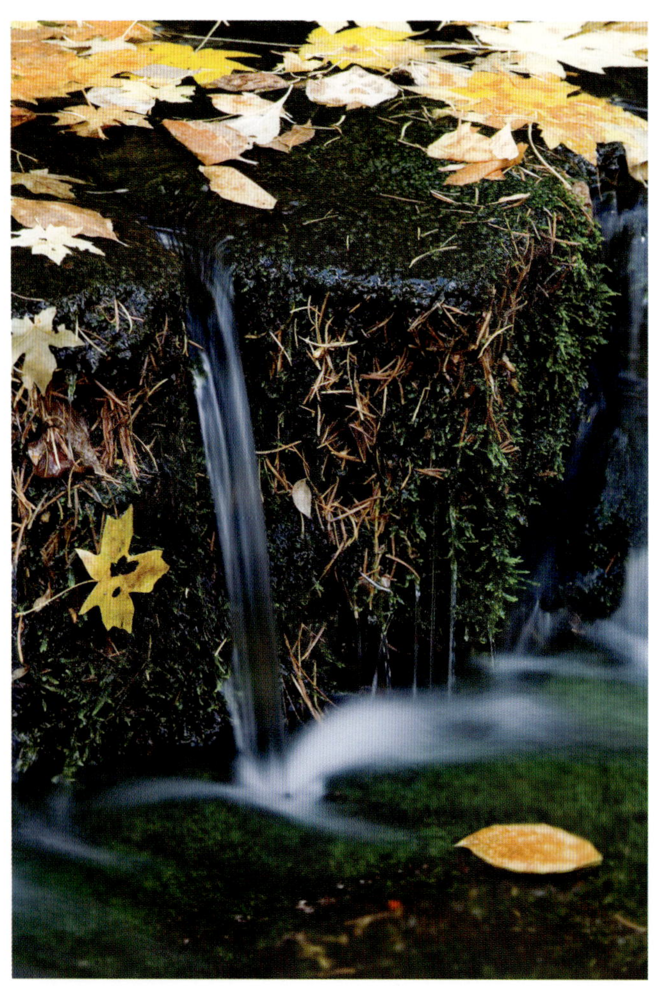

LEFT: **Yosemite National Park, California**
Fern Springs.

RIGHT: **Yosemite National Park, California**
The Ahwahnee Lodge.

PAGES 208 & 209: **Yellowstone National Park; Wyoming, Montana, Idaho**
Algae in Yellowstone geysers and thermal pools, which is often studied for its mysterious properties, including medicinal uses and potential sustainable-energy applications.

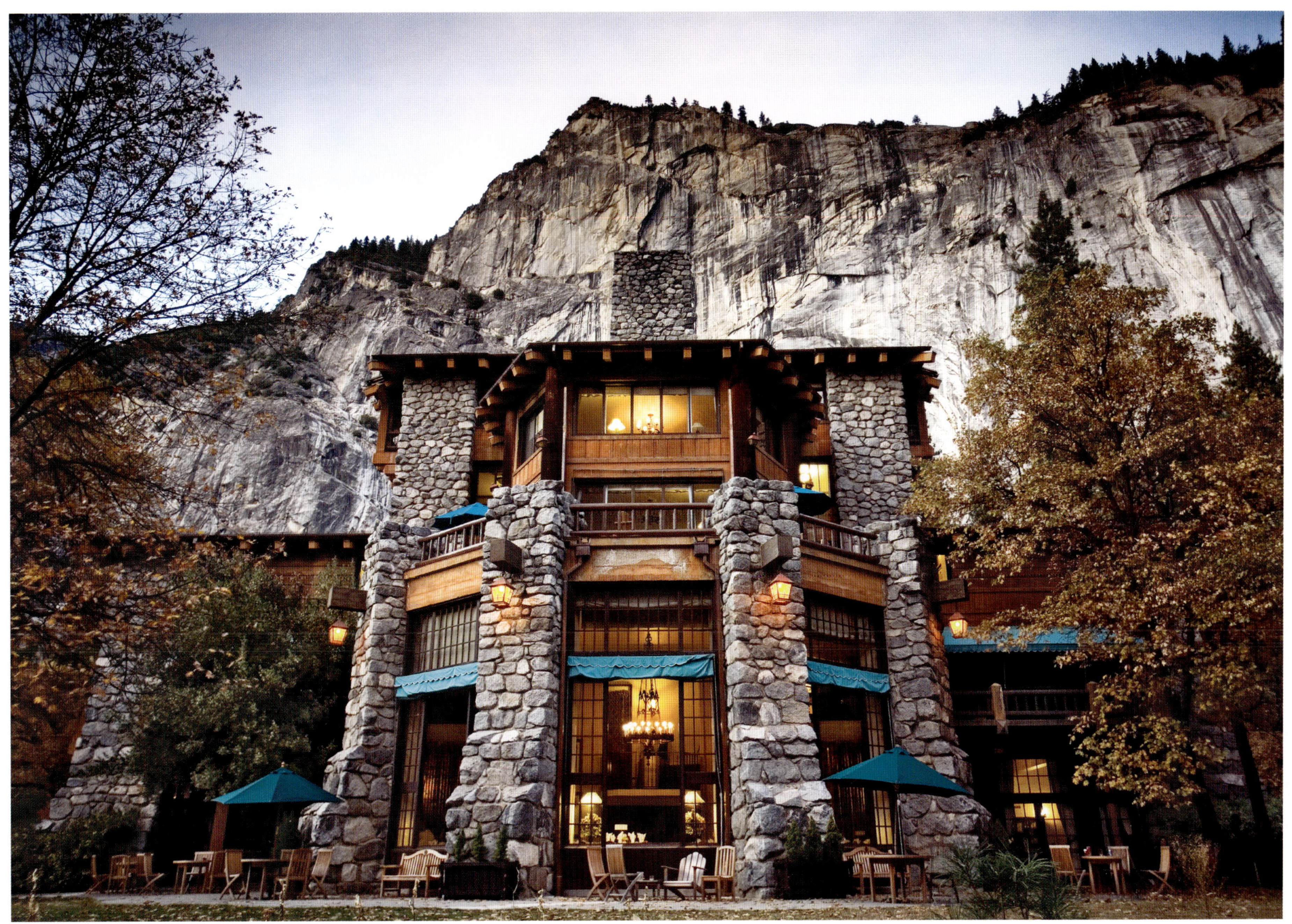

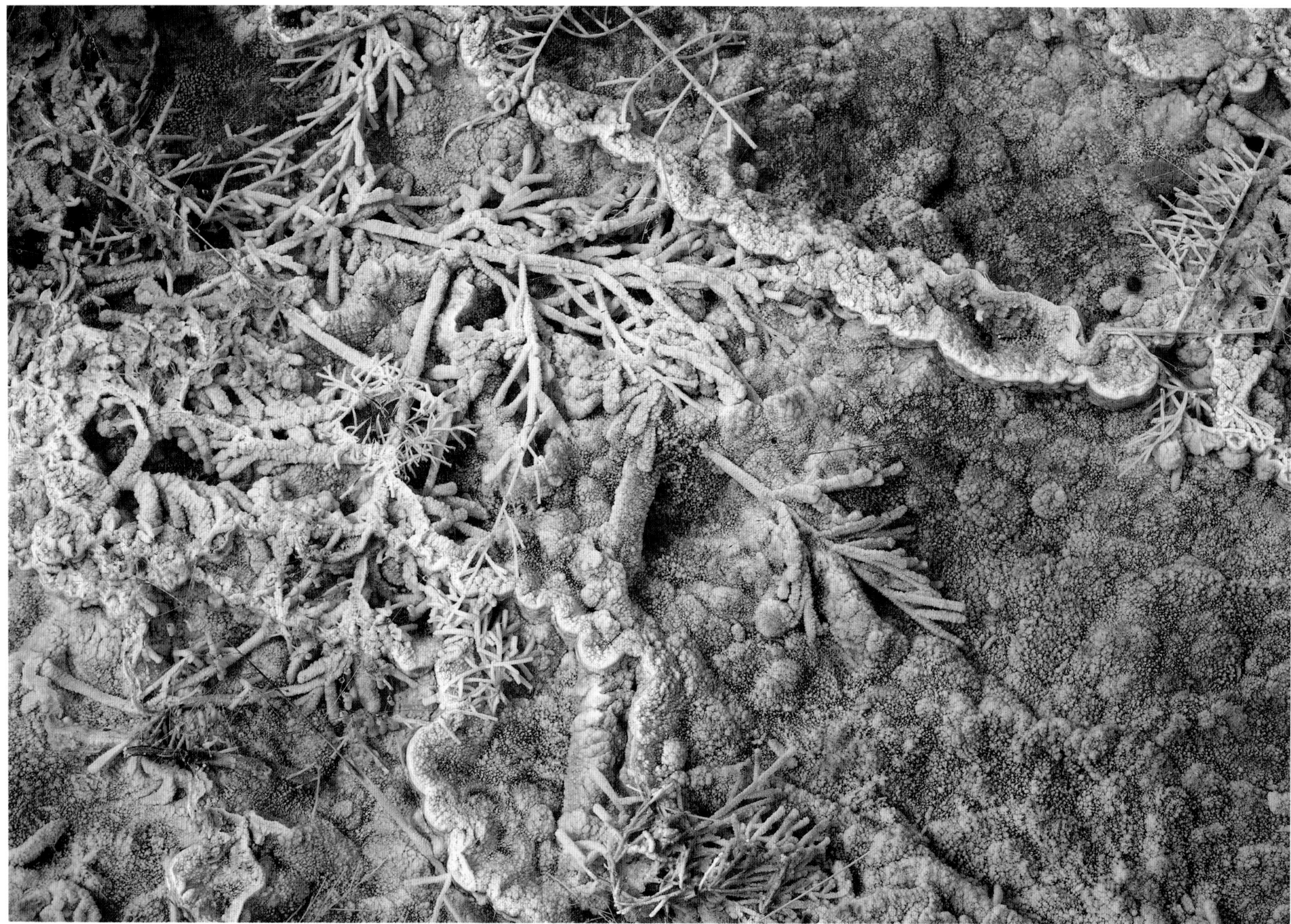

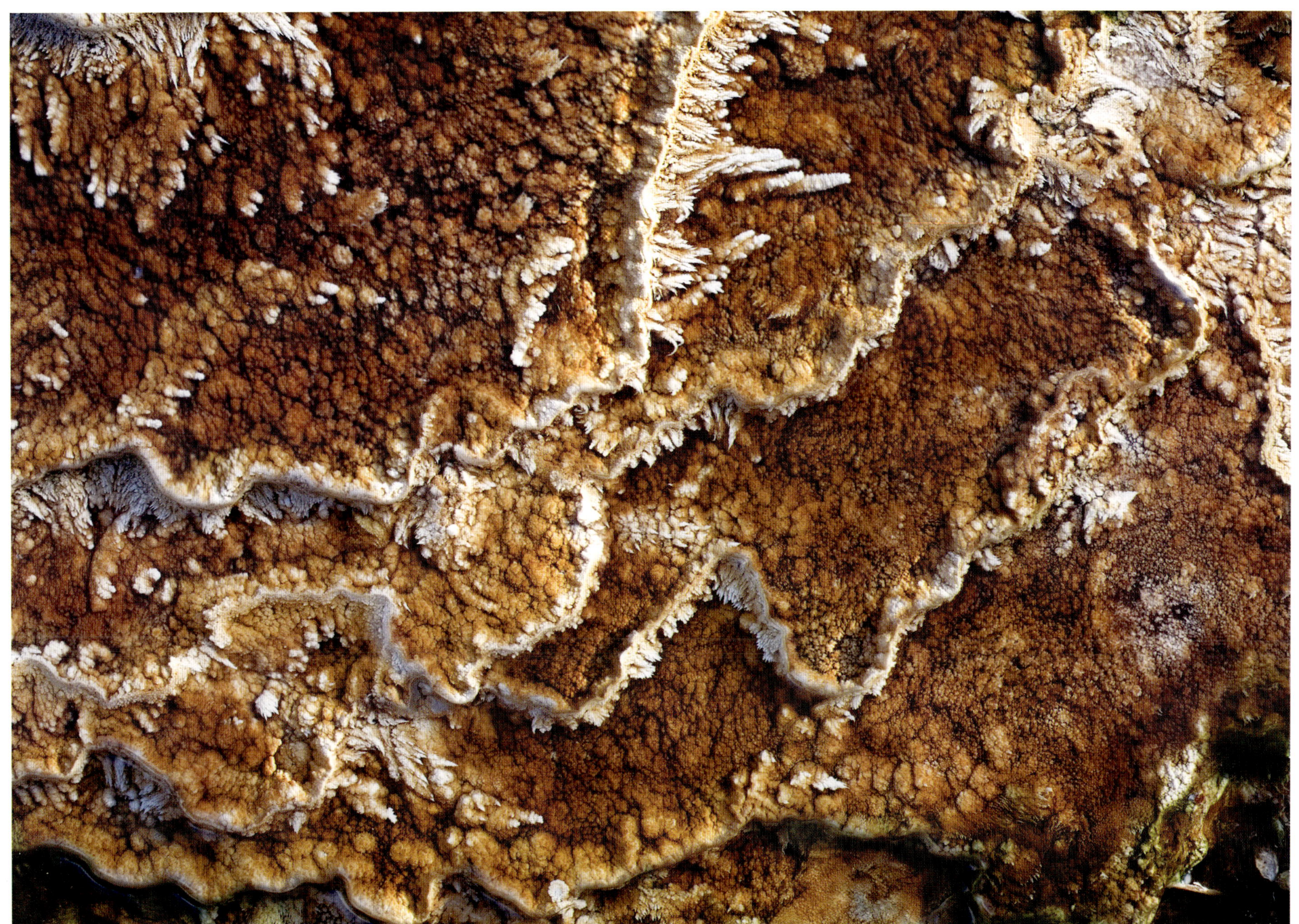

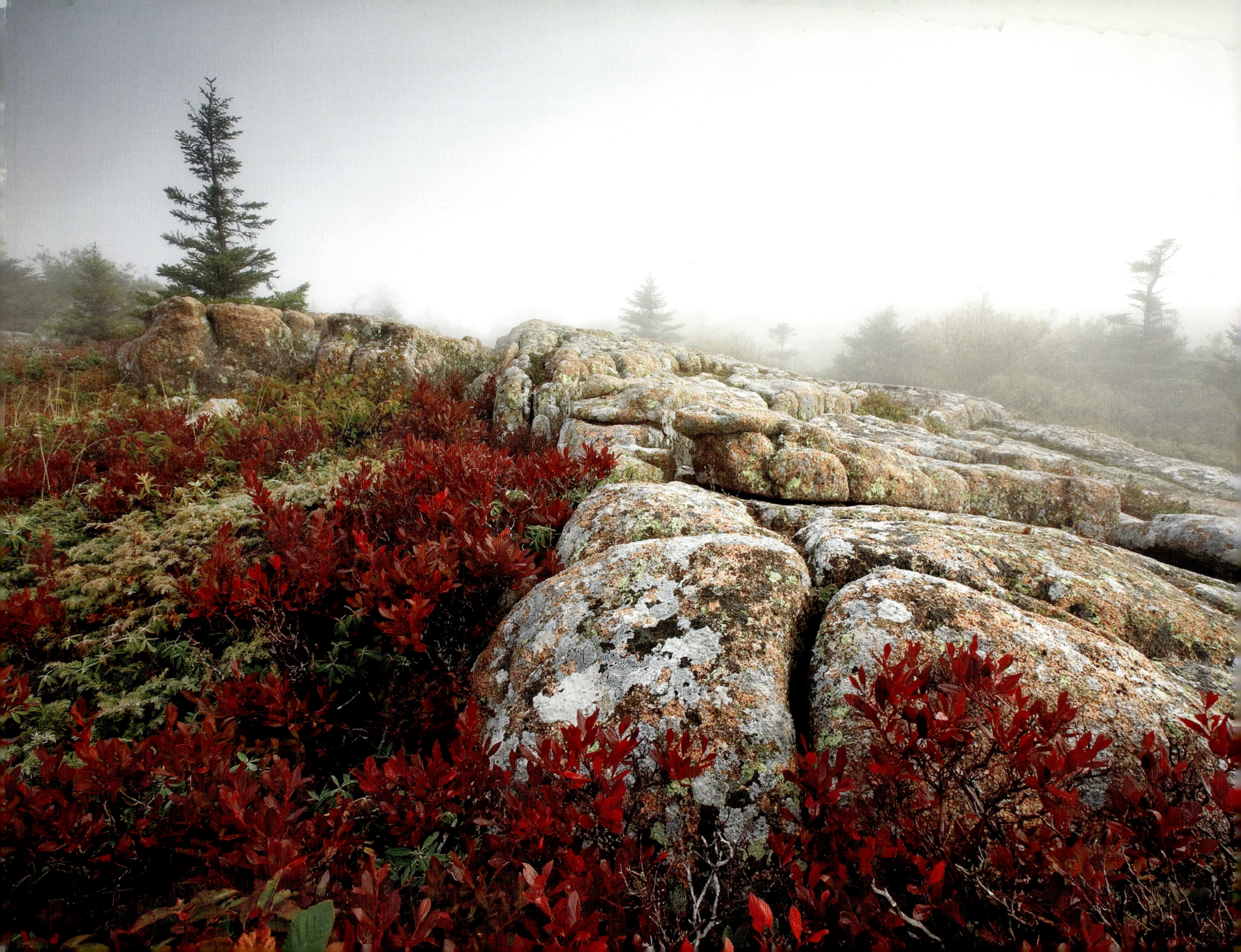

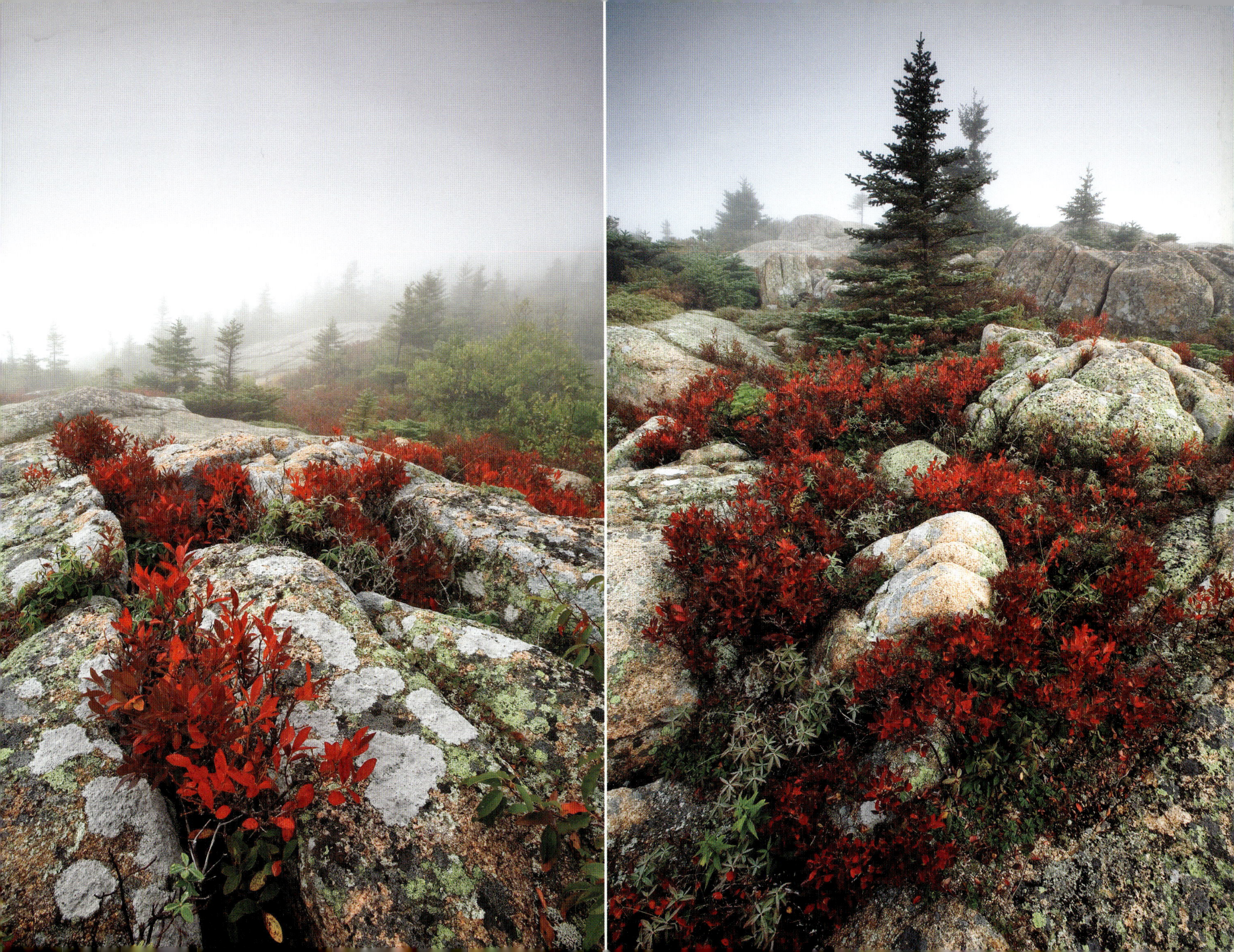

PAGES 210 & 211: **Acadia National Park, Maine**
The summit of Cadillac Mountain during heavy morning fog.

RIGHT: **Sequioa & Kings Canyon National Parks, California**
Giant sequoias stand sentinel among the green forests of Sequoia National Park.

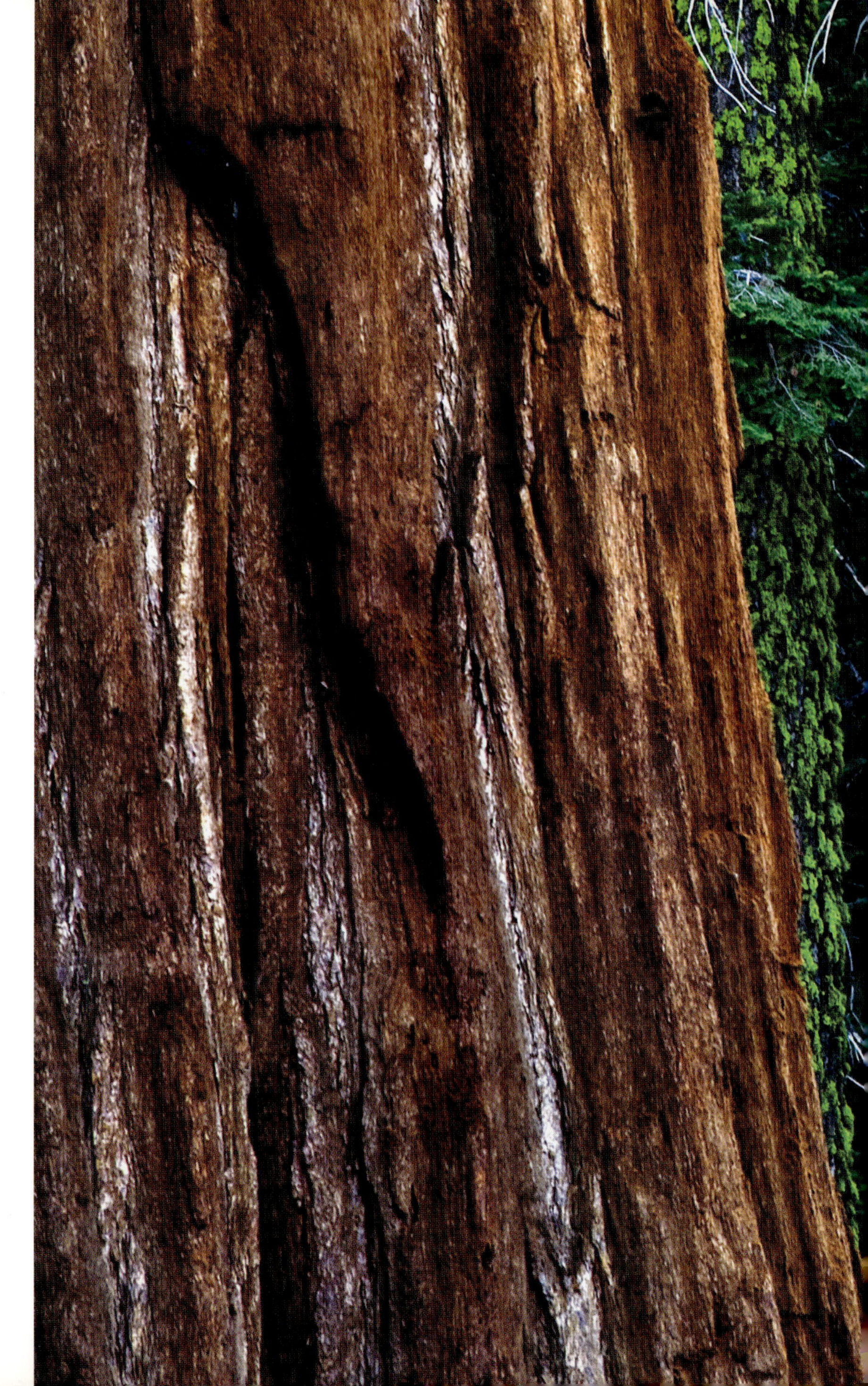

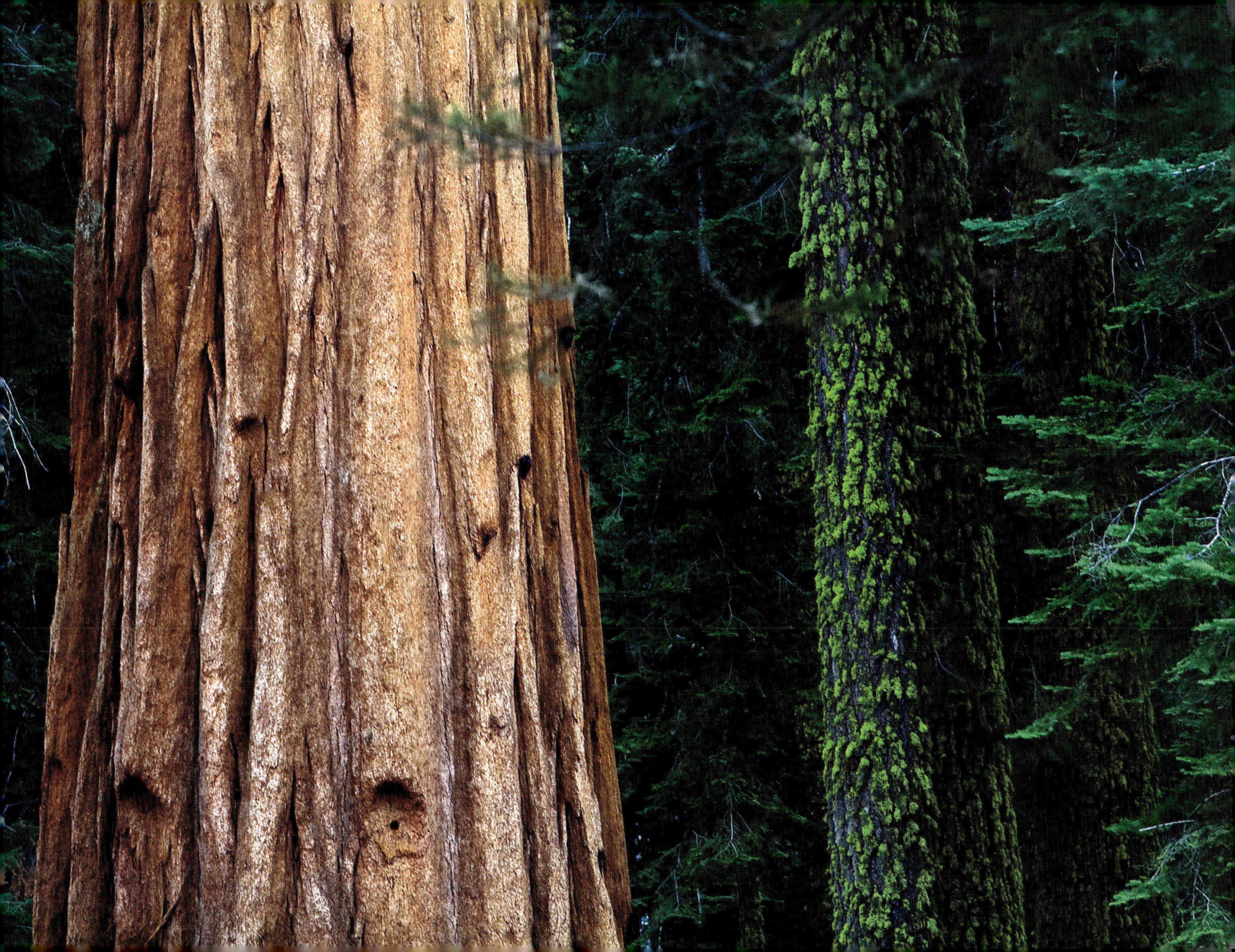

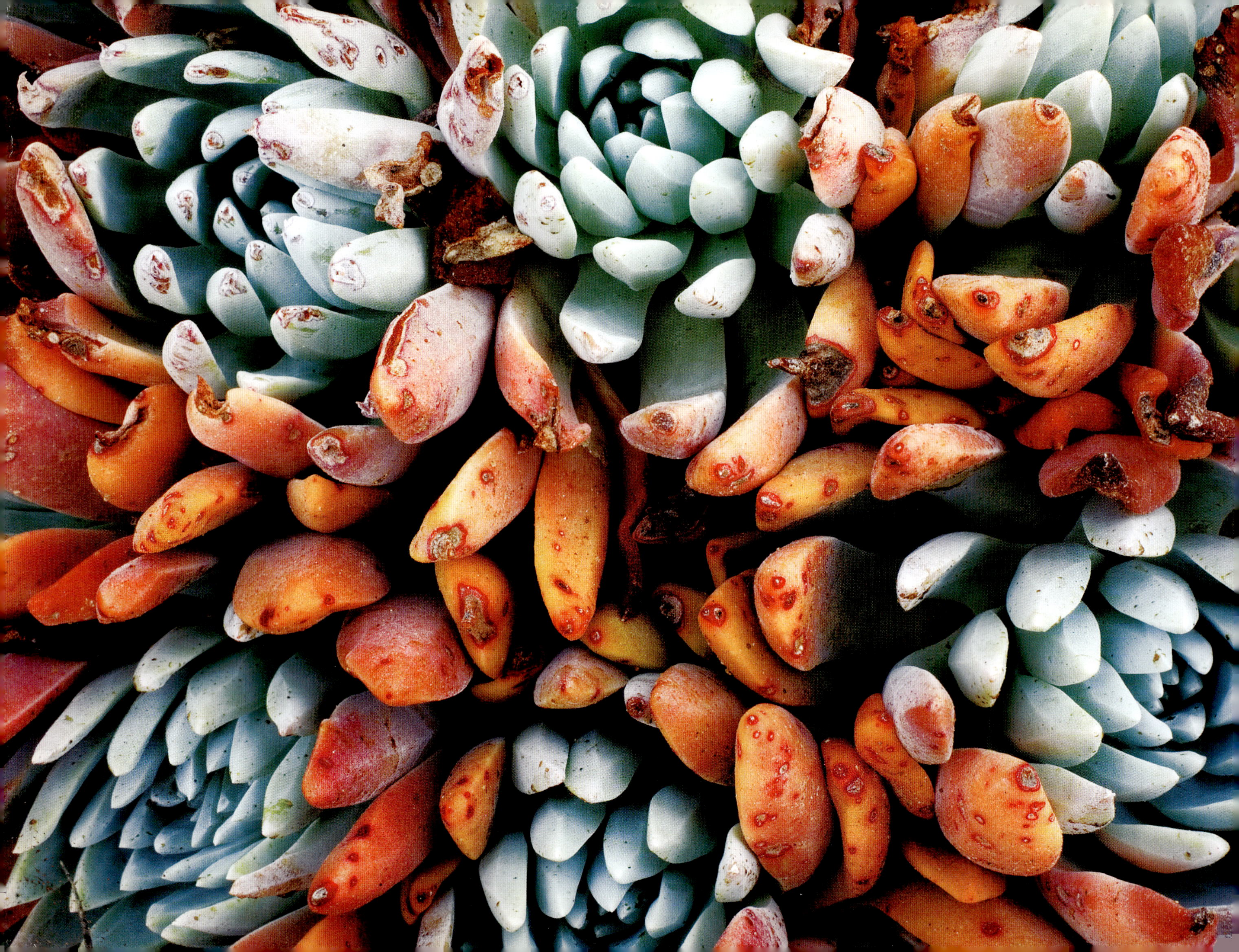

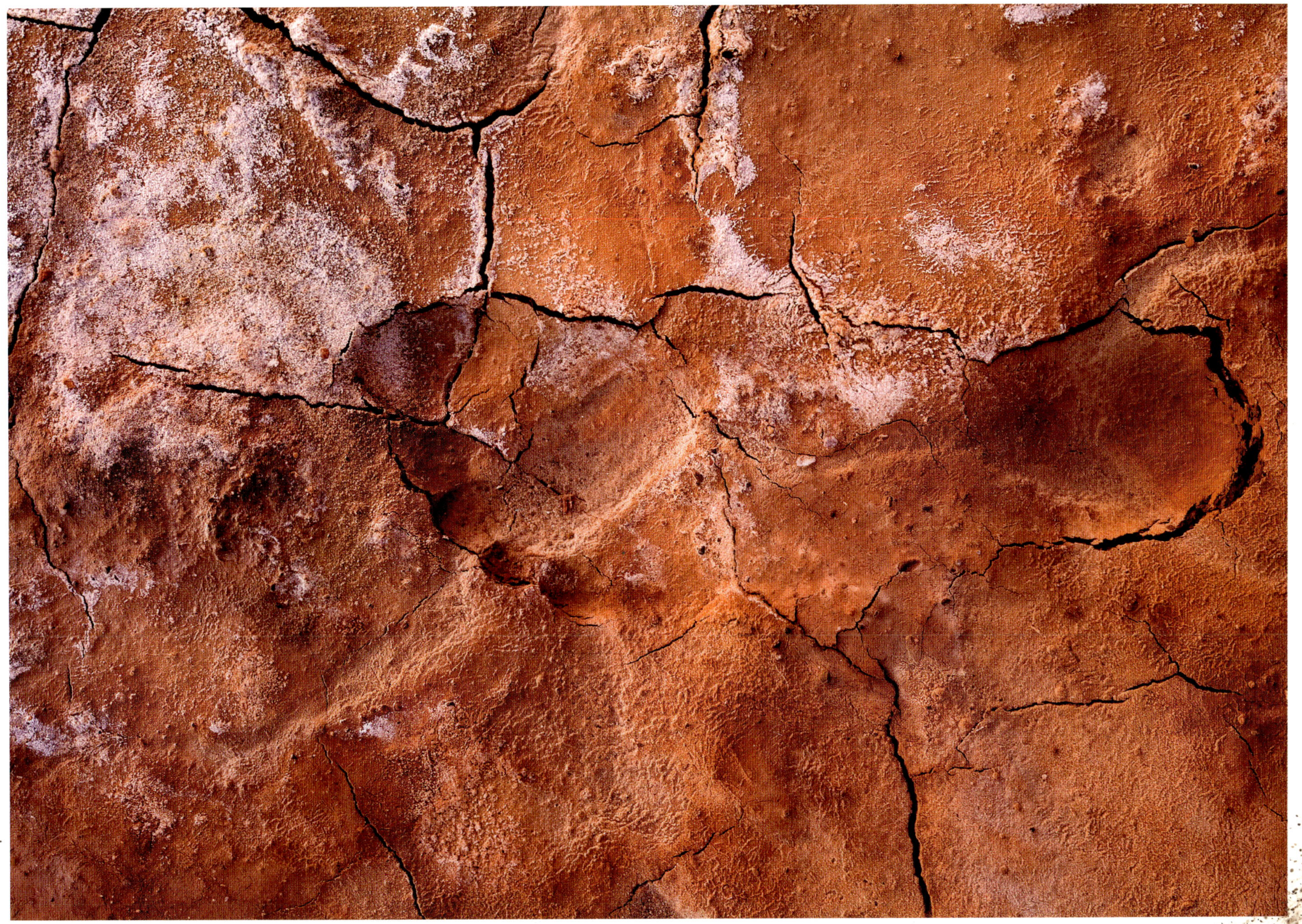

PAGE 214: **Channel Islands National Park, California**
Succulents, or live-forevers, flourish on Santa Cruz Island.

PAGE 215: **Death Valley National Park, California**
A footprint in the mud—sign of a recent human visitor.

RIGHT: **Big Bend National Park, Texas**
A scorpion glows bright green under a UV black light, which is often used by researchers to aid in their efforts to locate and study scorpions. This scorpion was the size of a pencil eraser. Photographing these guys under the black light was a nerve-wracking experience, as I needed total darkness to capture the effect. The exposure time was almost a full minute, which meant that the scorpion couldn't move, or it would be out of focus. To get it to stand still, I would gently blow on it, which would freeze it in its tracks. Meanwhile, I was hoping that in the darkness, no other scorpions were finding their way into my camera bag or into my shoes.

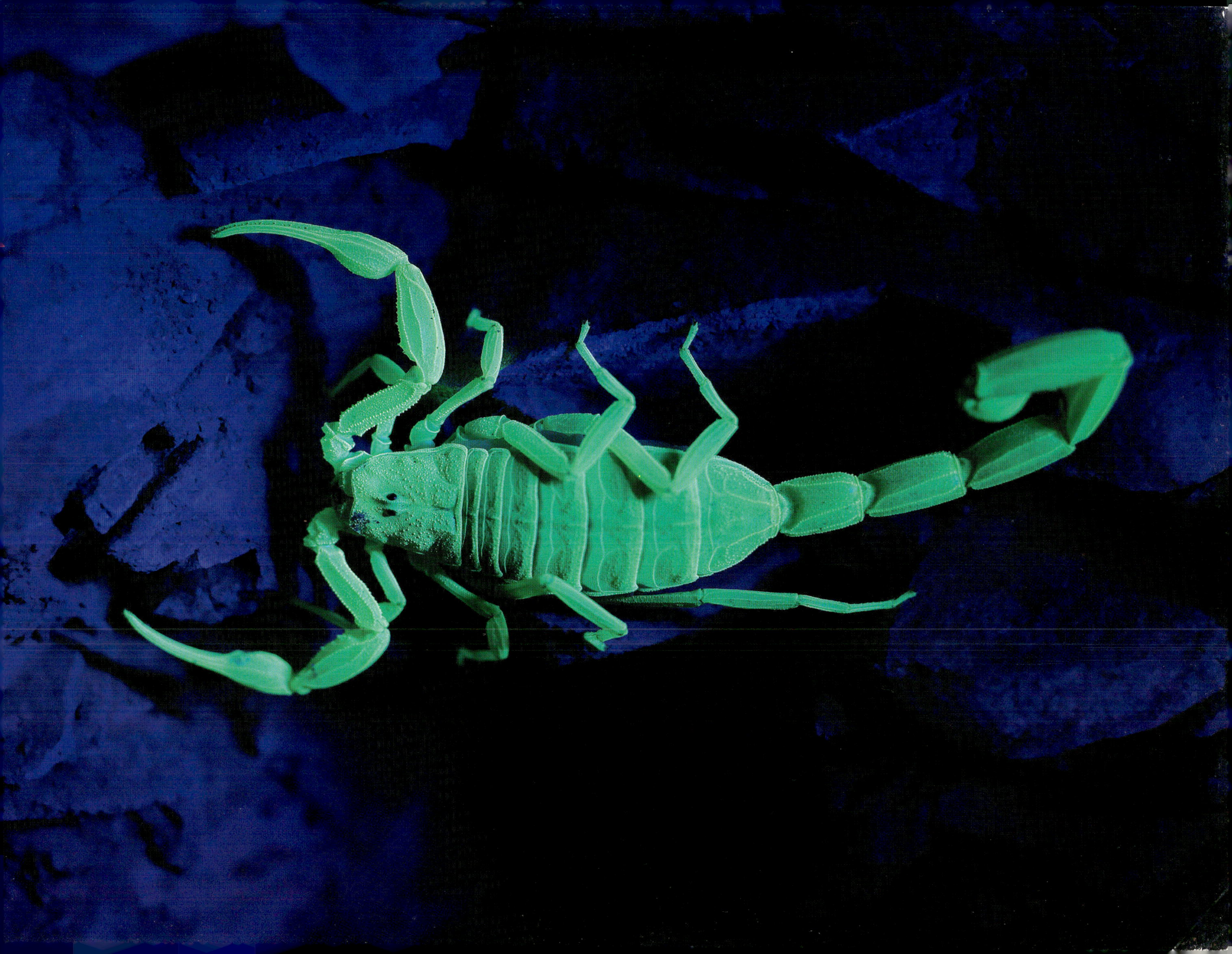

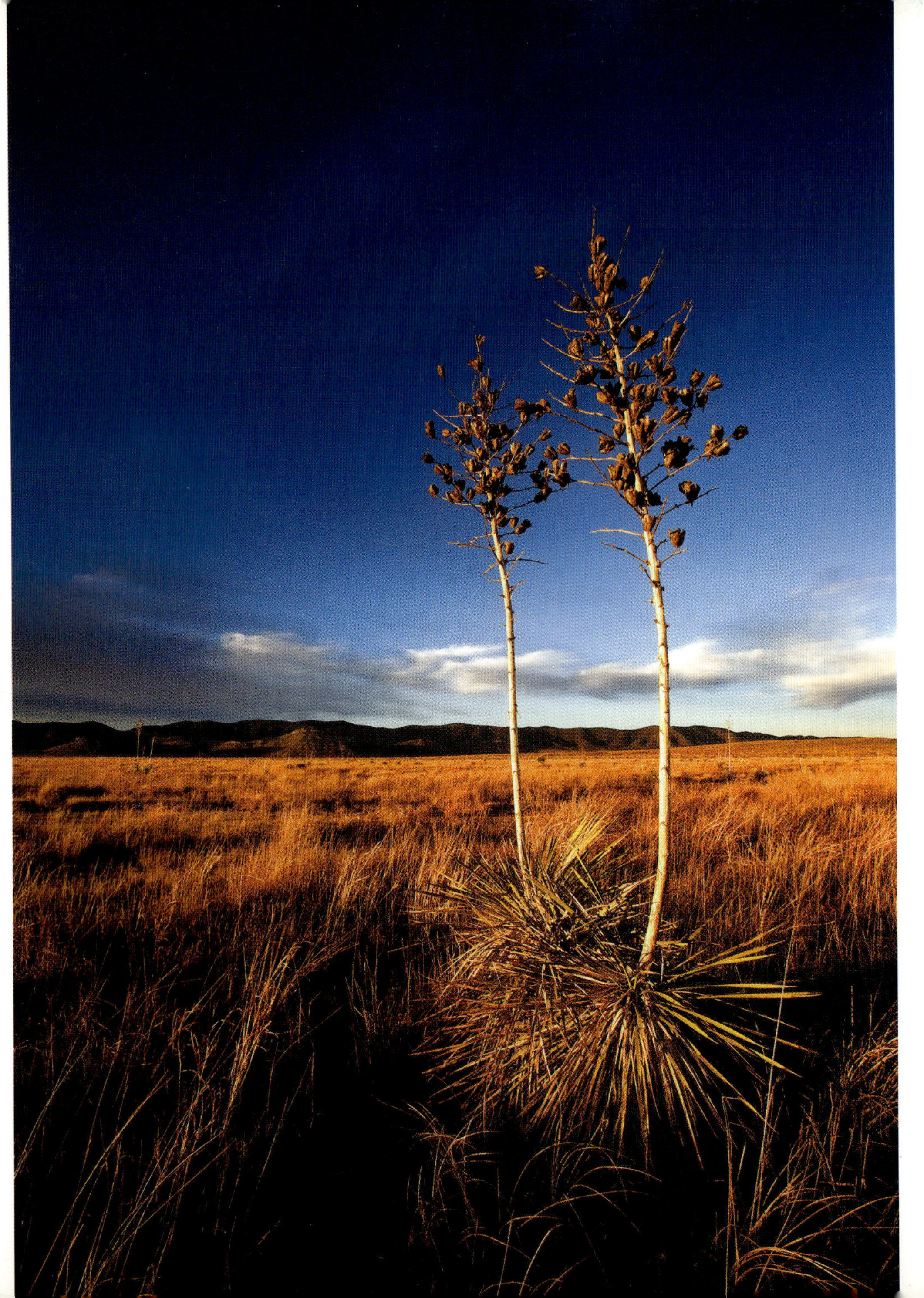

LEFT: **Big Bend National Park, Texas**
A yucca standing tall against a clear blue sky.

RIGHT: **Big Bend National Park, Texas**
A warm sunset light illuminates Casa Grande Mountain.

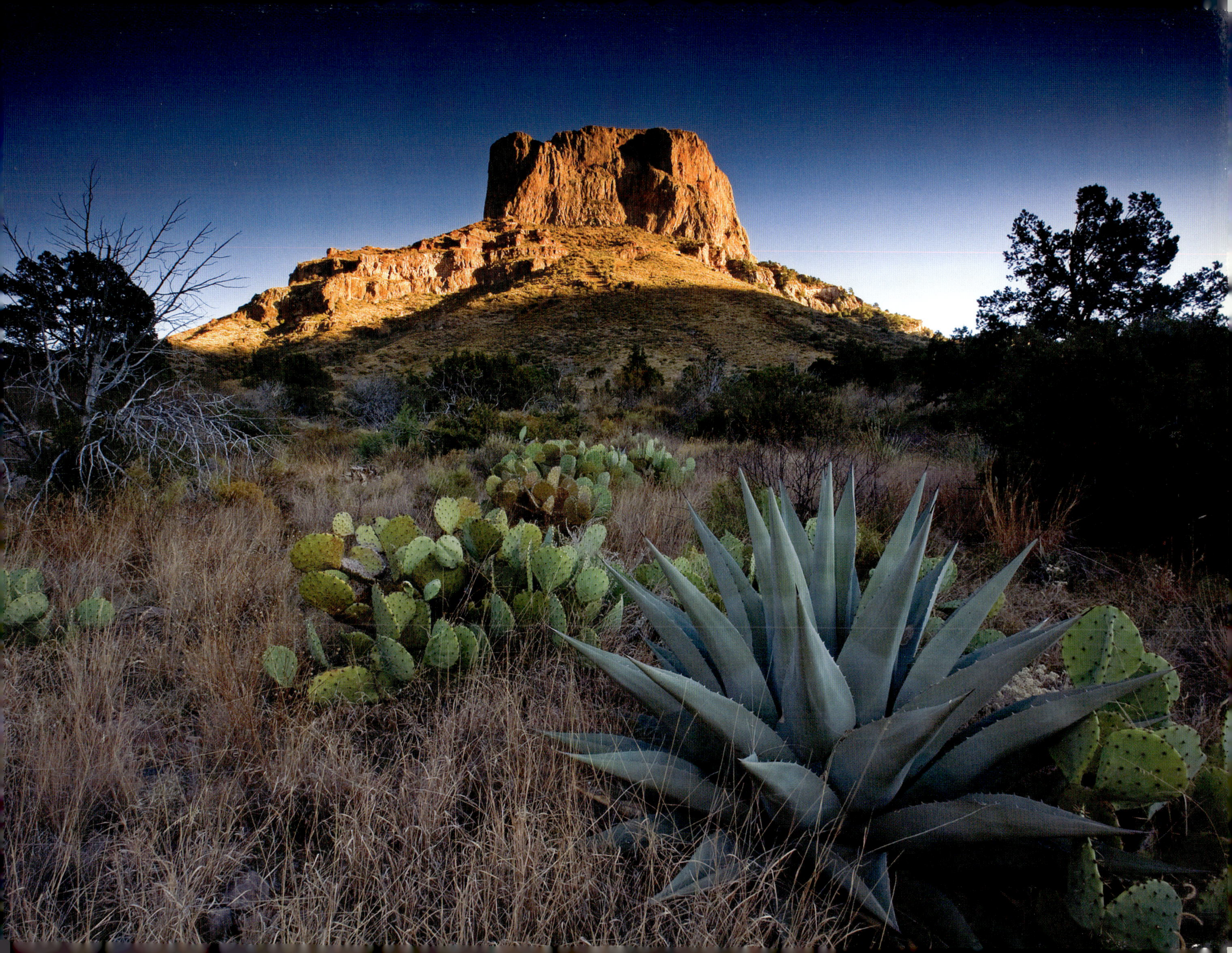

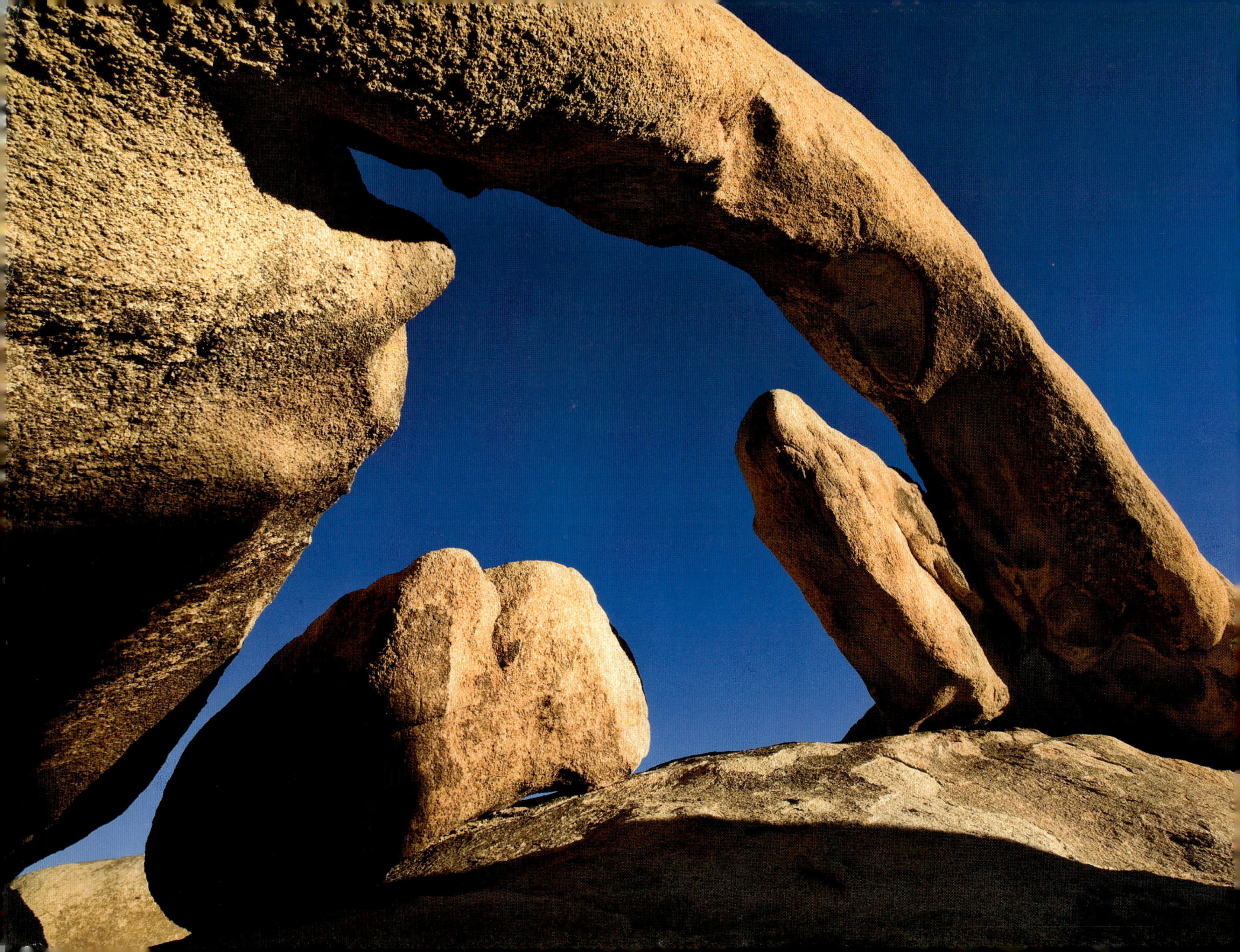

LEFT: **Joshua Tree National Park, California**
White Tank Arch.

RIGHT: **Saguaro National Park, Arizona**
Giant saguaro.

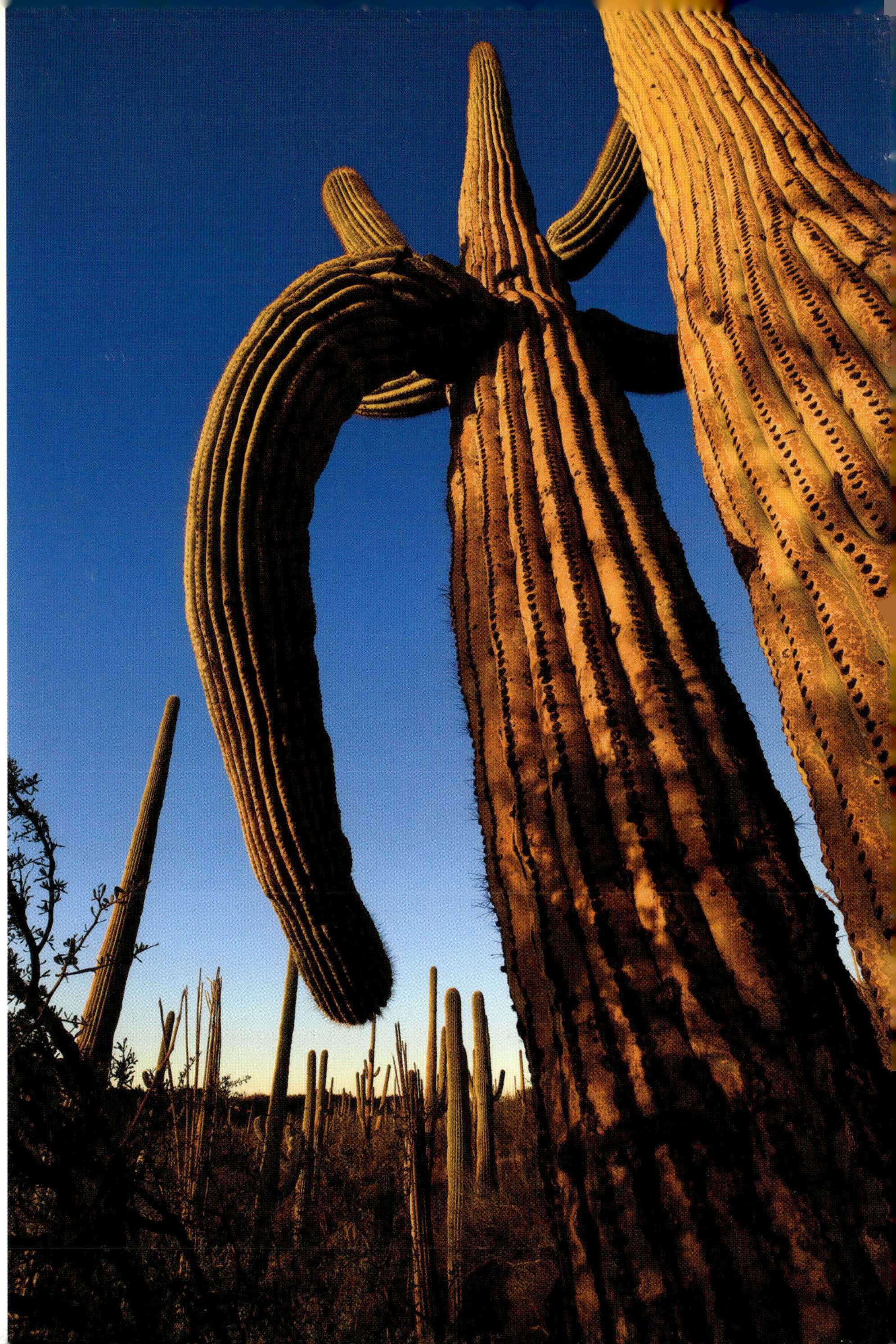

RIGHT: **Channel Islands National Park, California**
A jellyfish swimming through the kelp forest off of Santa Cruz Island.

INDEX OF NATIONAL PARKS PHOTOGRAPHS

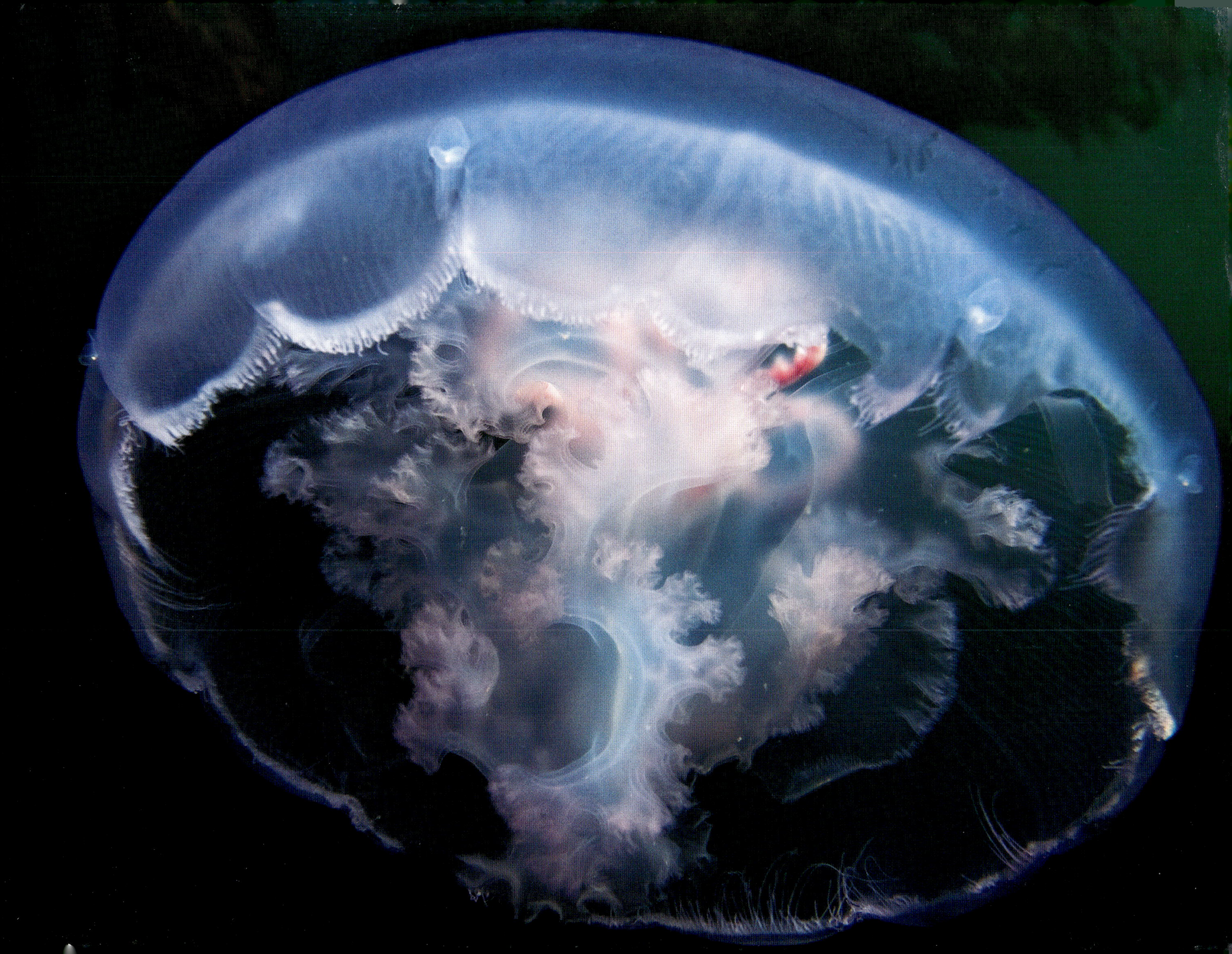

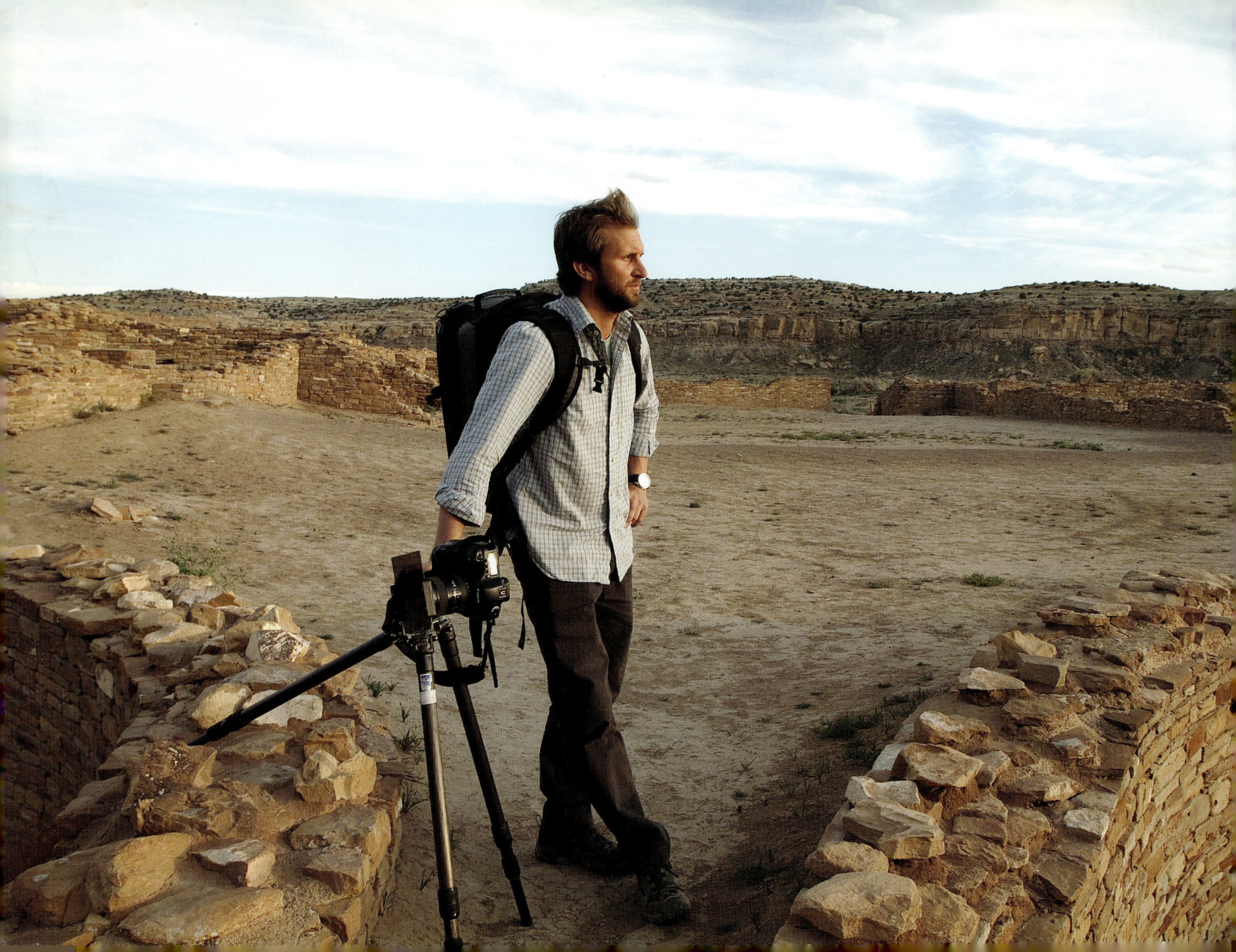

TECHNICAL NOTES

All of the original images in this book were shot digitally using Canon 5D cameras. The additional images added in this paperback edition were mostly photographed on the Canon 5D Mark II. I use two bodies—one armed with a 70-200mm f2.8 image stabilized lens and another one at wide angle, f2.8 16-35mm. In my bag, I also had a 24-70mm 2.8 lens, a 50mm 2.5 macro (which I am a huge fan of), a 2x teleconverter, 12mm and 25mm extension tubes, a couple of 580 EX strobes, and a variety of filters, cable releases and gizmos. At the end of the day, my camera bag weighs approximately 38lbs—not including my tripod.

In pursuit of making these images, the Canon cameras held up amazingly well, never failing me once. Not for lack of me trying to get them to fail—they were subjected to arctic conditions in Alaska and torrential rainstorms in Montana, and banged around on every rock in the Grand Canyon and Utah that I could find along the trails.

There is also a lot of discussion on the use of Adobe Photoshop. I believe in the utmost truth regarding the ethics of photography. No skies were added, no details removed in any of these photos except for the exorbitant amount of dust that manages to find itself stuck to my camera sensor. All images of wildlife were taken in the wild. All images were processed using Adobe Photoshop, and some contrast and saturation was added, but nothing beyond what would have taken place if I had been shooting with Fuji Velvia film. I'm a strong believer in the strong use of color in my images, and I've found many ways to pull out the beautiful saturation that happens naturally in our wild places, especially in the moments just before and just after the sun crests the horizon. I also use Lee filters and polarizers to help control my contrast and tonal ranges. The only colored filter I use is a warming filter, and I use it sparingly.

Everything you see in this book is accurately and faithfully representative of the scene that unfolded before me—a fact that should only serve to further inspire those who read it to realize with what these great treasures of our country really provide us.

LEFT: Photographer Ian Shive on location at Chaco Culture National Historical Park, New Mexico.
Photograph by James Shive.

ACKNOWLEDGEMENTS

Any creative project is inevitably a sum of all our parts, which includes many individuals from all aspects of our lives. First and foremost, I wish to thank my mother, who helps me find the perfect words for every photo; and my father, who taught me that every photo could be worth a thousand words. My grandparents, for their guidance and love and the lifetime subscription to *National Geographic* that began when I was five years old. Amy Leinbach Marquis, who has selflessly supported my photography from my first image of a national park. Scott Kirkwood, who has helped elevate the caliber of my work. Thank you to Elizabeth Andersen, who has tirelessly guided the promotional efforts and visibility of my work. Special thanks to Gianluca Lignola; Patricia Lignola; Russell Chadwick; the Merchant family; Nick Merwin; the Matijas family; Holly Fazio; Jeff Gallegos; Nate Rusch; Julie Solomon; Rob Sheppard; Lev Ginsburg; Steve Smith; Sarah Rutherford; Nicole Yin; Jay Reilly; Karine Aigner; Amy Walgenbach; Iain Morris; Frank Debevec; Paul Yarmoluk; Luba Yarmoluk; Grant Nemirow, Chris Geronimi, and the team at Terry Hines & Associates; Lee Donahoe; the Huang family; the Wardlow family; the Young family; Cheap Frank; my friends at the National Parks Conservation Association; my friends at the Nature Conservancy; my friends at the Sierra Club; my friends at A&I Photographic; *Outdoor Photographer* magazine; the American Society of Media Photographers; the North American Nature Photography Association; and my family at Sony Pictures Entertainment. And, of course, the team at Earth Aware Editions, who has always been so amazing to work with: Raoul Goff, Jake Gerli, Charles Gerli, Robbie Schmidt, Jason Babler, and Lucy Kee.

I'd also like to give recognition to the National Park Service for the important work that they do in helping to secure these amazing natural resources for future generations, and for the many individuals in the park service who have personally lent me their guidance and advice—without which this book could not have happened.

ABOUT THE NPCA

Our national parks protect some of the most beautiful, majestic, and awe-inspiring places on Earth. From mountains and rivers to forests and plains, to monuments to our history, our national parks open our minds and refresh our spirits. When you visit Yellowstone, Gettysburg, the Everglades, the Statue of Liberty, Mesa Verde, or any of the 391 parks, you see nature at its best and stand in the shadow of our heroes and ancestors.

But our national parks face a variety of threats—from air pollution and water pollution to global warming, adjacent development, and even a lack of adequate funding. That's why, since 1919, the National Parks Conservation Association has acted as the leading voice of the American people in protecting and enhancing our National Park System. The NPCA engages its 320,000 members and a broad range of allies to preserve our nation's natural, historical, and cultural heritage for our children and grandchildren. It's not just about preserving great places—it's about preserving an American legacy.

To learn more about our national parks, take action to protect them, or become a member of the NPCA, visit www.npca.org or call 1-800-628-7275. Members receive our quarterly magazine filled with words and images from Ian Shive and dozens of other talented conservation writers and photographers.

RIGHT: **Saguaro National Park, Arizona**
Cholla and saguaro at sunset.

PAGE 228: **Biscayne National Park, Florida**
Below the surface.

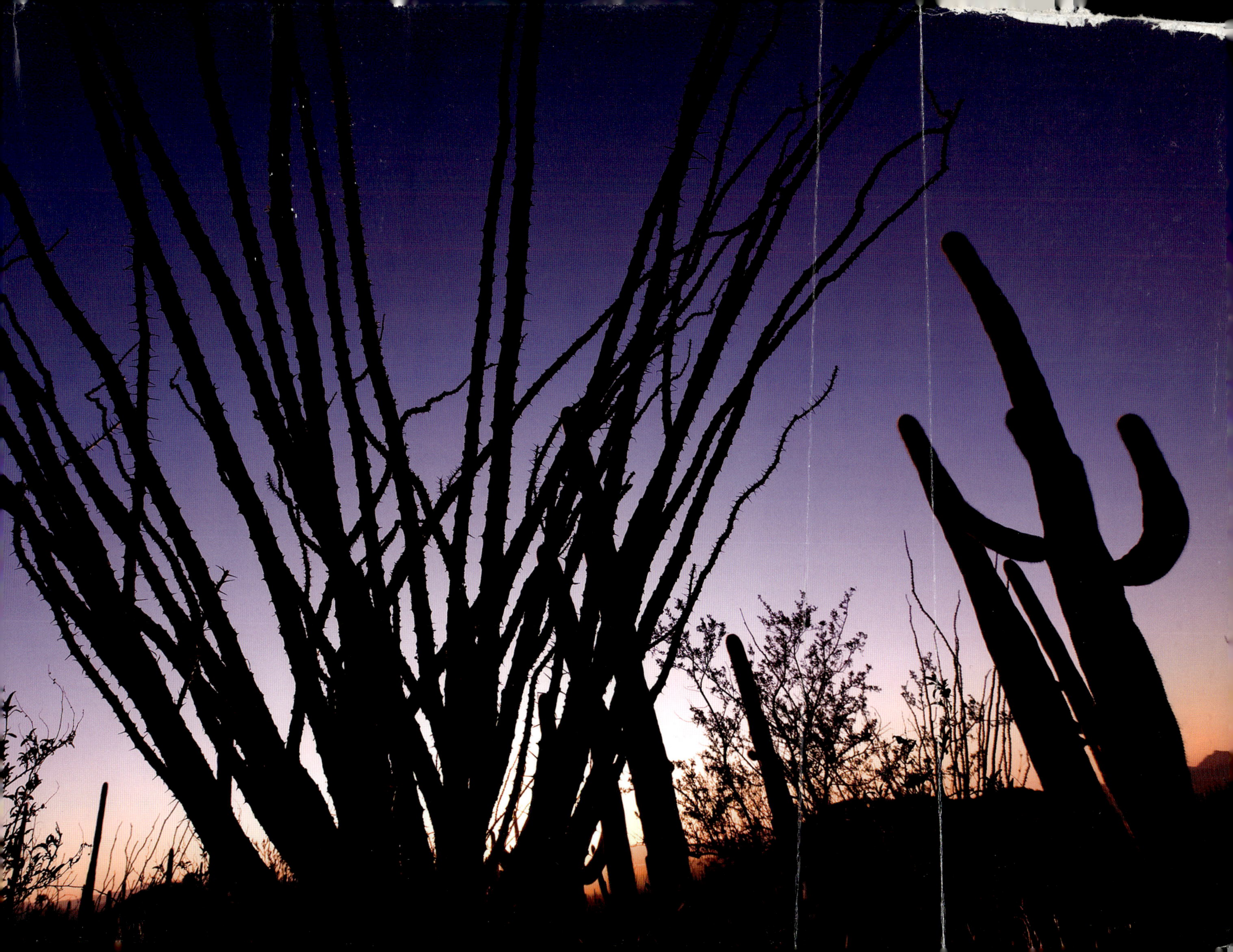

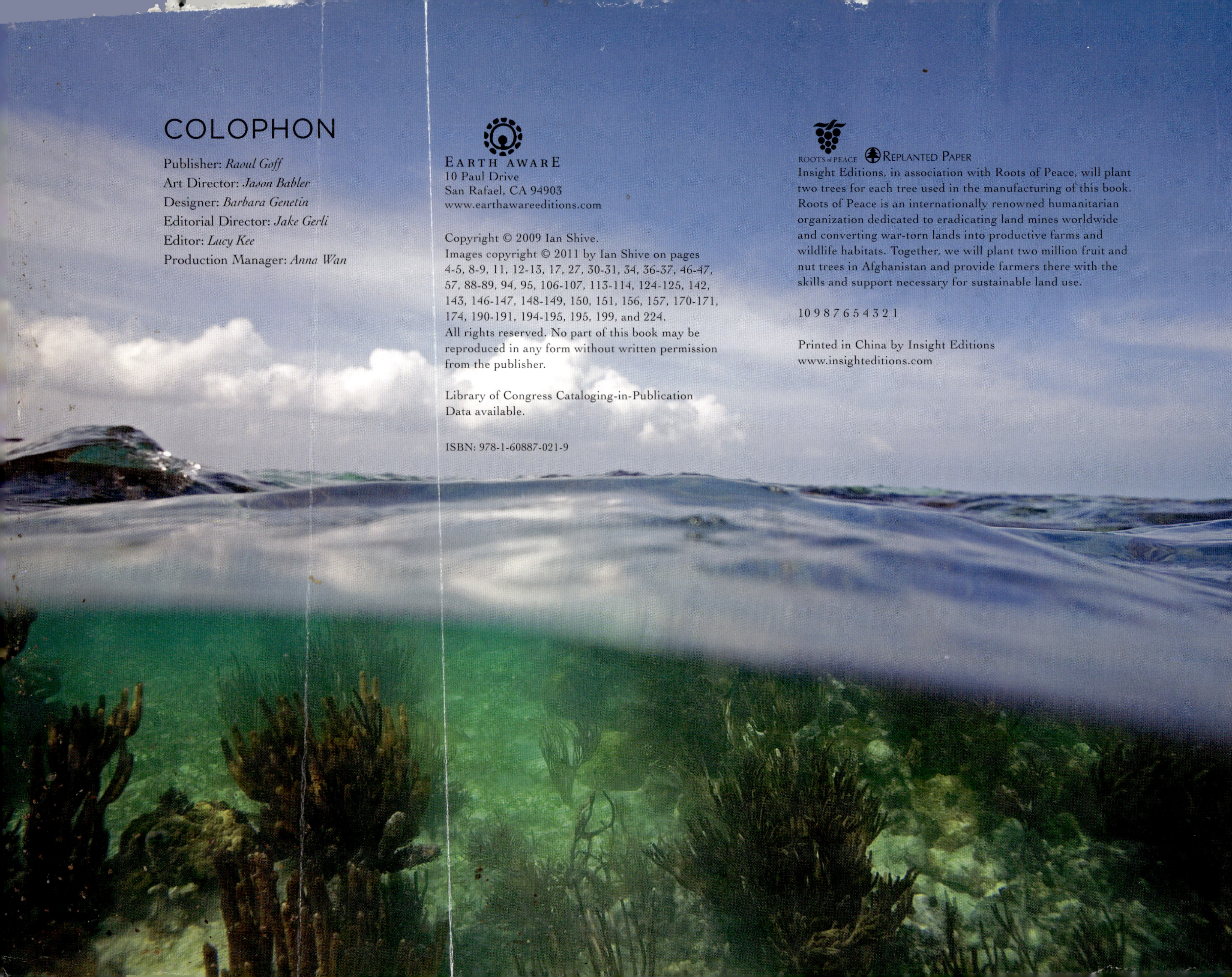

COLOPHON

Publisher: *Raoul Goff*
Art Director: *Jason Babler*
Designer: *Barbara Genetin*
Editorial Director: *Jake Gerli*
Editor: *Lucy Kee*
Production Manager: *Anna Wan*

EARTH AWARE
10 Paul Drive
San Rafael, CA 94903
www.earthawareeditions.com

Library of Congress Cataloging-in-Publication Data available.

ISBN: 978-1-60887-021-9

ROOTS of PEACE REPLANTED PAPER
Insight Editions, in association with Roots of Peace, will plant two trees for each tree used in the manufacturing of this book. Roots of Peace is an internationally renowned humanitarian organization dedicated to eradicating land mines worldwide and converting war-torn lands into productive farms and wildlife habitats. Together, we will plant two million fruit and nut trees in Afghanistan and provide farmers there with the skills and support necessary for sustainable land use.

10 9 8 7 6 5 4 3 2 1

Printed in China by Insight Editions
www.insighteditions.com